The Workingman in the Nineteenth Century

The Workingman
in the Nineteenth Century

Edited by
MICHAEL S. CROSS

TORONTO
Oxford University Press
1974

© Oxford University Press
(Canadian Branch) 1974

Cover design by
FRED HUFFMAN

ISBN-0-19-540220-0

Printed in Canada by
THE BRYANT PRESS LIMITED

Preface

The Introduction sets out some of the academic rationales for study of the working class in Canadian history. But there are other, more compelling reasons for that study. For too long the people's history has been submerged by historians writing out of their own middle-class experience. The working class has existed in a historical vacuum.

An increasing number of workers, and historians, are attempting to rectify that, to give the people back their history and help them discover their role in Canadian society. These documents may be a small contribution to that process.

Most of the research for this book was undertaken in the Public Archives, Ottawa, the University of Toronto Library, and the Toronto Public Library. Their staffs were universally helpful. Much of the work was done while the author was on leave with a Canada Council fellowship; that aid is gratefully acknowledged. My secretary, Wendy Watson, helped the process enormously by typing many of the documents. Above all, my gratitude to Fern Jeffries, resident proletarian.

M.S.C.

For Patrick:
he's a good mouse

Contents

Introduction

History, in its traditional form, has been past politics. An increasing number of historians, however, have come to see that that is only a small part of what history might be; they have come to see that the real task of history in our time is to re-create, appreciate, and analyse the full spectrum of past societies.

That means, pre-eminently, to attempt to understand the lives of the working people, the great mass of any society. Unfortunately it is a task that is inordinately difficult, which may be one large reason why historians have been reluctant to undertake it. In any century before our own, most working people were illiterate; most had little leisure for reflection and writing, even if they were literate; and most had no sense that their lives were of any interest to others. In other words, they lacked all of the attributes that led politicians and members of the upper classes to record their lives, and to pass those records on to historians. The stuff from which history is ordinarily written is lacking for the lower orders of society—diaries, correspondence, speeches, books, sympathetic newspapers. The story of working people must be reconstructed from other, more difficult evidence. Statistical material, travellers' accounts, surviving examples of domestic architecture, government reports, the judgements of those literate members of other classes who wrote about workers—these are some of the sources that must be sifted. A single collection of a politician's papers can give a rounded picture of such a man. The picture of the working people will be, at best, a blurred mosaic constructed from a thousand incomplete sources.

This book is designed to serve as an introduction to the study of the workingman in the nineteenth century. It will indicate some of that variety of sources. It may suggest some of the questions that must be asked before any true understanding of working-class life can emerge. But it is only an introduction. Statistical approaches, which may be among the most useful, are not represented. Such subjects as the architecture of working-class homes and working-class cities, the incidence of crime and violence, religion, and all too many others cannot be dealt with here. But the interested reader will find enough documents on enough aspects of working-class life to begin the process of re-thinking our history, from the bottom up.

Apart from the usual difficulties of dealing with a mass of relatively inarticulate people, the Canadian situation poses some special problems. It has been held by most Canadians, although less firmly than in the United States, that ours is not a class society. Class lines, if they do exist, are fluid; social mobility is easy and natural. This is the North American social myth. This national self-assessment makes it more difficult for people to understand the condition of working people in the nineteenth century when, patently, class lines did exist, when mobility was certainly less easy than it is today, and when people were conscious of class differences. It is important to wrench ourselves from the liberal ideology of the twentieth century and to look objectively at a nineteenth century in which society was structured in very different ways and in which people had different views about the order and the purposes of society.

What was meant by class in nineteenth-century Canada? The study of social classes has proceeded basically along two lines. The Marxist tradition has stressed 'objective' economic classes: people fit into social classes on the basis of their relationship to the means of production. The working class, then, is made up of those people who have no control over the productive capacity of society, who must sell their labour to survive. In contrast, North American social science has usually spoken of 'subjective' classes, classes defined by the way people actually perceived them. Status, rather than economic control, determines rank in society.

Both interpretations can find support in the conditions of nineteenth-century Canada. Power and influence were distributed on a complex weighting of economic influence and status, businessmen and professional men interreacting to create powerful and stable elites. Working people had their place defined both by lack of economic power and by subjective judgements about their proper place, judgements based on such intangibles as education, 'breeding', cultural sophistication. It is true that the phrase 'the working class' did not have wide currency in Canada. Those higher on the social pyramid in the first half of the century often referred to 'the lower orders'; later, the terminology was the more flattering 'the workingman'.

Whatever the phrase, those with power in society were defining a proletariat. This definition changed in important ways during the century. A tolerant view was based upon a combination of control and distance. Aristocrats who felt unthreatened by the lower orders tended to look upon them as curious but harmless beings. As cities grew and forced the 'better people' into physical proximity with the poor, as rebellion and riot showed the violent potential of the lower orders, and as industrialization turned the independent yeoman into the wretched labourer, the view of the lower class necessarily hardened after 1837 into an opinion of workers as threats to the stability of society. The change was signalled by new interest, on the part of the leaders of society, in developing institutions to control these dangerous elements—institutions such as police forces and schools. Labour organization later in the century reinforced fears of the lower class; the frequency with which troops were employed to crush strikes surely indicated this. Emphasis continued to be placed on schools and police as agencies of social control. Science added new concerns and new techniques as the century wore on. Disease was seen as a new threat from the lower orders and programs of vaccination and health education were established to check this newly perceived danger.

Some aspects of the view of the working class remained consistent. Workers were regarded by those above them as different, different not only in status but in outlook and capacity. They were seen as an unstable factor in the social order. And they were seen as a permanent factor. None of these assessments of the lower class were premised on easy, natural social mobility. Class lines were clear and permanent.

The consciousness of classes must be viewed primarily from above because of the difficulty of finding evidence about lower-class self-awareness. Traditions of deference, however, surely indicated not only a realization of the class system but an acceptance of upper-class evaluations. Unionization later in the century provides some additional evidence. For instance, demands by unionists for labour representatives in parliament showed a class consciousness and an awareness of the gulf between classes; the point of view of workers, they argued, could only be expressed by workers themselves. But trade unions also showed how complicated the class structure was. Unions in the skilled trades did not, ordinarily, attempt to pretend that they spoke for the working class at large. They saw skilled workers, artisans, as a class apart—separated from common workers in interests and viewpoint, as surely as they were separated from those above them.

Despite being relegated, in society's eyes and in his own, to an inferior position, the Canadian workingman in the nineteenth century had a major role to play in the development of this country. By immigrating to Canada in their millions, workers moved Canadian life from the forest to the city. The colonies of British North America in 1800 were home to a few hundred thousand people scattered over the countryside and in small towns. By 1900 the Dominion of Canada had a population of over five million, an increasing percentage living in large cities with populations in the hundreds of thousands. That alone profoundly altered the scale of Canadian life. The potentialities and problems of a large urban population were totally different from those of a small rural population. In their numbers, and in their imported skills, working people fostered the development of large-scale industry to replace the agriculture, staple trades, and small shops of the beginning of the century. As late as 1837 William Lyon Mackenzie could, with some sense of realism, propose banning industry from Canada, forbidding any business larger than a single-family unit.

The vast immigrant flow after that date, however, wiped away all traces of Mackenzie's rural utopia.

The workingman was the victim of this change as well as its agent. The growth of industry and cities closed off the options of both immigrants and native-born Canadians. The dream of an independent farming existence, which moved so many people to come to Canada, faded away for most. To establish a farm by the end of the century required moving to the Prairies, for the immigrant flow had filled up eastern Canada. In this new age of machines it also required finding the capital, not only to set up in the far west, but to purchase farm machinery. Few of those trapped in city factories could ever hope to find that capital.

Even those committed to industrial life, with no thoughts of escape to a farm, found their environment profoundly changed—not always for the better. In the most obvious sense it was changed by the growth of the city. The city offered more cultural activities, organized recreation, a greater range of consumer goods. But it was also crowded, impersonal, ugly. The typical Canadian in 1800 lived in an environment of green fields, forest, clean air. The typical Canadian in 1900 lived amidst lowering Victorian buildings, factories, and sooty air. His workplace was equally different. If he did not work on the farm in 1800, he worked in a small shop where he was in daily contact with his employer and a few other workers. By 1900 he might well work in a large factory, an impersonal plant where he never met his employer and knew only a few of the hundreds of fellow-workers, where his craft traditions were lost in the process of mass production. How different it was for his sense of accomplishment and self-worth to move from work in which he handcrafted an entire product to a situation in which he made only one component of a product he might never actually see in its completed form.

The social system in which the workingman functioned also altered. Immigration produced an unbalanced society. Canada received large proportions of the very lowest classes and of the gentry class, but relatively few from the middle classes of British society. Those who could afford to emigrate, those of the middle classes, tended to immigrate to the United States, where their capital and their skills would win them greater rewards. The gentry, forced out of Britain by declining economic fortunes and therefore difficulty in maintaining their social status, often wanted to remain within the British empire—the cradle of their lifestyle—and so deliberately chose Canada. The poor, cleared from the land by landlords or subsidized by the British government to ease the pressure of unemployment in the home islands, had little choice but to come to Canada; they could receive subsidies to do so or, if travelling on their own, they found it much cheaper to reach than the United States. Their motives, then, were often not very positive ones. They were pushed out of Britain rather than being drawn into Canada.

In the first third of the nineteenth century all the colonies of British North America had stratified societies, with social leadership and political power concentrated in a few hands. The prevailing ideology was deeply conservative, more concerned with maintaining a traditional social order than with achieving rapid economic progress. There were few to challenge the elites, for talent was spread thin. The lower class, used to deference, certainly did nothing to disrupt either the social or the economic order.

Continued immigration and economic expansion began to change all of this. In both English and French Canada a native middle class emerged to demand a piece of the action. A portion of this middle class, especially frustrated, finally came to the point of rebellion in 1837. Some farmers, frustrated by the already apparent shortage of good land and by their increasing debts, took part. So too did some labourers, perhaps an expression of early industrial alienation. In the Toronto area, for example, the shock troops of the rebellion were brewery workers and men engaged in iron work.

In the battle between the elites and those below them, the real winners were those members of the middle class who remained uninvolved. Political parties, responsible government, and Britain's dismantling of the old economic empire in the 1840s handed power over to the middle class. It was, of course, only partially peculiar Canadian circumstances that produced this shift. The last half of the nineteenth century, everywhere in the western world, was a time of middle-class dominance. Bourgeois economic activities prospered; so did bourgeois ethics. With the support of pseudoscientific followers of Darwin's theory of evolution, middle-class views on the need for competition, the rationality of unfettered capitalist enterprise, and the work ethic became the dominant ideology.

In Canada newer and sterner elites emerged. The old leadership of Toronto, for example, gave way to a very different one. The Strachans and J. B. Robinsons, aristocrats more concerned with leading a gentle life than with creating great wealth, were replaced by the William McMasters, the George Browns, the Daniel Masseys—dour men, Christian men, who saw financial success on earth as their key to salvation. They rejected the old elite's paternalistic attitudes towards the lower orders, its concerns for a gracious life at the expense of progress. The factory, not the parlour, was their natural environment.

Under such leadership the industrial city grew. For the workingman it meant greater economic opportunity. But it also meant crowded living space, large factories, the machine. Used to doing what had to be done in an unquestioning way, most workers probably thought little of the changes in their lives. But there are occasional hints that some workers, at least, realized what was happening to them—and did not like it. Shoemakers, traditionally the intellectual leaders among the working class, tried vainly to stop the march of the machine. Under the cover of the political rioting in Montreal in 1849, shoemakers attacked a factory and destroyed the sewing machines recently introduced there. It was wasted effort, of course. New machines were imported and the shoemaker, like his compatriots in other trades, saw part of his craft tradition disappear.

Trade unions were an obvious response, organizations to allow workers to assert some say over their futures. Unions began to emerge in the 1830s. Often founded by men with experience of unionism in Britain, they developed first in highly skilled trades such as printing. Although their demands were usually moderate, they met hard resistance. In Toronto, for example, union activities among printers were initially denounced by the radical politician, William Lyon Mackenzie. Unions faced entrenched employers, traditions of working-class deference, and a great mobility among their memberships. Not surprisingly, most unions were shortlived, collapsing until some serious economic pressure led to new union activity.

The growth of large-scale industry after 1860 presented such obvious problems for workers that larger, more permanent unions began to appear. Again, they were limited substantially to the skilled workers. With long craft traditions and a sense of their own worth, skilled workers could more easily develop a craft, if not a class, consciousness. Common labourers, engaged in a constant struggle to keep above the subsistence level, usually underemployed and moving from job to job, had little opportunity to do so. Even among the skilled workers, however, unions continued to have a difficult time. Economic expansion and a bitter and widely publicized printers' strike in Toronto in 1872 (discussed at some length in Chapter 5) produced a rapid growth of union activity in the early 1870s. A national labour body, the Canadian Labour Union, was formed. But employer hostility and economic depression blighted the movement; the national body died and many of the union gains were lost.

Despite setbacks, the union movement continued to grow after the mid-1880s. One reason was the extension of the franchise, and as a result a greater willingness by governments to meet the legislative demands of unionists, who were after all now voters. Another was the expansion of American unions into Canada. Firmly organized on a national scale by the American Federation of Labor, American unions were anxious to bring their benefits to Canadians. And, as American companies expanded in Canada, American unions were almost compelled to follow suit. Canadian workers were more than willing to support such expansion, often taking the initiative in inviting American unions. The creation of these 'international' unions brought greater expertise and greater financial resources to the support of Canadian workers.

Unions were able to win better wages for their members and to profit all workers by gaining legislative changes to regulate hours of work and to prevent the exploitation of the labour of women and children. But for most non-unionized workers, the vast bulk of the labour force, conditions remained hard. The economic cycle was depressed for most of the period from 1873 to 1896. Factory labour, hard to come by at times, became more inhumane as people became more and more supplements to machines. The solution for many workers was to vote against Canadian conditions with their feet. Between 1871 and 1901, something in the order of 1,500,000 Canadians immigrated to the United States. There was, of course, flow the other way as Americans moved to the Canadian West. But the net population loss to Canada in these thirty years was 800,000 people.

In response to these conditions, some workingmen went beyond traditional trade union demands. When asked what unions wanted, AFL president Samuel Gompers was fond of answering, 'More!'. This was not an adequate answer for some. Industrialization and the stress of depression had set many to questioning the basic structures of a society in which such things were allowed to happen. In England a socialist movement of some substance was being born in the 1880s. In the United States, in the same decade, a variety of responses was being pursued. The Greenback Party was attempting to establish greater equality by breaking the power of financial capitalism. Henry George, whose ideas won vast international popularity, proposed a single tax on land as a method of stopping speculation and re-opening American opportunity. And Edward Bellamy, in his book *Looking Backward*, speculated on the emergence of a humanitarian society in which the giant industrial trusts would come under public control. Both George and Bellamy won considerable popularity in Canada, single-tax clubs and 'nationalist' societies springing up to propagate their ideas. Henry George, in particular, set many workers to begin questioning the system, thus putting them on the eventual path to socialism.

Such class defiance could not capture the minds of many. The Canadian workingmen were too much products of their society, of that curious combination of British deference and American myths of economic opportunity. A working class so nicely conditioned would remain eminently exploitable.

The role of the workingman in the nineteenth century, then, was not one of great glamorous deeds, of revolutions, and epic struggles. It was simpler and more real, but no less significant for its humble nature. The time has come, surely, to begin the search for the real Canada, the Canada the workingman built.

1 | On Farm and Frontier

The vast majority of nineteenth-century Canadians were farmers. Although in Ontario the population balance was shifting towards urban areas by 1850, the country at large remained rural throughout the century. Farmers did not usually think of themselves as 'workers' in the same category as those who laboured in factories. And in terms of independence and range of activities, farmers often had more in common with the middle classes than with the working classes. Nevertheless, a book on the workingman cannot completely ignore the bulk of the population. Farmers, therefore, are treated primarily in the frontier stage of agricultural development, the stage of struggle and hard labour, the stage in which the farmer had little opportunity to emulate the middle-class entrepreneur.

The farmer moving out onto a thinly settled frontier, whether in eastern Canada before Confederation or on the Prairies later in the century, shared many of the characteristics, and the problems, of the worker entering a factory. For the emigrant from Britain, the wilderness environment was as different from the neat, cultivated landscape of his home country as the factory was different from the small-town shop for the urban worker. Whatever the rhetoric about the independence of the farmer, he often was as tied to the local merchant and to the money lender as the city labourer was to his boss. Exploitation knew no bounds; it flourished as well in the forest as in the city street.

The lines blurred even more because many farmers needed to generate cash income to supplement their farming. Whether to buy seed, or pay off debts, or buy more land, farmers often found themselves forced to seek other employment, to translate themselves temporarily into workingmen. The fur trade, timbering, labour on government public-works projects, these were pursued at various times by many farmers in need of ready cash.

The French-Canadian farmer had a special range of problems. The land he worked in the St Lawrence heartland was often tired from too many centuries of cultivation. His farming techniques were notoriously archaic. Generations of British officials and agricultural experts attempted to get the habitant to improve his farming, to revitalize his land. But traditional agriculture was an important part of the way of life French Canadians were attempting to maintain under alien rule. Recommendations for changes, then, however well meant, could often seem to be attacks on

French-Canadian culture. An additional check on improvement was the ancient feudal landholding system, the seigneurial system, that persisted into the 1850s. The results of these problems are indicated in excerpts from an article by geographer Cole Harris, the leading expert on the seigneurial system.

For French Canadians a traditional outlet from the agricultural distress of Quebec was the fur trade. Until 1821 Montreal was a major centre for the trade, and even after that date some French Canadians found employment in the lower ranks of the Hudson's Bay Company. An account of the French-Canadian voyageurs at the beginning of the century by British traveller George Heriot describes this traditional life.

Early farm life was similar throughout English Canada. Transportation was always a problem, making it difficult to get produce to market and increasing social isolation. Clearing the land was difficult everywhere in the eastern forest. The readiness of Canadians even now to bulldoze trees in their subdivisions is perhaps a legacy of pioneer hatred of the ever-present barrier of the forest. A tight family organization was necessary, for there was always more work than there were hands to do it. Similarly, co-operation among neighbours was much more than mere friendliness; it was an economic necessity. Only joint action could get barns raised, stumps cleared, and quilts made.

The persistent problem of inadequate means of transportation is discussed in an 1824 letter from the New Glasgow settlement in Lower Canada. An article on the New Ross settlement in Nova Scotia describes the farm routine of the Ross family, natives of County Cork, Ireland, who settled in Nova Scotia in 1816. A sharp contrast is offered by the agricultural community in New Brunswick. The forest was an even greater barrier there, but also a greater opportunity. New Brunswick agriculture lagged behind that in the other colonies because so many men were lured away from the farm by the high pay and the adventure of the timber trade. Agriculture remained, even in the 1840s, undeveloped and casual, often pursued by squatters who moved freely from one lot to another, never sinking roots. The author of the New Brunswick account was Abraham Gesner, who was employed by the provincial government in the 1840s to survey New Brunswick agriculture and make recommendations for improving it. Gesner made other contributions to Canada; he was the inventor of kerosene, which revolutionized domestic life by providing a cheap, practical fuel for home lighting.

Upper Canada, the later Ontario, was the richest agricultural area in eastern Canada, the nation's wheat basket until replaced by the Prairies at the century's end. The hardships of starting out even there are illustrated in an excerpt from Catherine Parr Traill's *The Backwoods of Canada*. Mrs Traill was part of an upper-middle-class group who settled near Peterborough, and who left a number of vigorous and literate accounts of pioneer life. She came from a prominent literary family in England, which also made a considerable impact on Canada: her sister was Susanna Moodie, who wrote probably the most famous account of the Canadian frontier, *Roughing It in the Bush*; and her brother, Samuel Strickland, was an official of the Canada Land Company and author of *Twenty-Seven Years in Canada West*.

Farm life was often lonely and boring, an endless repetition of routine tasks. The farm diary of P. H. Gosse of Compton, Lower Canada, well illustrates this. Even Christmas was a day like any other: '. . . I repaired the stable divisions, . . . carried over two sled loads of Oat straw, & brought 15½ bus. Oats to the house.' There was more social contact as the country filled in. Farm life after Confederation is described in the diary of David Nelson, who lived near Peterborough, Ontario.

Success was elusive. Canniff Haight, in a book published in the 1880s, discussed the elements needed to make it on the farm. He also included a comparison of prices between 1830 and 1880, showing a remarkable price stability over the fifty-year period. Improved transportation and increased agricultural production apparently compensated for any inflationary drift. For some, success was always over the horizon. W. A. Robertson was born in Scotland, but his family moved to Flamboro West Township in Upper Canada when he was still an infant. Family problems and the difficulty of finding a viable trade drove him, like so many others, ever further in the search for success. He was not essentially different from those who pursued the chimera from farm to farm, hunting the promise they thought Canada held out for them. Robertson, after exhausting his possibilities in Upper Canada, set out for the gold fields of the Pacific Coast, only to be discouraged by stories he heard of conditions there. After wandering the United States for a time, he joined the Union army in the American Civil War. After the war he did go west to British Columbia to prospect—with no great success. For men like Robertson, there always had to be 'a next year country' where fortune waited.

A more prosaic but more solid experience of the Western frontier was pursued by the settlers who began to fill in the Prairies in the 1880s and 1890s. The process of settling-in emerges in an account by the Saskatchewan Archives, compiled from questionnaires returned by pioneer settlers in that province. Even in the early stages of Western settlement, however, certain problems emerged. One of the most disturbing for young farmers was the lack of women. A letter from an anxious young man at Arran, Manitoba, expresses in its humour a considerable degree of desperation. More telling in the long run, and less easy to rectify, was the departure of young men from the farm, the subject of an editorial from the *Manitoba Free Press*. If this was a problem in the new West, how much more serious was it in the East, where the cities held out an eternal lure to the young and restless.

Other industries absorbed much of the manpower on the frontier. Many farmers went into timbering and other trades out of compelling necessity. However John Langton, another of the middle-class pioneers of the Peterborough region, was more systematic than most in assessing the possibilities open to a distressed farmer. The course Langton eventually chose was to enter the timber trade. Three documents illustrate the development of that trade during the century. John MacGregor's account of timbering in New Brunswick in the 1820s shows the forest life at its most unruly and, for bored farmers, its most appealing. In Ontario fifty years later the trade was more orderly and the workers were professionals rather than moonlighting farmers. Even then however there was a sense of adventure to be found in few other activities. Finally an elderly French Canadian describes to a sociologist his experiences in Quebec timber camps at the end of the century.

Among the most precarious of frontier economic activities was fishing. Fishermen were at the mercy of fish supplies, unreliable markets, and the merchants who advanced them cash and supplies. The distance of the fishing frontier from sources of agricultural products was an additional hazard. The report of an 1817 famine in Newfoundland underlines this; there was ample money, but no food to buy with it. The way in which fishing was carried out is described in an account of the Labrador fishery in 1897 taken from a Toronto newspaper.

A declining factor throughout the nineteenth century was the old Canadian staple, the fur trade. The cut-throat competition between the North West Company and the Hudson's Bay Company ended in 1821 when the companies merged. The result was the end of the Montreal fur trade and the end of the fur trade's influence on settled Canada. In the North of course the fur trade was still king. Like other frontier trades it became more businesslike and more prosaic as the century wore on. An account from the *Winnipeg Times* of 1883 shows how the once glamorous fur trade had taken on the characteristics of any large business.

While the fur trade declined, the exploitation of mineral resources became ever more important. The most dramatic developments were in British Columbia and the Yukon, scenes of the great gold rushes of the century. The gold rush of 1858 opened up a colony that had been a sparsely-settled fur reserve. If few of the gold seekers grew rich prospecting, they did begin the settlement of British Columbia. Even more attention was focused upon the Klondike gold rush of 1898. This great adventure, immortalized in the verse of Robert Service, was even more ephemeral than the British Columbia rush. It ended as quickly as it had begun, bringing gold wealth to few of the tens of thousands of prospectors. Conditions in the Klondike are described in a letter to their English parents by two young hopefuls, Arthur and Joseph Robinson.

LIFE ON THE SEIGNEURY

Cole Harris, 'Of Poverty and Helplessness in Petite-Nation'. *Canadian Historical Review*, LII, 1, March 1971, 47-50. Reprinted by permission of the author and of the publisher, University of Toronto Press.

The few emigrants who crossed the Atlantic to the lower St. Lawrence in the seventeenth and early eighteenth centuries were, for the most part, poor and dispossessed people who had only a toehold in French society before they crossed the Atlantic. . . . Along the lower St. Lawrence they found an abundance of land that, when cleared, yielded a higher standard of living than that of most French peasants. They found an opportunity to settle along the river, away from official eyes, and in a setting where their lives could not be controlled. And they found in the untrammelled life of the fur trade contact with largely nomadic Algonkian Indians whose rhetoric, courage, and apparent lack of régime they admired and emulated.

Out of this emerged a habitant population characterized by bravado, insouciance, and a considerable disdain for authority. The habitants lived boisterously, spending their income, enjoying the independence and modest prosperity of their lives in the côtes, and perhaps too, the Indian girls along the upper Ottawa; a style of life that grew partly out of their French background but probably more out of the opportunities of a new land. They had brought few institutions with them, and needed few in Canada. The Canadian seigneurie was neither a social nor an economic unit, the parish was only slowly emerging as a social unit at the end of the French régime. The village was almost absent; collective open-field agriculture never appeared. The côte did become a loose rural neighbourhood, as time went on neighbours were frequently kin, and, after perhaps the earliest years, the nuclear family was always important. In the background was the colonial government, eager to promote the settlement of the colony, paternalistic, tending to side with the habitants in disputes with the seigneurs. The government could not impose itself on the habitants, but it could offer certain services—inexpensive regional courts, for example, or the right of free appeal to the intendant. In operating hospitals, orphanages, and poorhouses, the religious orders did the same. Such support only increased the independence of the habitants who were not forced to compensate for an oppressive officialdom by a tighter social organization at the local level.

In the century after the Conquest, this way of life had slowly changed. Habitant mobility was constrained by the declining relative importance of the fur trade and, after 1821, by its loss to Hudson Bay; by English-speaking settlement in Upper Canada; and by growing population pressure along the St. Lawrence lowland. Farm land was becoming scarce as

any injury which may be sustained on the voyage. The men are engaged at Montreal four or five months before they set out on their journey, and receive in advance their equipment, and one-third of their wages. Each man holds in his hand a large paddle; and the canoe, although loaded within six inches of the gunwale, is made to move along with wonderful expedition. The *voyageurs*, or navigators, are of constitutions the strongest and most robust; and they are at an early period inured to the encounter of hardships. The fare on which they subsist is penurious and coarse.* Fortified by habit against apprehension from the species of difficulties and perils with which they are about to struggle, they enter on their toils with confidence and hope. Whilst moving along the surface of the stream, they sing in alternate strains the songs and music of their country, and cause the desolate wilds on the banks of the Outaouais, to resound with the voice of chearfulness. They adapt in rowing their strokes to the cadence of their strains, and redouble their efforts by making them in time. In dragging the canoes up the rapids, great care is necessary to prevent them from striking against rocks, the materials of which they are composed being slight and easily damaged. When a canoe receives an injury, the aperture is stopped with gum melted by the heat of a piece of burning charcoal. Fibres of bark bruised, and moistened with gum in a liquid state, are applied to larger apertures; a linen rag is put over the whole, and its edges are cemented with gum.

The total number of men contained in the canoes, amounts usually to about three hundred and seventy-three, of which three hundred and fifty are navigators, eighteen are guides, and five are clerks. When arrived at the grand depôt, on Lake Superior, part of these ascend as far as the Rainy Lake, and they are usually absent from Montreal about five months. The guides are paid for this service thirty-seven pounds sterling, and are always provided suitable equipment. The wages of the person who sits in the front of the canoe, and of him whose office it is to steer, are about twenty-one pounds sterling each; those of the other men, about twelve pounds ten shillings of the same money.

To each man, a blanket, shirt, and pair of trowsers are supplied; and all are maintained by their employers during the period of their engagement. The advantage of trafficking with the savages† is likewise permitted, and some individuals procure by this means a profit amounting to more than double their pay.

When, in ascending the Outaouais, the voyagers approach the rapids, they draw the canoes to the shore, excepting one, which they join in dragging up, and lodge in a place of security. Another is in like manner conducted to the head of the torrent, and they thus continue to drag until the

---

* Chiefly the grease of the bear, and a meal, or coarse flour, made from Indian corn.
† A term in use at this period to refer to the native people.

whole are assembled. At the portages, where waterfalls and cataracts oblige them to unload, the men unite in aiding each other to convey the canoes and goods across the land, by carrying the former upon the shoulders of six or eight men, and the latter upon the back. A package of merchandise forms a load for one man, and is sustained by a belt which he places over his forehead.

They form their encampments at night upon islands, or upon the borders of the river. The murmuring sound of the streams, the wildness of the situation, and remoteness from the habitations of men, added to the nocturnal gloom, powerfully invite the imagination to indulge itself in a train of melancholy reflections. On the north-east shore, about sixty miles higher up than the falls last described, is the site of an old French fort called Coulogne; and six miles farther is that of another, named Defon. At a distance of seventy-two miles from the latter, is point *au Baptheme*, so denominated, because the rude ceremony is here performed of plunging into the waters of the Outaouais, such persons as have never before travelled thus far. An ordeal from which exemption may be purchased, by the payment of a fine. The land here rises into hills, whose summits are conical, presenting a scene rugged and romantic.

The torments inflicted by legions of musquitos and flies, in journeying through these wildernesses, are intolerable to an European; but the hardy Canadians seem to disregard them, or to be little subject to their attacks. . . .

In travelling to the north-west by the Outaouais river, the distance from Montreal to the upper end of Lake Huron is nine hundred miles; the journey may be performed in a light canoe, in the space of about twelve days; and in heavy canoes, in less than three weeks, which is astonishingly quick, when we reflect on the number of portages, and powerful currents to be passed.

About one-third of the men we have mentioned, remain to winter in the remote territories, during which they are occupied in the chace, and for this service their wages and allowances are doubled. The other two-thirds are engaged for one or two years, and have attached to them about seven hundred Indian women and children maintained at the expence of the company; the chief occupation of the latter is to scrape and clean the parchments, and to make up and arrange the packages of peltry.

The period of engagement for the clerks is five or seven years, during which the whole of the pay of each is no more than one hundred pounds, together with cloathing and board. When the term of indenture is expired, a clerk is either admitted to a share in the company, or has a salary of from one hundred to three hundred pounds *per annum*, until an opportunity of a more ample provision presents itself.

The guides, who perform likewise the functions of interpreters, receive, besides a quantity of goods, a salary of about eighty-five pounds *per annum.* The foremen and steersmen who winter, have about fifty pounds sterling; and they who are termed the middle men in the canoes, have about eighteen pounds sterling *per annum,* with their cloathing and maintenance.

The number of people usually employed in the north-west trade, and in pay of the company, amounts, exclusive of savages, to twelve hundred and seventy or eighty men, fifty of whom are clerks, seventy-one interpreters and under clerks, eleven hundred and twenty are canoe-men, and thirty-five are guides.

PROBLEMS OF A NEW SETTLEMENT

Montreal Gazette, November 10, 1824.

NEW-GLASGOW SETTLEMENT.

1st November, 1824.

Mr. EDITOR,—We are in a pitiful predicament, although possessing lands of the first quality as to soil, although the settlers are quiet industrious people; although there is no disagreement among the neighbours; and although we have had our labours repaid this season with a plentiful crop, and got it all safe secured, yet Mr. Editor we are in a pitiful predicament, and in this you will agree with me when I tell you that from the wretched state of our roads, we are for a considerable part of the year completely locked out from all communication with our neighbouring settlements. We were induced to fix upon this settlement, having understood that government had liberally granted money to make a road to our door. This road has never been completed. The swamps are not wooded; the bridges rock like cradles. The raveens are so steep in the banks that a horse might as well ascend the side of a house as climb them. In the months of May and June the water in many places is three feet deep, on what is called the road. Would you Mr. Editor believe, although our roads are left in this state, the person who contracted to make them is said to have received £1000 of the public money for this job.

I have heard it always said that the law was a tedious and vexatious thing; but it is truly marvelous that this road should have been the subject of litigation for upwards of four years. Surely there is a snake in the grass:—I beg you will give our case publicity, say something about it which may meet the eye of those in power, in order that they may search and discover where the fault lies and with a voice of authority demand justice to have its course.

We were in lively hope that this road matter was relieved from the quibbles of law by its having become the subject of arbitration, and that the decision would have been final; yet strange to tell, this *decret arbetrat* has either died in the birth or perished in its cradle, or perhaps it has not got sufficient nourishment to make it speak, yet. Surely these gentlemen are somewhat allied to the stoics and incapable of commiseration, when they can be either directly or indirectly the means of hemming in and imprisoning so many of their fellow men for 9 months in the year, or who if these attempt to scramble through the roads as they are, appear like frogs coming out of a bogg. Give us your opinion Mr. Editor, what is to be done? shall we petition the executive government or the Judges of the Court, or what shall we do in this case? The press is said to be a mighty Engine, perhaps it may arouse some from their lethargic state of indifference and make them urge the completion of this tardy business with effect.

In addition to this depressing and distressing impediment to our prosperity we have another complaint, viz. the want of a mill—there being none within nine miles of us, and that same, but an indifferent one.—So that what with the badness of our roads and the distance we have to travel to a mill, it would be cheaper for us to buy our flour from the people who bring it from the surrounding settlements, during the short period they can get access to us, than to grind what we raise ourselves, at the nearest mill.—Our worthy seignor promised us a mill two years ago, but having some disputes about his title deeds, he was desirous to have it settled before going to the expense of erecting a mill. From the want of it we are the daily sufferers. Will you publish what is the law or custom on these matters in cases like ours, and you will oblige the New Glasgow settlers particularly yours, &.—*Philo.*

FARM LIFE IN NOVA SCOTIA

J. Lynton Martin, 'Farm Life in Western Nova Scotia Prior to 1850'. *Collections of the Nova Scotia Historical Society*, XXXVII, 1970, 68-72. Reprinted by permission of the Nova Scotia Historical Society and the author.

Today, with our more advanced knowledge of physiography, soils and agricultural practices, we often wonder why settlement was attempted in many parts of the province which we now consider sub-marginal for agriculture. There are two points we should keep in mind: first, twenty acres looked like a large piece of arable land to a man with nothing but an axe, a hoe and a strong back, and second, many of the smaller farms, even in the earliest times, were considered a place to build a home and raise food and clothing for the family, with the major part of the cash income derived from work elsewhere.

This is well illustrated by the organization of the Ross family. In 1835, William, the eldest son, was married and lived at home, but was responsible for the operation of a grist and saw mill. He helped out on the farm at peak periods, and the other boys helped him in the mill when required.

The second son, Irlam, is presumed to have died by this time, and George, the third son, was primarily responsible for the farm operations. However, in stormy weather and during slack periods, George served as the community shoemaker, having learned his trade from Jacob Hiltz of the nearby Forties Settlement.

The next son, Edward, helped George on the farm, did William's bookkeeping for the mill, and operated a small store with supplies he brought in from Halifax. He also bought cattle, butter, hay, barrels and other produce of the district and sold it in Chester, Lunenburg and Halifax. He later became Justice of the Peace and collected county rates, paid pensioners, and controlled statute labor.

Lawson worked at home until 1835, but then left for St. Martins in New Brunswick and after several years there, he went on to Boston where he remained until he died. This illustrates the fact that surplus labor left the small farms and even migrated from the Province in the second generation.

James, the youngest son, worked with his brothers on the farm and at the mill, and Mary, the eldest child married Andrew Kiens, a son of John Kiens the former Quartermaster of the 5th Battalion, 16th Regiment, and she went to live on the Kiens farm across the lake.

Rosebank Cottage was built in the Cape Cod style so common to much of Nova Scotia. A large central flue provided five fireplaces—one in the cellar, three on the main floor and one upstairs. The fireplace in the cellar was lighted in January and February to prevent the vegetables and potatoes from freezing, but in the coldest weather even this precaution was not always successful. On numerous nights water froze in all the bedrooms and in the kitchen.

When the weather was suitable, the farm routine included cutting and hauling firewood for the house and logs for the mill, threshing grain in the barn, cutting underwood in preparation for land clearing, and hauling hay from the marshes. Two kinds of firewood were harvested—pole-sized wood was cut, limbed and dragged home in tree lengths with the oxen. A load of this wood was called a drag. The bigger wood was cut in shorter lengths and was hauled on a sled. It was called sled wood.

Hay from the natural meadows provided most of the fodder for cattle and horses. It was cut and stacked on the marshes in the fall, and when the ground was frozen and covered with snow, it was hauled home. Threshing and cleaning barley, wheat and oats was a laborious process with flails and winnowing basket. One man could thresh from three to five bushels of grain in a long day, and many winter days were required to get the grain ready for the mill.

Oxen and horses were taken to Russell's blacksmith shop to be sharp shod, and sleds were built at home and taken to Russell's for ironing. When mild spells occurred during this period, much hardship resulted since everyone depended upon the snow for the heavy hauling of the year, and to facilitate travel to Chester Basin and Kentville.

Stormy weather found the farm folks busy with threshing, weaving wool and linen, mending shoes, repairing equipment and writing letters. When the snow disappeared following heavy rains, underwood was cut on the rough lands and then heavy wood in preparation for burning, and logs were cut for the sawmill. Traps were set for fur-bearing animals because even rabbit and wildcat skins could be sold on the Halifax market.

In March, the last of the hay was hauled from the marshes and most of the traps were picked up and brought in. Logs and firewood were cut and hauled, and with spring just around the corner fence poles were harvested and more land was prepared for burning. Potatoes in the cellars began to sprout, and they had to be picked over, and of course there were always the odd jobs like going to the swamp for a fine hackmatack to make a sled tongue, or locating some fine ash for axe handles. When snow conditions were right, a group of men often gathered with guns, snow shoes and dogs and sought out the moose in their winter yards.

In April, the seemingly never ending task of cutting firewood continued and the job of cutting land for burning was finished. Fence poles were cut and hauled home and the old fences were repaired and new ones built. Wooden-framed spike tooth harrows were made and new handles were put in the hoes. By the end of the month, ploughing usually began in New Ross, although the folk in Chester were often able to plough the first week of April. And of course, this was the month for maple sugaring.

In May and June, clouds of smoke rose above the forest clearings all over the countryside because this was the time for piling and burning land. It was common practice to clear and burn new land for at least a part of the potato and grain crop each year. Edward Ross noted that 'in new settlements like Sherbrooke it is generally the chief dependence of a crop as whatever may be the cause ploughed potatoes seldom turn out well.' Extra help was sought and six or eight men piled and burned the brush and trees. When the fires were out, the men were joined by women and the potatoes were laboriously hacked in with hoes. In 1838, six men

THE NEW BRUNSWICK SQUATTER

Abraham Gesner, *New Brunswick; with Notes for Emigrants* (London, Simmonds & Ward, 1847), pp. 244-7.

The system of clearing in New Brunswick differs a little from that pursued in Canada. A tract of ground having been selected, all the under-brush is first cut away—this is most easily done when the ground is frozen—and it is desirable also to remove such small trees as are suitable for making the fences. The large trees are then felled and "junked up" (cut into logs) from ten to fifteen feet in length, the limbs are lopped off, and the closer they lie to the ground, the better will they afterwards burn. The trees are sometimes felled in windrows (long heaps of fallen timber)—a plan which operates against the equal burning of the surface and the distribution of the ashes.

The time for chopping varies. It is generally admitted that the under-brush should be cut in the beginning of winter, and the large trees in the ensuing spring, before the sap has ascended to the branches. In August or September the chopping is fired, and much labour is saved by obtaining *a good burn*. Most frequently the fire consumes all the brushwood and limbs, and nothing remains but the charred logs and extinguished brands. In the autumn, these are rolled together with handspikes, or drawn by oxen, into large piles, where they are burned. This work is most frequently performed by a number of settlers, who unite and assist each other in the laborious task. Almost every man collects his neighbours, if he have any, and makes a *piling frolic*. After the labour of the day is ended, and the company have partaken of the refreshments prepared by the females, it is not uncommon to hear the fiddle strike up, and the party engage in the merry jig and reel. This system of mutual assistance is considered beneficial; it removes little jealousies in society, and cheers the heart of the settler amidst his struggles to redeem the soil; yet I have observed, that men who plod on alone and single-handed are as successful as those who adopt the other course. After the piling, the heaps of wood are fired, generally in the evening, when the whole surface is in a blaze, and the anxious settler remains up all night to roll the ignited logs together.

In Canada, the ashes are collected while they are dry, and safely stored in water-tight log-sheds until winter, when they are carried to the potash manufactory and sold. There are no *asheries* in New Brunswick, and the alkali is allowed to mix with the soil.

Choppings are sometimes made in the winter, and burned in the spring: in such instances, the labour of "clearing off" is greater, but a crop is obtained in the same season. After all the timber has been consumed, or drawn off to make the fences, the surface of the earth is broken by a crotch-harrow, drawn by horses or mules. The harrow is in the shape of the letter V, with a row of teeth in each side. The wheat, or other grain, is then sown broadcast. About two bushels of wheat are required for an acre. Some sow the grain upon the unbroken surface. The harrow is again applied, and hacks are employed to cover the grain around the stumps. The price of clearing an acre of land ready for the harrow is from £2 10s. to £4, currency, according to the quality and growth of the timber upon it. The wheat sown as above almost universally yields a good crop. At the time of harvest it is stacked, unless the proprietor has erected a barn for its reception. Two crops of wheat are seldom taken from the same piece of ground in two successive seasons, although potatoes are sometimes planted on the same field two and three years following.

With the wheat, timothy and clover seed are sown; the first crop is therefore succeeded by grass for hay, the value of which is much increased by the demands of the lumber parties, who frequently pay as high as £5 per ton for the fodder of their oxen. The ordinary price of wheat is 7s. 6d. per bushel.

Besides potatoes, these new lands produce turnips, cabbages, and all kinds of vegetables, and also the leguminous plants, without the aid of manure. Over and above paying the expense of clearing the land, the cost of seed, the labour of sowing and harvesting, the first crop yields a profit. Many settlers and squatters, therefore, prefer clearing a new piece every year, to the cultivation of tracts from which the timber has been already removed. In consequence of this propensity to level the forest, large fields are seen in every quarter overrun by raspberry bushes, sprouts, and a young growth of trees, the land having been abandoned as soon as the first crop was secured. These results are also favoured by the cheapness and abundance of land, and, all taken together, have produced a very remarkable class of persons called squatters.

These men will remove their families into the deep recesses of the forest, where, to use their own phrase, they "knock up a shanty," and commence chopping. They are all expert hunters, and at fishing quite *au fait*. Their stock consists of a cow and a pig. The former, during the summer, finds her own living, and wears a large bell upon her neck, to inform the dairymaid of whereabouts in the wilderness she is feeding. When the little stock of provisions is nearly exhausted, deer, partridges, or salmon and trout, are quickly supplied. Maple sugar is exchanged for flour, which is sometimes drawn over the snow on toboggans to great distances. The squatter is also a trapper, and, during the winter, collects a quantity of fur. The crop raised by one of these men and family in a season will more than supply them with food for a year; and their clothing is purchased with the proceeds of the furs, maple sugar, brooms, axe-handles, and other articles of their own manufacture. If the owner of the land appear to meddle with his affairs, the squatter looks upon him with cool indifference, or leaves his residence to repeat the same operation in another quarter. The Government seldom interferes with these men when they fix their abodes on Crown lands; and if their clearings are taken up by persons who obtain grants, an allowance is made to them for improvements. Their number in the Province is about 1600, exclusive of persons who have made partial payments for their lands.

Viewed under any light, the squatter is a useful man: he is the true pioneer of the forest—the advanced guard of the agricultural army; and often, from his knowledge of the country, skill, and kindness, he proves to be the benefactor of the disheartened immigrant. We stop not here to inquire into the lawfulness of his pursuits, knowing that they have resulted from the humanity of the Government, and that they will be given up to steady industry when the country shall be widely inhabited.

THE FRONTIER FARM

[Catherine Parr Traill], *The Backwoods of Canada: Being Letters from the Wife of an Emigrant Officer* (London, Charles Knight, 1838), pp. 97-105.

I have listened with feelings of great interest to the history of the hardships endured by some of the first settlers in the neighbourhood, when Peterborough contained but two dwelling-houses. Then there were neither roads cut nor boats built for communicating with the distant and settled parts of the district; consequently the difficulties of procuring supplies of provisions was very great, beyond what any one that has lately come hither can form any notion of.

When I heard of a whole family having had no better supply of flour than what could be daily ground by a small hand-mill, and for weeks being destitute of every necessary, not even excepting bread, I could not help expressing some surprise, never having met with any account in the works I had read concerning emigration that at all prepared one for such evils.

"These particular trials," observed my intelligent friend, "are confined principally to the first breakers of the soil in the unsettled parts of the country, as was our case. If you diligently question some of the families of the lower class that are located far from the towns, and who had little or no means to support them during the first twelve months, till they could take a crop off the land, you will hear many sad tales of distress." ...

Many persons, on first coming out, especially if they go back into any of the unsettled townships, are dispirited by the unpromising appearance of things about them. They find none of the advantages and comforts of which they had heard and read, and they are unprepared for the present difficulties; some give way to despondency, and others quit the place in disgust.

A little reflection would have shown them that every rood of land must be cleared of the thick forest of timber that encumbers it before an ear of wheat can be grown; that, after the trees have been chopped, cut into lengths, drawn together, or *logged*, as we call it, and burned, the field must be fenced, the seed sown, harvested, and thrashed before any returns can be obtained; that this requires time and much labour, and, if hired labour, considerable outlay of ready money; and in the mean time a family must eat. If at a distance from a store, every article must be brought through bad roads either by hand or with a team, the hire of which is generally costly in proportion to the distance and difficulty to be encountered in the conveyance. Now these things are better known beforehand, and then people are aware what they have to encounter.

Even a labouring man, though he have land of his own, is often, I may say generally, obliged to *hire out* to work for the first year or two, to earn sufficient for the maintenance of his family; and even so many of them suffer much privation before they reap the benefit of their independence. Were it not for the hope and the certain prospect of bettering their condition ultimately, they would sink under what they have to endure; but this thought buoys them up. They do not fear an old age of want and pauperism; the present evils must yield to industry and perseverance; they think also for their children; and the trials of the present time are lost in pleasing anticipations for the future.

"Surely," said I, "cows and pigs and poultry might be kept; and you know where there is plenty of milk, butter, cheese, and eggs, with pork and fowls, persons cannot be very badly off for food."

"Very true," replied my friend; "but I must tell you it is easier to talk of these things at first than to keep them, unless on cleared or partially cleared farms; but we are speaking of a *first* settlement in the backwoods. Cows, pigs, and fowls must eat, and if you have nothing to give them unless you purchase it, and perhaps have to bring it from some distance, you had better not be troubled with them, as the trouble is certain and the profit doubtful. A cow, it is true, will get her living during the open months of the year in the bush, but sometimes she will ramble away for days together, and then you lose the use of her, and possibly much time in seeking her; then in the winter she requires some additional food to the *browse* that she gets during the chopping season, or ten to one but she dies before spring; and as cows generally lose their milk during the cold weather, if not very well kept, it is best to part with them in the fall and buy again in the spring, unless you have plenty of food for them, which is not often the case the first winter. As to pigs they are great plagues on a newly cleared farm if you cannot fat them off-hand; and that you cannot do without you buy food for them, which does not answer to do at first. If they run loose they are a terrible annoyance both to your own crops and your neighbours if you happen to be within half a mile of one; for though you may fence out cattle you cannot pigs: even poultry require something more than they pick up about the dwelling to be of any service to you, and are often taken off by hawks, eagles, foxes, and pole-cats, till you have proper securities for them."

"Then how are we to spin our own wool and make our own soap and candles?" said I. "When you are able to kill your own sheep, and hogs, and oxen, unless you buy wool and tallow"—then, seeing me begin to look somewhat disappointed, he said, "Be not cast down, you will have all these things in time, and more than these, never fear, if you have patience, and use the means of obtaining them. In the mean while prepare your mind for many privations to which at present you are a stranger; and if you would desire to see your husband happy and prosperous, be content to use economy, and above all, be cheerful. In a few years the farm will supply you with all the necessaries of life, and by and by you may even enjoy many of the luxuries. Then it is that a settler begins to taste the real and solid advantages of his emigration; then he feels the blessings of a country where there are no taxes, tithes, nor poor-rates; then he truly feels the benefit of independence. It is looking forward to this happy ful-filment of his desires that makes the rough paths smooth, and lightens the burden of present ills. He looks round upon a numerous family with-out those anxious fears that beset a father in moderate circumstances at home; for he knows he does not leave them destitute of an honest means of support."

In spite of all the trials he had encountered, I found this gentleman was so much attached to a settler's life, that he declared he would not go back to his own country to reside for a permanence on any account; nor is he the only one that I have heard express the same opinion; and it likewise seems a universal one among the lower class of emigrants. They are en-couraged by the example of others whom they see enjoying comforts that they could never have obtained had they laboured ever so hard at home; and they wisely reflect they must have had hardships to endure had they remained in their native land (many indeed had been driven out by want), without the most remote chance of bettering themselves or becoming the possessors of land free from all restrictions. "What to us are the sufferings of one, two, three, or even four years, compared with a whole life of labour and poverty," was the remark of a poor labourer, who was recount-ing to us the other day some of the hardships he had met with in this country. He said he "knew they were only for a short time, and that by industry he should soon get over them."

I have already seen two of our poor neighbours that left the parish a

twelvemonth ago; they are settled in Canada Company lots, and are getting on well. They have some few acres cleared and cropped, but are
obliged to *"hire out"*, to enable their families to live, working on their
own land when they can. The men are in good spirits, and say "they shall
in a few years have many comforts about them that they never could have
got at home, had they worked late and early; but they complain that their
wives are always pining for home, and lamenting that ever they crossed
the seas." This seems to be the general complaint with all classes; the
women are discontented and unhappy. Few enter with their whole heart
into a settler's life. They miss the little domestic comforts they had been
used to enjoy; they regret the friends and relations they left in the old
country; and they cannot endure the loneliness of the backwoods.

THE FARM ROUTINE, THE 1830s

Journal of P. H. Gosse, 1836-1837. PAC, MG 24, 163.

1837.
　　Th. Jany. 19. Recd. 6/10 from Mr. Doncaster for his son's tuition.
　　Sat. Feby. 4th. Being at home today, I cut a large Cedar, on the bank
of the river, & divided it into lengths for about 24 Rails.
　　Sat. Mar. 4th. My school being ended, I returned home, bringing with
me a Colt of Fisher's on trial.
　　Mar. 6th. Cleaned my Stable, Etc. in the forenoon: in the afternoon I
cut 6 Rails on the river.
　　Mar. 7th. Cut a few more rails & broke out a path: then brought them
up with the Sled.
　　Mar. 8th. Cut Cedar sufficient for about 15 rails: then, as it rained, I
mended my coat.
　　Mar. 9th. I cut = 20 rails in the forenoon.
　　Mar. 10th. In the forenoon I cut on Bill's farm, a large round Birch, to
make a Roller, & wheels for a truck. In the afternoon I cut = 10 Cedar
rails.
　　Mar. 11. I fetched home the Birch log, & cleaned the Stable.
　　Mar. 13. I recd. $2.01 from Doncaster, school money. I bought 15 ft.
Maple Plank, 16 ft. Birch Board, 2 Maple Axles, & pr. Sled Shoes for
which I paid (with the sawing to order) 4/.
　　Mar. 14th. Bought of G. Barker, 11 bush. Oats @ 3/. In the afternoon
I cut = 9 Rails.

Mar. 15th. I cut = 44 Rails.

Mar. 16th. I went to Ascot: & bought ½ bush. Pease for 5/.

Mar. 17th. I walked to the village, on some errands.

Mar. 18th. As it rained all day, I did little but assort some letters.

Mar. 20th. I hauled up 5 loads of Rails, being all I had cut. I received £3. 15/. from W. Jones, school money. I bought Fisher's Colt for £5. 10/.

Mar. 21st. I moved some hay from my stack, I went to Ths. Parker's. I made a helve for my axe. Jas. Huntington began to thresh wheat.

Mar. 22nd. I went to the village, & to the Mill.

Mar. 23rd. I with Jas. H. winnowed 3 bushs. wheat, & ½ bush. Hay-seed. In the afternoon I got out my sled, & fitted on the box, in which I took over the chaff.

Mar. 24th. Being unwell, I was indoors and made a headstall. Sold Th. Parker 5 cwt. of Straw, at 1/.

Mar. 25th. I cut = abt. 60 Rails.

Mar. 27th. J. Huntington having given up threshing, I spent the fore-noon vainly seeking other assistance. In the afternoon I winnowed 2¼ bush. wheat, ¼ bush. barley, & ½ bus. Hayseed.

Mar. 25th. I cleaned my Stable in the morning; in the afternoon I cut = abt. 48 Rails.

Mar. 29th. I hauled up 3 loads of Rails: engaged Mr. Moore & Mr. Head, to thresh at 10p. bushel.

Mar. 30th. I cut a large Spruce for Mill logs, & cut two butts.

Mar. 31st. I cut the other two butts of the logs. The men finished the wheat, 5¾ bushels, & ¾ bush. Hayseed. I sawed the axles & planks to size.

April 1st. I endeavored, but vainly to handle the Mill logs, & was forced to leave them. I drew two Cedar logs as far as the bridge, but could not get up the bank.

Apl. 3rd. I went to Lenoxwille & Sherbrook with samples of Wheat, Barley, & Hayseed: but got no offers for the first two, & only 10/. p. bush. for the last.

April 4th. Cleaned the Stable. Saw the barley winnowed,—12 bushels, ½ bus. hayseed.

Apl. 5th. Carried over 1 load of Barley Straw, & 1 load of Barley chaff. I cut 4 mortices for Cart.

Apl. 6th. I cut 4 more mortices. Afternoon winnowed the wheat & chaff again, I got ½ bus. Hayseed, & ½ bus. (indeciph) grain.

Apl. 7th. I borrowed a 2 in. Auger, mended & shod my sled.

Apl. 8th. I cleaned the Stable, mended my coat & did some small jobs.

Apl. 10th. I took over a load of Straw & a load of chaff. Made two cart axles.

Apl. 11th. I hauled my last load of Straw: & split the logs at the bridge into 27 Rails.

Apl. 12th. I lost the morning in preparing to go to Sherbrook. Made an Axe helve.

Apl. 13th. I endeavored to go to Sherbrook, with the cart, but was forced to return. I mended the wheel, which had broken.

Apl. 14th. I went for a sled-load of slabs, but could haul only five! Aftn. cut 8 mortices.

Apl. 15th. I split 42 Rails.

Apl. 17th. I hauled up the Rails at the bridge. Aftn. fitted the uprights & crop pieces of Cart.

Apl. 18th. I made a Roller of cart & fitted the tongue. In the evening I split 20 Rails.

Apl. 19th. Worked all day about the Roller.

Apl. 20th. I walked to the Village.

Apl. 21st. Went to Sherbrook, & sold my hayseed.

Apl. 22nd. Went again to the village.

Apl. 24th. Cleaned the Stable. Worked at Roller ½ day, & Cart ¼ day: Split 8 Rails.

Apl. 25th. Worked all day at the Cart.

Apl. 26. Took a tug to Ramsdill's to be mended. Aftn. hauled 4 loads (of 15 bu.) Maple leaves on potato ground.

Apl. 27th. I exchanged my half-bushel for a dead yearling, which I hauled to the loghouse, & covered with earth. I spread the heap of leaves. Split 30 Rails.

Apl. 28th. Went to Doncaster's. Worked at Cart ½ day.

Apl. 29th. I grafted 7 Plum trees; spread the ashes on Orchard Field; & transplanted a Beech 2 ft. high.

July 1st. We ploughed between potatoes ¾ day. I began to dry the small cow.

July 3rd. We hoed 3½ rows Potatoes. T. churned 2½ lb. Butter. Put the cows in Barber's pasture.

July 4. We hoed 10½ row Potatoes. I posted up.

July 5th. We hoed 6 rows. I picked the sprouts from our store potatoes.

July 6th. I rode to Sherbrooke. T. hoed 4 rows Potatoes.

July 7th. We hoed 12½ rows Potatoes. T. dug in cellar.

July 8th. We called on Templeton in forenoon. Hoed 4½ rows Potatoes.

July 10. We finished hoeing Potatoes. Peas are in blossom.

July 11th. We twitched some stumps in the Pasture, abt. ¾ day. T. churned abt. 4 lb. Butter.

July 12th. We picked Potatoe sprouts in forenoon.

July 13th. Cut down some dead apple trees, & eradicated the suckers in Orchard.

July 14th. I scraped the apple trees: attended divine Service in aftn. Made a poke for horse. Wheat in Birch Fd. is in ear.

July 15. I went to Sherbrooke & Compton on business. Oats (first sown) are coming in ear.

July 17. We dug in the cellar.

July 18th.	Do.	Do.	T. churned.
July 19th.	Do.	Do.	
July 20th.	Do.	Do.	½ day.
July 21st.	Howed 10 rows Turnips.		
July 22nd.	Do.	10 rows	Do. — latter Oats in ear.
July 24th.	Do.	4	Do.	worked ½ day at Cellar.
July 25th.	Do.	6	Do.	Buckwheat is in flower.
July 26th.	Do.	8	Do.	
July 27th.	Do.	5	Do.	Put up Bennett's fence & dug a

little in cellar.

July 28th. We finished hoeing the Turnips.

July 29th. We dug in cellar in forenoon. I cut wood, & T. went to the mill.

July 31st. I went with the cows to the Bull, without success; which occupied the forenoon; aftn. we transplanted 3 rows Turnips, & T. went to the mill.

Sept. 29th. T. Started for New York. I was confined with a sore foot, & churned. . . .

Oct. 2nd. I cleaned the Timothy seed, & mended the headstall.

Oct. 3rd. Took a grist to the mill: carried home the winnowing machine, & brought up a twitch.

Oct. 4th. Put a post in the cellar, made a poke for the horse, & helped Mr. Bill to unload wheat. All my wheat was housed today. Reaped my barley.

Oct. 5th. I was very ill, & confined to the house.

Oct. 6th. Tho' still unwell, I sowed about 3 acres in Orchard with time they [timothy?] seed, & picked most of my apples, a great part of which are frozen in the trees.

Oct. 7th. I harrowed 1½ acre of the Grass seed & hewed a hog's trough.

Oct. 9th. Drew ½ bush. Turnips. Helped Mr. Bill to harvest the oats. Aftn. I churned.

Oct. 10th. Confined by a gathered foot.

Oct. 11th. Cut a Maple which I drew up in three twitches, & partly cut up.

Oct. 12. Rainy weather: indoors all day.

Oct. 13th. Catching the horses, cutting wood, etc. occupied the morning: aftn. I ploughed green sward in log house Field.

Oct. 14th. Went to Mr. Bill & Mr. Bostwick for labor; took from the mill 20 bu. of Woolsweepings.

Oct. 16th. Mr. Allen & I dug & took in 20 bu. Potatoes.

Oct. 17th. I dug & got in 7½ bu. Potatoes.

Oct. 18th. Mr. Bill & I dug & got in 26 bu. Do.

Oct. 19th. In the morning I boiled 2 bu. Potatoes for the Pig: aftn. I helped to pick Potatoes. Mr. Bill & Mr. Allen were at work & we got in 37 bush.

Oct. 20th. Rain: I churned in forenoon: aftn.—stowed the Potatoes.

Oct. 21st. Boiled 2 bu. Potatoes: & got up 3 twitches.

Oct. 23rd. Mr. Allen dug & picked 9 bu. Potatoes. I being very ill with Rheumatism, only carried them in.

Oct. 24th. 25th. & 26th. Confined to the house by sickness.

Oct. 27th. Mr. Bill dug & carried in 5 bu. Potatoes, when as it rained hard, he went home.

Oct. 29th. I got up a twitch of firewood.

Oct. 30th. Went to see Mr. Thomas in forenoon. Aftn. took 2 bu. Buckwheat to the mill.

Oct. 31st. Got up some sticks from the stable, & morticed them, & cut some more. . . .

Dec. 25th. Being at home today, I repaired the stable divisions, which had fallen down, carried over two sled loads of Oat straw, & brought 15½ bus. Oats to the house.

THE FARM ROUTINE, THE 1870s AND 1880s

Diary of David Nelson, 1864-1886, Otonabee, County of Peterborough. PAC, MG 29, B21, pp. 1-2, 34-6.

DAY BOOK

For 1870: January (10) sawing wood at Aunt Margaret's (11) went to Harvey with Lydia (17) rained all day (25) James drew his wheat to Allandale (28) Jane English died   February (9) Brown's sawed our wood (27) Sacrament day.   March (16) snowed about 18 inches (22) William Weir was here (27) snowed about 18 in.   Aprile (1) raised Johns house (3) roads are getting bare (5) I quit using tobacco and Mr. Andrews was here (13) Mrs. Jones Rittle died (18) very high water (19) nearly all the Briges on the Allandale river washed away (24) the water is still rising (25) Allandale mill dam washed away (29) started to sow   May (7) water is falling (14) cousin Andrew Nelson came home from the states (19) old Mrs. Nicholls died at Allandale   June (13) David Gunn died at Allandale (17) raised Johns stable (29) started to cut the hay   July (9) new potatoes to dinner (13) Uncle James died (22) Miss Lane buried.

August (2) Peter Gillespie died (9) Grandfather Esson died (12) Maggie went to work at Leitches (17) finished the harvest   September (1) sowed the wheat (3) Mary Jane Fife and I went to Harvey (28) Andrew Nelson was married   October (1) Joseph Brodie brought down his oxen (5) John moved down to his other place (11) county show at Norwood (17) young James Lang died (22) sold the butter to Walter Renwick.   November (7) killed the pigs (22) thrashed (23) voting for the Railroad   December (14) John Landerville died.

January 1883—(1) Went to Mrs. Davidson's funeral and voting for the Councillors, Wood Grady & Anderson elected (2) Arthur and I went to Pterboro (3) Mrs. Humphries & Mrs. Dinsdale were here (4) making a handsleigh and James is at Toronto convention (5) Nettie Weir and Jimmy was here (6) Little Jimmy Weir and I went to Peterboro (7) Sunday (8) Reform Convention at Norwood (9) took a load of wheat to Peterboro Conservative Convention at Norwood (10) Geo. Read brought out, a pretty cold day (11) went to Peterboro with a load of wheat and Daniel Essons child was buried (12) cleaned a load of oats and made a rack (13) a stormy day (14) Sunday (15) appointed assessor salary $65.00 and Joseph Hooper was here all night (16) Bella went up home to a quilting bee and it is a beautiful day (17) went to Peterboro with a load of oats @ 43¢ (18) David Kerr died (19) family gathering at James and it is very stormy (20) went to Peterboro with fall wheat at 92¢ per bus. (21) Sunday cold and windy (22) went to Peterboro with fall wheat at 92¢ and it is a very cold day (23) a very hard frost this morning (24) went to Peterboro with wheat and Carrie Speirs died this morning (25) a nice day   took down the grist (26) started to assess the Township and went to the funeral (27) assessing in the S.E. corner (28) Sunday (29& 30) assessing over East (31) took 2 sheep to Peterboro to Moffatt. . . .

April, 1883—(1) Sunday fine weather (2) cutting logs for to saw (3) getting out logs and the snow is very deep about 3 feet in the woods and swamps (4) thawing a little and Uncle Robert Nelson died last night and Peter McFarlane Sr. died today (5) rained a little all day and we went to Uncle's funeral (6) changed some oats at Wm. Millers and the snow is going fast (7) Bella and I went to Peterboro with butter and eggs in the cutter (8) Sunday (9) the snow is over 3 feet deep in places yet (10) Jane Agness & Rosilla Fife were here with the cutter (11) Lydia Bryam married to Andrew Shearer (12) copying the assessment roll (13) fine weather and the fall wheat looks splendid and the snow is going slowly (14) Bella and Aggie Jane and Janet & I went to Peterboro on the cars and Aggie & Janet got theor photos taken (15) Sunday a thunder shower tonight (16) Mrs. Bell from Smith came here tonight to bury Fred (17) returned the assessment roll and the snow nearly gone (18) started to plow (19) rained all last night and all forenoon and the ground is very wet and Helen

Renwick died tonight (20) Geo. C. Rodgers drowned at Peterboro, the ground is very wet (21) went to Peterboro (22) Sunday (23) a very hard frost this morning and we sowed some wheat this afternoon for the first [time] and Mrs. Alexander Esson died (24) sowed some barley (25) an awful cold day and very hard frost and I went to the funeral (26) a hard frost this morning and raining this afternoon (27) cold backward weather (28) went to Peterboro with butter and eggs (29) Sunday (30) hard frost every morning. . . .

July 1883—(1) Sunday   James & Jane and Lizzie Lang was here (2) went up to John Langs and Edwin Braden was here (3) a terrible storm of thunder and lightening and rain and hail tonight killed 2 cows for Geo. English (4) heavy thunder this morning (5) building a fence between Bryams and James and it is very warm and Mrs. Thos. Walker was buried (6) a heavy rain tonight (7) went to Peterboro and it is a heavy rain and the ground is awful wet (8) Sunday James Bowie was here (9) working at Sylvesters kitchen (10) raised Sylvesters kitchen (11) started to cut the hay (12) cutting hay and it is raining tonight again and Mrs. Humphries was here (13) working at Sylvesters and Thos. Richardson went to Peterboro (14) turning and raking hay (15) Sunday   rained all forenoon and John Lang and his wife were here (16) Thomas English started to work for me (17) at the hay (18, 19, 20, 21) busy at the hay and it has been a nice dry week, James Lang got his leg broken on the 18th (22) Sunday (23) finished cutting hay (24) Bella and I went to Peterboro with the wool and sold at 18½¢ per lb. (25) finished the hay (26) Thos. English and I was working at Sylvesters house (27) started to cut the fall wheat (28) cutting wheat (29) Sunday (30) cutting wheat and barley (31) cutting wheat and barley. . . .

October 1883—(1) Went to Charles Nelsons pea thrashing (2) raining a little and Arthur came here from Harvey (3) Arthur and I went to Peterboro, it is the show day in East & West Peterboro (4) Archy Byram is here digging potatoes (5) finished the potatoes (6) at the manure (7) Sunday (8) went to Lakefield to hire Thos. English (9) a beautiful day pulling carrots (10) Thos. English started to work for me and Robert Esson was married and Lydia and Janet came down from Harvey (11) a very nice warm weather (12) Keene Shaw for the Township (13) rained all day (14) Sunday (15) drawing out manure (16) went to Charles Nelsons thrashing and thrashed some at home (17) thrashing at home (18) took little Mabel down to Dr. Massie she is very sick and we took in the carrots (19) Dr. Massie was here seeing Mabel (20) Dr. Massie was here and we took in the turnips (21) Sunday Dr. Massie was here (22) Dr. Massie was here and Mabel is a little better and I got 2 little pigs from Wm. Nelson and it is very cold weather (23) nice ploughing weather, shut in the pigs (24) ploughing (25) sold the butter to Campbell McNeil @ 20¢ per lb. 736 lbs. and took a load of barley to the Station (26) took the barley to the station 250 bus. @ 60¢ per bus. (27) a beautiful day (28) Sunday (29) raining (30) ploughing and helping Charley Nelson to clean his wheat and Uncle Robert Esson was here (31) went to Peterboro for stove-pipes.

MAKING IT ON THE FARM

Canniff Haight, *Life in Canada Fifty Years Ago* (Toronto, Hunter, Rose & Co., 1885), pp. 125-8.

The secret of their success, if there was any secret in it, was the economy, industry and moderate wants of every member of the household. The clothing and living were the outcome of the farm. Most of the ordinary implements and requirements for both were procured at home. The neigh-bouring blacksmith made the axes, logging-chains and tools. He ironed the waggons and sleighs, and received his pay from the cellar and barn. Almost every farmer had his work-bench and carpenter's tools, which he could handle to advantage, as well as a shoemaker's bench; and during the long evenings of the fall and winter would devote some of his time to mending boots or repairing harness. Sometimes the old log-house was turned into a blacksmith shop. This was the case with the first home of my grandfather, and his seven sons could turn their hands to any trade, and do pretty good work. If the men's clothes were not made by a mem-ber of the household, they were made in the house by a sewing girl, or a roving tailor, and the boots and shoes were made by cobblers of the same itinerant stripe. Many of the productions of the farm were unsaleable, owing to the want of large towns for a market. Trade, such as then ex-isted, was carried on mostly by a system of barter. The refuse apples from the orchard were turned into cider and vinegar for the table. The skins of the cattle, calves and sheep that were slaughtered for the wants of the family, were taken to the tanners, who dressed them, and returned half of each hide. The currency of the day was flour, pork and potash. The first two were in demand for the lumbermen's shanties, and the last went to Montreal for export. The ashes from the house and the log-heaps were either leached at home, and the lye boiled down in the large potash ket-tles—of which almost every farmer had one or two—and converted into potash, or became a perquisite of the wife, and were carried to the ashery, where they were exchanged for crockery or something for the house. Wood, save the large oak and pine timber, was valueless, and was cut down and burned to get it out of the way.

I am enabled to give a list of prices current at that time of a number of things, from a domestic account-book, and an auction sale of my grandfather's personal estate, after his death in 1829. The term in use for an auction then was vendue.

	1830.	1880.
A good horse	$80.00	$120.00
Yoke of oxen	75.00	100.00
Milch cow	16.00	36.00
A hog	2.00	5.00
A sheep	2.00	5.00
Hay, per ton	7.00	12.00
Pork, per bbl.	15.00	12.00
Flour, per cwt.	3.00	3.00
Beef "	3.50	6.00
Mutton "	3.00	6.00
Turkeys, each	...	1.50
Ducks, per pair	...	1.00
Geese, each	...	.80
Chickens, per pair	...	.40
Wheat, per bushel	1.00	1.08
Rye "	.70	.85
Barley "	.50	1.00
Peas "	.40	.70
Oats "	.37	.36
Potatoes "	.40	.35
Apples "	.50	.50
Butter, per pound	.14	.25
Cheese "	...	.17
Lard "	.5	.12
Eggs, per dozen	.10	.25
Wood, per cord	1.00	5.00
Calf skins, each	...	1.00
Sheep skins, each	...	1.00
West India molasses	.80	.50
Tea, per pound	.80	.60
Tobacco	.25	.50
Honey	.10	.25
Oysters, per quart	.80	.40
Men's strong boots, per pair	3.00	...
Port wine, per gallon	.80	2.75
Brandy "	1.50	4.00
Rum "	1.00	3.00
Whisky "	.40	1.40
Grey cotton, per yard	.11	.10
Calico "	.20	.12
Nails, per pound	.14	.4

Vegetables were unsaleable, and so were many other things for which the farmer now finds a ready market. The wages paid to a man were from eight to ten dollars, and a girl from two to three dollars, per month. For a day's work, except in harvest time, from fifty to seventy-five cents was the ordinary rate. Money was reckoned by £. s. d. Halifax currency, to distinguish it from the pound sterling. The former was equal to $4.00, and the latter, as now, to $4.87.

NEXT-YEAR COUNTRY

W. A. Robertson, Reminiscences, 1832-1911. PAC, MG 29, B26, pp. 23-35.

. . . [A] few days after I got a chance to go and learn blacksmithing in a small country shop with a man named Geo. Powell. He was not much of a mechanic except he could shoe horses pretty good. When my Brother heard I was going to Powells to learn Blacksmithing he ordered me out of the house. The house I had help to build and all the rest of us helped to build. For that act I never forgive him as he never asked me to do so. And I made him pay for it in after years. . . .

I worked with Mr. Geo. Powell trying to learn my trade three years and four months or from Novb. 13th 1849 untill March 1853. It was a hard place to put a youth, as he kept a way side tavern and our spare time was put in the baroom. It was no wonder I learned to be very profane and its a wonder I did not learn worse, but I was determined I would not learn to drink and I did not touch it all the time was there. . . . I learned my trade as well as might be expected in a shop where the sphere was so limited. I fell in love with several young girls and generally got over it without danger to myself or any of them. Mr. Powell and I fell out in March 1853 and I struck out and hunted for a job as a smith and followed that untill the next autumn when I went to Kincardine in Ont. and went in Partnership with my cousin John Campbell and started a Blacksmith shop there. He was teaching school, but after we started he quit teaching. There was not much get up to him. The country was too new and there was no money in it, and in the following spring I quit the shop and went back to work in Hamilton in a carshop for two or three months. Then I went back to Kincardine and done the ironwork for some mills that Mr. McPherson was building as I had promised to before I left there in the spring. While there a young girl that I will not name tried hard to get me to marry her but I could not think of getting married without more cash besides I wanted to see more of the world and I did not want to tie myself down in Ontario. So I came back that autmn and started to build a large stone shop in Freelton near my old home on the Brock road. But I did not get it finished untill next summer and then I started in good shape. But the luck of our Family seamed to follow me. I took in Partners two good mechanics. One Ephm. Walker a waggonmaker and Geo. Sutherland a woodworker and painter—had they been steady men we would have done well enough but I was somewhat reckless and they were far worse. After a while Sutherland run away with considerable of our funds and crippled us and after a year or two I got a good chance to sell the stock and rent the shop and I done so. But in an evil and unlucky hour I traded the shops [and] . . . a dwelling house . . . for 6 lots in the Northwest peninsula of Ontario. The land was good but it was not all paid for. But it had some fine white pine on part of it and a company was under agreement to build a sawmill on a lot of land they had there on a stream called the Sable and I was to get the job of running it. But they never built the mill and they eventually lost their land and timber and I lost mine. . . .

In the beginning of 1860 seeing there was no use of fighting any longer to retreive my self I made up my mind to go to British Columbia . . . I was extremely sorry to leave in that way but there was no help for it as the way the law was then it was imprisonment for debt as there was no bankruptcy law . . . When I got to New York . . . I met many returning from the Pacific Coast and they all gave it such a hard name they skared me from going at that time and after a months time in New York seeing the sights I started on the tramp and was in Philadelphia, Pittsburg, Cleveland. I worked a while in Cincinati then I went on down the Ohio to Cairo and up the Mississippi river to St. Louis and on to Burlington, Devonport and worked a while in Eau Clarien in Iowa. . . I went on and got a job at a place called Huntley and I worked there for about a year altogether.

SETTLING-IN IN THE WEST

Lloyd Rodwell, 'Saskatchewan Homestead Records'. *Saskatchewan History*, XVIII, Winter, 1965, 11-15, 20-3. Reprinted by permission of *Saskatchewan History* and the author.

Settlement under the free land grant system was established by Order-in-Council in 1871. In the succeeding years the passage of Dominion Lands Acts made many changes in the regulations under which homesteads were obtained but in general they allowed for settlement on a 160-acre farm upon the payment of a registration fee of $10.00. In order to receive a patent for the land, the farmer had to reside on it for a specific period and show his serious intentions as a settler by making improvements on the land. By means of second homestead entries, pre-emption rights and purchased homesteads, the settler was able to expand his holdings. . . .

Occupations other than farming are sometimes listed on the application for patent, the most common of these being teaching, the ministry, blacksmithing, or storekeeping. Many teachers and clergymen found in the very early days that they had to farm in order to provide themselves with necessities or possibly additional income. Thus clergymen and teachers worked a homestead near the school or mission at the same time they were carrying on other duties in the community.

The hardships faced by the pioneers are rarely mentioned on the application for patent; more often these difficulties are described in the correspondence asking for an extension of time in fulfilling the homestead duties or when applying for extra time in which to pay seed grain debts. But one application for patent had the arresting words "The Armless and Legless Wonder of Moose Jaw" written in quotation marks after the name of the applicant. In the application, the farmer stated ". . . in the winter of 1887-8 I was frozen losing both legs and arms and did no active work personally after that though I had a crop or two put in and some plowing done after that." While this farmer was in hospital, neighbours put up a house for him to meet the homestead regulations, but the kindness shown by some was not shown by others as he reported that a frame stable he had built was stolen while he was in hospital. Subsequently he earned his living by selling "notions" in the district. Officials of the Department of the Interior considered that he had fulfilled the requirements to get his patent and it was issued shortly after he applied for it.

Under the homestead regulations, a settler could abandon the land he had first chosen and enter on another homestead. He had to state his reasons for abandoning the land and the information given on this form reveals the situation faced by many farmers. . . .

The abandonments show that lack of a good water supply was one of the main problems faced by some settlers. Two farmers wrote on their abandonments that:

> Unfortunately I cannot live on it, since there is no water to be found. The cattle must be driven 4 or 5 miles to a watering place, and we have to go 5 or 6 miles for drinking water. I have hunted all over the homestead, and can find no water. What is the farm to me if I have no water.

> ———

> We tried for water in 4 different places 3 wells we went down 60 feet and one 106 feet without finding water. At the time of thrashing last fall we had to drive 30 miles for water to do our thrashing with.

In 1886, one farmer near Pense thought he could solve the water problem by digging in ravines. He offered to buy a quarter section adjacent to his homestead at $1.25 per acre because it had ravines and he would be able to get water which, until that time, he had been unable to find on his own homestead:

In spite of failing crops for the last three years and my neighbours all leaving, as you may see by the number of cancelled sections round me, & those who remained to get their deed have removed there houses after fulfilling the regulations. I have persevered in trying to get water and thought I was successful after digging 124 feet and boring 50 feet but it has been an endless expense for the last two years. . . I paid in the first place for digging and Kerbing a well 97 feet & boring 50 feet $195. As there was no water a man witched the land so I dug where he indicated and had to remove my house, dairy & stable. The present well cost $291 the first outlay and as it was impossible to pump by hand I had a geared Windmill erected which with the pump cost me $400. And now it is useless, and all the time this work has been going on I have had to haul water & melt snow and last winter I lost two valuable mares & their colts, I believe from no other reason than lack of water. It is utterly impossible for me to carry on this farm without water.

Although some settlers lacked a suitable water supply, some had too much. One farmer was flooded out after being on the land for three years. One can assume that another settler was a trifle exasperated at the amount of water on his land for when he abandoned it he wrote "Land was only fit for pasture. Now only fit for ducks." Droughts, if not of the proportions of the one in the 1930's, were all too prevalent from the early days of settlement. One farmer, who with his wife and six children lived in a sod house 16 by 24 feet for three years, finally abandoned his homestead after having successive crop failures. He also mentioned a lack of school facilities, another common reason for leaving certain localities:

In 1893 I put in ten acres of crop and received no return from Drought. In 1894 I put in forty acres of crop and received twenty bus in return and having eight of a family to support with no other means of support was forced to abandon [the homestead] Another reason four of my children are of school age and there is no school nor likelihood of any as the settlers have all left.

The settler who followed this farmer on the same piece of land only stayed on it from June to August in one year and then abandoned it. The third settler was more permanent. He stayed on the land and got a patent for it but he only cropped the same amount of land which the first settler had broken and used the remainder for grazing purposes.

There were other reasons for abandoning land. One farmer had his entry inspected because a neighbour complained that when the occupant filed on it he made a false statement claiming that there was less hay land on it than allowed for grazing purposes. The file does not contain the results of the inspection but the occupant left the land to settle elsewhere. His stated reason for leaving the land was "The immigration of foreigners

and the exodus of all the English speaking settlers from these parts . . .
now there are a number of Galicians around and I would be the only
Englishman for miles." Another homesteader left his quarter section because there were no Mennonites settling in the district as he thought there
would be, so he wanted to go to a district where there were some. One
farmer abandoned his land when he made an incorrect entry on it because
he could not find the survey mounds. Another settler could not speak
English and he was told to detrain at the wrong land location. Instead of
getting off the train west of the third meridian, he was put off west of
the second meridian, about 180 miles short of his destination. It was not
until the land agent investigated a double entry that the error was discovered. One farmer deviated a mere six miles off course from his intended destination. He gave the following reason for abandoning his
entry "I filed in error on this land being intoxicated at the time. . . I had
entered for [other] land two days previously but being drunk at the time
could not remember." Possibly this entrant should have swapped homesteads with another who abandoned his quarter section because there were
too many "alcohol" lakes on it. Of course, it is more probable that he had
difficulty spelling "alkali" rather than was guilty of overlooking a good
thing when he had it. It is entirely possible that many settlers did not give
complete reasons for abandoning their land, but one homesteader showed
that he was master of telling a lot in a few blunt words when he abandoned his homestead for one seven miles away. He wanted to move his
children seven miles closer to school and seven miles further away from
his wife's relatives. . . .

The file of one Moosomin district farmer covers a period from 1884 to
1904 and tells of the difficulties he faced in his attempts to farm his land,
raise a family and pay off his debts. On December 9, 1884, this farmer
filed on his homestead quarter. He had come from England, where he had
been employed as a clerk, under the auspices of the Canada North-West
Land Company to whom he was indebted for $250.00. This amount was
more than likely a travel advance or an advance made to get him established on the land. It was charged against his land and before the patent
could be issued in his name, he would have to repay the advance and
interest at not more than 6%. In 1887, the farmer received seed grain
from the Canadian Government for which he had to repay $37.00. This
Seed Grain Lien constituted a permanent charge against the land, and it
would have to be paid before title to the land could be issued. In March
1888 the farmer applied for an extension of time on the repayment of the
lien because he had been unable to get a machine to thresh his crop. In
April of the same year he filed his application for patent and this showed
that by 1887 he only had 22 acres cropped and a further 15 broken, his
livestock consisted of one team of oxen and two cows. The homesteader,
his wife and 9 children lived in a house 16 feet by 32 feet. In reply to his

application for patent he was advised that it would be issued as soon as the liens against the land were discharged. On December 25, 1888 he wrote to the Department:

I find it utterly impossible to raise the amount due for seed grain that the government so generously supplied, having only enough wheat & barley left for seeding 45 or 50 acres in the ensuing year; after reserving the above I have not enough left for Bread for my large family (I have a wife & nine children). . . . My crop of 25 acres only averaged 8 bushel & I had to pay for stacking, cutting & threshing. Having to work out for sustenance.

The Department replied that he would be given until the next harvest to pay the seed grain lien provided he paid at the current market prices with interest at 6%. By the end of 1889 his debt with the Canada North West Land Company, which also had not been paid, amounted to $333.75 of which $83.75 was interest. In 1890, the homesteader was forced to get more seed from the government and that year he claimed that he got the first "decent" crop since going on the land. He requested that the Department use its influence to prevent the land company from pressing him for his debt because:

. . . If the said company are allowed to push me . . . all my terrific struggle and labour will have gone into their coffers and myself a little better—if at all—than a beggar. You will judge of my prospects when I tell you I hope to seed down sixty—& if possible to even extend to seventy—measured acres next year. This year I farmed 45 acres.

The farmer felt that a couple of good crops would set him up in the country for life but his hopes were not realized. There is no indication in the file as to the results of the 1891 crop but in December 1892 the collection of some of the seed grain liens had been placed in the hands of Winnipeg lawyers and to them the homesteader wrote:

I am most anxious and willing to discharge this obligation, and have been trying for a long time to make enough headway to enable me to start making payments; but the absolute need of the barest necessaries of life for my large family of ten members, and the fearful struggle with fire (one crop with Hay & Stables entirely destroyed) & Drought and Hail (one year since the year of the fire, I had only 80 Bushels of grain and the next 300) I am just at present without the change of one Dollar, and my fine crop of 70 acres, to which I most anxiously looked to reduce if not clear up, this claim, having suffered from the two latter causes and gophers, is, unless it pans out far better than appearances bids me to hope, about enough to feed my family with bread groceries (clothing I cannot begin to hope for, although greatly needing them for those members who must face the fearful winter on piled and burned land on the Ross Farm for eight days, and then with the help of several women they planted 41 bushels of potatoes in seven days. In November, they harvested 164 bushels, a small crop by today's standards. In 1835, they harvested 440 bushels but we have no record of how much seed was planted.

Grain was sown broadcast and harrowed with the burnt-land harrow, or in extremely rough areas was covered with the hoe. The burnt land was often planted with the same crops for two or three years until yields dropped and weeds became troublesome. By this time, most of the stumps were well rotted, and it was a relatively easy job to clean up the field and seed it to hay, or to leave it in the rough state and use it for pasture.

Dung was hauled from the barn in a two-wheeled cart and spread on the improved ground. It was ploughed in, for the most part with wooden ploughs, although a few cast-iron models began to appear after 1820 imported from England, and after 1835 from the United States. The ploughed ground was harrowed with a square spike-toothed harrow and the grain was broadcast by hand. The land was then harrowed once more, and after about 1820, the seed was firmed in the ground with a roller made from a log.

By the first of July, planting was finished except for the turnips which were usually left until about July 15th. The early part of the month was used for fencing crop land, hoeing potatoes, statute work on the roads, and the wild strawberry harvest. Now and again a barn or house-raising frolic was organized, and spinning frolics occupied the women folk.

After the middle of the month, the haying equipment was checked, repaired or remade. Scythes brought in from Halifax (imported from England or Scotland) were fitted with home-made snaths, old rakes were repaired and new ones made up, new handles were fitted to wrought iron pitch forks, and wagon and cart ladders were repaired. Mowing began on the uplands about the end of the month, and on the marshes about the middle of August. It was seldom completed before mid-September.

The upland hay near the house was usually mowed by the men working in pairs. The women helped by raking and shaking it out to dry. It was then cocked up and hauled to the barn either on a two-wheeled cart or a wagon. Four-wheeled wagons were not common until after 1835.

The marshes and many of the burnt-land clearings were often some distance from the house, and the marshes were too wet to use oxen or horses. Thus a party of six or eight men usually went from one meadow to another to handle this chore. They mowed the hay, dried and raked it, and piled it into cocks. Ricks were built at convenient locations, and the cocks were then carried on two poles by men working in pairs. The hay was stacked on the ricks where it remained until it could be hauled home over the frozen ground in winter.

these vast open plains this winter) and provide seed for one more effort. I expect the threshers after it freezes up, but cannot see any hope of clearing up the amount yet, as to stock for sale, I simply have but 2 Cows (10 Dollars due in trade on one of them) and this years calf, an old beast for beef for the pot, and a team of ponies (one small) barely able to pull me through needed labour.

Later he wrote to the Secretary of Dominion Lands:

> . . . I have been most anxious to pay this amount out of this crop but regret to tell you it is utterly impossible. I have only three small stacks of wheat off 75 acres of crop—part of that only fit for feed—having suffered from Drought & Hail & Gophers, so that I cannot expect so much as grist for my large family of ten., after my seed is secured added to which I have not been threshed. I have nothing I can sell having only two cows (one with $10.00 to pay on) and a calf, and a team of ponies.

The reply from the Secretary of Dominion Lands was to the effect that if both the borrower and his sureties joined in a request for an extension of time, it would be granted until April 1, 1890 but a further extension could not be granted unless a request was sent to the Minister of the Interior. On February 19, 1893 the homesteader wrote to the Minister, outlining the poor crop he had had that year and mentioning that he would have to save from it enough grain to seed 50 acres of wheat and that he would have to purchase oats, barley and potato seed. His letter went on:

> I have suffered real hardship and privation for years—you will better understand this if you know what a family of 10 hearty boys and girls consume; 100 lbs. flour and 4 Bushel potatoes—when I have them—barely sufficient for ten days: i am nearly beside myself at times to clothe their dear half naked bodies; which, I solemnly declare to you, have literally with three small lads been staring me in the face through the recent blizzards, I am willing to make affidavit of the truth I utter if you wish it.
>
> I beg to ask for one more trial to get a good crop to pay this debt. . . i pray you therefore to grant me this generous favour and do not push my surety, who is a poor man almost as hardly able to pay as myself. . . .

In reply, the Department of the Interior extended the time of payment until January 1, 1894, and the file contains nothing more about the debts until 1904. By that time the seed grain debt had increased to $95.00, of which $50.00 was principal and the balance interest. The debt with the land company had increased to $550.00. In the intervening years, the homesteader's family had grown up and the homesteader himself had left the farm and entered the real estate, loan and insurance business. His sons, on whom he had depended to look after the farm for him in his old age, had also left the farm and it was uncultivated. The homesteader had been in the real estate business only two years and was still struggling to make it a paying concern. Part of his reason for leaving the land was that he was fifty years of age and was no longer able to carry on the arduous work on the farm. He was relying upon his land, which he claimed was worth about $10.00 per acre, to provide for his need in his old age.

In order to get the patent issued, he had to clear the land of debt by borrowing $550.00 from an investment company. He also paid off the seed grain lien. Thus by 1904 he was able to get clear title to the land on which he had settled in 1884. The experiences of this farmer were typical of many who came to Canada ill-prepared and ill-equipped for farming under Western Canadian conditions. Many farmers incurred larger debts than this farmer, the interest sometimes increasing the debts by three times and well into the thousands of dollars, but few files are readily found having letters as revealing of the homesteaders feelings as this particular file. Unfortunately, the homestead records contain more information about the unsuccessful farmers than about the successful. Records for successful farmers usually contain a few documents, and the success of the farmers is shown by the amount of land cropped and the improvements made. This information usually needed no correspondence to support it. On the other hand, unsuccessful farmers, or those facing difficulties wrote many letters to the Department. It must be admitted that the Department generally was as lenient as it could be when the plight of the settlers was made known to it.

THE YOUNG FARMER'S PLAINT

Winnipeg Daily Times, April 11, 1883, p. 4.

In a fit of desperation a young fellow writes from Arran, Manitoba, to a friend at Galt, Ontario, as follows: "Tell me if any of the girls are married yet. If not, just tell Mrs. —— to keep them all for me and I will take them off her hands. Lots of my friends here would give a big premium for a good wife, and they couldn't get a better than Susie or Kate. We can buy most every thing else out here, but a wife cannot be got for love or money. So we must grub along; but when I think of the home comforts I left and then of the days of dish-washing and dirty shirts into which I have come, I get mad."

KEEPING THEM DOWN ON THE FARM

Manitoba Morning Free Press (Winnipeg), June 12, 1893.

THE BOY AND THE FARM.

This is the subject of an article in the Toronto Week, in which the position is taken that we should no more expect the country boy to remain on the farm than that the city boy should be sent to it if it be discovered that his aptitudes fit him for that kind of life. A plea is made in behalf of the country boy that he should be given the same liberty to consult his tastes and inclinations in the choice of a calling as we accord without question to the sons of merchants and professional men. "Why not," asks the Week, "permit the law of natural selection to operate freely in the case of farmers' sons as well as in that of the sons of merchants and professional men in the cities? And why should not parents in town and city, tradesmen, business men, professional men, on the same principle, note carefully the tastes and aptitudes of their boys, and encourage those of whom there are doubtless many, who seem specially fitted for agricultural or horticultural pursuits, to choose their future callings accordingly; not, indeed, by stinting their education, but rather by giving them every facility for thorough culture, both general and special, to fit them for successful and honorable lives in those congenial lines!"

There is no reason why the law of natural selection should not be allowed to apply in the one case as freely as in the other. That has never been the subject of controversy, so far as we know. The lament has been that the boys of the period are displaying a constantly growing disinclination to a life on the farm, and the question so often discussed has been whether this dissatisfaction is not encouraged by that dangerous thing of a "little learning" which comes of our present system of education. The whole question indeed is well summed up in the criticism which was made a day or two ago in this city on the proposal to expend $150,000 on a normal school building. It was said that Winnipeg to-day is swarming with college students and graduates who have no employment, no means, and who have been unfitted by their so-called education to turn their hands to any useful work. They cannot be absorbed here, and the result is that our colleges of all kinds, commercial, medical, theological and what not, are merely agencies for swelling the exodus to the United States. Without entering into the question of liberty, which no one raises, it will have to be admitted that this is a deplorable state of things if true. And that it is true to a very large extent we can all testify of our personal knowledge. Is there no way by which this evil can be checked? Is it not possible by some means to persuade the country boy who comes in for his college course to carry back his education to the farm, and not only that but to persuade the city boy whose object in life is just as aimless to go with him? Neither need we raise the question of natural selection. Four times out of five they are as fit for life on a farm as for anything else, and on the farm there is an opening for all of them, which in the public interest at least it will be better for them to embrace than to go off to another country.

The Week expresses the belief that a change from country to city and from city to country has a beneficial effect on the physical and intellectual strength of the nation. No doubt of it, and sufficient of that change is constantly going on through perfectly natural and healthy causes, and will continue to go on though we regulate the national life even so strictly. There is no monopoly of talent in the cities, as it says. Everyday almost comes up from the country some budding genius whose ambition must seek the larger theatre of the cities for its complete development. That is natural, and inevitable, and altogether right. It is the application of the law of natural selection. But while we vindicate this right we may do something to dissuade the victims of a crude and misleading education, who impose upon themselves the dangerous belief that they too are called to forsake the farm. How to go about it, however, is the question that puzzles. The conviction is growing stronger that our educational system is responsible for the influences which unsettle so many of the youths of the country. They do not come up to the cities in ones and twos, according to the law of natural selection but in hundreds and as if their minds had been poisoned or perverted. The Week cannot but recognize the evil, although it attributes it more to a false standard of success in life which we set up in city and country alike.

ALTERNATIVES TO FARMING

W. A. Langton, ed., *Early Days in Upper Canada: Letters of John Langton* (Toronto, Macmillan Company of Canada Limited, 1926), pp. 199-201. Reprinted by permission of The Macmillan Company of Canada Limited.

Oct. 21, 1844

The complaints are universal of the difficulty of making a living by farming, and I feel no doubt, after giving it a fair trial, that in the present state of affairs it is not to be done. Still I cannot bring myself to think of giving up the farm, for the chances will certainly improve every year and in time even farming alone will probably become more profitable. Were there any other means of making a little money to help the farm, the kind of life is one which I should prefer to any other, and though agriculture alone is a poor prospect, you may live better on a small sum on a farm than anywhere else. The question is what other means of money-making there are, and it is a question which I have asked myself and others five hundred times without getting any satisfactory answer. Ways of making money there doubtless are, but almost any I can think of involve the necessity of moving to a more civilized neighbourhood and it is exactly this which I want to avoid. A steamboat would have the advantage of improving the country more perhaps than anything, but the chances of profit are not very encouraging and the risk and capital to be expended are great. At present the thing is out of the question because the public works from want of funds are at a standstill and it will be probably two years before the whole line will be opened. A distillery on my own creek in connection with the farm, and a store principally intended to buy grain for the distillery would I believe produce enough, but there are objections even in the way of this. My mother is most decidedly and strongly opposed to it on the score of morality, as she thinks a facility of procuring whiskey would be an injury to the country. Besides this a bill has been introduced into our House of Assembly for imposing an excise of sixpence per gallon on whiskey (about thirty per cent. on its value), which will have the effect of throwing the business into large establishments. This I conceive would be the case even in a cash country like England, but in a country like this, where it is always difficult to obtain cash for any article whilst the tax would have to be paid in money, I think it would have the effect of entirely knocking small distilleries on the head . . . [A distillery] would very well dovetail into a farm for, besides consuming the surplus grain, the feeding of pork and beef is one of the main profits of a distillery and the farm might be principally devoted to rearing stock. The store would certainly pay and that permanently, but it requires there to be something else to bring customers to a store. Those who brought their grain to the distillery would lay out the proceeds at the store, but if the former were given up they would take their grain and with it their custom elsewhere, and leave for the unsupported store only the custom of those who had no grain to sell. I think I have before said to you that I know of no money-making business in Canada except the Law, storekeeping, tavern-keeping and perhaps I may add horse-dealing. The two latter we will altogether omit. Storekeeping is decidedly the most money-making and is carried on with very little capital, but it appears to me that those who make it pay are invariably those who have started with next to nothing and have gradually crept up in the world, increasing their business as their capital, custom and experience increased; I hardly recollect an instance of any who have succeeded in planting a full grown tree.

TIMBERING IN THE 1820s

J. McGregor, *Historical and Descriptive Sketches of the Maritime Colonies of British America* (London, Longman, Rees, Orme Brown, and Green, 1828), pp. 164-8.

The timber trade, which, in a commercial as well as political point of view, is of more importance in employing our ships and seamen, than it is generally considered to be, employs also a vast number of people in the British Colonies, whose manner of living, owing to the nature of the business they follow, is entirely different from that of the other inhabitants of North America.

Several of these people form what is termed a "lumbering party," composed of persons who are all either hired by a master lumberer, who pays them wages, and finds them in provisions; or, of individuals, who enter into an understanding with each other, to have a joint interest in the proceeds of their labour. The necessary supplies of provisions, clothing, &c., are generally obtained from the merchants on credit, in consideration of receiving the timber which the lumberers are to bring down the rivers the following summer. The stock deemed requisite for a *"lumbering party,"* consists of axes, a cross-cut saw, cooking utensils; a cask of rum; tobacco and pipes; a sufficient quantity of biscuit, pork, beef, and fish; pease and pearl barley for soup, with a cask of molasses to sweeten a decoction usually made of shrubs, or of the tops of the hemlock tree, and taken as *tea.* Two or three yokes of oxen, with sufficient hay to feed them, are also required to haul the timber out of the woods.

When thus prepared, these people proceed up the rivers, with the provisions, &c., to the place fixed on for their winter establishment; which is selected as near a stream of water, and in the midst of as much pine timber, as possible. They commence by clearing away a few of the surrounding trees, and building a camp of round logs; the walls of which are seldom more than four or five feet high; the roof is covered with *birch bark,* or boards. A pit is dug under the camp to preserve any thing liable to injury from the frost. The fire is either in the middle or at one end; the smoke goes out through the roof; hay, straw, or fir branches are spread across, or along the whole length of this habitation; on which they all lie down together at night to sleep, with their feet next the fire. When the fire gets low, he who first awakes or feels cold, springs up, and throws on five or six billets; and in this way, they manage to have a large fire all night. One person is hired as cook, whose duty is to have breakfast ready before daylight; at which time all the party rise, when each takes his *"morning,"* or the *indispensable dram of raw rum, immediately before breakfast.* This meal consists of bread, or occasionally potatoes; with boiled beef, pork, or fish, and *tea* sweetened with molasses; dinner is usually the same, with pease soup in place of *tea*; and the supper resembles breakfast. These men are enormous eaters, and they also drink great quantities of rum, which they scarcely ever dilute. Immediately after breakfast, they divide into three *gangs*; one of which cuts down the trees, another hews them, and the third is employed with the oxen in hauling the timber, either to one general road leading to the banks of the nearest stream, or at once to the stream itself; fallen trees and other impediments in the way of the oxen are cut away with an axe.

The whole winter is thus spent in unremitting labour: the snow covers the ground from two to three feet from the setting in of winter until April; and, in the middle of fir forests, often till the middle of May. When the snow begins to dissolve in April, the rivers swell, or, according to the lumberers' phrase, the *"freshets come down."* At this time all the timber cut during winter is thrown into the water, and floated down until the river becomes sufficiently wide to make the whole into one or more rafts. The water at this period is exceedingly cold; yet for weeks the lumberers are in it from morning till night, and it is seldom less than a month and a half, from the time that floating the timber down the streams commences, until the rafts are delivered to the merchants. No course of life can undermine the constitution more than that of a lumberer and raftsman. The winter snow and frost, although severe, are nothing to endure in comparison to the extreme coldness of the *snow water* of the *freshets*; in which, the lumberer is, day after day, wet up to the middle, and often immersed from head to foot. The very vitals are thus chilled and sapped; and the intense heat of the summer sun, a transition, which almost immediately follows, must further weaken and reduce the whole frame.

To stimulate the organs, in order to sustain the cold, these men swallow immoderate quantities of ardent spirits, and habits of drunkenness are the usual consequence. Their moral character, with few exceptions, is dishonest and worthless. I believe there are few people in the world, on whose promises less faith can be placed, than on those of a lumberer. In Canada, where they are longer bringing down their rafts, and have more idle time, their character, if possible, is of a still more shuffling and rascally description. Premature old age, and shortness of days, form the inevitable fate of a lumberer. Should he even save a little money, which is very seldom the case, and be enabled for the last few years of life to exist without incessant labour, he becomes the victim of rheumatisms and all the miseries of a broken constitution.

But notwithstanding all the toils of such a pursuit, those who once adopt the life of a lumberer seem fond of it. They are in a great measure as independent, in their own way, as the Indians. In New Brunswick, and particularly in Canada, the epithet "lumberer" is considered synonymous with a character of spendthrift habits, and villainous and vagabond principles. After selling and delivering up their rafts, they pass some weeks in idle indulgence; drinking, smoaking, and *dashing off*, in a long coat, flashy waistcoat and trowsers, Wellington or hessian boots, a handkerchief *of many colours* round the neck, a watch with a long tinsel chain and numberless brass seals, and an *umbrella*. Before winter they return again to the woods, and resume the pursuits of the preceding year. Some exceptions however, I have known to this generally true character of lumberers. Many young men of steady habits, who went from Prince Edward Island, and other places, to Miramichi, for the express purpose of making money, have joined the lumbering parties for two or three years; and, after saving their earnings, returned and purchased lands, &c. on which they now live very comfortably.

TIMBERING IN THE 1870s

Joshua Fraser, *Shanty, Forest and River Life in the Backwoods of Canada* (Montreal, John Lovell & Son, 1883), pp. 23-5, 36-8, 43-7, 330-1, 347, 349-53.

Monahan's shanty, built under his own supervision, is a capital specimen, of its kind, of backwoods architecture. It is warm, roomy, lightsome, and "doesn't smoke." Smoke is the pest of the shantyman's domicile. It requires very considerable mechanical ingenuity, and practical experience, so to construct the camboose and the opening in the roof immediately above it, with its log chimney of few or many feet in height, that the smoke may escape freely and fully. Even with the best and most *experimental* precautions there are few shanties but will smoke sometimes. It depends greatly upon the weather: when the atmosphere is damp, foggy and depressed it is often impossible to prevent it. Our shanty is one of the best in this respect I have ever been in; and in it, until I moved to the mill quarters, I spent a most comfortable and happy time.

Monahan's "gang" of forty men is a fair sample of the shanty *genus homo*; English, Scotch, Irish and French are its constituent elements, and among them are some splendid specimens of physical humanity.

Shanty life would be monotonous in the extreme, were it not for the vigorous exercise in the open, bracing air, and the redundant health, with its natural accompaniment of high animal spirits, which is almost continually enjoyed.

Still the men have their amusements: at night when supper is over, it is a cheery sight to see them round the roaring fire, in the full enjoyment of that sweetest of all rest which follows after hard, lengthy, and healthy labor in a bright, keen atmosphere, surcharged with ozone and oxygen, and impregnated with the balmy odors of the pine, balsam, spruce and tamarac.

Cards, chequers, reading if they have books—and they always have where I am—an occasional dance, song and story, all accompanied by the merry strains of the fiddle, and, better than all, a *camaraderie* which pervades the whole—make the long winter evenings pass quickly and pleasantly, until it is time to turn in under the warm blankets, to sleep that sweet, sound and refreshing slumber, which only strong men in the redundance of health and animal life, without care or thought of the morrow, can obtain and realize. . . . .

Now there is no doubt that . . . [a] low estimate of character is tolerably correct as applied to the average shantyman of many years ago. But it does not hold true now in any sense whatsoever. A great change for the better has been wrought in the character and conduct of these men. I don't believe that, take them as a whole, there is a more sober, orderly, and well-behaved class of laboring men in the world than our backwoods and river lumbering men. To compare them with the working men of our towns and cities, such as ship laborers, canal or railroad navvies, or laborers generally on our large public works, would be, I consider, an atrocious libel upon them—a comparison not to be entertained for a moment. This is the unanimous testimony of all the competent authorities I have consulted on the matter, and, as far as my own experience of twenty years goes, I *know* it to be the case.

Swearing is at a discount among them. Lewd conversation and songs are not tolerated. Liquor is not allowed in, or near the shanty. And, as we shall see further on, they welcome and listen with great attention and respect to the preaching of the Gospel.

I account for this great change in the morals and habits of this class on two grounds:

First, there is a different class seeking work and being engaged by the employers from what used to be. A few years ago the great bulk of the men were hired at Ottawa and Quebec, and were principally French Canadians, of the lowest class. Now, since the sawn lumber business has assumed such large proportions, the drive on the river is comparatively short, generally over by the first of June, consequently a much larger number of the farmers' sons in the vicinity of the works are seeking employment, as they generally can get home in time for sowing the crop; and as they are a much more steady and reliable class, and just as able-bodied and skilful workmen, they are more readily engaged than any others. The number of men who engage in the fall to go through to Quebec is but a fraction of what it used to be, and the number of French Canadians who work in the woods is now reduced to a minimum.

Hence the *personnel* of the shanty is greatly changed, and that vastly for the better, within the last few years.

One of the most important personages about the shanty is the cook. If you wish to enjoy yourself, and have some fair measure of comfort, you must keep on good terms with him. . . .

He is the oracle of the establishment, and his opinion is consulted by every one connected with it. Not only by the magic power of good cooking, but by his general disposition and temper, he exerts an influence in the shanty which greatly affects its general peace and comfort. Hence the employer selects the cook with great care, and gives him the highest wages, often double what an ordinary working man can command.

And you would be amazed at the general excellence of the cooking that is done by these fellows. Where will you find such bread as is made in their immense pots, buried in and covered over by the hot ashes at the end of the *camboose*? Not a particle of the strength and fine flavor of the flour is lost by evaporation, as in the case of a stove or open oven: it is all condensed in the bread. Then it is strong and firm, and yet—and this is the mystery to me—it is light and porous as that of any first-class housewife's.

And what shall we say about the beans? They are simply *par excellence.* They are baked in the same kind of pot as the bread, the lid being hermetically sealed to the rim by dough, and then buried in the hot ashes. The beans are first thoroughly sifted, washed and boiled; and then large slices of fat pork mixed with them. The pot is then placed in its deep bed of hot ashes, and, as in the case of the bread, not a breath of steam or of the essence of the bean allowed to escape. The fat pork becoming dissolved by the heat, and of course neither fried nor boiled as in other processes, becomes amalgamated with the beans, and when the whole is considered sufficiently cooked, a mess is ready, which, for succulency of flavor and savory richness of nutrition, will completely throw into the shade the famous pottage for which Esau bartered his birthright.

It is strong food, of course, the very strongest, I believe, in the world. A person who is accustomed to the ordinary dishes of domestic cooking must be cautious how he attacks it at first. If he takes too heavy an allowance, as he is strongly tempted to do on account of its savoriness, he will be very likely to throw his stomach into convulsions. But it is the grandest food in the world for shantymen, whose vigorous open-air exercise in the keen oxygenated atmosphere enables them to digest food which would upset and demoralize the stomach of a town or city man.

Beans have entirely superseded peas, and are now one of the staple articles of shanty diet. There is a staying power in them which I believe is possessed by no other food, that is, when prepared in the way I describe. I have often taken a large tin plate-full in the morning, and then tramped the whole day through the woods, till after dark, and yet felt no pressing sensation of hunger or fatigue. . . .

There is a great improvement now-a-days, not only in the *cuisine*, but also in the *materiel*—the food itself provided for the shantymen. Years ago pork, tea and bread were the sole food of the men, and sometimes not too much of that, nor of the best quality either. In nothing in shanty life is there a greater change noticeable than in this matter. Now, not only is the food superabundant, but also of the most varied and best quality. Compared to the other laboring classes, our shantymen fare sumptuously every day. What do you think of such a bill of fare as this, which constitutes the daily routine of my friend C—'s *menu*: Mess pork, *fresh* beef, bread, tea, dried apples stewed, syrup, beans, potatoes, sugar, often butter, *fish*? What laboring men in the world have such living as this, and what more, or, better could the heart of a strong healthy working man possibly desire? . . .

I deny most emphatically that the general influence of shanty life in the woods during winter is prejudicial in itself to a good, fair tone of character and morals. If anything, apart from perverse extraneous influences, it is the reverse. The plain, strong, healthy food—the pure, keen, bracing atmosphere—the heavy, unremitting physical exertion, the regular routine life week in and week out—and the total abstinence from intoxicating liquors, all combined, have a tendency, if not to elevate, at least not to lower the ordinary standard of human morality.

But I must confess that a certain change takes place in these aspects of character when the drive commences in the spring. The river life is more calculated to unsettle good resolutions and habits, and to develop the harum-scarum propensities of human nature than that of the winter. It is a life of irregular, unsettled and changeful interest, and is beset with new and peculiar temptations to the ex-hibernated shantyman.

If he is grogily inclined, he has now frequent opportunities of gratifying his appetite. Every few miles on the river side there are low taverns, or shebeen shops, licensed and unlicensed, where rank vitriolized poison, under the name of good-whiskey, is sold by the glass or bottle to the thirsty drivers.

These places are hot-beds of abominations. They awaken and revive in full force the long repressed devil of strong drink which has been lying dormant, perhaps almost extinguished, by the lengthy winter sojourn amid the pure bracing influences of the forest. Now it is that, upon occasion at least, the river-man can, if he pleases, give full fling to all that is sensuous, low, and debasing within him. On Saturday nights especially, when the week's work is finished, and he can sleep off the effects of a debauch on the Sunday, these river-side shabeens are often the scenes of frightful orgies, and of most inhuman and brutal "fights" between rival gangs of other "drives."

Those encounters in their ferocity, bloodshed, and often serious and even fatal consequences, beggar all description. When the devilish passions of those rough and powerful men are thoroughly roused by the demon of whiskey, then they become more like wild beasts, and infuriated madmen than human beings. . . .

The "settling up" in Quebec is an anxious time for both the lumber merchant and the shantyman. . . .

As soon as the raft is "snubbed" within the booms at Quebec, and put in its most presentable shape for the inspection of the buyers, then the "boss" comes aboard with a bag of money, and with his clerk pays to each man the amount coming to him. Very many of these fellows, especially the French, can neither read nor write, and are in a state of uncertainty as to the actual amount coming to them; their account for clothes, tobacco, advances to their families, dockings for lost time, etc., have in most cases made a considerable hole in their year's wages, in some instances entirely eaten it up, with even a balance against them. But in general there is a pretty fair sum coming to them, varying in amount from a hundred to three and even four hundred dollars. Sometimes there may be a hot row between the parties, when some man thinks he has been wrongfully charged with advances or lost time; but almost invariably the boss has the better of the dispute, for while the poor fellow has nothing but his memory, or counting upon his fingers, to rely upon, the mysterious entries in the clerk's book tell dead against him, and the boss summarily closes the matters by telling him "to take it or leave it, just as he likes," and calling up another man. As a general thing, however, there is very little difficulty in settling, and the moment Bill, Pat, or Louis receives his money his anxiety is over, and, like a boy out of school, he is ready for any fun or frolic that may turn up.

Like Jack Tar when he gets into port, the poor shantyman has now to run the gauntlet of the very worst and vilest temptations that can assail a man. For the past ten months or more he has toiled, take it all in all, as no other class of working men have to do; during that time he has led, as a rule, a careful, abstemious, saving life, twenty-five dollars would probably cover all his necessary personal expenses. Under the wholesome influences of rigid discipline, arduous but healthy work, abstinence from intoxicating stimulants, and continual life in the open, bracing air, one would naturally suppose that both mind and body would be so tempered and strengthened as not only to be able to withstand the strongest temptation to vicious and sensual indulgence which the flesh and the devil could present, but also to have a positive distaste and repugnance to them. And so it would be with well-balanced, high-toned and rightly-trained dispositions; but, alas, few of the shantymen possess these offsets against temptations to aid them in maintaining these wholesome influences of the past year's life. In the revulsion of their position from restraint and abstemiousness, there is also a revulsion of their feelings as to indulgence and licentiousness. In the first burst of his absolute freedom and idleness the thoughtless shantyman is too apt to go headlong into every indulgence that presents itself, and you may be very sure the devil is at his elbow to help him on. As he leaps with a light heart and a heavy pocket from the raft on to the shore he is at once beset with a host of hell-runners in the shape of calash drivers, boarding-house agents, brothel sirens, and crimps and sharpers of the blackest stamp. "Come and have a drink, my jolly buck," is generally the first salutation that greets his ears, and in the joyous hilarity of his soul, the poor fellow thinks it only "good manners," and right fellowship to comply; and though with many an inward resolution to take care of himself, and many a knowing wink to himself that he knows what he is about, he soon becomes helplessly entangled in the devilish wiles of those who, without pity or remorse, will strip him of his last shilling. He supposes that he may take a few glasses with perfect safety, and have a good time for a day or two, and then draw off and go to his home or work, none the worse in body or pocket. But Satan never palmed off a blacker deception upon human credulity than this which the shantyman imposes upon himself. The liquor with which he is plentifully plied is poison of the blackest and rankest kind, and on account of his long abstinence from all intoxicants produces a more immediate and potent effect than it otherwise would. As the fiery spirit mounts to his brain, and his pulses, already exhilarated, become doubly so under its influence, he soon loses all caution and self-command. His love of ostentatious spending and open-handed treating give themselves full fling—he treats right and left, and delights in being the hero of a thirsty crowd of spongers and thieving vagabonds, and flourishes his bank notes and tosses them on the counter with the air and tone of a millionaire. Of course the upshot of the whole business can be readily surmised. Between bad whiskey and worse men and women he is plucked as clean as a Christmas goose, and in an incredibly short time too. I have known several instances of men who have received between two and three hundred dollars, coming back to their employer before twenty-four hours without a cent in their pocket, and in the direst distress and shame begging to be taken out of this "cursed hole," and have their passage paid back to their homes or to Ottawa.

TIMBERING AT THE TURN OF THE CENTURY

Horace Miner, *St. Denis: A French-Canadian Parish* (Chicago, University of Chicago Press, 1963), pp. 279-81. Reprinted by permission of The University of Chicago Press and the author.

At nineteen I went to the *chantier* with my brother. We had never been out before. At the first camp we were with a lot of English. We could not understand them, and they could not understand us. We were there one day, and the next day we went to the second camp. There was a big lake between the first and second camps. I had brought two horses up to work, and I had to take them to the other camp. There was no road around the lake, so we just followed the shore; and when the trees were right down to the water, we would go out into the lake. The first work we had at the second camp was cutting wood for the "cook." Then they took us out into the forest. If I had ever had any experience in the *chantier*, it would not have been so hard to understand the directions they gave me in English. After a few days I had to take down a horse which had gotten a bad foot, I think from keeping its feet in the water so much when we came around the lake. . . .

The hard thing about work there was the long walks. We walked three or four miles a day to get to work. That was bad. Sundays we played with axes on the [frozen] lake. You swing the ax low and let it go, and it will slide far, far, far. There are other men still farther away to slide them back again. One man, Louis Dionne, who was really *capable*, big, and strong, used to play in only a shirt and pants with bare head and feet. He kept moving all the time *par exemple*.

The second year we understood a little, and it was better. It was not the wood which was difficult but the language. We had had lots of experience cutting wood for our own family. One day a big storm filled a little stream so that the men would not have been able to get back to camp without wading through it. The "foreman" came and tried to explain it to us, wanting to know if we knew how to make a bridge. We couldn't understand a thing he was saying; so I went with him to see what had happened. He showed me the stream; and at first I thought the word "bridge" must mean "stream," but then I realized he wanted to make a bridge. It's aggravating not to understand anything. It was worse for them to hire a man and not have him understand anything. That "foreman" was always smiling and laughing. The "foreman" at the first camp looked "rough."

The prettiest pine I saw while I was there was eleven inches through at the end of sixty-two feet. It got smaller so gradually that the sides were almost like that stick over there. There is much better wood in other regions, but that's the best I ever saw. I saw a cedar that was four feet through. It was so large and got small so quickly that the "foreman" told us to leave it alone.

The second year I took up two horses; and when I arrived at the camp there was no one there. Later in the day a "foreman" came there. The next day he told me to take care of the horses. I told him that was easy: I had spent my life taking care of horses. My brother and he went to a place on the lake where they were opening a new camp. They went in a small steamboat. There were two Indians at the new camp to help them. The next day my brother and I took the horses down to the new camp. There was a road cut around the lake this time. On the way it began to rain. When we arrived at the camp we found that the Indians had taken a piece of birch bark about three feet square and set it up slanting on four posts. They and two other men were all standing under it. We couldn't get a piece of birch bark to cover us and the horses, though (*laughing*). Making the new camp was the nicest work I ever had while I was up there. We knew the "bosses"; and if there was any hard work, they would give it to someone else. That was the nicest time during my two years in the *chantier*. Sundays we would *promenade* on the lake. Louis Dionne had hollowed out a log and made a boat. A boat like that "rolls" M'sieur! We would take his "logue" when we could not get one of the "boats" of the camp. He even put a birch-bark sail on his boat. I stopped the *chantier* because I had to work for my uncle at Mont Carmel. I would have kept it up until I got married had it not been for that. A lot of families went to the States in the summer and left their lands uncultivated. Then they would return in the winter when there was nothing to do, and spend part of the money they had earned. We always thought it was better to farm in summer and then go to the *chantier* in the winter. I never went to the States because there was always plenty to do at home.

FAMINE ON THE FISHING FRONTIER

Montreal Gazette, June 9, 1817.

HALIFAX, May 7—The following letter exhibits a melancholy picture of the distress of the inhabitants of St. John's N.F. and which, perhaps, does not equal, or at least exceed, in representation, the sufferings experienced at the different out-harbors of the Island:

Extract of a letter from St. John's, N.F. dated 5th April, 1817
"Our condition in this Island generally is deplorable, the consequence must be serious if relief is not received from some quarter soon: all the

stores here are completely empty; the surplus of provisions that were in the navy stores is exhausted, and we have but a few tierces of flour to recover from the commisariate stores. Families of the first respectability are drained of the provisions they laid in for their own support. There are 2500 people supported by the charitable institutions, 1000 others by the inhabitants in messes where they get a dinner every day; biscuit is baked from the flour we receive from the King's stores, and sold by small quantities to such as are able to purchase. The whole of our stock is not sufficient to support us three weeks.—The Magistrates have described our state to your Governor. Let us beg of you to use your endeavors to have relief sent—There is plenty of cash to purchase with, if provisions were to be had. For God's sake make our wants as public as possible, so that we may get succour."

THE FISHING FRONTIER

Evening Star (Toronto), July 10, 1897, p. 2.

St. John's, Nfld, July 9—Only Americans and Canadians fish the Newfoundland Banks. The Newfoundlander himself goes to the Labrador coast for his season's fishing. Now at St. John's and for several weeks past, the fishing vessels have been leaving port bound for the scene of the summer's fishing, making sure to start so early that in all stress of wind and weather they may surely be at the grounds when the capelin come inshore, with the cod behind them. Hundreds of little schooners are at the wharves, taking aboard supplies and fishing gear, and, every skipper and crew are hurrying to their start for the days are slipping away and the capelin may be looked for any time after May 30 off the Labrador coast.

The streets of St. John's are filled with a strange assemblage of people, seen there only twice in the year when the fishing schooners set out for Labrador and when they return. There are the passengers, the fishermen with their families, that the schooners carry up to the shore of the bleak peninsula and leave there until they take them aboard for Newfoundland, in October. They have come from up and down the coast, far and near, and throng the wharves, as eager to embark as the schooners' companies are.

Let us see what sort of people these migratory fishing folk are, and how they are likely to fare in their voyage to Labrador.

Here is the schooner Rowena Tucker, getting ready to cast off hawsers when she shall have completed her lading by taking aboard her passengers. She is a fairly lined and balanced little craft of perhaps seventy tons measurement; looks as if she could sail and ride out bad seas and weather, although she is dingy to the eye and there has been no waste of paint and labor in keeping her bright and clean.

CLOSELY STOWED.

Her hold is stowed to within five feet of the decks with household furniture, flour, meal, pork, tea, nuts, trawls and fishing contraptions generally. There are so many fishing boats upon the decks that it is a marvel how the sailors are ever to get about to work the ship, and every boat is packed to the gunwales with dunnage. And there on the wharf are 150 people, men, women, children, who are the passengers the Rowena is expected to take to Labrador, one thousand miles away. . . .

To an American watching this embarkation the other day it seemed a miracle where the passengers could have stowed themselves, and how they should live through the one or two or three weeks trip to Labrador, but few people in St. John's and least of all the fishermen themselves, think of this method of human packing as anything else than natural and proper. It being sanctioned by immemorial usage. . . .

With such lading the fishing schooners are swarming up the coast. By the 10th of May the last one will have gone. They may be expected to weather storm and sea and arrive on the Labrador coast in time for the passengers to have disembarked and got settled in their shore quarters by the first of June. Some of them have tents, most return to houses which they have occupied in former years, hovels with a single room built of the dwarfed Labrador spruce and fir.

While the women attend to all household matters, the men set at once to the getting ready of handlines, trawls, nets, seines and cod traps, and have the fishing boats where they can be launched at short notice. Sometimes during the first week of June somebody raises the cry that sends every boat into the water up and down the coast.

"The capelin!"

The black waves that roll up against the cliffs have become suddenly alive and their surface flitters at the jumping of the capelin—the little fish which on the New York and New Jersey shores is called the frost fish— and the fishermen know that the cod are following them shoreward. The fishing season has begun off Labrador.

Every day henceforth, when wave and weather permit, the fishermen are out early and late in their boats taking cod. The Labrador cliffs fall steeply down into water so deep that the fishing is all done close to shore. The cod are of fine quality and great catches are often made, but there are many days that the fishermen cannot put out in their boats.

Sometimes on a fall day, with a still sea the ground swell comes in rolling thirty feet high over exposed rocks, and dashing sixty feet high against the cliffs. At signs of its coming the fishermen have to make for shore and pull their boats above its reach. There may be weeks with such a sea breaking against the cliffs that no boat can put out. When the fishing is lucky and the catches are brought in the women and large children lend a hand in splitting and spreading the fish upon the flakes to be salted and dried.

In this way twenty thousand Newfoundlanders pass the summer and early autumn along the Labrador coast. For the simple supplies they used they go to the trader, who furnishes them on credit, and he allows them a certain price per quintal on the fish they bring him. . . .

The end comes about the middle of October. The weather has become cold and ice has formed on the inland water. There have been two or three days of poor fishing and then the word is passed that the cod have stopped biting off shore. Then the fishing schooners work back to the coast, vessels perhaps are sent from St. John's, and so the twenty thousand fishermen, with their kits and families, are taken back to Newfoundland.

There is a settlement of accounts with the traders, and, if the season has been good, the fishermen have something to live on through the winter. If not, they manage to live somehow. It is not for the interest of the traders that they should starve, and so it goes until the next season's migration to Labrador.

THE FUR FRONTIER IN THE 1880s

Winnipeg Daily Times, April 13, 1883, p. 5.

Mr. G. S. McRae, a Hudson Bay employee, who has just arrived in the city from York Factory with the mail, gives the following account of that post.

York Factory is 180 miles south of Fort Churchill and is the most northern Factory on the west shore of Hudson Bay. It consists of a large store or depot, and in addition there is the clerk's house, the master's house, and another building in which the doctor and the overseer reside; there is also a house for the Episcopal clergyman, a trading and sale shop, the men's house, and several workshops and a few other buildings now unoccupied on account of the furs being sent to England by the States, instead of by vessels calling at the Factory as formerly. . . . [A]ltogether there are about 23 white people at the factory of whom three are women. In addition there is an Indian and half-breed population of about 160 souls. . . .

At six a.m. during the summer months a bell rings and all hands begin work and work until eight o'clock when breakfast is taken. Dinner is served at one o'clock, one hour being given for that purpose, and work continues until 6 p.m. During the summer evenings the employees amuse themselves as best they can, some playing quoits, the majority however walking about when the mosquitoes will permit them to do so. During the winter season dog driving, trapping and shooting is the principal amusement, Sunday being the great day for it. There is a splendid library at the factory and anyone can get books from it by paying a small subscription, the chief men paying an annual fee of $1, others an annual fee of 5 shillings, which sums go for the purchase of new books and the repair of old ones. Christmas week is a great week for amusement. There are lots of fiddlers at the factory, some of them Indians, and regular dance parties take place, in the joiner's shop, the dusky maidens being the fair partners, and they step the Rockaway, the Curfew Lancers, the York Factory Breakdown, the Hudson Bay Jig, and the Polar Bear Walk Around to their hearts content. The Indian women go into the dance with great spirit, and will dance down any white man at the Factory. Biscuits and tea are served out at these parties, which takes the place of the usual supper, and the fun is great. There is a piano and a melodeon at the settlement, the former being the property of the doctor, and his wife is a capital pianist; the latter is the property of the clergyman. There is also a melodeon in the church, but there is no regular choir.

The work at the settlement is diversified. There are three boat builders, a blacksmith, a joiner, three coopers and carpenters, a man to attend the cattle, of which there are about sixteen head, and the rest of the employees are variously employed, some cutting and hauling wood, some dog driving, some fishing, and one or two making boat sails. . . .

The chief factor at York Factory, Mr. Fortescque, like the chief factors elsewhere, has supreme power. He is a magistrate and can punish delinquents. Liquor being unobtainable, rows and disputes very seldom occur, but there is a small lockup for the refractory. Last summer and fall quite a few deaths occurred among the people at the post, the chief cause being scrofula. All the people are members of the Church of England except the Indians, who are pagans, but there isn't a Roman Catholic in the place.

B.C. GOLD FEVER

William Carew Hazlitt, British Columbia and Vancouver Island (London, G. Routledge & Co., 1858), pp. 134-8, 140-3.

We cannot better illustrate the progress of the gold fever than in the words of the "Own Correspondent" of the Times at San Francisco. The narrative is somewhat extended; but the style is so graphic and so vigorous, there is so much incidental landscape and manners prevailing, and the subject so full of interest in every respect, that the reader will think the space well appropriated.

"San Francisco, Thursday, June 14th, 1858. "On the morning of the 5th, just as the last mail steamer was about to leave for Panama, a steamer arrived from Vancouver's Island with further news of the most glowing and extravagant tenor as to the richness of the new gold country in the British possessions. My last letter was then posted. . . .

"The only way in which I can give an intelligible statement in a moderate compass is to *sift the facts* from the mass of correspondence and personal details at hand. The following is the experience of a man from San Francisco, well known here, connected with a business firm in this place, and whose statement is worthy of credit. He left San Francisco in April, and, in company with seven others, ascended the Frazer River 275 miles. I will let him tell his story in his own way, interposing only such remarks of my own as will be explanatory of his 'terms' and of the localities mentioned. 'We prospected all along coming up from Fort Hope to Sailor's Bar, several days' travel, and in some places got two bits to the pan and in some places five cents.' Two 'bits' may be set down as of the value of a shilling sterling. 'We camped and commenced mining at Sailor's Bar,' about twenty-five miles above Fort Yale, 'which has rich diggings, in some places paying as high as six bits to the pan.' The 'pan,' most readers know by this time, is a small tin basin with which the miner 'washes' the gravel containing the gold. 'When I arrived miners were making as high as six ounces a day to the rocker.' These are enormous earnings. Six ounces of gold, at its market value of $16 the ounce, would be nearly 20*l.* sterling as the product of the daily labour of two men, which a 'rocker' should have to work it efficiently—one to 'fill' and another to 'rock,' and not hard work either, barring the inconvenience of being in the water. Such results were frequent in the early times of California mining, when the soil was 'virgin.' 'We mined along the banks of the river (the Frazer), and the average was from two to three ounces per day to the rocker. Miners are at work all along the banks of the river,' for twenty-five miles above Fort Yale. 'They average from two to four ounces a day.' These returns refer to mining carried on on such 'bars' of the Frazer River as were exposed; but the rise of all of the water from the melting of the snow in the mountains far up rendered the work uncertain till August, when the waters subside for the season. 'The river sometimes rises three feet in a night,' and, as a consequence, 'a man cannot make his expenses there. . .'

"The special correspondent of the *San Francisco Bulletin,* a reliable authority, writes from Fort Langley, twenty-five miles up the Frazer, under date May the 25th, that he had just come down from Fort Yale—

the locality above spoken of—where he found 60 men and 200 Indians, with their squaws, at work on a 'bar' of about 500 yards in length, called 'Hill's bar,' one mile below Fort Yale and 15 miles from Fort Hope, all trading posts of the Hudson's Bay Company. 'The morning I arrived two men (Kerrison and Co.) cleaned up 5½ ounces from the rocker, the product of half a day's work. Kerrison and Co. the next day cleaned up 10½ ounces from two rockers, which I saw myself weighed.' This bar is acknowledged to be one of the richest ever seen, and well it may be, for here is a product of 15½ ounces of gold, worth $247½, or 50l. sterling, from it in a day and a half, to the labour of two rockers. 'Old Californian miners say they never saw such rich diggings. The average result per day to the man was fully $20; some much more. . . .'

"The preceding imperfect sketch describes the sunny side of the picture. But the sun does not always shine upon the miner in New Caledonia; and so, to be impartial, we must have a look at the shady side. Overlooking the disagreeables and risks of the voyage from San Francisco, made at high rates of fare, in crazy old vessels, not one of which is really seaworthy, where men and women are crowded 'like herrings packed in a barrel,' to borrow a comparison from one of the 'cargo,' as a misery of short duration—only five to six days—we come to where the miner finds himself dropped on the beach at Victoria, Bellingham Bay, or elsewhere.

"Now his real difficulties and hardships commence, and his helplessness becomes painfully apparent. He is from 100 to 250 miles from the mines, without food and without shelter, in a variable climate. Several of his fellows tell the tale of his troubles in a few short but significant items:— 'Canoes are very scarce; the price has risen from $50 and $80 to $100 each. Many parties have built light boats for themselves, but they did not answer.' 'We have got up, but we had a hard time coming.' 'Jordan is a hard road to travel; lost all our outfit, except flour. Our canoe was capsized in the Falls, and was broken to pieces. Six other canoes capsized and smashed the same day near the same place. Four whites and two Indians belonging to these six canoes drowned.' Provisions high up the river are exorbitant, of course, as they can only be brought up in canoes requiring long 'portages.' Here's the tariff at Sailor's Bar and other bars:— 'Flour, $100 a barrel, worth in San Francisco $11 to $12; molasses, $6 a gallon; pork, $1 per lb.; ham, $1 25c. per lb.; tea at one place, $1 per lb., but at another $4; sugar, $2 per lb.; beans, $1 per lb.; picks, $6; and shovels, $2 each. There were no fresh provisions.' I should have been greatly surprised to hear that there had been. 'At Fort Hope there was nothing to be had but dried salmon.' 'At Fort Langley, plenty of black flour at $9 a hundred, and salt salmon four for $1.' What lively visions of scurvy these provisions conjure up! The acme of extravagance was not arrived at, however, until the poor miner came to purchase auxiliaries to his rocker. At Sailor's Bar 'rocker irons were at an ounce of gold each

($16), and at Hill's Bar $30.' This 'iron' is simply a plate of thin sheet-iron measuring eighteen inches by twenty inches, perforated with round holes to let the loose dirt pass through. I priced one of them, out of curiosity, at a carpenter's shop in San Francisco this morning—$2½. In England this thing would be worth 2s. At Sailor's Bar it would be worth 3l. 4s., and at Hill's Bar it would fetch 6l. Quicksilver was also outrageously high, but not being of such prime necessity as 'rocker irons,' didn't come up to their standard of value. At one place it was sold at $10 per lb.; but at Fort Langley a man bought one pound, paying $15 for it, and had to carry it a great distance. The price in San Francisco is 60c. the pound (half-a-crown), and on the Frazer River 3l. 'Nails brought from $1 to $1 50c. per lb. One lot of a dozen pounds brought $3, or two bits a nail,' which, being interpreted into Queen's English, means 1s. a nail! These are some of the outgoings which tax the miner's earnings in a new unpeopled country; but these are not his only drawbacks. 'There being no boards to be had, we had per force to go in the woods and hew out our lumber to make a rocker,' causing much loss of time. Then came the hunt for nails and for the indispensable perforated 'iron,' which cost so much. But, worst of all the ills of the miner's life in New Caledonia, are the jealousy and the audacious thieving of the Indians, 'who are nowise particular in seizing on the dirt of the miners.' 'The whites,' being in the minority, and the Indians being a fierce athletic set of rascals, 'suffered much annoyance and insult' without retaliating. What a trial to the temper of Oregon men who used to shoot Indians who came within range of their rifles as vermin in California in 1848 and 1849!

GOLD RUSH DAYS IN BRITISH COLUMBIA

R. Byron Johnson, *Very Far West Indeed: A Few Rough Experiences on the North-West Pacific Coast* (London, Sampson, Low, Marston, Lowe & Searle, 1872), pp. 47-51, 79-81, 114-16, 191-2.

My resolution got a little shaken on the following day by an excellent offer I received from a member of the legal profession, with whom I had struck up a casual acquaintance, and who advised me strongly not to go to the mines. 'A miner,' said he, 'is but the means of conveying money into other people's pockets: he is simply our agent, though he wouldn't acknowledge that position. I can name to you a hundred miners who have made fortunes, and lost or spent them, for perhaps two who have been able to stick to them. We townspeople have nothing to do but sit on our beam-ends, and wait for these hard-working, deluded creatures to come and pour wealth into our laps! ...'

Emigrants thronged the streets, buying broken-down mules and Indian ponies, and loading them with provisions and mining implements, packed in so ill a manner that one could well imagine how little skin would remain on the backs of the wretched quadrupeds when their journey was completed. The number of falls in the street sustained by inexperienced tyros in trying the qualities of their equine purchases was great, for Indian horses have an unpleasant habit of buck-jumping, hard to resist even in a Mexican saddle.

Many auctions were to be seen at street corners; the goods for sale consisting of articles utterly useless for up-country purposes to their possessors, such as dress suits, dressing cases, and other things of the kind, which had been crammed into the trunks of the emigrants under the idea that they were indispensable. One of the items I saw was an iron washstand, with fittings complete, which its owner had regarded with much complacency as 'just the thing for that country, you know,' until he found he should have to carry it on his back for three or four hundred miles, if he wished to avail himself of the prodigious facilities for open air ablutions *en route* which it offered. The prices realised were, of course, ridiculously small, as no one wanted such superfluities, and the money spent on them in the first instance would have been far better carried in the pockets of the luckless wights. The only outfit a man who intends to rough it ought to carry, is a few rough strong clothes and woollen shirts.

Criers paraded the streets, shouting forth the hours of departure of various steamboats for New Westminster (the capital of British Columbia, and the next place on the way to the mines) and the fares; which latter, as there was considerable opposition, were very low. Parties of sober old miners, clad in blue or red shirts, with their 'pants' tucked into knee boots, their belts showing the usual jack-knife and revolver, their heads crowned with wide felt hats, and their backs laden with small well put-up packs, consisting of a pair of blankets, enclosing a spare shirt and pair of socks (with the addition, perhaps, but not in many cases, I expect, from the bearer's appearance, of a piece of soap), wended their way quietly to the wharves, and got on board the expectant steamers. Here and there, a green youth fresh from home was toiling along under a load of Heaven knows how many pounds weight (hundredweight I was going to say) of traps; the greater part of which he would probably relinquish at the end of the first day's tramp, a prey to the jackal instinct of some prowling denizen of the forest. Scattered over the town, groups of dirty and stolid Indians, in many-coloured blankets, with their squaws and little red-skins—none of the family at all representing Mr. J. Fenimore Cooper's ideal—watched the scene with the air of grand spectators, for whom it had been specially prepared; occasionally making remarks among themselves in their own tongue upon the passers-by; doubtless, too, in unflattering criticism, judging by the sympathetic guffaws of the listeners. The whole place seemed to be in a most unwonted state of bustle and uproar; the only commensurate excitement I can think of, which might be seen at home, would be in a remote country village on its annual fair-day. . . .

I forgot to include John Chinaman amongst the inhabitants of this region; but the Chinamen form the largest section of the dwellers here. This much-enduring and industrious race are generally to be found in little clusters, at work upon the diggings deserted by the whites; and sometimes one meets a string of them migrating in search of a fresh field of enterprise, with all their worldly belongings in a pair of baskets suspended from either end of a pole carried across their shoulders. This mode of carrying is peculiar to the Chinaman, and he is so strongly conservative that he never adopts any other method. I once remember seeing one of these worthy people packing a quarter of beef; as he could not split this in two, so as to balance it on his pole, he adopted the following ingenious expedient. He cut a much longer pole (about twelve feet long) from a young fir-tree, tied the beef to one end of it, and a stone of about thirty pounds weight at the other; the end with the beef attached to it he kept near his shoulder, while the other end with the stone on it projected far in front of him, and thus balanced the heavier load next him; but John's ingenuity seemed rather heavily handicapped with a thirty pound penalty.

The patient industry of the race cannot, however, be too highly commended; they will work diggings that a white man will not look at—thus preventing a vast amount of waste—and will, doubtless, at the end of the year, by means of their frugality, save more than their white brother is likely to, in spite of his higher gains.

When they have accumulated a little money, their ambition is usually to set up a laundry business (for they almost entirely usurp that useful trade in California and the other gold countries in the North Pacific) or a store; and there are some Chinese firms in San Francisco whose trade far exceeds that of any American or European houses, and whose names are indeed more widely known and more highly respected. Owing to the scarcity of females, too, a great many Chinese find employment in the towns as domestic servants.

It is the fashion on the Pacific Coast to abuse and ill-treat the Chinaman in every possible way; and I really must tell my friends the Americans that in this respect they show an illiberal spirit utterly unworthy of them. The Chinese are really, as citizens, most desirable members of a community; they are hard-working, sober, and law-abiding—three scarce qualities among people in their station. Prior to the abolition of slavery, the colour of his skin was the avowed objection against the Celestial, and special ordinances were even passed to render his evidence unavailing against a white in a criminal court. Since the conclusion of the War of Secession, this objection to colour has been recognised as illogical, and therefore other outcries have arisen—he works too cheaply, so the great Irish element is in arms against the competitor who threatens to disturb its vested right of one day's work and two days' drunk for every day's pay. Which system of labour benefits society most all open-minded persons may judge.

Poor John! he is treated like a dog, bullied, scoffed at, kicked, and cuffed about on all occasions, his very name made a slang term of reproach; and yet, withal, he betrays no sign of meditated revenge, but pursues his labours calmly, and is civil and polite to all. He is close-fisted in his dealings with the whites, as he well may be, considering his treatment, and I really think the balance of honesty is in his favour. . . .

B.C. INDUSTRY IN THE 1870s

Rev. George M. Grant, *Ocean to Ocean: Sandford Fleming's Expedition Through Canada in 1872* (Toronto, J. Campbell, 1873), pp. 309-10, 322-4.

At various points on the river, all down the road, miners are still to be found. These are chiefly Siwashes and Chinese, who take up abandoned claims, and wash the sand over again, being satisfied with smaller wages than what contents a white man. Their tastes are simple and their expenses moderate. None of them dream of going to the wayside hotels, and paying a dollar for every meal, a dollar for a bed, a dollar for a bottle of ale, or twenty cents for a drink. The Chinaman cultivates vegetables beside his claim; these and his bag of rice suffice for him, greatly to the indignation of the orthodox miner. The Siwash catches salmon in his scoop net from every eddy of the river, and his wife carries them up to the house and makes his winter's food. These two classes of the population, the one representing an ancient civilization, the other scattered nomads with almost no tribal relationships, resemble each other in appearance so much that it would be difficult to distinguish them, were it not for the long tail or queue into which the Chinaman braids his hair, and which he often folds at the back of his head, instead of letting it hang down his back. The Pacific Indian is Mongolian in size and complexion, in the shape of the face, and the eyes. He has neither the strength of limb, the manly bearing, nor the dignity so characteristic of the Indians on the east side of the Rocky Mountains, but he is quite as intelligent, and takes more readily to civilized ways.

Salmon are the staple of the Siwash's food, and these are so abundant that they generally sell them for ten to twenty five cents apiece; and ten cents in British Columbia is equivalent to a penny elsewhere, for there is no smaller coin than the ten cent piece in the Province. Servants here and on the Fraser river would probably bargain as they used to bargain when hiring in Scotland, that they were not to be expected to eat salmon oftener than four times a week, if there was the slightest necessity of their making any stipulation. But masters and mistresses know their places too well to dream of imposing that or any other condition on them. We passed several Chinamen travelling along the road, each man carrying all his worldly goods suspended from the ends of a pole slung across one of his shoulders. So habituated are they to this style of carrying weight, that when they possess only one bundle, inconvenient to divide, they are said to tie a stone to the other end of the pole to balance the load. Whether this is meant as a joke or not, I shall leave as a puzzle to my readers. . . .

At 10 a.m. the united party started for Burrard's Inlet, and arrived in two hours. . . .

A steamer, so diminutive and toy-like that each man stepped on board tenderly for fear of upsetting or breaking her, was in waiting to take us across the Inlet to the large saw-mill of Messrs. Moody, Diety and Nelson. Thirteen million feet of lumber were exported last year from this, and about as much from another mill on the south side of the inlet owned by a company. All the lumber is the famous Douglas Fir. Logs four to five feet in diameter were being hauled up and sawed by two circular saws, the one placed vertically over the other, as it is easier to work on such huge subjects with two ordinary sized than with one very large saw. The workmen represented the various nationalities scattered everywhere along the Pacific coast, Whites, Chinese, Siwashes and Kanakas or Sandwich Islanders.

The aborigines work well till they save enough money to live on for some time, and then they go up to the boss and frankly say that they are lazy and don't want to work longer. They are too unsophisticated to sham sickness, or to strike. Another habit of the richer ones, which to the Anglo-Saxon mind borders on insanity, is that of giving universal backshish or gifts to the whole tribe, without expecting any return save an increased popularity that may lead to their election as Tyhees or chiefs when vacancies occur. An old fellow, big George, was pointed out to us as having worked industriously at the mill for years till he had saved $2,000. Instead of putting this in a Savings Bank, he had spent it all on stores for a grand "Potlatch," summoning Siwashes from far and near to come, eat, drink, dance, be merry, and receive gifts. Nearly a thousand assembled; the festivities lasted a week; and everyone got something, either a blanket, musket, bag of flour, box of apples, or tea and sugar. When the fun was over, big George, now pennyless, returned to the mill to carry slabs at $20 a month. His reputation mounted to an extraordinary height because of so magnificent a potlatch, and he stood a good chance of the Tyheeship; but two rivals, Supple Jack and Old Jim, were preparing to outdo him; and if Siwashes are at all like civilized beings, the "popularis aura" shall fill their sails before long. . . .

The workmen at the mill live in comfortable little houses perched on rocks at the foot of a lofty wooded hill overhanging the shore. There is no soil except what has been made on the beach from chips and sawdust. Round the nearest point is a small tract diligently cultivated by a few Chinamen. The men have a large reading-room with a harmonium, and a well selected library. No intoxicating liquors can be sold on the premises. Their pay is good and they save money. The manager of the mill on the other side of the Inlet told us that he would give $200 a month to any competent overseer we would send him.

KLONDIKE GOLD FEVER

Arthur and Joseph Robinson Papers, 1898. PAC, MG 29, C15.

> Vancouver, B.C.
> Sept. 4th, 1898.

Dear Father & Annie,

You will, I have no doubt be very pleased to know we are once more in civilized parts & when I inform you we are in the best of health you will know that we are very lucky although we are considerably poorer than when we started out. This however does not trouble us as we went in prepared for disappointment & in exchange for our capital we have gained experience which I would not have missed for a great deal. . . .

I will now endeavour to picture to you the state of affairs in Dawson. This city of tents is situated on low marshy land which lies between steep mountains and the river, which is almost stagnant for a considerable distance close to the bank & crowded with boats making it difficult to effect a landing. There are no sanitary arrangements & as I suppose the population is nearly 20,000 this in conjunction with the bad water makes disease very prevalent,; typhoid was raging when we left, & son of the man who bought our outfit falling sick with it & being sent to the hospital where he will probably end his days as they say it is of so malignant a nature that few recover. Last winter there was only work for about one fifth of the inhabitants & as many of the claims are too poor to work & the majority have proved blanks & worst of all no more rich strikes have been made you may judge what chance there is for the average man in

Dawson & many of the poor fellows are practically destitute. . . . In the whole Klondike there are about 30 claims which are undoubtedly very rich, about 60 which pay fairly well & 120 which pay their way & the whole country is pegged out for about 40 miles round Dawson hill tops & all, & unless a man can afford to grease the officials hands you can't obtain access to the records.

If you would like to cut cordwood or lumber you have first to obtain a logger's license at a cost of $125 & then to proceed over 70 miles up the Yukon to get clear of the timber limits & to cut hay one must pay a similar sum for a permit. The whole country is a mass of bribery & corruption, apropos of which an English gentleman remarked to me "What a treat when we get back under our own pure government at home once more" & another said "Dawson's all right if you are in the pull," & one man said to another "I can't afford to keep a woman & I can't get a woman to keep me & I'm no good at cards or gambling, so what's the use of me remaining in Dawson. . . ."

We amalgamated with two gunners who had formerly served in the British Navy & for the last 8 years had been in the employ of the Chinese government having fought in the Battle of Wei-Hai-Wei holding a fort there for a fortnight against the Japs who concentrated the fire from their ships & also from the captured forts on this particular one. In their party was a Kootenay miner & we whipsawed lumber & built two clinker built boats with which to ascend the river & we beat everything except canoes. . . . We had resolved to get up to the falls & kept proceeding notwithstanding the discouraging reports of many returning miners until we had got 40 miles up to the mouth of the famous Blackhill Creek & here we stopped & pegged out claims on Kingston Gulch & sunk several holes without finding anything although at its mouth I washed out coarser gold than any I had yet seen. The deepest hole on this gulch was sunk by a big party of Germans & French Canadians who went down 20 feet to bedrock & sunk the last 10 ft without a fire, result no gold, but leaves nearly as green as when growing only slightly tinged with yellow around edges. On the beaches of this gulch there was an old prospect hole out of which young poplars were growing probably 10 or 12 years old. We worked there for 3 weeks having to return every few days to the mouth of creek for more grub & this means work & no mistake. Packing over the Chilcot or White Pass Trails was hard but when it comes to shouldering from 50-60 lbs & proceeding 20 miles or more per day up a rough mountain stream you realize what packing means when the only trails are moose & bear packs where you get the best travelling, the worst is over the swamps which literally swarm with mosquitoes & into which you sink over your boot tops thereby releasing the noxious gases generated below the thick covering of moss & these extend for miles, now & then it becomes necessary to fell a tree in order to cross the stream & often for hours at a stretch one winds through an almost impenatrable forest where the windfalls obstruct your way at every step, or painful progress is made along a steep hillside flanking the stream beneath you & into which one false step would hurl the unlucky one. This walking is very hard on your feet as you are treading on the uppers all the time & Sid's & mine were raw with blisters & yet we used to keep tally with all our party which was 7 in number & even ask them not to rest as the perspiration &c would then congeal causing us great pain on once again starting until lubricated with sweat again.

Work | 2

In an age when a large percentage of the population lived at or below the poverty line; when ten to twelve hours was a normal working day; when opportunities for recreation, especially within the inner city, were few: in such an age, the workplace was the centre of the workingman's universe.

By modern standards most workplaces were uncomfortable, unsafe, and rigidly disciplined. Whether they were unreasonably so in the context of nineteenth-century conditions is a matter of controversy among historians in Canada, as it is among historians in Britain and the United States. This is part of a general argument that still rages among social historians over the impact of industrialization on the lower classes. On the one extreme it is argued that the rise of industry meant a higher standard of living, improved working conditions, and all of the advantages of urban civilization for working people. On the other, industry is seen as destroying self-sufficiency, driving workers into inhumane factories, exploiting them for the advantage of the industrialists: in short, the factories as Blake's 'dark Satanic mills'.

There is obviously evidence to support either view. Throughout the last half of the nineteenth century, people poured into the cities and towns, voluntarily deserting the farms for employment in factories. Would they have done so if conditions were oppressive? Hours in factories were long, but surely no longer than the workday on the family farm. Discipline on the job was often severe, but it could be argued that this was inevitable when employers were forced to deal with a workforce new to industrial conditions and new to co-operative labour. The factory was a hard school, but it taught workers skills and attitudes towards labour that allowed them to make their way up in the new society, that allowed them to profit from the opportunities held out by an industrialized and urbanized Canada.

Yet was the decision to leave the farm really voluntary, did it say anything about the superior advantages of the factory and the city? Pressure on the land supply may have been the key factor, leaving little choice for younger sons of farmers but to migrate to the city. Industrialization perhaps played another role; increased use of farm machinery reduced the need for farm labour, again driving people towards the factories. And the control by the middle class of the press and other means of communication helped create a climate favourable to industrialization, casting urban life in an unrealistically favourable light. Farm labour had been hard, it was true. But, say some historians, it was not so alienating, it did not remove choice and a sense of self-worth from its labourers. Man in the factory was an employee, not an independent worker as on the farm; he was stripped of any sense of accomplishment by being divorced from the end-product of his labour. Discipline in the factory was indeed severe, and served only to alienate the worker further and force him into a sense of dependence and lack of confidence.

And so the argument goes on. Some of these themes are illustrated in the documents that follow. The best single source on the nineteenth-century factory is the Royal Commission on the Relations of Labor and Capital in Canada, which reported in 1889. Its two reports and five volumes of evidence provide an unequalled collection of views and opinions on the state of industrial Canada. An excellent selection from the Royal Commission material has recently been published under the editorship of Greg Kealey (*Canada Investigates Industrialism*, University of Toronto Press, 1973).

Our first selection gives some statistical data on age and sex distribution in factories in the early 1880s, and on hours of labour. It is followed by two illustrations of the problems workers faced in the age of *laissez-faire*. The Toronto *Globe*, then Canada's most influential newspaper, argued against government interference in work conditions on the grounds that people should make their own decisions about the conditions under which they laboured. While prepared to make some concessions in regard to children, the *Globe* assumed all adults were in the position to make a rational choice about how long they should have to work. This editorial was written in response to a bill introduced into the House of Commons to regulate the hours of employment for children. It was one of a lengthy series of such bills introduced by an M.P., Dr Bergin, all of which met with little response. From the Royal Commission of 1889 comes some testimony on the legal bias in favour of employers and against employees.

The company town has always characterized the resource industries in Canada. Such towns, where the company controlled stores, housing, medical facilities, and most other social institutions, obviously placed workers under more than usual control by their employers. Two documents illustrate conditions in Nova Scotia coalmining company towns. Some of these towns would become the scenes of bitter and bloody strikes in the twentieth century. That workers in the West also had problems is shown in a letter reprinted from a Winnipeg newspaper. Traditionally the worst of all factory conditions were those found in cotton mills, where large numbers of women and children were employed. Some testimony from the Royal Commission describes conditions at a New Brunswick mill.

As industrialism advanced society was faced with a new range of problems. One was technological unemployment. Olivier Benoit, a Montreal shoemaker, testifies about the impact of machinery on his trade. More pressing on the public conscience were the problems of child and female labour. A series of documents comment on these issues, and on the ways in which employers maintained discipline in factories largely occupied by children. No studies have yet been done to determine how widespread harsh discipline was in such workplaces. The circumstantial evidence of the Royal Commission would seem to indicate that fines were quite commonly levied for tardiness, poor work, or damage to machines. Much less prevalent, but still not uncommon, were more drastic methods such as beatings, incarceration in 'black holes' in factory basements, and even the arrest of young workers for indiscipline.

Few would have defended the 'sweating system', but it was nevertheless allowed to continue. The sub-contracting system usually employed in the garment industry led to serious abuses and the vicious exploitation of poor women and recent immigrants. The federal government established a Commission upon the Sweating System that reported in 1896. Its report, part of which is reproduced below, was generally complacent, accepting industry arguments that sweating was not widespread in Canada. A young reporter for the Toronto *Mail and Empire* did not agree. The *Mail and Empire* was part of the so-called 'people's press', a muckraking newspaper that professed to espouse the interests of the lower classes. This article was one of a series exposing conditions among immigrants in Toronto. What gives it special interest is that the article was written by a cub reporter for the *Mail and Empire*, one too unimportant to win a byline on his story; that young reporter was William Lyon Mackenzie King, later prime minister.

THE FACTORY

Report of the Commissioners appointed to enquire into the working of the mills and factories of the Dominion, and the labour employed therein. Canada, *Sessional Papers*, xv (1882), v.9, no.42, pp.9-10, 14.

Total number visited, four hundred and sixty-five . . .

CLASSIFICATION OF LABOUR.
Number of hands at work.

The total number of hands engaged at these factories is 43,511, classified as under:

Classification.

Children under 10 years, males	104
" " " females	69
Children between 10 and 14 years, males ..	1,263
" " " females ..	823
Adults, males	26,308
" females	12,735
Married females	324
Unclassified	1,885

TABLE SHOWING THE HOURS WORKED PER WEEK IN THE VARIOUS FACTORIES.

Working day and night	11	Working 59½ hours per week ..	11
"	75 hours per week ..	1	"	59	"	..112
"	72	"	.. 1	"	58½	"	.. 12
"	66	"	.. 1	"	58	"	.. 28
"	65¾	"	.. 1	"	57½	"	.. 4
"	65¼	"	.. 1	"	57	"	.. 19
"	65	"	.. 1	"	56	"	.. 11
"	64½	"	.. 3	"	55½	"	.. 1
"	64¼	"	.. 2	"	55	"	.. 14
"	64	"	.. 4	"	54	"	.. 11
"	63¾	"	.. 1	"	53	"	.. 9
"	63½	"	.. 2	"	52½	"	.. 3
"	63	"	.. 9	"	52	"	.. 7
"	62½	"	.. 6	"	50	"	.. 2
"	61½	"	.. 2	"	48	"	.. 1
"	60½	"	.. 2	Not known	5
"	60	"	..167		

HOURS OF LABOUR: THE LAISSEZ-FAIRE VIEW

The *Globe* (Toronto), January 6, 1881.

Dr. Bergin's Bill to regulate the hours of employment in factories of young persons is a well-meant endeavour to protect children and young persons from the mental, moral, and physical deterioration consequent upon too early and arduous application to labour. The main provision of the Bill is that no young person between the ages of 13 and 18, and no woman of any age, shall be employed in any factory, mill, or workshop except between half-past six in the morning and half-past six in the evening. On Saturdays there is to be one hour allowed for meals, and on the other five days there are to be two hours allowed, of which one hour shall be before nine in the morning and the second hour before two in the afternoon. The hours of labour thus fixed would be extremely distasteful to the mass of our working population. This climate is not a suitable one in which to indulge in such a practice as getting up from a warm bed in time to walk a considerable distance on an empty stomach. Nearly all operatives would prefer to commence work at seven or half-past, having had a breakfast at home; then to have their dinner hour from twelve to one, and leave off work at six. It will be urged that Dr. Bergin's Bill applies only to women and young persons, but it is plain that the general hours of employment must be the same for all hands. In many factories the absence of the set of work people who perform certain processes would unhinge the whole establishment. Dr. Bergin's Bill, by lengthening the hours during which machinery must be kept in motion, would injure the employers, and if it conferred any benefits on the persons whom it is intended to protect, it would cause ill-feeling among the grown men, whose hours of leisure it would abbreviate without increasing their pay.

Another clause of the Bill prohibits the employment at overtime of women or young persons under eighteen. If this clause were to pass in its present form, it would amount to a simple prohibition of all overtime work in some factories. It is of course desirable that women should not overwork themselves, but the less the state interferes between the employers of labour and those of the work people who have attained full growth and intelligence the better. The subject of the employment of women would be best regulated by leaving it to the factory owners, who would soon find it to their interests to adopt regulations similar to those in vogue in England and continental factories. In those factories a fund is formed and applied to the encouraging of women to cease work for a sufficiently long time before and after the birth of their children to prevent injury to the constitution of mother or infant. As to the preventing of overtime work by young persons under eighteen, no hard and fast line can be drawn. We fail to see that a strong girl or lad of sixteen or seventeen would receive any injury from an additional hour or so of well-paid work occasionally.

What we would like to see effected would be the absolute prohibition of the employment in factories of very young children; and the regulation of the employment of such children and young persons who are employed, the regulation being directed to securing that education shall proceed along with the work. No child under fourteen or fifteen should be allowed to work in a factory unless the employer can give satisfactory evidence that the child has attended school for at least twenty-six weeks of the preceding year. Some provisions ought to be made for securing that the Act shall not become a dead letter as soon as passed. It is suggested that the School Inspectors would be excellent officials to entrust with the carrying out of the Act. As they are not Dominion appointees, it would be necessary to provide for payment for their services according to the work done. This would be an active incentive to diligence, and would prevent similar lax practices to those prevailing in New England from becoming common in Canada.

LEGAL RIGHTS OF WORKERS

Canada, Royal Commission on the Relations of Labor and Capital in Canada, 1889. Evidence—Quebec, pp. 210, 212-14.

CHARLES J. DOHERTY, Advocate, Montreal, called and sworn.

Q.—Will you state to the Commission the position occupied by working men as apprentices with regard to the application of the law relating to the masters and apprentices? A.—I understand your question to refer to the by-law of the city of Montreal. Of course the by-law is before the Commission, and can be seen for itself. I have had some practical experience in the working of it as counsel for working men, who have been arrested under its operations. The result of the observation I have made of the practical working of the by-law, would lead me to the conclusion, that it certainly could not at its origin have been intended to govern the relations between the employers and employees as we ordinarily find them at the present day. Under its operation, the employee finds himself liable to a sentence of imprisonment for absenting himself without permission, or for refusing or neglecting to perform his just duties, or to obey the lawful commands of his master or mistress. The by-law does not on its face provide for any exemption from this penalty in consequence of what might be considered legitimate excuses. To give an instance. In one case in which I was concerned where the employee was prosecuted for having left the service of the employer, and where the foreman, that is the employee, tendered evidence to establish that he ceased to work because his master refused to pay him the rate of wages agreed upon, and insisted on deducting a certain amount for materials the employee had spoiled, and where the employee in addition tendered evidence to establish that he was not responsible for the spoiling of the work and had not spoiled it, it was held that under the by-law that such facts, even if established beyond a doubt, would constitute no defence and no justification of the employee's action, and that he would notwithstanding such evidence being made and the fact being established, that he was without blame with reference to the matter in dispute between him and his master, that nevertheless he would be liable to imprisonment, and that the only recourse he would have would be by civil action at the end of his term, that is when his wages became due.

Q.—Has not the court decided that when an apprentice was employed for a year his wages payable weekly, he was obliged to work the whole year round whether he was paid weekly or not, and at the end of that time he could come before the court, and sue for his pay?   A.—The decision in its practical effect would actually amount to that, but provided the master alleged any reason for the refusal of the pay; inasmuch as the court in that case refused to interfere in the question who was right or who was wrong as regards the payment of the wages, and holding that the employee should be imprisoned for refusing to work, leaving him as his recourse as to the payment of his wages before the civil courts. He might sue each week if he choose.

By Mr. WALSH:—

Q.—In the case of the journeyman there was a plea of spoiling materials you say; that in itself might constitute a plea, but in the case of the apprentice there was no plea of that kind brought against him I understand? A.—The case I spoke of was not the case of an apprentice. The by-law is called "An Act with respect to masters and apprentices," but it covers very much more than apprentices, and it has been held to cover the case of every employee working under a contract with his employer.

Q.—Does that by-law exist as law to-day?   A.—Yes; it is a by-law of the City of Montreal.

By Mr. FREED:—

Q.—Does it apply to workingmen working under verbal contracts? A.—Yes; if they are engaged before one or more witnesses.

Q.—For what length of time?   A.—For one month or for a longer or shorter period.

By Mr. HELBRONNER:—

Q.—Supposing an employer should refuse to pay an employee, and the employee should take out an action, would it not be possible under Section One for the employer to prevent his employee from suing him in Court? A.—I don't see there could be any protection for the employee from such a provision. The provision being simply that if an employee absents himself, without permission, by day or by night, he will be liable to the penalty, which is a fine not exceeding $20.00, and imprisonment not exceeding thirty days—no option being given to the court as regards both punishments.

Q.—Is it to your knowledge that employees have been sentenced to fine and imprisonment for not having furnished a certificate of a doctor, for absence in case of sickness? A.—No; that is not my personal knowledge.

Q.—Will Section 1 of this by-law not have the effect of preventing an employee from executing all his civil duties, and his duties toward his family in case of sickness or death? A.—The letter of the by-law, I think, certainly would do so. I don't know of any case where it has been interpreted in view of facts of that nature; but the letter of the by-law makes the absenting of the employee dependent on the permission of the employer—there is not anything said about cause or reason of his absence. I think, for instance, under that by-law, a man wishing to absent himself on voting day could not do so without permission.

By Mr. WALSH:—

Q.—That would entirely depend on the master? A.—That certainly is the reading of the by-law.

Q.—So he could prevent that man from executing one of the rights belonging to all freemen? A.—Yes; I don't see there is any protection for employees in a case of that kind.

Q.—That expression, "by day or by night," is very broad; it does not specify any length of time. You might work a man for a week, with cessation under that by-law, I suppose, as there is no definite period mentioned in it? A.—No; there is nothing stated in regard to any limiting period. I presume the court would hold that a man was entitled to his customary rest. Of course, all effected by custom.

By the CHAIRMAN:—

Q.—And by the decision of the judges? A.—Yes; I think the wording of the by-law should be different for the protection of working men and employees.

By Mr. HELBRONNER:—

Q.—Is not an employee, who leaves his master's employ without giving fifteen days' notice, liable to both fine and imprisonment? A.—Yes.

Q.—And when an employer discharges an employee, is not the employer liable to fine and imprisonment? A.—I don't see it stated in the by-law that he shall be liable to fine or imprisonment for the discharge of his employee.

Q.—Look at Section 2? A.—Section 2 says that he should give him the notice. The only section providing a penalty to be inflicted on the master is Section 5.

By Mr. WALSH:—

Q.—What is the penalty in that case? A.—It is fine or imprisonment, at the option of the magistrate. The wording is this: "Having any just cause of complaint against his or her master or mistress or employer, for any nuisance, defect, insufficiency of wholesome provisions or food, or for cruelty or ill-treatment of any kind." I don't see anything about his being fined for discharging an employee.

By Mr. HELBRONNER:—

Q.—Section 2 provides only for the payment of fifteen days salary? A.—Yes; it would appear to me that if a master discharged an employee without justifiable cause, the employee would be left to his action for damages.

By Mr. WALSH:—

Q.—That would indicate that the section is drawn so as to cover the old indenture system by which the apprentices were living in the house of their master? A.—Yes; it would give one that impression.

THE COMPANY TOWN

Canada, Royal Commission on the Relations of Labor and Capital in Canada, 1889. Evidence—New Brunswick, pp. 61-2.

JAMES KENNEDY, President Phoenix Coal Company, St. John, N.B., called and sworn.

By Mr. CLARKE:—

Q. Where are your mines situated? A. Nova Scotia.

Q. How many hands are employed in your mines? A. We employ 150 hands at present.

Q. How many boys are in your employ? A. There are about eight or ten, I should think. Of cutters we have seventy or eighty.

Q. These are all men, I suppose? A. Yes.

Q. How many hours a day do the cutters work, as a rule? A. They work piece-work, and they generally work about ten hours.

Q. What would the average wages of the cutters be? A. Some of them are better than others, and some work steadier. I think that $1.50 would be about the average, although some of them make over $2 a day—that is, taking the wages by the month.

Q. Do not some earn a good deal less than $1.50? A. Yes; that is taking them by the month.

Q. Do you employ many unskilled laborers? A. We have about forty or fifty, I suppose—that is, surface men.

Q. What wages do they earn? A. They ought to earn from $1 to $1.50.

Q. Are they constantly employed? A. They will be after this. Our mine has only opened in connection with the Intercolonial Railway since the first of the year. Before that there were four months in the year we were shut down, on account of navigation being closed. On this account we could not reach here from the mines from December to April, but now we have opened a branch line of railway from the mines to Maccan, Nova Scotia, so there will be no more necessity of the men losing any time, and they will have steady work all the year round. . . .

Q. Are there plenty of houses there for your miners? A. There are.

Q. Does the company own the houses? A. We own most of the houses —the company does.

Q. Do you make a profit on these houses, or do you let them at cost? A. We make a small rental charge for them.

Q. What would be an average rent for these houses? A. $2 to $2.50 a month.

Q. Have you any idea of what it cost to build these houses? A. They cost about $300 for a single house; some of the double houses may have cost $400 or $660.

Q. How many rooms are there in each tenement of a single house, or half of a double house? A. In a single house there would be a kitchen, and a bedroom or two; in fact, I was never in them.

Q. Can you give us the sizes of the houses over all? A. No; for I never took the dimensions of them.

By Mr. WALSH:—

Q. They are something like on a straight line? A. I have never seen the inside of them.

Q. Have you ever heard any complaints about them? A. I never heard the people complain about them; the sleeping apartments are up-stairs.

By Mr. FREED:—

Q. Are provisions found near your mine or do you send for them from a distance? A. We get them mostly from St. John.

Q. Then they are dearer than they are in St. John? A. No; in the summer they go up by schooner, and there is not much difference in the price; there is only a little freight added on.

Q. Is there any farming community around you? A. Yes; there is a fine farming country all around; the railway branch goes through a fine country.

Q. Could not the farmers of the district supply you with the provisions you want in the mine? A. Yes; but the flour is drawn from St. John and the merchants of St. John get the benefit of their own investment. The company has no store of their own at the mines. The men opened a store there last fall, which they run themselves and to a certain extent they buy their provisions wholesale.

Q. Do you know whether they are satisfied with their venture? A. I do not; I have not heard; it has not been going long enough to tell much with certainly; I know they buy their flour by the car-load.

Q. Do they sell their provisions only to stockholders or to all comers? A. I think they sell to all comers.

Q. Do you know whether their prices are lower than the same goods can be bought in the local stores? A. I could not say, for I have never bought anything from them myself and have never inquired particularly into the matter.

Q. You do not think they have carried it on long enough to know whether it is a financial success? A. The object of the store is to benefit the men. There is a great deal in the management of these things as to whether it will pay and I cannot see why, if it is well managed, it should not pay; but it has not been long enough going to form an idea as to whether it will pay or not.

Q. What would be the ages of the youngest boys employed in the mines? A. I suppose about fifteen years of age.

Q. What wages do they receive? A. Some get 65 cents, some 75 and some 90 cents a day.

Q. Are there schools situated convenient to the mine? A. There is a school and two churches. It is a good school; a new church was built there last year.

Q. Are not the miners anxious to get their boys employed in the mines about as quickly as they can do so? A. Yes.

Q. Are they anxious to get them employed too early to get a good common English education? A. I do not think so, because work of that kind takes quite a lump of a boy to do it. We have no use for children of tender years; we have no use for children of ten or twelve years of age. A boy has to be about fifteen or sixteen years of age before he is of any use to us.

Q. Do the children get as good an education as the average of children throughout this country? A. I do not know of anything to the contrary.

A COAL MINER TESTIFIES

Canada, Royal Commission on the Relations of Labor and Capital in Canada, 1889. Evidence—Nova Scotia, pp. 444-9.

ALEXANDER MC GILLVRAY, miner, Little Glace Bay Mine, sworn.
     By Mr. FREED:—

Q. What mine do you work at? A. The Little Glace Bay Mine.

Q. What company operates that mine? A. The Little Glace Bay Mining Company.

By Mr. WALSH:—

Q. Who is the superintendent of the mine? A. Mr. Rigby.

Q. How many men and boys are employed in the mine? A. I could not give a very definite account, but I think there would be about 45 pairs of men employed.

Q. You are a coal cutter? A. Yes.

Q. About how many hours a day do you work? A. We generally go down about 6 o'clock in the morning and come home sometimes as early as 4 o'clock. We generally come home from 4 to half-past 5 o'clock.

Q. About how many days in the year are you able to work? A. I could not tell the exact number of days we work.

Q. Can you tell us approximately? A. No.

Q. Are you paid by the ton? A. Yes.

Q. How much are you paid per ton? A. In some parts of the mine we are paid from 41 to 43 cents—there is a difference of two cents between different parts.

Q. That would be according to the thickness of the seam? A. Just so. . . .

Q. Are you able to tell us how much you earned last year? A. I cannot exactly say, but I can tell you how much I earned for several months.

Q. State that? A. It would be $198.60 for April, May, June, July, August and September. The figures are: For April, $22.51; May, $27.87; June, $38.50; July, $25.13; August, $33.94; September, $40.67.

Q. Was this what you made clear? A. No; powder, oil, doctors, school and rent were to be deducted.

Q. For September did you get in a full month's work? A. I am not quite sure, but I don't think so.

Q. Did you get some work every month? A. No.

Q. Some months you were idle for the whole month? A. Yes.

Q. How much time have you worked since last September? A. We worked October fairly steady, I think, and the best part of November, and I think a little in December. In January I think I was idle altogether; in February we were idle; in March we worked.

Q. Did you get a full month's work? A. No.

Q. How many days have you worked during the present month? A. Very few; in March I earned $25 or $26.

Q. In the year closing this March did you do as well as in former years? A. I think it would compare favorably.

Q. It would be a fair average year? A. Yes; I think so.

Q. Do you own a house? A. No; I live in a company's house.

Q. Do many men who work in your mine own houses? A. Yes; quite a number.

Q. Have they paid for them out of their earnings in the mine?   A. I am not in a position to know, but I think some of them have done so.

Q. How many rooms are in the house you occupy?   A. The houses are generally composed of three rooms. In some instances they have more than that. A block is divided into four dwelling houses; when it is not full you will have more rooms, but when it is full you will have two bedrooms and a large kitchen.

Q. What rent will you pay for that?   A. $1.50 a month.

Q. How many families get water from one well?   A. There are two wells that I know of.

Q. How many families get water from them?   A. I don't know.

Q. How many families live around them?   A. I suppose 30 or 40.

Q. Not more than 40?   A. No; I don't think.

By Mr. WALSH:—

Q. Are these wells in the middle of the population?   A. No; there is a part of another row of houses which has no well.

Q. Do they come to these wells?   A. They go for water wherever they can get it most conveniently.

By Mr. FREED:—

Q. Is there a privy for each family?   A. No.

Q. How many families resort to one?   A. I don't know. There is one on the premises owned by the company.

By Mr. KELLY:—

Q. Did you ever work in any other mine than this one?   A. Yes; a short time.

Q. In this province?   A. Yes.

Q. How do the wages here compare with the wages at other mines?   A. I am not in a position to say. I think they are something about the same; they may be a shade better.

Q. How often are you paid?   A. Once a month.

Q. Would fortnightly payments be of benefit to the men?   A. It is my impression that they would.

Q. They would be in a better position to purchase goods?   A. I think so.

Q. Do you belong to the Miners' Association?   A. Yes.

Q. Have they presented the question of fortnightly payments to the management?   A. Not that I know of.

Q. Do the men complain of fortnightly payments?   A. Yes; they do.

Q. But they have never presented their case to the management?   A. No.

By Mr. FREED:—

Q. Does the company for which you work have any store?   A. One of the company owns a store; I think it is the president.

Q. If you trade there is the amount taken out of your monthly payments?   A. Yes.

Q. Does it make any difference if you don't trade there? A. I don't think it does.

Q. Do you get as good value there as in other stores? A. I don't think.

Q. Can you do as well there as if you had cash in hand to buy? A. No; not near.

Q. Yet you think you are free to trade wherever you please? A. Yes; as far as the store is concerned.

Q. When the mine is running short time do the men run in debt to any extent? A. Yes; I think most of them do.

Q. Are there many boys employed in the mine? A. I think there would be 15 or 16 drivers.

Q. How many cutters are employed in the mine? A. I think there are three or four.

Q. Do you know what the trappers get? A. I am not sure whether it is 40 or 50 cents.

Q. What do the drivers get? A. I think it is from 50 to 70 cents.

Q. Do you know what the laborers get? A. Some of them get 80 cents a day—I don't know whether any get more than that or not. This is a comparative list of prices in the stores.

By Mr. WALSH:—

Q. How is the school tax and the doctor's tax levied? A. The school tax and the doctor's pay are levied separately in the mine in which I am employed. The doctor's pay is 40 cents a month, and the school tax 15 cents a month.

By Mr. HAGGERTY:—

Q. Do you pay 15 cents for the school every month? A. Every month that there is work.

Q. Has that been talked over with the manager? A. Yes.

Q. What was the result? A. He would not alter it.

Q. Do you consider that that tax is legal? A. I do not.

Q. Have you presented it to the school inspector? A. We have not.

Q. Would you not get more satisfaction by representing it to the proper authorities? A. If they have any authority to deal with it.

Q. You are aware that you must pay a school tax any way? A. Yes; we pay a school tax beside that.

Q. Do you know what your personal property is assessed at? A. I cannot tell.

By Mr. WALSH:—

Q. What amount of taxes do you pay altogether independent of school tax? A. We pay $1 for statute labor, $1 for poll tax and 30 cents for poor rates.

By Mr. HAGGERTY:—

Q. You have heard the testimony of the other witnesses? A. Yes.

Q. Do you agree with it generally? A. They are from a different colliery and I am not in a position to say. I agree that fortnightly payments would benefit the men generally.

Q. Would the average wages you get be an average for the rest of the men? A. The average would be $242 for the year.

Q. That is from April to the end of March? A. Yes.

By Mr. FREED:—

Q. Look at this paper (memorandum handed to witness) that is the statement of your account for the month of July, 1887? A. Yes.

Q. You cut sixty-six tons and a half of coal? A. Yes.

Q. For which you are credited $33.53? A. Yes.

Q. And you cut two cubic yards for which you were credited $1.60? A. Yes.

Q. Making a total of $35.13? A. Yes.

Q. Against this you were charged rent $1.50, coal 25 cents? A. Yes.

Q. How much coal did you receive for that? A. About two loads.

Q. You are charged for the hauling and not for the coal? A. I think so.

Q. You are charged with oil 80 cents? A. Yes.

Q. Did you use that amount of oil in one month? A. I think so.

Q. You are charged with powder $3.24? A. Yes.

Q. Was that one month's supply of powder? A. I am not sure, I have had less than that some months.

Q. Have you ever had as much as that? A. I can't say.

Q. You are charged for school 15 cents? A. Yes.

Q. For doctor 40 cents? A. Yes.

Q. For tally 30 cents? A. Yes.

Q. That is for the man the miners employ to watch the tally? A. Yes.

Q. You are charged for store account $28.49? A. Yes.

Q. Would you run that much every month? A. No.

Q. This would probably include some book account? A. Yes.

Q. So the credits and the debits for the month exactly balance each making $35.13? A. Yes.

Q. You received that month no cash? A. No.

Q. Is it generally the case that at the end of the month no cash is coming to you? A. On many occasions.

Q. Do you get all your family supplies at the store? A. Most of them.

By Mr. WALSH:—

Q. Have you any other figures you can give? A. I think that is all.

By Mr. FREED:—

Q. Are the boys who work in the mine generally able to read and write? A. I cannot say that they all are.

Q. What is the age of the youngest boy working in the mine? A. I don't know that there is any younger than 12.

Q. Do you think the boys are well treated? A. Yes; so far as I know.

Q. You have not seen any of them beaten? A. No; nor heard of them being beaten.

Q. Do they work the same hours as coal cutters? A. Sometimes they are done ahead.

Q. Do they get a full day's pay? A. Yes; in general.

Q. Do you enter the mine by a slope or a shaft? A. By a shaft.

Q. Are the men carried up and down? A. They have to go in the cage the coal is carried in. This is a memorandum for last year, showing the total amount of earnings for the several months, and the amounts paid for rent, coal, powder, oil, school, doctor and tally. (Witness hands in memorandum).

ACCOUNT of earnings for months of 1887

	Total amount Earned.	Rent.	Coal.	Powder.	Oil.	School.	Doctor.	Tally.
	$ cts.	$ cts.	cts.	$ cts.	cts.	cts.	cts.	cts.
March	11.62	1.50	0.50	0.36	—	0.15	0.40	0.30
April	22.51	1.50	0.25	1.80	0.50	0.15	0.40	0.30
May	27.87	1.50	0.55	1.26	0.50	0.15	0.40	0.30
June	38.57	1.50	0.38	2.80	0.80	0.15	0.40	0.30
July	35.13	1.50	0.25	3.24	0.80	0.15	0.40	0.30
August	33.94	1.50	0.25	2.60	0.90	0.15	0.40	0.30
September	40.67	1.50	0.38	2.52	0.80	0.15	0.40	0.30
October	35.38	1.50	0.38	1.44	0.80	0.15	0.40	0.30
November	26.55	1.50	0.37	2.16	0.60	0.15	0.40	0.30
December	14.58	1.50	0.63	0.36	0.40	0.15	0.40	0.30

By Mr. GIBSON:—

Q. Is the amount required for school purposes a fixed sum? A. Yes; I never saw it more or less.

Q. How is it collected? A. It is stopped off in the company's office.

Q. Does the municipality authorize the collection of the tax by the company in any way? A. Not that I know of.

Q. Then they collect it without authority? A. That is our impression.

By Mr. KELLY:—

Q. Have the miners a voice in the election of a school trustee? A. They had last term for the first time so far as I am aware of.

Q. Are any of the miners elected school trustees? A. There was one for this district this year.

Q. Did he never take into consideration the amount paid for school purposes by employés in the mine? A. I don't know.

Q. You don't know how much is levied each year for school purposes on the district? A. I could not say, but I could get the amount. (Witness puts in a memorandum of earnings of several miners.)

By Mr. FREED:—

Q. This is a statement of the earnings for the year 1887, of Daniel and Alexander McDonald? A. Yes.

Q. They earned in that year for riddled coal, $394.83—unriddled $231.82—bank $42.45? A. Yes.

Q. What do you mean by bank? A. That is when they were banking coal.

Q. The total is $669.10? A. Yes.

Q. Giving each man for the whole year $334.55? A. Yes.

Q. The statement also gives the earnings for the same year of Richard and Joseph Beaver? A. Yes.

Q. They earned for riddled coal $156—for unriddled $119.34—for bank $25.05—being a total of $300.39, and giving each man $150.19 and a half? A. Yes.

Q. The average of the whole per man would be $240.37? A. Yes.

Q. Now can you explain how it is that two of those men earned more than twice as much as the other two? A. No; I only took them as the highest and the lowest.

Q. You think that the average between these two would be a fair average of the earnings of the men in the pit? A. I think it would not [be] far off it.

Q. What circumstances would warrant two men making so much and the other two so little? A. I think the coal was easier to cut, and the men were better.

WORKINGMEN'S PROBLEMS IN THE WEST

Winnipeg Daily Times, June 12, 1883, p. 4.

To The Editor of the Times.

SIR,—I notice in your report of the employment market you have quoted figures that are altogether misleading, and which will, if allowed to be published, do injury to a very deserving and useful class of settlers—I refer to mechanics and labourers. You quote carpenters wages at $3 to $4 per day, and laborers from $2.75 to $3. These figures are far in advance of the fact. The idea of contractors giving boom wages at a time when work is so scarce and men so plentiful is absurd. If the quotations were about half the figures you make use of they would come nearer the truth, and that, too, with the supply of hands far in excess of the demand.

I suppose you will be loath to publish anything like this for fear it should act as a check on emigration, but most of your readers will agree with me when I say that if intending emigrants of the class here spoken of were told the truth and given to understand just what they might expect when they get here, there would be less dissatisfaction and less cursing the country than what is being heard almost every day on the streets at present. Numbers know already from bitter experience that it is not very pleasant to be lured to a country like this where it costs so much to get here and so much to live when one does get here, and expecting, too, to be able to get work at once at good wages only to find that one can only get about half what he was led to expect, and then getting a job by mere chance after a week or two of diligent search. You will do a very great service to a great number of the good and desirable settlers if you will publish the matter just as it is, so that parties in the East who may be contemplating coming out here, and who probably have good jobs may be able to find out how things are here at present, and so be able to see before leaving their present employment that they would be disappointed if they did come, and also be in the way of their fellow tradesmen who have already fastened themselves here by investing what means they had when they first came. There are hundreds of mechanics here now who have invested what means they brought with them in a homestead and pre-emption, and who have to depend on their earnings to redeem themselves and carry their undertakings out successfully. They will be very tightly pinched and in some cases, probably will have to leave the country altogether, and run a very great risk of loosing their all by the scarcity of employment and low wages consequent upon the great excess of supply over the demand. Such matters as this appearing in one of the principle papers of the country would no doubt cause a great many to regard the country with suspicion, but the old adage will apply in this case very forcibly that "a bird in the hand is worth two in the bush." Far better make some effort to keep those that are here than to keep on encouraging others to come only to crowd others out and glut the whole market. It is a fact that hundreds of carpenters have left good jobs in the East this spring and come up here, induced to do so by such reports as I have referred to, and it is needless to add that they have been grieveously disappointed. It is not the fault of the country by any means that this state of things exist. No doubt, as money gets more plentiful things will brighten up, but not before a great many will be pretty badly stripped. Why it would not be advisable to have the true state of affairs published so as to warn mechanics to keep away during the tight times, and benefit both themselves and their fellow tradesmen up here, I am at a loss to find out.

It seems the press generally think they are doing the country a service by advising all of that class to come that can possibly get here, but how it is benefitting the country, taking everything into consideration, I fail to see. All they do for the country is to spread a little cash while they remain but the harm they do may be reckoned by the members of capitalists that will be prevented from coming by the adverse reports of the country. These disappointed ones will be sure to circulate when they get back East.

Yours, &c,

A MECHANIC

Brandon, May 30.

CONDITIONS IN A COTTON MILL

Canada, Royal Commission on the Relations of Labor and Capital in Canada, 1889. Evidence—New Brunswick, pp. 189-90.

Miss ELLEN MC LEAN, Operative in Park's Cotton Mill, called and sworn.
By Mr. FREED:—

Q. In what department are you employed?   A. In the reeling-room.

Q. Are many hands employed there?   A. There are about twenty hands.

Q. Are they mostly ladies?   A. Yes.

Q. About what would be the fair average wages a week in that room for skilled hands?   A. About $6 a week.

Q. How long must a person work at that particular branch before being expert at it?   A. Well, about two or three years.

Q. What would they be able to earn when beginning in the reeling-room?   A. One dollar and fifty cents.

Q. And then their wages are advanced according as they become more expert?   A. Yes.

Q. After you learn the business do you work at piece-work?   A. Yes.

Q. Altogether?   A. Yes.

Q. How many hours a day do you work?   A. Eleven and a-half.

Q. Do you have any time out of that eleven and a-half hours for meals?
A. Three-quarters of an hour for dinner.

Q. Do you work the same hours on Saturday as on other days?   A. Half a day on Saturday.

Q. What would be the ages of the youngest girls you have known to work in that department?   A. Nine years old.

Q. Have any so young as that been employed recently?   A. Well, I could not say; they are not in our room.

Q. What would be the age of the youngest girl now employed in that room?   A. Seventeen years old.

Q. Do you get constant employment all the year round?   A. Yes.

Q. Are there any fines in your department for inferior work?   A. No; I have never known any.

Q. Are any fines imposed for being late in the morning? A. Yes; there have been, but I never was.

Q. Have you known any fines to be imposed lately? A. No; not lately.

Q. Is the room comfortable to work in? A. Yes; quite comfortable.

Q. Is there any machinery in the room which is dangerous at all? A. Well, no; none.

Q. Is the room uncomfortably warm in summer or is it reasonably well ventilated? A. It is ventilated just by the windows.

Q. They are kept open, so as to get a draft through? A. Yes; they are lowered from the top.

Q. How frequently are you paid? A. On every Saturday.

Q. When does the week for which you are then paid end? A. On Wednesday night.

Q. Are you always paid in full? A. Yes.

Q. And always in cash? A. Yes.

Q. Do the hands in that department frequently change, or do they remain there pretty constantly? A. Some of them change.

By Mr. HEAKES:—

Q. Do the young women in your department eat their lunch in the factory at the dinner hour? A. Yes; a good many of them.

Q. Do they eat in the place they have been working in, or is it eaten in a separate room? A. In the same room.

Q. Is the ventilation in the room such that it is close in summer time? A. There is just the windows opened.

By the CHAIRMAN:—

Q. It blows pretty hot in summer in St. John? A. Yes.

Q. Is there any dust arising in the room? A. No; only when sweeping.

Q. How many stories high is your room in the factory? A. Four stories high.

Q. Is there any fire-escape? A. Well, not out of our room; there is out of the other room.

Q. Underneath? A. No; in the room out of ours.

Q. Do the doors open outwards or inwards in your room? A. Outwards.

Q. Would the average wages, considering your room all round, be $6 a week? A. No.

Q. What would be the average wages? A. What I generally make is $4.

Q. Are there many of the young women making under $4? A. Yes; from $3 and $2 a week.

Q. Are there any little girls there that earn under $2? A. No, not any.

Q. What would be the average of your room, please? A. The highest wages?

Q. No; the average wage between the highest and lowest? A. About $3.

THE MACHINE AND THE CRAFTSMAN

Canada, Royal Commission on the Relations of Labor and Capital in Canada, 1889. Evidence—Quebec, pp. 364-5.

(Translation)

OLIVIER DAVID BENOIT, Boot & Shoe Maker, of Montreal, called and sworn.
By Mr. HELBRONNER:—

Q.—Are you a boot and shoe maker? A.—Yes, sir.

Q.—Do you work by the day, or by the piece? A.—By the day.

Q.—Can you tell us if wages in the boot and shoe trade have increased in the past ten years? A.—No; I beg your pardon. They have been lowered, instead of increased. They have been lowered by about 15 to 20 per cent in certain branches.

Q.—Are young people employed in your trade? A.—Yes, a few; but only a few among very young people.

Q.—Are there young people, who are employed in your trade, engaged as apprentices, or to do certain lines of work, and help other workmen? A.—It is only as helps in the factory.

Q.—Do they serve a certain number of years before they are looked upon as mechanics? A.—As soon as they get a chance of increasing their wages by taking the place of a mechanic, or even of a man who has a family to work for, they do so.

Q.—They cannot be regarded as boot and shoe apprentices? A.—No; they cannot be so regarded, because there is the machinery. Every one works in his particular branch; and, naturally, if you work in one branch for twenty years you cannot make a boot, nor even a shoe.

Q.—These young people are, therefore, unable to make a pair of boots or shoes after they have done what they call their apprenticeship? A.— They have no apprenticeship at all, and when they leave a factory, they are skillful in only one branch of the trade. Take myself, for example; it is about twelve years since I left the factory, and about twenty years that I am working, and I am able to do only a single branch of my trade.

Q.—There are very few boot and shoemakers to-day, who are able to make a pair of boots or shoes? A.—There are in the factories very few boot and shoe men who can make a boot or shoe; they are so few, indeed, that they can hardly be found at present. In other words, the boot and shoe makers of old times and the boot and shoemakers of our time are not the same men, because the boot and shoe men of the old times could make a shoe or boot, make the uppers, sole it, or make the pattern and put it on the last, and then finish it and put it on the foot, whereas to-day, as a general rule, all the men working in factories, especially the large factories, are able to do only one kind of work, as to set a heel or sew a sole, or set the uppers, because to-day perfected machinery has replaced hand work.

Q.—This means that to-day a perfect machine can make a boot or shoe or a series of machines can make a boot or shoe without the help of workmen and only assisted by young people?   A.—That is true in a great measure.

Q.—Has the introduction of machinery in the boot and shoe trade, resulted in a lowering of wages?   A.—Yes; and that is the reason that I came here, before this Commission to say that our wages have been lowered, and not only the wages but the work has decreased, inasmuch as to-day one machine most certainly takes the place, on an average, of five or six men.

Q.—Does machinery have, as a result, the lowering of prices in boots and shoes?   A.—Well, machinery brought on competition, and competition has been spread and been distributed over hand work, I think, and I am certain that, so far as the goods themselves go, if they have been lowered in price, it is the workmanship that has suffered.

By the CHAIRMAN:—

Q.—What you are asked is this—whether the prices that rule to-day are the same as the prices of other days, that is, a boot or shoe of the same quality is cheaper to-day than it was before the introduction of machinery into the boot and shoe trade. Is that so?   A.—It is precisely the same thing with the exception of the few cents more or less one way or the other.

By Mr. HELBRONNER:—

Q.—Do you believe that it is possible to make boots or shoes by hand as cheaply as they are turned out by the machinery?   A.—There is a house here, in Montreal, which began about five or six years ago to make boots and shoes by hand. The two members of the firm, at the time that they started, were not very well up in means—as I could prove to you, and to-day, after having worked five or six years at the handworking of boots and shoes they have realized a handsome fortune. Lately, however, machinery was introduced into that house; the employer had to give it up only a few days ago. He said that if the machines had not entered his factory he would never have allowed them to enter.

By the CHAIRMAN:—

Q.—It follows hence that it is possible to make a boot or shoe as cheaply by hand as by machinery, and machinery has been of no injury to you at all, if you can make shoes as cheaply by hand?   A.—I do not see how you can say that machinery has not injured us.

Q.—But if you can make a shoe as cheaply by hand as by machinery how can you make out that machinery is harmful to you?   A.—Yes; but you must consider that one machine can be put down as equivalent to twenty men, and that I, for instance, may be thrown upon the street. In that case who enjoys the benefit? It is the man who manufactures.

CHILD LABOUR

Canada, Royal Commission on the Relations of Labor and Capital in Canada, 1889. Evidence—Ontario, pp. 1151-2.

*   *   *, Ottawa, called and sworn.

Q.—What is your age, past?   A.—I am twelve years past.

Q.—Do you work at the Chaudière?   A.—Yes; in the box factory.

Q.—How long have you been working there?   A.—Four weeks on Tuesday.

Q.—What kind of a machine is it that you work at?   A.—I do not work at a machine at all; I just carry the blocks and another man puts it on the machine.

Q.—The machine you take these blocks from is it a sawing machine? A.—Yes; the boys carry the blocks and pile them on the bench, and I carry them from the bench.

Q.—What hours do you work?   A.—From six o'clock in the morning till six o'clock at night.

Q.—How long are you allowed for dinner?   A.—One hour, all but ten minutes.

Q.—What wages do you receive?   A.—Twenty-five cents a day.

Q.—Have you known any little boys to get cut in the place where you are working?   A.—No little boys. There is a man who got his finger cut off.

Q.—Where this man got his finger cut off, could you get yours cut off too?   A.—Working around the saw.

Q.—Yes?   A.—He was working the edger; it is not the same kind of a machine that I carry the blocks to.

By Mr. BOIVIN:—

Q.—What size are the blocks? Are they heavy pieces of wood?   A.— The blocks are not heavy, they are thin ones.

By Mr. HEAKES:—

Q.—Can you read and write, my little boy?   A.—Yes, sir.

*   *   *   , of Ottawa, called and sworn.

By Mr. CARSON:—

Q.—What age are you?   A.—I am fourteen in August.

Q.—Where do you work?   A.—I work at Mr. Booth's mill at the Chaudière.

Q.—How long have you been working in the box factory?   A.—Since the 25th of April I have been working in the mill.

Q.—What were you working at last year in the box factory?   A.—I was working on the butting-saw last year.

Q.—What age would you be in August last?   A.—Thirteen.

Q.—What age were you when you commenced to work?   A.—I was twelve and a-half years old when I began this work.

Q.—What hours do you work?   A.—From six to twelve; then we have an hour for dinner—not quite an hour, because we start work again at five or ten minutes to one, and then we work until half-past six at night. We quit work at six o'clock on Saturday.

Q.—Are there any boys working there younger than you are?   A.—Yes.

Q.—What ages are they?   A.—Eleven and twelve years of age.

Canada, Royal Commission on the Relations of Labor and Capital in Canada, 1889. Evidence—Quebec, pp. 314-20.

(Translation)

PIERRE PLEAU, Machinist, of the city of Montreal, sworn:

By Mr. HELBRONNER:—

Q.—Have you been employed in cotton factories?   A.—Yes, sir; for some fifteen or eighteen years.

Q.—At Montreal?   A.—In the United States and at Montreal. I have worked in Montreal for four years. I was foreman for four years at the Ste. Anne manufactory.

Q.—Does the Ste. Anne Manufactory belong to the same people as the company which is called the Hochelaga Hudon Factory?   A.—Yes, sir.

Q.—According to your remembrance how many men were employed by the company when you were there?   A.—I cannot speak for the whole factory; but I can answer for my department. In my department, at the time that I worked there, I had from 60 to 70 men employed under me.

Q.—How many young women and women were there?   A.—On an average during the year, there might be from 34 to 36 young women.

Q.—Were there any children in your department?   A.—There were little boys and little girls. Among the 34 or 36 persons whom I have just mentioned, there were small young girls from 13 to 14 years of age.

Q.—Which was the youngest child employed in your department?   A.—The youngest child who worked under me was about thirteen years old.

Q.—Were there in the Ste. Anne Mills children younger than this, in the other departments?   A.—I have seen such; but they did not work under me.

Q.—What age might they have been?   A.—They did not appear to me to be above ten years old.

Q.—At what hour did work begin?   A.—In my time, work began at twenty-five minutes past six.

Q.—How long is it since you left the factory?   A.—It is now ten months.

Q.—At what hour, in ordinary times, did work cease? A.—Work ceased at a quarter past six.

Q.—At what hour had you your dinner? A.—We had three quarters of an hour for dinner, but generally speaking the hands were forced to resume work after a half hour. The engine was set in motion after the half hour, and the speed started immediately after the half hour.

Q.—Was there much overtime made? A.—Last winter, that is a year ago last winter, we worked for two months time up to a quarter past seven; but only in my department.

Q.—Did they give you any time to rest in the afternoon? A.—No; no rest. When the girls wanted to eat they were not allowed to go out and I sent out a little girl of twelve or thirteen years, who was employed in changing the work, to get a little lunch and thus they eat while working.

Q.—Has it ever happened that you worked later than a quarter past seven in your department? A.—Yes. We have worked up to nine o'clock at night.

Q.—You have worked up to nine o'clock at night for several days in succession? A.—We have already worked up to three nights in succession during the same week. . . .

Q.—Did they allow any time for rest when they made you work up till nine o'clock at night? A.—Not more than when we worked up to a quarter past seven.

Q.—If I understand you properly, then, you worked from a quarter to one in the afternoon, until nine o'clock in the evening, without any rest? A.—Yes; without rest; only he came to me, towards three o'clock in the afternoon, and he said to me: "You will notify your men that they will work to-night till nine o'clock."

Q.—Without stopping? A.—Yes; without stopping. I myself gave them a chance. I gave them the privilege of sending out for something to eat. I said to them: "Send one of your sisters, or one of the little girls, to get food, if you have none." When he asked me in the forenoon to tell the hands that we should work at night, I said to the hands at noon: "Bring some lunch with you, we shall have to work till nine o'clock to-night."

Q.—Why did you have to work till nine o'clock at night? A.—I cannot say. It seems to me that a couple of times I heard the manager, and the other foremen, say that they were working also for the other factory—for the Hudon Company below, who were in arrears with their work, and had not enough filling or warp.

Q.—But you were not given time to eat, you had to eat during your work? A.—We had to eat during our work.

Q.—So that the children of whom you speak, who were only thirteen years old, were forced to work from a quarter to one, in the afternoon, till nine o'clock at night, without stopping, and without taking time to eat? A.—Yes; just the same as grown people.

Q.—Did it happen often that you had to work thus until nine o'clock at night?   A.—During the time that I was foreman, that happened, generally, every fall, for seven or eight weeks running. We worked every second night. ...

Q.—Could you give us some examples of cases where you saw fines imposed?   A.—This very evening, I was around among a few neighbours, and I think that I have, on my person, some forty envelopes, in which fines are set down. I could show them to you. I should not wish that the names be known.

Q.—How are wages paid at the present time?   A.—At the present time, the wages are paid every fortnight.

Q.—Then, they are the envelopes of the fortnight that you have with you.   A.—Yes; these envelopes all belong to the same family. In the last five months, I believe that there have been docked off over $30.00 for fines. There are fines of $2 on a single pay. I might have others, if I had more time. There is another parcel of envelopes all belonging to the same family.

Q.—May you produce these envelopes before the Commission?   A.—No; I promised to return them to the parties who placed them in my hands; if I had known that you wanted any, I could have brought you lots more.

Q.—Is there any by-law concerning these fines pasted up in the factory?   A.—No; not at all. What they do, is this; they will go and talk to the party, and if that party answers coarsely, they will break out swearing and say: "I will fine you 50 cents," and then they go off.

Q.—Who does that?   A.—It is the first foreman.

By the CHAIRMAN:—

Q.—What is the name of the foreman?   A.—James Skead.

By Mr. HELBRONNER:—

Q.—What is, to your knowledge the highest fine that has been imposed?   A.—I believe that it was five dollars.

Q.—All at once?   A.—All at once. It was imposed on a boy for having broken a roller.

Q.—Had he broken it voluntarily or maliciously?   A.—No; it was an accident.

Q.—How much, to your knowledge did that boy earn per day?   A.—That boy, I believe earned fifty or fifty-five cents per day. I cannot say exactly what were his wages. ...

Q.—Is it to your knowledge that the factory, in which you worked, sought workmen, or workwomen, or children in the country?   A.—In our factory I have no knowledge that they went to seek for them, but I know there were those who came from the other factory, whom they had sent agents to search for. I know that there was a Mr. Gideon Thibaudeau, for whom they searched in the Saguenay, but I cannot exactly say where.

They called them "the Saguenay" at the factory.

Q.—Were there many whom they called "the Saguenay" at the factory?
A.—Yes; there were many of them.

Q.—Did these people receive the same wages as those who were engaged in Montreal? A.—No; they had to wait five or six weeks, sometimes two months to be able to get the wages of the others. They had a sort of apprenticeship to put in.

Q.—Among the people, whom you call "the Saguenays," were there many children? A.—They are, generally, all large families.

Q.—Is it to your knowledge that among those "Saguenay," there were children who went to Montreal without their family? A.—I knew girls who were sufficiently old, who were sixteen or seventeen years old, and boys, also, of sixteen or seventeen years, who were here without their families.

Q.—These girls, and these boys, of course, boarded with strangers?
A.—Yes; occasionally, they had acquaintances, cousins, or relatives from "the Saguenay," they all came from the same place.

Q.—When people were brought from the "Saguenay," is it to your knowledge that the factory was always in want of hands? A.—No; they had enough of them.

Q.—Is it to your knowledge that, when the hands from "the Saguenay" were qualified to work, the factory discharged the old employees? A.—Yes; that happened more often, even, than otherwise. People from the town held out for their rights, you see, when they required them to do too much, and they turned them out.

Q.—Is it to your knowledge that families living in Montreal, and discharged from the factory, to give place to the Saguenay people, were compelled to emigrate to the United States? A.—I knew one family which went to the United States.

Q.—Did you see, during the four years that you passed in the factory, any accidents? A.—There was one—one only to my knowledge—on account of their negligence. It happened to me, myself, by their fault. It might have been a serious accident, and I might have been killed. I fell from three upper stories.

Q.—Did you hear the people whom you call the "Saguenays" complain that they did not pay them their promised salaries? A.—I never heard them speak. I never had many of them working for me, it was a few of the young people—the small boys. The greater number of them worked at the Hudon Cotton Factory below.

Q.—Did you ever see these children badly treated in the factory? A.—Once I saw one of these small boys taken by the arm and cuffed, but most generally their money was taken from them and fines were imposed upon them.

Q.—What was, to your knowledge, the highest fine that a boy had to pay during a month?   A.—There were small boys who earned twenty-five cents per day, and during the month of four weeks they sometimes had a dollar or seventy-five cents stopped; this was as they were quiet. There were small girls also who paid fines.

Q.—In speaking of accidents, is it to your knowledge that a young girl had her hand cut in the factory?   A.—That happened in the spinning room department. I worked in the guard room where I saw it. I went to her help, because it was my business to pass there. . . .

Q.—Generally speaking, what was the conduct of the young girls and the young men in the Ste. Anne Factory?   A.—Pretty free.

Q.—Did the Superintendent of the Ste. Anne Mills impose fines when he saw a young man conducting himself improperly?   A.—No; never.

Q.—Had you children who worked with you in the factory?   A.—I had one daughter only who worked there. She left at the same time as I did.

Q.—You did not wish to have her in the factory when you left?   A.—No.

Q.—Why?   A.—On account of the regulations, and sometimes when one is with the wolves one must howl.

Q.—What was, in your opinion, as the father of a family, the moral condition of the Ste. Anne Factory during the time that you worked there?   A.—For myself whilst I was there, I saw several girls or women—and I believe girls—whom the Superintendent should not have allowed to work in the factory, in the condition in which they were, in the presence of other young girls of thirteen and fourteen years and of small boys of from ten to eleven years.

Q.—Did you see any reprehensible acts committed in the Factory?   A.—I saw things pretty "tough" as we say.

Q.—Did they occur often?   A.—Yes; several times; but, as they were people above me, I had nothing to say.

Q.—Do you mean to say that the Manager and the Superintendent of the Factory did not maintain order in the establishment?   A.—No; in this particular, they were a little too free with certain women.

Q.—When you left you took your daughter away with you, as you did not wish to leave her in the Factory?   A.—Yes; she left at once—about seven or eight days after.

PARENTS AND CHILD LABOUR

Fourth Annual Report of the Inspector of Factories. Ontario, *Sessional Papers*, xxiv (1892), v, no. 25, 7-8.

I found very few children (males between 12 and 14 years of age) this year at work. Even fruit and vegetable canning factories, which four years ago employed so many without regard to age, during the season, by the adoption of machinery, can to a large extent do without them. The corn is hulled, the peas podded, the cherries pitted and the apples prepared by machinery nowadays, dispensing almost entirely with child labor; even where light manual labor is required the canners prefer older hands to do it. The abundance of fruit and vegetables this year made business very brisk in the canneries. The Legislature this year passed the Truancy and Compulsory School Attendance Act by which all children, with certain exceptions, under 14 years of age shall be sent to school. By this Act the truant officer can visit factories and send out to school many of the boys under 14 years that are legally working under the Factories' Act. This law, if generally enforced, will take out of factories the greater part of any children at present employed. The Act only came in force in July of this year, and so far I have not learned of any children having been removed from their employment under its provisions. Although the proportion of boys under 14 years of age at work in factories is very small, there is ample opportunity for this new law to do good work in a few of the localities I visit. I have accidents reported this year to six boys under 14 years that might have been averted had the Act been in force earlier. Of course this law does not apply when school is not in session, nor during holidays. Below I give a copy of two letters, one to me, and the other to an employer, which will go to show that the restrictions of the Factories' Act in regard to age, while on the whole good, do in particular cases incur a hardship on individuals:

.   .   .   May 28, 1891.

MR. BLANK,—

MY DEAR SIR,—Could you not give Mrs.   .   .   's daughter employment. Of course she is a minor, but they are badly in want, and I do not think that anything would be said.

Yours truly,

.   .   .

Mayor.

The other is addressed to me as follows:

DEAR SIR,—I take the privilege of asking your consent, if you will kindly allow me to go to work. I have no father, and mother has worked and supported us for six years past. Her health is failing and she cannot stand such hard labor any more. I had to stop out of school two weeks at the summer examination or I would be in the fourth book, but I had so much headache that I could not stand it. I am nearly 13 years old; am in the senior third class.

From yours sincerely,

. . . .

P.S.—Mother spoke to the truant officer about it, and he said we should write you will you please apply (reply.)

From these letters will also be seen the reason why females, sometimes very young ones too, work in factories, and not always at such work as they would choose, but frequently at such work as they can obtain.

STREET BOYS

C. S. Clark, *Of Toronto the Good. A Social Study* (Montreal, Toronto Publishing Co., 1898), pp. 81-5.

You can scarcely walk a block without your attention being drawn to one or more of the class called street boys.

Every morning, rain or shine, summer or winter, a perfect swarm of boys make their appearance at the offices of the different newspapers, and boarding the early cars, they have papers to all parts of the city in time to catch the earliest pedestrian or street railway passenger. The World, on account of its condensed form, has a very large sale amongst those who live in the outskirts of the city, as by the time one reaches the city he is master of the news of the day. But the boys who sell the morning papers are comparatively few in number. The newsdealers control a large amount of this trade, and the efforts of the newsboys centre on the evening papers, large numbers of which are sold all over the city. The great stand for the boys is on the corner of Yonge and King streets, and at the railway stations, where in the mornings you hear the cry "Globe, Mail & Empire, World," while in the evening, "Globe, Mail & Empire, News, Telegram and Star" is rattled off as [fast as] their tongues can utter them. Some little fellows, however, of limited capital confine themselves to the Telegram, and at six o'clock the streets are full of little shavers, yelling "six o'clock Telegram." At the time of the Whitechapel horrors, it was a rare harvest for them, and sometimes when there was no Whitechapel murders on the boards, they called it out anyway. These lads are as a rule bright, intelligent little fellows, who would make good and useful men if they got a chance, but some of them are simply stupid. Some of them have no shoes, no coats, and even their shirts are merely apologies for such, and yet they are rarely, if ever, sick; they can nearly all swim, and enjoy themselves in the summer time, but the cold must necessarily tell upon them in time. Some of the boys live at home, but the majority are wanderers in the streets, selling papers generally, and sometimes forced to beg. In the summer time they can live out all night, but in the winter they are obliged to patronize the cheap lodging houses, the newsboys' home or St. Nicholas home.

Some of the more careful ones have done well, from a financial standpoint. Davy O'Brien, who for years stood at the corner of King and Yonge streets with unfailing regularity, deposited thirty dollars every two weeks in the Home Savings and Loan Company's office, and in addition thereto, he owns a house and lot on Duchess street, the value of which is at least eighteen hundred dollars. Some time ago when the Mail reduced its subscription price to four dollars in the city, the boys were unable to compete against the office, but the company agreed to sell the morning paper at 25c. a month per copy, if they were paid for in advance, this would be a cent a copy. Davy promptly took the matter up and paid for two hundred and fifty copies in advance each month and then sold them to the other newsboys, at a cent and a half a copy. Other boys have records equally good but which have not so bright a side financially. One young chap who used to stand at the corner of Bay and King streets is now in one of the offices learning to be a pressman. He was a reliable, honourable boy, and those with whom he dealt learned this, and when an opportunity presented itself he was rewarded by an appointment to a vacant apprenticeship. Another is now in the mailing department in one of the city papers. He, likewise proved himself worthy of confidence and received this position. Both of those boys are on the way towards making respectable and useful citizens.

In addition to the newsboys proper are also the youths who carry routes for the morning papers. Each paper employs from forty to fifty of these boys, and while the remuneration does not exceed two dollars a week, it is quite an item, inasmuch as the majority of the boys work during the day at some other business or go to school. It requires some enterprise and considerable self sacrifice, as they are required to be up at five o'clock in the morning but their work is finished by seven.

Again there are boys who carry evening papers to subscribers of their own. These are for the most part boys of respectable parentage, and who attend school. They are required to pay for their papers every day, and pay an average of seven cents a dozen, their profit being five cents. Some of these lads make several dollars per week, and have accounts at the savings' banks. They are sure to get along in the world, and their enterprise and pluck demonstrate beyond a doubt their ability to take their places in the battle of life. The boys who carry the morning routes are among the most respectable in the city, and must be of good moral character.

One of the boys employed by one morning paper was the son of the pastor of a most prominent city church.

A good many of the regular newsboys sell the newspapers in the early morning and black boots part of the day, taking up the newspapers again in the evening. Their ages run from ten to sixteen years. A few are older, and one or two men follow this avocation in the street. A boy provides himself with a box with a sliding lid, and a rest for the feet of his customer, a box of blacking and a pair of good brushes. All these articles are kept in the box, when not in use, and the owner carries this receptacle by means of a leather strap fastened to it, which he slings across his shoulder and trudges on with his box on his back. They are generally sharp, shrewd lads with any number of bad habits and little or no principles, and are averse to giving much information with respect to themselves; when asked how much they earn, they give evasive answers, but one dollar is supposed to be the average daily earnings of an industrious boy. The price of a new outfit or kit is perhaps worth a dollar, but second hand outfits can be bought at the junk dealers for much less. Some of the larger boys spend a considerable portion of their earnings for tobacco and drink, and they patronize all the theatres, their criticisms of which are really worth hearing, and their imitations or rather mimics of the different comedians are most creditable and put to shame the baser imitations we are obliged to listen to as being original and which we vociferously encore. The course of life which they pursue leads to miserable results, as when a newsboy gets to be seventeen years of age he finds that his avocation is at an end, it does not produce money enough and he has acquired lazy, listless habits, which totally unfit him for any kind of work. He becomes a vagrant and perhaps worse, and a wanderer all over the country. A boy of seventeen has visited nearly all the large cities of the United States, and the stories they tell of their experiences in Chicago in particular are absolutely revolting. The crime that banished Lord Somerset from London society is committed according to their reports, every night in some of the lodging houses in Chicago.

Like all matters of people who are compelled to reside in the city, the newsboys are, of course, the special care of that august body, the police force, which sought to tag the boys like dogs, and by consulting the chapter on the police force, you will see the opinions of some of the citizens on the subject. At a meeting held in connection with criminal matters, the following report is taken from a city paper:

Sir Daniel Wilson thought the prison was no place to send a boy to. Whipping soundly was the best treatment for boys of all classes who were refractory. The badge system of making newsboys register at police headquarters, Sir Daniel thought, would have been quite successful had not the newspapers given their voices against it. The system of compelling boys to go to school for two hours a day had not been thoroughly successful, because the boys left the respectable lodging houses in order that the police inspectors could not get at them so easily. The badge system must be carried out thoroughly or not at all. Radical were Sir Daniel's ideas as to the treatment of adult criminals. "When a man comes to thirty years of age," he said, "and has been convicted of burglary twice, I think it is ridiculous to lock him up for but two years or so, and on the third conviction I would send him to prison indefinitely, for I regard such men as wolves who live to prey on the community."

I call particular attention to the remarks anent the newsboys, and would say for the information of others that when one of the police officers called at a certain office the clerk who sold the papers did his utmost to make himself as offensive as he possibly could, and declared his intention of selling to every boy or girl who asked for papers, whether their age was five or fifty.

"Two members of the police force insulted me one night, and anything that I can possibly do to obstruct them in a constitutional way, I purpose doing," he observed in explanation, and suffice to say he kept his word. Any boy, tagged or untagged got all the papers he wanted in that office at least.

Other legislation has been passed for the benefit of the boys not necessarily newsboys, but as the boys are now almost restricted to looking cross-eyed on the street, and eating their dinners, I give the expressions of Saturday Night on the subject of the restrictive legislation proposed for their benefit:

Only those who have studied criminal procedure can understand what a roaring farce more than half of it is. Only those who have watched the discussion in Parliament have the faintest conception of the vast amount of a[b]surdity which was eliminated during the discussion. Hanging for sheep stealing was nothing compared with some of the dreadful things proposed to do to people. Then look at the Cigarette Act, which is intended to correct the habits of the young as regards the use of tobacco. Since Dominion day it has been law in this province that all persons under eighteen years of age are prohibited from buying, using, or having tobacco in their possession, and those who sell or give it to them are liable to heavy fines. They should frame a Spanking Act intended to prevent the squalling of babies, the chewing of gum and refusal to take the matutinal bath. Enactments should be provided for the imprisonment of boys who insist on sliding down hill to the detriment of their trousers, and for the making of dreadful examples of girls who let their stockings sag around their ankles. By proper attention to these domestic details the responsibility of parents may be greatly decreased. All they will have to do shall be to provide nourishment and raiment for their offspring, the policeman will do the rest. What a delightful vista is opened for the coming parent when the Kodak theory of parental responsibility is perfected. They will bring the child into the world, the police magistrate will do the rest.

This is given to demonstrate the absurdity of half of the restrictive legislation passed, and the absurdity of making children, or anyone else for that matter, good or virtuous by Act of Parliament, and Saturday Night adds:

The perfection of public schools has endowed the state with the right of even compulsory education. So far we could not quarrel with the idea of government. Unfortunately so many parents were unable to educate their children or even contribute to their education in a technical sense, that to prevent illiteracy the state was forced to invest itself with proper powers. Following in the wake of this, Sunday schools, imitating the Catholic example, relegated the religious education of the child to what may be called professional teachers. The mother, no longer feeling called upon to tell the sweet story of Christ's sacrifice to the child at her knee, had more time to devote to the designing of new gowns for herself and offspring. The father, relieved of his teaching duties, could spend more time at the club or in that odd mixture of secular and religious work designed to benefit the heathen and extend the tenets of his denomination. There is a general outcry for more religious teaching in the schools. Even the careless parent is observing that the proxy system has not yet been perfected, that neglect in providing parental precept and example is having its effect. Of course, parents are not impressed with the idea that they ought to do some of this sort of thing themselves. They feel that the schoolteacher ought to do it, that there is too much long division and too little divinity taught in the schools. The policeman having become the guardian of the childish habits with respect to liquor and tobacco, the nursery business should be extended to the Fire Brigade, who could no doubt be profitably employed in their spare moments in washing the knees of the school children and giving dirty little boys their bath before going to bed. I think the whole business would be laughable if it were not an innovation of that outrageous and fool idea that good boys and good girls and good men and good women are to be made by statute.

I wish to point out to those people who [are] so ready to clap a boy or young man into gaol for committing some offence against society that society itself might exert some influence to reclaim these people. I have in my mind one particular case, which is but an example of hundreds. A young chap of eighteen, who had spent three years in the Reformatory, met me one night and asked me for some money. I gave it to him, and he told me part of his history, which I have since followed through the newspapers. He has been in the Central once or twice, and is in prison to-day, I believe. On several occasions I have given him money, and the economical use he would make of it convinces me that he would have been honest if he could. I have seen him wait around day after day where work was going on, in the hope of being employed. He once walked a distance of forty miles to get employment, and was unsuccessful. Would it not have been better to have some place where such people could go and stay when out of employment, than to run them in as vagrants? Might not a large share of missionary money—spent in foreign lands—be better employed in feeding and lodging the outcast? I was much struck by the explanations of a parcel of Toronto women of some scheme to which they contributed their money. It was to provide for East India Widows! It made me laugh when I read it. East India widows, Chinese and other Asiatic races having Canadian money spent for their benefit and to teach them a religion they do not want, while boys in Canada who steal because they are starving, are filling our prisons. Singular is it not? I may possibly be mistaken in regard to the objects of this particular missionary society being the assistance of India widows, but it was something just as ridiculous, if that were not it.

The same hysterical asses that live to-day appear to have lived in the times of the immortal Dickens, and I submit an example of his satirical references to foreign missionaries, being from Bleak House:

Joe is brought in. He is not one of Mrs. Pardiggle's Tockahoopo Indians, he is not one of Mrs. Jellyby's lambs, being wholly unconnected with Boorioboola Gha, he is not softened by distance and unfamiliarity, he is not a genuine foreign savage, he is the ordinary homemade article. Dirty, ugly, disagreeable to all the senses in body, a common creature of the common streets, only in soul a heathen. Homely filth begrimes him, homely rags are on him, homely parasites devour him, homely sores are in him, native ignorance the growth of English soil and climate sinks his immortal nature lower than the beasts that perish. Stand forth, Joe, in uncompromising colors. From the sole of thy foot to the crown of thy head there is nothing interesting about thee.

Some time ago Mr. Harry Piper made a practice of taking a cartload of flowers through the Ward for distribution to the ragged children of poverty there. If I had my choice of a record when I stand before God on the last day, I would far rather it should be as a dispenser of such blessings as Mr. Piper's, or contributions to the newsboys' home, than all the glory of assisting missionaries in foreign countries where they are not wanted, but, of course, it is to be remembered that the former get no newspaper mention made of their actions and the latter do.

When I was on the staff of a newspaper published in this city, a lady came into the office to demand a free advertisement for the meeting of her pet missionary society. I took precious good care that she did not get it. That women could go to that newspaper office and with venomous persistency could haggle over the price of an advertisement regarding foreign missions, yet as she swept up the steps of that office she must have passed numerous half starved little newsboys sitting on these same steps who were far better objects for her missionary labors than any foreigners could be, yet I do not doubt, judging from the sneering, venomous-looking mouth and the disposition whose devilishness I had a fair example of that day, that this woman would consider herself contaminated had her skirts touched one of these little fellows she had passed.

NEWSBOYS AND JUVENILE DELINQUENCY

Canada, Royal Commission on the Relations of Labor and Capital in Canada. Evidence—Ontario, pp. 161-5.

W. H. HOWLAND, Mayor of Toronto.

Q.—Now, as to the class known as newsboys in Toronto, are they mostly immigrant boys or native boys? A.—Well, you could get that information better from the newsboys' institution. My opinion is, that they are neglected children, some of them the children of widows trying to earn a little; but the majority are neglected children, and it is ruinous to a boy to become a newsboy, in nine hundred and ninety-nine cases out of a thousand. When I was in Chicago the other day, I saw many of these boys; they all knew me. There are several runaways among them, and they asked me to see their parents here. I found them respectable working people earning their livings, except in one case where the man was a drinking man though a good mechanic. They told me that their boys were all right until they began to sell newspapers on the street at eleven and twelve o'clock at night, but then they got demoralized. I met a number of those boys and they were all alike in that respect. My judgment is, that if we were really paternal in our management of children, they would not be allowed to be on the streets at late hours at night doing any business of that kind.

Q.—Would you advise a law by which the police would be permitted to drive these boys home after a certain hour? A.—It does not require police; the school system could be so simply extended to do it all that the wonder is that it is not done. In Glasgow the school system is a paternal one. The chairman of the school board goes into these districts and has the parents and children come before him and he enquires into their mode of living, and so on, and if any cause prevents them from going to school he gets it removed some way. The system, as I said, is paternal, but the authorities take a great deal of trouble. I have, with some trouble, persuaded our Police Commission that the great bulk of our petty crime has been committed by boys just in this way. I persisted in bringing it before the board until they consented to allow a suitable policeman to be put on duty for thirty days, to go about in plain clothes and try to break up these gangs of boys who assemble on the streets.

Q.—You are *ex-officio* a police commissioner? A.—Yes. The result has been that we have broken up twenty of these gangs, ranging from five to twenty-five. They were systematically organised as a general thing, the head of the gang being a boy who was convicted once or twice before the Police Court. They were systematic gangs, organised for all kinds of mischief, and in a great many cases they indulged in petty stealing. He has succeeded in breaking them up, and it has made an immense difference already. In some cases the parents were got to send the boys to school or to work, and now the Commission has made an order that this shall be done regularly once a month or as often as necessary. I am satisfied that in every city a large portion of the petty crime is done by these boys, and you would be surprised at the perfect organization they have amongst themselves for the purpose of discussing and planning how to carry out their mischief. At first there were one or two things that struck me very strongly. One of them was the way in which every window in a vacant house would be broken, and I found that it was one of their plans to assemble together by a pre-concerted arrangement, armed with stones, and with one volley they would break every window in the house, and then they were off like a shot. There is no such thing as a boy being really criminal at heart until he gets to be about thirteen or fourteen; it is all surface depravity up to that time; and I don't believe in the necessity of allowing boys to go to the devil at all if they are properly managed; I think it's a sheer waste, the result of bad government and bad management.

Q.—What proportion of the boys in Toronto do you think are absolutely homeless? A.—I don't know that you could say that of any boy. There is a certain number who are regular residents of the Newsboys' Lodgings. There was a boy in my office yesterday, an incurably bad boy you might say, because we have not got the machinery to cure such cases just now. He is between thirteen and fourteen; he moves about from place to place; he has been helped several times to work, but he will not stay at work. He should have been taken care of and dealt with before being allowed to drift down into criminal life. That boy may be called homeless, but it is by his own determination.

Q.—Boys cannot be sent to the Penetanguishene Reformatory, unless they are actually convicted of crime? A.—No.

Q.—Do you think that a reformatory for boys not convicted of crime would be a good institution? A.—Do you know the principle of our industrial school?

Q.—Well, perhaps, it would be as well for you to state it, so that we may get it on the record? A.—I have been convinced all the way through that it is a wrong principle to treat boys as criminal under any circumstances, that there is no necessity for it, and that a child should be treated as a child, and on an altogether different system from the one we pursue. Now, our industrial school is modelled on the English system, and the particular point about it is this—that there is nothing in the world about it that has the prison taint. If, we have ourselves a boy who is unmanageable we send him to the strictest boarding school that we can find, the one having the best manager. That is what we do for our own boys, because we have the means to pay a couple of hundred dollars a year for it. But the workingman cannot do that; he has no play ground near his house, and when the mother is busy in the house, and the father is at his work, the boy is on the street, subject to bad influences until he gets unmanageable. The parents cannot manage him; they have not the time nor the opportunity to get him really under control. Now, to say that that boy becomes a criminal, and is to be treated as a criminal, because he commits an offence against the law—to send him to a place with the criminal taint —under such circumstances is simply an outrage. The principle of the industrial school is nothing more nor less than a compulsory boarding-school, attached to our school system, for boys who are unmanageable; and if the parents cannot pay the expense the municipality pays it. If they can pay, they do so, so that they are not under any obligations to the municipality. Now, that institution has got no cells and no bars over its windows; it has not even a high fence around it—the fence is one, which when I was a boy I could have jumped over with a running jump. There is nothing in the world about it which would prevent a boy from escaping, if he tried. Of course, they do escape sometimes—we have had four cases. Of course, if they went as far as Japan we would get them back. One got as far as Sarnia, and another as far as Point Edward; a third was found in the city, but we got them all back. One of them came back from his mother's home. They are not put in cells, they have no criminal treatment; they are treated as you would treat boys in school. If it is necessary to give them the strap, they get it, though there is but little of that. At first when a boy is brought before the Police Court, instead of being brought up in the open Court he is taken to the judge's room. The judge talks with him, and has a talk with the parent; he looks into the case, finds out from the parents what the fault is, and what they think about it, and if he thinks it is wise to do so he simply writes an order to the school, and they take the boy, and keep him for five years, if necessary. There is one boy that we have already restored to his parents. He had simply got uncontrollable, and lost his head and judgment, and when he had been there for three months the home feeling was restored. The parents were living in rather a bad neighborhood; they moved to a better neighborhood, and the boy was taken back to them, and now he is as good a boy as any. He would have been ruined if he had been sent to a jail or handled in that way. Therefore, I say it is an outrage to treat boys as criminal, when you can answer every purpose in that way.

Q.—It does answer the purposes? A.—Yes; I wish you could go out to Mimico and see it. At present we do not teach them with any intention of teaching them trades. My theory is that we have too many in the different trades in the city now, but there is any amount of land in this country and we take the boys and teach the great majority of them, who are physically suitable, so that they may be useful to farmers. They are taught so that they can do anything about a farm, the handling of horses, sowing, planting, the use of implements, simple carpentering work, mending harness, so that when we give the boy out to a farmer he finds him posted in the very things he wants. There will not be any trouble in placing them and eventually they will be holding land of their own and we will have good citizens manufactured out of so-called bad boys. You would be surprised at the work these boys are able to do under the carpenter's instructions; they are so quick and clever that they require less teaching than you have any idea of. Our theory is that in the common schools we have no education which is worth anything which does not educate a boy perfectly. We should train him to use his mind, his hand, and his eye together and when you thoroughly train him to do that, when he is turned out, he will be able to learn any trade, and will not be merely stuffed up like the boys we are turning out of the public schools. They are taken away from school at twelve or thirteen when they have just education enough to fit them to be shop men or book keepers or something of that kind. By our system we are raising a miserable class of this kind of whom we have a superabundance already, a class whose wages are very low. There are married men who are working as book keepers and in other occupations of that kind, who have large families who get perhaps seven dollars a week and some even four or five dollars a week. They are educated to a point which just makes them unfit to go into manual occupations and they go into callings where they have almost to starve for the rest of their lives.

Q.—Is that not due to a false idea of gentility rather than to defective education? A.—Yes; but the proper thing is to teach every boy at school a manual training; I don't mean to teach him a trade but to teach him to use his mind, his eye, and his hand together. Most of the boys when they come out of school have fingers so clumsy that they are good for nothing.

I was at the manual training school at Chicago; it is rather more of an aristocratic institution; the boys who come out of it become foremen and managers of work, but it has been very successful. They are now starting an ordinary high school in that way but they do not go far enough. They teach some of the boys in this way; they take an ordinary class and begin with, say, a block of pine wood; they are asked about it, its nature, where it grows, the purposes to which it can be applied, and so on. Then they are taught to draw mortices on a blackboard; after which they go to a bench and are taught to do the work themselves and you would be surprised at the results which are attained. This is on the principle of complete training but it is not trade training, because I am convinced that you have to go back to the old system of manual training, the old guild system, to some extent, not only to get men to learn their trade properly but to give them a better opinion of labor and to remove silly objections to manual training. I might illustrate that from our own experience. I was not inclined to be a very quiet boy when I was young, and when I was at Upper Canada College I took a fancy for printing and it was not long before I had a good stock of everything connected with printing. I used to put in all my spare time working at it and knowing the number of boys of my time who went to the dogs I am certain that made a great difference to me. I believe it was of enormous value to me, and I think that interesting boys in these things will have the best practical effect in keeping their minds off the things which will injure them—to say nothing of the more material benefits they will receive.

Q.—I will ask you to refer back for a moment. You spoke of these gangs of boys; were they made up to any extent of newsboys?   A.—No; I don't think so. To give you an idea of how these boys get hold of the training of the common school I will mention the case of one little fellow of about thirteen. He had been up many times before the police magistrate who however looked upon it as ridiculous to bring him up—he was very small for his age and he used to turn him off. That boy was a perfect little thief. I have often seen him with a string of school boys at his heels watching around the fruit stores and teaching these schoolboys to steal. We bring before the police court in Toronto about a thousand girls and boys every year and these children are in touch with the children of our public schools. Now it is all wrong. It is marvellous how these boys follow a leader; they go through a regular process of electing a leader.

Q.—There are natural leaders of boys, just as there are of men?   A.— Yes; and they generally lead them through some gratification or through some bold leadership in mischief.

Q.—This school at Mimico might be called a primary technical school? A.—That would not be a bad term for it.

Q.—Would you carry the technical education of the ordinary schools further than that?   A.—No; I would not. My theory is—and I think it will eventually work into practice—that we have to go back to the guild system in order to determine the education of apprentices. If you are to have first class workmen you must have a definite system of apprenticeship and carry it out.

Q.—Are not the conditions of production so changed that these old conditions of apprenticeship are no longer useful? A.—No; I don't think so. I don't think there ever was a better system than the old craft system by which you determine exactly an apprentice system so that men could not be considered workmen until they have gone through a certain training. I will not go into the particulars but I am satisfied that it has got to be done. The main difficulty now between workmen and employers is that boys are engaged as workmen and take the place of skilled labor the result being that it is unjust to skilled labor and does not give us first class workmen.

Q.—Would there be economy in employing skilled and therefore dearer labor rather than employing unskilled and therefore cheaper workmen? A.—I think the best is always the cheapest; that has always been my experience. It is always cheap to employ a thoroughly skilled man; he looks to the consequences, and even if he is only to make a hole in a wall he looks further to see if it will lead to other damage.

Q.—You would not employ a bricklayer to carry a hod? A.—No. It would not be wise to do so.

Q.—Then in any craft you would not require a skilled laborer to do unskilled work? A.—No; certainly not; it would be a waste of time and good material.

Q.—If there was any kind of a law forbidding an employer to put unskilled workmen at rough work you would say that would be a hardship on the employer? A.—If I were to answer that you would probably get me into some technical position in which I would not be very strong.

Q.—No; I confine myself to general principles? A.—Well, the general principle is that work is of a kind either requiring skilled labor or not. The case of a bricklayer carrying a hod is a clear one. It does not require a bricklayer to carry a hod, and in anything connected with carpenters' work if there are rougher portions to be done by apprentices, those apprentices should be called on to do it, but they should do it under a system which trains them to be skilled men. The result is simple in its effects; you will always have men going through, but you will have skilled workmen. You will always have enough labor under a proper system, within scope of the guilds, to do anything which would not require the time of the men, who could be put at more valuable work.

Q.—Referring again to technical schools, do you think that technical education should properly be taught in the common schools? A.—You understand just how far I carried that idea just now. You cannot educate boys to be fit for tradesmen's or workmen's positions in the common schools. But this manual training I speak of would be simply part of his education; he would be receiving that training which would make him a perfect man. That training would be common, perhaps, to twenty different occupations; it would be necessary to fit the boy for any one of them. Just as we are giving in our common schools a certain intellectual and moral training, we should give the pupil also a certain manual training, which will make him more facile, take away his objections to manual labor, and give him an interest in it. In the Old Country, I believe they are pursuing a capital plan with regard to apprentices, and the result is that they are getting capital workmen.

Q.—You would combine primary technical education with ordinary public school education? A.—Yes, I would; I think our public schools are terribly imperfect at present. They are turning out bookkeepers and shopmen; training men into labor of that kind where they are not needed, and are not productive to themselves or the community. They are destroying good workmen by destroying an interest in the very things they should take an interest in.

Q.—You think the common school education should take into account, more than it does now, the actual lives of the people in the way of educating them for the actual battle of life? A.—Yes; I think so. I would make no exception; I would make every boy go through this manual training.

Q.—Familiar with the use of tools? A.—I would have his mind, his eye, and his hand trained together—made a perfect man, who can apply himself either physically or mentally. Of course in some countries, Austria for instance, everybody has to acquire a trade; I believe the Emperor of Austria is a tinsmith, for instance, and I see no reason why we should not have that system here.

DISCIPLINING THE WORK FORCE

Canada, Royal Commission on the Relations of Labor and Capital in Canada, 1889. Evidence—Quebec, pp. 29-30, 24-6.

(*Translation*)

EDOUARD MIRON, Journeyman Cigar-maker, of Montreal, sworn.
    By Mr. HELBRONNER:—
    Q.—You are a workman cigar-maker? A.—Yes.

Q.—How old are you? A.—Twenty-two years of age.

Q.—At what age did you go into apprenticeship? A.—At sixteen.

Q.—How long did you serve? A.—Three years.

Q.—How much did you make the first year? A.—$1 the first year, $2 the second and $3 the third.

Q.—When you began your apprenticeship did you make an engagement with your employer? A.—Yes.

Q.—You signed it? A.—Yes, sir.

Q.—You were ten years old then? A.—Yes, sir.

Q.—Were you ever sent before the Recorder? A.—I was never sent before the Recorder but was taken up.

Q.—By whom were you taken up? A.—I cannot give his name.

Q.—Were you taken up by a factory hand where you worked, or by a policeman? A.—By a policeman.

Q.—What for? A.—Because I had lost an afternoon to go to the circus.

Q.—How did that matter turn out? A.—He had to pay the whole thing.

Q.—Were you taken to the police station? A.—Yes. I was locked up from one o'clock till ten in the evening in a cell at the City Hall.

Q.—That was the day after you went to the circus? A.—I went to the circus on the Saturday and was arrested on the Monday following.

Q.—You were not at the factory on the Saturday? A.—Yes. I worked there.

Q.—Did you get pay on that Saturday? A.—Yes.

Q.—You had no fine to pay for the day you missed? A.—No, sir.

Q.—He simply forfeited your day, then? A.—Yes.

Q.—You mean that you went to the factory on Saturday morning, when he kept back your money and had you arrested on Monday? A.—Yes; between noon and one o'clock.

Q.—You do not remember in what year, thereabouts, you were arrested? A.—It was in my second year of apprenticeship.

Q.—What year was that? A.—About five years ago.

Q.—At night you were let out? A.—Yes, because my father sought Mr. DeMontigny and got a writing from him to let me go. Without that I could not get away.

Q.—Did you pay any fines during your apprenticeship? A.—Yes.

Q.—Do you remember how much? A.—I could not tell you the amount. I paid too much.

Q.—Do you remember what was the highest fine you paid in a whole week? A.—It was not much at a time. It was fifty or sixty cents.

Q.—A week? A.—Yes.

Q.—Did you pay fifty or sixty cents the first year you worked? A.—No.

Q.—Did you pay any fines the first year you worked? A.—I do not remember.

q.—Did you pay many fines?   a.—Often. Nearly every week I had fines to pay.

q.—Why?   a.—Sometimes it was because we were sick and lost time. If we did not fetch a doctor's certificate we were fined fifty cents.

q.—Do you mean that they kept fifty cents from you over and above the time you lost?   a.—Yes. When we lost any time, and they asked us why, and we did not tell, they kept back fifty cents at times, although not always.

(*Translation*)

THÉOPHILE CHARRON, Journeyman Cigar-maker, aged 14, of Montreal, sworn.

By Mr. HELBRONNER:—

q.—How old are you?   a.—I was 14 on the 10th January last.

q.—When you call yourself a cigar-maker, you mean that you have served your apprenticeship, do you not?   a.—Yes, sir.

q.—How long?   a.—Three years.

q.—You began working at 11 years?   a.—Yes, sir.

q.—What wages do you get now? Are you paid by the piece?   a.—Yes, sir.

q.—You receive the same wages as the workingmen?   a.—Yes.

q.—What wages did you get during your apprenticeship?   a.—One dollar a week for the first year, $1.50 for the second year, and $2 for the third year. When I worked extra I got more. . . .

q.—Did you have any fines to pay during your apprenticeship?   a.—Yes, sir.

q.—Many?   a.—A good number.

q.—Do you remember how many?   a.—No.

q.—Do you remember the most you paid in one week?   a.—Twenty-five cents.

q.—This is the highest you paid?   a.—Yes, sir.

q.—How many hours did you work a day?   a.—Sometimes ten hours, other times eight hours. It was just as they wanted it.

q.—Do you remember why you paid these fines?   a.—Sometimes for talking too much; mostly for that.

q.—You were never licked?   a.—Yes; not licked so as any harm was done me, but sometimes they would come along, and if we happened to be cutting our leaf wrong, they would give us a crack across the head with the fist.

q.—Was it usual to beat children like that?   a.—Often.

q.—Were you beaten during the first year of your apprenticeship?   a.—Yes, sir.

q.—That is, you were beaten at eleven years?   a.—Yes, sir.

Q.—You were never sent before the Recorder? A.—No, sir.

Q.—How much do you make nowadays? A.—That depends. I have not yet made my full time since I am a journeyman.

Q.—Have you worked since the 10th January? A.—Yes, sir.

Q.—How much have you made a week, thereabouts, since the 10th January? Which was your best week? A.—$4.45.

Q.—Why did you not work more? Was it for lack of work? A.—Yes, sir.

Q.—Have you seen other children beaten? A.—Yes, sir.

Q.—Did you see them beaten worse than yourself? A.—No, sir.

Q.—Do you know of a factory where there is a blackhole? A.—Yes, sir.

Q.—Have you seen children put in that blackhole? A.—Yes, sir.

Q.—How old were these children? A.—I could not tell the age.

Q.—Younger than yourself. A.—No, sir.

Q.—Why were they put into the blackhole? A.—Because they lost time.

Q.—Who put them into the blackhole? A.—The man who kept the press.

Q.—Do you know whether this man wears a constable's medal? A.—Yes, sir.

Q.—Do the children cry out? A.—No, sir.

Q.—Were they taken to the blackhole brutally? A.—No, sir.

Q.—How long did they stop in the hole, as a general thing? A.—Some of them stopped there till seven o'clock.

Q.—When were they put in? A.—In the afternoon.

Q.—Was it seven o'clock in the evening or seven hours of time? A.—Seven o'clock in the evening. They put them in during the afternoon until seven in the evening.

Q.—At what time do the men leave the factory? A.—Generally at five o'clock and sometimes at six.

Q.—Do you mean to say that those children were kept in the blackhole after the men had left the factory? A.—Yes, sir.

Q.—Who let them out? The same that put them in? A.—Yes, sir, I think so, but I never saw him.

Q.—Was this blackhole heated? A.—I don't know, sir.

Q.—In what floor of the factory is this blackhole? A.—In the cellar.

Q.—Is there a furnace in the cellar? A.—Yes, sir.

Q.—Is the blackhole near the furnace? A.—No, sir.

Q.—Is there a window therein? A.—No.

Q.—When children were shut in there, you never heard them cry to get some one to let them out? A.—No, sir.

Q.—At what age did you quit school? A.—At ten years and a half.

Q.—Can you read and write? A.—A little.

Canada, Royal Commission on the Relations of Labor and Capital in Canada, 1889. Evidence—Nova Scotia, pp. 129-30.

EDWARD GILFOY, carding room employé in Halifax Cotton Mill, sworn and examined.

By Mr. HEAKES:—

Q. How long have you worked there? A. Four years.

Q. How old are you? A. Fifteen.

Q. Are there many boys employed in the carding room? A. Yes.

Q. Any younger than you? A. Yes.

Q. What is about the age of the youngest? A. Twelve or thirteen years of age.

Q. Are there any of the girls there younger than that? A. I think there are.

Q. You do not know for certain? A. No.

Q. What wages do you get? A. $5.25 a fortnight full time.

Q. What wages do the boys and girls who go to work for the first time get—what did you yourself get? A. $1.50 a week.

Q. That is three dollars a fortnight? A. Yes.

Q. Are there any fines imposed in your room? A. Yes, sometimes.

Q. What are those fines imposed for? A. Sometimes about the machinery getting smashed.

Q. And for being late? A. Yes.

Q. Are you ever fined for playing? A. Yes; sometimes.

Q. I suppose boys and girls there will play sometimes? A. Yes.

Q. Are you pretty well treated? A. Yes.

Q. Have you ever seen boys or girls getting whipped? A. Yes.

Q. What for? A. For playing.

By the CHAIRMAN:—

Q. Who beat them? A. The boss.

Q. Would that be the foreman or the manager? A. The foreman.

Q. Did he whip them very hard? A. No; not very.

Q. Just gave them a slap? A. Yes.

Q. Do you work the same hours as the other witnesses? A. Yes.

Q. Do you find it very hard to work so many hours a day? A. I do sometimes feel it pretty hard.

Q. You are pretty tired at night? A. Yes.

Q. Do you have much time for play? A. No.

Q. What time in the morning have you to be up in the winter? A. A quarter to six or six o'clock.

Q. How far have you to go to work? A. About a quarter of a mile I think.

Q. And if you are late three or four minutes what is said to you? A. If you are late five or ten minutes you are fined for it.

Q. Do they allow you five minutes in the morning? A. They blow a horn twenty-five minutes after six and that is so as to allow you to get in—so they say.

Q. Have all to be there sharp on 6.30 to start work? A. Yes.

Q. You say that you are well treated? A. Yes.

Q. Is there any drinking water in your room? A. No.

Q. Have you far to go for it? A. It is down in the next flat downstairs.

Q. It does not take long to go that far? A. No.

By Mr. FREED:—

Q. How long did you go to school? A. About three or four years.

Q. Did you learn to read and write? A. Yes.

Q. Did you learn any arithmetic, grammar or geography? A. No.

Q. Do you know any children in the mill not able to read and write? A. Yes.

Q. You think there are some? Do you know of them yourself? Are there many? A. Only a few, I think; not many.

Q. How old are those children now? A. About 11 or 12, or something like that.

Q. Do you think they never went to school at all? A. I do not know about that.

By Mr. ARMSTRONG:—

Q. Have the little girls ever been whipped by the foreman? A. I have not seen any girls whipped.

Q. Have the boys ever been slapped to such an extent that they would cry? A. No; I do not think so.

Q. Have the boys ever been checked for going down too often for drinking water? A. Yes.

Q. Have they been checked by the foreman for going too often, in his opinion, for drinking water? A. Yes.

AN ACCIDENT

Canada, Royal Commission on the Relations of Labor and Capital in Canada, 1889. Evidence—Nova Scotia, pp. 176-7.

JOSEPH LARKINS, biscuit maker, sworn:

By Mr. HEAKES:—

Q. How old are you? A. I am 11 years.

Q. What is the matter with your hand? A. It got hurt in the machinery.

Q. How? A. It got caught in the rollers.

Q. What rollers? A. The rollers of a cracker machine,—a biscuit machine.

Q. How long were you working in the biscuit factory?   A. About seven weeks.

Q. Was it part of your work to look after the machinery?   A. No; I was taken in as a packer and was then put to work on the machinery.

Q. How much wages did they give you?   A. A dollar a week first, and then a dollar and a-quarter.

Q. How much do they give you now?   A. Nothing at all.

Q. How long is it since you were hurt?   A. Nine weeks Thursday.

Q. And have they not given you anything?   A. No; except for the week when I was hurt.

By Mr. KELLY:—

Q. Did you ask for employment?   A. My mother asked for a job for me, and they said I could get a job biscuit packing; then they changed me to where the machinery was.

By Mr. FREED:—

Q. How long were you working at the machinery before you were hurt? A. I could not say.

Q. What were you doing at the machinery?   A. I was brushing the dough off according as it came through.

By Mr. KELLY:—

Q. Are other boys of your age employed in the concern?   A. I could not say. There was a boy about the same size.

By Mr. HEAKES:—

Q. Did you lose any fingers?   A. I lost one.

Q. Did you lose any of the joints of the others?   A. I think I will lose a second finger.

By Mr. KERWIN:

Q. Who paid the doctor?   A. I could not say.

By Mr. KELLY:—

Q. Who took you to the doctor?   A. A man who was there. The doctor put seven or eight stitches in.

FEMALE LABOUR

Canada, Royal Commission on the Relations of Labor and Capital in Canada, 1889. Evidence—Nova Scotia, pp. 6-9.

W. H. GIBSON (of Doull & Miller, manufacturers of clothing), sworn.
By Mr. WALSH:—

Q. You represent the firm of Doull & Miller here in connection with the clothing department?   A. Yes.

Q. How many men do you employ, that is how many hands altogether do you employ in the manufacture of clothing? A. Well, it varies at different seasons of the year.

Q. Give us the average? A. There are just a hundred hands working now, but that is hardly a fair average; about a hundred and twenty-five would be a fair average.

Q. How many of those have you employed in the building? A. We have at present fifty-five.

Q. The balance would be outside? A. Yes.

Q. How many of those are men, I mean journeymen tailors? A. Eleven.

Q. What is the average wages of these journeymen tailors? A. About nine dollars.

Q. How many of your hands are women? A. There are forty-five employed inside.

Q. How many small children have you employed inside? A. None.

Q. Those inside—are they paid by the day or by the piece? A. By the piece, except a few who are paid by the week. There are three or four paid by the week.

Q. Have the kindness to tell us the wages per week earned by those women? A. They average three dollars a week all around.

Q. Then all the other hands are outside on piece work? A. Yes.

Q. Could you tell us about the average earnings of those people outside? A. I have taken them altogether. They average three dollars a week inside and out.

Q. Are you aware whether the people outside employ any help? A. I think nothing outside their own families. They may have a little assistance from some members of their own family.

Q. Have you ever had any labor troubles among your people? A. No. The only troubles we have are pic-nics.

Q. As a general rule are your hands pretty industrious? A. Yes; we have no labor troubles.

Q. Your men for the most part are sober and industrious? A. Yes.

By Mr. HEAKES:—

Q. Has there been any increase in the wages of your people in the last seven or eight years? A. No.

Q. Has there been any decrease? A. No; the wages are about the same.

Q. Do you furnish your hands with constant employment all the year around at the rates named? A. Yes.

Q. Have you separate conveniences for male and female help? A. Yes.

Q. How are they separated? A. They are practically one, with a division between the two.

Q. They are side by side? A. Yes.

Q. Is there any screen to prevent the men from seeing the females go in? A. No.

Q. They can see one another go in? A. Yes.

By Mr. ARMSTRONG:—

Q. Have you any system of fining the employés? A. No.

Q. When goods come in from outside are they examined? A. Yes.

Q. Suppose they don't pass the examination what happens? A. The people have to make them right.

Q. Are they sent back? A. No; they are kept until they come for them. When they come the error is explained and they are asked to rectify it.

Q. Are they charged for any damage done? A. Yes; where any actual damage takes place; if the goods are botched in the making they have to pay for them.

Q. Is the charge enforced? A. Yes.

Q. It depends on the inspector whether he sends the garment back, or charges? A. Yes.

By Mr. KELLY:—

Q. What is the average amount paid for vests? A. Well, each house has its own charges. It would depend on the style of the garment and whether it has a collar or not and on the style of the collar.

By Mr. HEAKES:—

Q. Do you make shirts? A. Yes.

Q. Flannel shirts? A. Yes.

Q. Have you any objection to stating how much you pay per dozen for the making? A. From a dollar a dozen to two dollars, according to the quality.

By Mr. KELLY:—

Q. Have you fire escapes connected with the work rooms? A. We have doors leading to the adjoining warehouses and ladders to the roofs, put in, of course, under the supervision of the board of fire wards.

By Mr. HEAKES:—

Q. Do you make overalls? A. Yes.

Q. How much a dozen do you pay? A. It is according to how they are made.

Q. How much do you pay for making common overalls? A. There are some so common they could hardly be called overalls at all; we pay from sixty cents a dozen up.

By Mr. ARMSTRONG:—

Q. When charges are made for bad work what is done with the garment? A. The operative can take it at the actual cost.

By Mr. CLARKE:—

Q. What ready-made clothing comes into competition with you? A. That from the upper Provinces, that is, Montreal, and some local houses.

By Mr. ARMSTRONG:—

Q. Are your hands paid weekly or fortnightly? A. Fortnightly.

Q. Do they prefer that? A. We do it for our own convenience.

Q. Do they ask to be paid more frequently? A. No.

Q. Don't you think it would be a convenience to them? A. No; not to the class of people we employ.

Q. Are they wealthy people? A. No; but they are an industrious class; their money is perhaps more useful to them every two weeks.

Q. Can a person pay rent and support a family on five or six dollars a week? A. No; they don't have families.

Q. You say the average wages is three dollars a week? A. Yes.

Q. How much would the people who receive that amount pay for board? A. The girls mostly live at home and it does not cost them anything.

Q. Do you ascertain whether the girls you employ live with their parents? A. No.

Q. I suppose it is a matter of indifference to you? A. We don't care where they live.

Q. You don't know how much they pay for board? A. I suppose they would pay from two dollars to two and a half.

Q. Have you any in your employ that earn less than three dollars? A. Yes; that sum is the average.

Fourth Annual Report of the Inspector of Factories. Ontario, *Sessional Papers*, XXIV (1892), V, no. 25, 6-7.

One effect of this depression in manufacturing is towards some relaxation in the working hours of females in some branches. Another effect is, owing to the ease in which older help can be obtained, to do away largely with the employment of children (males between 12 and 14 years of age) in many industries, which has made the Inspector's duty in this respect comparatively light. Though I am of the opinion that should a fair improvement in the demand for manufacturers show itself, the number of children employed would materially increase. . . .

The following are the weekly working hours of females in some of the principal trades in Toronto, west of Yonge street. Baking powder, 55; bookbinding, 50 to 55; baby carriage trimming, 54; boots and shoes, 49; brooms and brushes, 55; binding and other twine, 48 to 50; caps, 49 to 50½; coffin trimming, 50; corsets, 47 to 50½; clothing, 50 to 57½; cigars, 44½ to 50; envelopes, 53 to 55; electro-typing, 48; fringe and tassels, 54; fancy boxes, 54; furs, 53; hats, straw and felt, 52½; india rubber goods, 50; jute and cotton bags, 49; knitting, 54 to 60; laundries, 55 to 60; millinery goods, 49; overalls, 47½; paper bags and boxes, 49 to 53; printing, 56; rope making, 60; soap, 52; thread spooling, 52½; tobacco, 52; trunks and valises, 52½; ladies' white wear, 50 to 56; window shades, 53; wall papers, 51½; umbrellas, 54.

In some of the above industries two sets of hours are given, that means there are more than one establishment on that class of goods, and their working hours vary. I give the shortest and longest.

In some trades the hours are the same in all the factories. In other cities the hours are about the same, but in the smaller places are somewhat longer. In some of the above mentioned trades males are also employed, and usually their hours are longer, generally ten hours a day. From what I see, read and gather in conversation, from employers and employed, I feel convinced that the tendency is towards shorter hours than at present prevails, where 60 hours a week is the allotment.

Many factories shut down from two to ten weeks in the winter, and others such as those engaged in manufacturing harvesting implements do so, or greatly slacken down in the summer, when the sales for the year are done. Some cotton mills have not made one-half time with full staff in the two previous years; though this year, owing to a number of the principal mills on grey goods coming under the control of one company and thus working to better advantage, the cotton trade has improved. Not long ago I noticed that one company had declared a dividend of seven per cent., and no doubt other companies also have divided profits. I observe that the number of occupations in which females are employed is gradually being enlarged, and it is now not at all uncommon to find them doing work that fifteen or even ten years ago would have been considered as out of harmony with public opinion, for the employer to ask them to do, such work at that time being considered proper for males only. There are various reasons for this to which I need not allude, but I cannot in my own mind justify all the reasons. I frequently meet with persons who think that females should not work in factories, but instead, sufficient wages should be given to fathers and brothers to enable them to keep the girls at home, and thus not go into competition with male labor. But there are many trades in which at least a portion of the work is more suitable for females, and can be better done by them; though in the clothing and other wearing apparel branches of trade, males do in some cases operate the sewing machines and do the ironing of shirts. So it seems that if females are encroaching on the field of labor which was formerly considered as exclusively belonging to males, the latter, on the other hand, are spreading out on the territory devoted to female labor. In mentioning the occupations in which females are employed, I refer only to this Province, particularly to the western district. In other countries, in the old world, females have long been doing most laborious work, much of it under most degrading conditions, which are being slowly improved by legislation.

THE SWEATING SYSTEM: CONDITIONS IN THE WORKSHOP

Report upon the Sweating System in Canada. Canada, *Sessional Papers*, XXIX (1896), no. 61, 22-7.

Mr. GUROFSKY.—
. . . You will find that in many of the places that many of the bundles are not only used to sleep on, but to nurse sick children on while the women work at the sewing machines. Of course, in large establishments, such as I work in, where many hands are employed, the clothing is not used for bedding.

The COMMISSIONER.—Do the wholesalers or manufacturers keep themselves informed or make inquiries as to the sanitary condition of workshops or dwellings in which their clothing is manufactured?

Mr. GUROFSKY.—In several years of experience, I never heard of a wholesaler inquiring as to the workshop where their work was done. I doubt whether many wholesalers or foremen ever see the establishments in all their lifetime. People work for them for years and bosses and foremen know nothing of them beyond the street and number of the house in which they reside. . . .

The COMMISSIONER.—Is there much work given out by contractors to persons who work in their homes?

Mr. GUROFSKY.—Well, Mr. Wright, as far as I know, a few sub-contractors have gone into that part of the work. There is one fellow in particular getting in that work on ladies' work. One on Front Street—Fine is his name—14 Front Street, West, I think—has recently gone into the business. You will find his record in the police court. Not less than fourteen girls left him in one week. Several of them had been in the police court for non-payment of wages. He sub-contracts on all kinds of work. Eaton's have also gone into that kind of business.

The COMMISSIONER.—Which Eaton's?

Mr. GUROFSKY.—T. Eaton's. They are making up their ladies' work on that kind of business. They give their people piecework. They contract with the contractor, who gets the rake-off.

The COMMISSIONER.—Eatons get all their work done by contractors, do they not?

Mr. GUROFSKY.—Some of it.

The COMMISSIONER.—Does the practice prevail to any considerable extent among manufacturers or wholesalers, of giving out work directly to people who make it up in their homes?

Mr. GUROFSKY.—They carry that out to a large extent with most of their small work, all children's work goes out in bundles of five, or six or a dozen. To some extent the same thing is carried on in coats of the lower grade and pants. It is only within the last two or three years that two or three pant establishments have started to make up bundles in large quantities, but the bulk give only three or four to one woman, and in that way send them all over the city.

Mr. CAREY.—I know of cases where work is given out from large wholesale houses to manufacturers to the women.

Mr. GUROFSKY.—Several large ready made clothing establishments in this city do the same thing, although of course they buy some clothing ready made.

Inspector BARBER.—We suppose that the great bulk of ordered clothing for the trade is done in the same way.

The COMMISSIONER.—That question will come up later. Is it usual for people who make up clothing at their homes, for manufacturers or contractors, to employ assistance not members of their own families?

Mr. GUROFSKY.—They always get some one who will work for less than nothing. All have some one to help them.

The COMMISSIONER.—What is the nature of this assistance; are those they employ males or females; adults or children?

Mr. GUROFSKY.—They do mostly children's work in the branch shops: very few men work in the branches except in the larger shops. In the wholesale houses young girls come in who want to learn the trade.

The COMMISSIONER.—Are such employees usually paid by the piece, or do they generally work by the day or week?

Mr. GUROFSKY.—Myself and those here to-night are all paid by the week, but in some of these places, Eaton's establishment, for instance, they pay them by the piece.

The COMMISSIONER.—Speaking more particularly of employees who work in private houses.

Mr. GUROFSKY.—As far as I know both piecework and week work.

The COMMISSIONER.—Are there many shops or places where clothing is made that do not come under the provisions of the Factories Act? I think the statement made by Mr. Brown covers this question.

Mr. GUROFSKY.—Hundreds of them.

Mr. JURY.—What the Commissioner should do to satisfy himself is to walk up and down Bay Street for a few hours any day in the week and see the great number of women staggering up and down with great bundles of clothing; some of the poor creatures hardly able to walk.

Mr. CAREY.—Yes, he would see baby carriages used to carry these bundles.

The COMMISSIONER.—I asked that question largely to make way for the next one. Are there many children employed in such shops or places who are under the Factories age?

Miss CARLYLE.—I do not think so.

Inspector BARBER.—The School Act that we have now requires children between eight and fourteen years of age to go to school and in this city, at least, I think that that law is pretty well enforced.

Inspector BROWN.—I think that it could be regulated. There are many places which do not come under the Act where girls under fourteen are employed.

Mr. JURY.—To the Commissioner. Does not your question apply to places that do not come under the Factory Act?

The COMMISSIONER.—Yes, only to such places.

Mr. O'DONOGHUE.—I know of my own experience that there are children under age working in the factories.

Mr. GUROFSKY.—I could take you to places where the children are making pants with their mothers. These children are under the school age. They are employed sewing on buttons, and the like of that. I know some of the factories where the inspectors go, in which the children work after school hours.

Inspector BARBER.—In those circumstances you ought to let the inspectors know.

Mr. GUROFSKY.—They are their own children (the people who run the factories). You might go a dozen times and not see them working there but I might see them any day.

Mr. TODD.—Then the factory inspectors would have some difficulty in locating these cases.

The under age question is a hard one to get at. A gentleman I know—a foreman in a factory where a large number of boys and girls are working—has often told me that boys come to him whom he believes are under age. He tells them that he cannot employ them unless they are over fourteen, and of course they immediately swear that they are over that age. You cannot get the registry of births because not one boy in ten is registered.

Mr. GUROFSKY.—There is a place where you can go to-morrow, a tailor shop on Hagerman Street, where, should they not notice you coming, you will find a whole family of children working.

The COMMISSIONER.—How many hours constitute a day's work in shops where the day or week system obtains?

Mr. GUROFSKY.—As far as our coat shop is concerned where a large number of men are employed, the hours are from 7 to 6 and to 12 o'clock on Saturdays. There was one shop where I worked all hours, where only one or two men are employed. The balance of the employees are girls. The hours are from 7.30 to 6 and to 12 o'clock on Saturdays.

Mr. O'DONOGHUE.—There is one establishment near my place where the hours are from 7.30 to 6 and to 12 o'clock Saturdays.

Mr. GUROFSKY.—The men in my shop have to be there at 7 o'clock, but the girls come in at any time up to 7.30.

The COMMISSIONER.—How many hours daily do piece hands usually work?

Mr. GUROFSKY.—In Eaton's, where they work piecework regularly, the hours are from 8 to 6, but there is a place on Elizabeth Street, where you can go at eleven and twelve o'clock at night and five o'clock in the morning and find them working. They never seem to be doing anything else.

Mr. O'DONOGHUE.—With respect to that place on Elizabeth Street, it appears to me they never sleep. It is on the east side of the street.

The COMMISSIONER.—Do you mean Rosen's place?

Mr. GUROFSKY.—Yes, they are all piece workers there, both men and girls. They do a lot of work for Eaton's.

The COMMISSIONER.—They work for Eaton's pretty much altogether, I think.

Mr. GUROFSKY.—There is another place on Edward street, where they make pants. You can go along there any time and find them working.

The COMMISSIONER.—The place of Rosen's comes under the Factory Act, I think.

Miss CARLYLE.—Yes.

Mr. GUROFSKY.—I don't think that there are six working there now, not including their own family.

The COMMISSIONER.—Still if they have six with their own family that will do.

Mr. O'DONOGHUE.—Speaking in regard to the time in factories, I would just like to ask the inspectors, do they find the Factory Act now very specific so that the question as to what constitutes a day's work and what constitutes overtime cannot be avoided by an employer so desiring? Can employers in their factories now so arrange the work so that night work can be counted as part of the day's work or otherwise? As a manufacturer would it be possible for me to so arrange my men as to run them day and night?

Inspector BROWN.—Have you reference to men alone? because the Act does not apply to men alone.

Mr. O'DONOGHUE.—I am speaking of where the Act does apply, can the employer so arrange his time table?

Inspector BROWN.—So long as he does not make his men exceed sixty hours per week each.

Mr. GUROFSKY.—In Eaton's or any of these large establishments the power is never turned off. The employees eat their dinner in five minutes, put the rest of the meal hour in at work.

Inspector BARBER.—The law definitely fixes sixty hours per week as the working week, and there is no possibility of the employer making any alteration in the forms left him, by which he can exceed those hours. . . .

The COMMISSIONER.—I noticed in the evidence given before the United States Congressional Committee that it was said by some witnesses that they had to work away into the second day to make up the first day's work.

Mr. GUROFSKY.—That is often the way in the states. In our own shop we generally manage to finish so many coats a day. The work, however, is so arranged that we start in the morning and finish at night. We have not made a bargain with the boss that we do so many coats a day, yet it is commonly understood that it is to be done. My head man sitting here will bear me out in the statement that we feel if we do not get through there will be trouble.

The COMMISSIONER.—You realize that if it is not done some one else will get your place.

Mr. GUROFSKY.—That's about it.

Mr. SNIDERMAN.—Some days the boss expects too much, then we make a kick. We generally do twenty-six coats a day each. . . .

The COMMISSIONER.—What are the usual wages for hands who work by the week?

Mr. GUROFSKY.—For men who are operators—there are not many of us here—the best men get $11 a week, and the wages run down to $5 and $4. This gentleman here (pointing to Sniderman) is the only man in Toronto who gets over $11 per week. At one time pressers used to get $2 per day. Now, instead of having one man to press the whole garment they have four. One for the seams, one for the collar and so on. They pay these men from $3 to $5 per week where formerly one man would do the whole thing and make $12 per week. He had been paid as low as $9 per week and as high as $14.

The COMMISSIONER.—How about the women?

Mr. GUROFSKY.—They run all the way from seventy-five cents.

The COMMISSIONER.—A week?

Mr. GUROFSKY.—Yes, up to $6, and I doubt if there are half a dozen women earning over $6. The usual wages is $3 to $4.50; but $3 is a fair wage.

The COMMISSIONER.—Speaking of these girls, are they supposed to know the trade?

Mr. GUROFSKY.—Those earning seventy-five cents know some branch of it.

The COMMISSIONER.—What is the average age of the women employed?

Mr. GUROFSKY.—Oh, all ages—16, 17, 18 and up to 30 years of age.

Mr. O'DONOGHUE.—Do you think that $4 or $4.50 is above the average?

Mr. GUROFSKY.—Taking them as a whole I doubt if they would average $4. I may say that there are five men in my shop. Our average wage is $12. The girls there average $4. It has been my experience that in shops where men are employed the wages are higher than where no men are employed. Having the men in the shop has the tendency to increase wages of both girls and men.

Inspector BROWN.—With reference to wages of women. On one occasion

I accompanied a reporter to a number of shops in the city making inquiries. I remember one shop where we went and the wages paid ranged from $1 to $3.50 per week for a finisher. When asking the employer how they could sustain themselves on such small means he replied that he only got thirty-seven and a half cents each for making coats and could not afford to give any higher wages.

Mr. GUROFSKY.—It is only within a short time that the wages have gone up to the average I mentioned. There has been a scarcity of hands—many having gone over to the United States, and the wages have gone up for those who remain.

The COMMISSIONER.—How about children's wages?

Mr. GUROFSKY.—They generally work for nothing, learning the trade.

The COMMISSIONER.—Is the tendency, as judged by the experience of recent years, toward higher wages or lower?

Mr. GUROFSKY.—I could not do justice to that question. My wages have gone up some recently for the reason I mentioned, a scarcity of hands.

The COMMISSIONER.—For a number of years past what has been the tendency?

Mr. GUROFSKY.—To lower.

Inspector BARBER.—My experience has lasted over some years, and as I have taken an interest in the matter, I have found that the warehousemen were beating down the prices to the contractors; and while many contractors reduce the prices to their workers, in other cases contractors tell me that they were paying the same prices to their workers as formerly and thus losing themselves. Some of these contractors have gone to taking work away from other contractors.

Mr. GUROFSKY.—That is a fair answer to the question.

Mr. JURY.—In 1873-4-5 and 6 just after I first came to Toronto, firms like Robert Walker and R. J. Hunter, both used to make up large quantities of stock work in their slack time. They used to pay $3.50, $4 and $4.50, for their best made overcoats. These men tell me there are no such prices paid now.

Mr. GUROFSKY.—You can get the best stock made coat now for $1.50 and the money for cotton, etc., comes out of the pockets of the workers.

The COMMISSIONER.—In such divisions of the trade as show tendency to higher wages, does the rise appear to be due to combinations among the employees, to better prices for the finished clothing, or to a scarcity of competent workmen? Or is it to be accounted for in any other way?

Mr. GUROFSKY.—In some instances the tendency has been to increase the wages because there is a scarcity of competent operators. But in the others where there is no lack of finishers, pressers, etc., the wages have gone down. The wages have also gone down in the lower grades of operators. In my branch, wages have gone up owing to the scarcity of competent hands. It is the same way with the girls. A number of experienced girl operators got married recently, that has had the tendency to make the wages of remaining competent girl operators go up.

The COMMISSIONER.—Then I understand your answer to be that in cases of increase in wages in any branch of the work it is due to a scarcity of competent workers in that branch?

Mr. GUROFSKY.—Yes.

THE SWEATING SYSTEM: THE 'PEOPLE'S PRESS' REPORTS

The *Daily Mail and Empire* (Toronto), October 9, 1897, p. 10.

There is possibly no phase of industrial employment so frequently spoken of and so little understood by those who are fondest of treating of it, as the sweating system. The term itself has something about it which savours of human sacrifice, as the result of brutal oppression, and has been used in this sense to denote all manner of tyranny, and often a condition of depravity. The term "sweating," when properly used, denotes a condition of labour in which a maximum amount of work in a given time is performed for a minimum wage, and in which the ordinary rules of health and comfort are disregarded. It is inseparably associated with contract work, and is intensified by sub-contracting in shops conducted in homes. . . . Although the sweating system exists in a number of occupations, it is the garment-making industry (comprising men's clothing, ladies' cloaks and suits, undergarment, and shirt-making branches) that has given it its real significance. Garments lend themselves readily to such a system of manufacture. Sewing is a branch preeminently suited for the home, and a coat or blouse is as easily manufactured there as in a factory. Merely working at home on some article of manufacture is not in itself so objectionable, it is that the rate of wages paid for labour is, as a rule, so low when the sweating system has come into vogue that work from early morn till late at night will scarcely suffice to procure the necessaries of a bare existence. But even this is not the worst feature of the evil. The combination of living apartment and factory, and the employment of outsiders therein, constitute the detrimental features which in time become a menace to the community.

Here is the process in its simplicity and detail. A large wholesale house will undertake the manufacture of ready-made clothing. A quantity of cloth is bought at wholesale rates. It is put in the hands of the designer, who designs the styles of clothing for the season's trade. He is usually also the foreman, and controls the letting out of the work to the contractors and other individuals who may apply. These latter, on learning that the house has a quantity of garments which it wants manufactured, apply to the foreman, who makes a contract with them to make up so many articles at a stipulated price.

THE SUB-CONTRACTOR.

Now the persons stipulating for the contract may do one of two things. They can, in the first place, take the articles home and work individually or with the assistance of their families upon them, or they may engage a number of hands to work for them, and take the garments to a shop, where, with the aid of the hired help, their manufacture is completed. In the first case, owing to the fact that one individual has to do nearly all the work upon each garment, only a very few can be completed in the allotted time, and the amount realized in consequence is very small. In the second case, a large number of garments are manufactured owing as a rule, to the minute subdivision of labour, but the contractor desirous of realizing a profit much above the running expense of his shop, pays those in his employ a sum which is frequently below a living wage. In a large shop there may be engaged in the manufacture of a single coat no less than 16 different individuals, each of whom works at a special line, and, after completing one stage in the process of manufacture, passes the garment on to the next, who is skilled in his line, and so on, till the article is completed. But there is frequently another stage. The contractor as a rule does not have the button-hole making and finishing or "felling" done in the shop, but sub-contracts this work, or it is returned to the foreman of the wholesale house, who contracts for that part again. The "felling" and button-hole making are usually done by women at their homes, and very often by the whole family. Under such an arrangement it is easily seen that, aided by competition, prices and wages must continue to fall and the work-day be lengthened until the limit of human endurance is reached. The limit, it seems, has been touched through the task system, an arrangement in the coat-making branch by which the contractor and the employees engage in a sort of competition, under which the contractor agrees with his employees to solicit work from the warehouses at a figure perhaps refused by another, provided they (the set of hands) are willing to do a certain task for a "day's work" for so much wages, even though it takes two or three days to do the specified "day's work." This set, of course, can work as many hours in a day as it chooses, the only limit being that of endurance.

WHERE THE SWEATING BEGINS.

So much for the system as it is. In reading it over it seems to fit so nicely that there appears no objection. All that is needed is the introduction into it of human life, men and women, living human beings with hearts as well as hands, and possibly feelings also, to see the iniquity which, not only may be, but usually is, worked at every stage. More than this, if it were possible to accurately do so, instead of the word "home," a description of the home should be given; instead of the term "shop," a description of the place which is spoken of as such, and instead of the simple non-committal "contractor," a portrayal of the man who hires life and blood, and knows as a rule how to buy it at the cheapest rate.

In order that exceptional conditions may not be cited there will here be given a description of conditions as actually seen, and information as actually related to a representative of The Mail and Empire in a few hours' rounds, in which he visited some of the places where clothes are being made. And that it may not be said he chose the worst of cities, the conditions here related were those seen in Toronto scarcely a fortnight ago. The first shop was visited shortly after day-break. It was one of the common kind, a combination of the home and factory. An ordinary small frame building with two large rooms on the ground floor. The front one was filled with five girls, one a mere child, and four young men: the family, the father, mother, and four children, two of them were infants, were washing themselves, and eating breakfast in the room behind, there being a wide open space between the two rooms. It was vests that were being made. Working alone, the father said he would be unable to finish more than three a day. He had contracted to make the vests complete at from 17 to 25 cents each: the cloth was supplied him, but he had to provide his own thread and silk, and have the garments sent for and delivered. His son helped him every day, and his wife when she had time. He worked frequently till midnight, and was always up at sunrise. He did not say what he paid his hands, who worked ten hours a day, but admitted that after paying them he was scarcely able to clear enough to keep his family clothed and fed. They looked, indeed, as though both had been wanting for some time.

AN ITALIAN OPINION.

Next an Italian and his wife were seen. They had been forced to give up the work as it had run them into debt. While they were working for a leading wholesale house they had hired four men at $5 each a week, two boys at $1 each, and one young girl at $4. Frequently they had worked themselves from four in the morning till eleven at night, and then were unable to keep out of debt. They had made Norfolk jackets, which required to be lined, pressed, etc., at from 26 to 40 cents each. After paying for gas, rent on machines, house rent, etc., they could not make ends meet.

A woman with a large family, some of whom were sick, was the next person visited. She was about to move to a new residence, and the clothes at which she had been working were lying with a heap of rubbish on the dirty floor. She could hardly speak with a consumptive cough, which is fast taking her life away. She had worked at the garment trade for many

years, but had been unable to save enough to permit of her children getting a proper schooling. A little girl, sixteen years of age, who was thin
and sickly in appearance, stood by her side and related how she had
worked for eight years past for a large wholesale house, most of the time
at $2 a week. She now intended to help her mother at the machine. She
had a little sister, nine years of age, who also sewed at a machine. Another
sister got $2 a week in a large shop for making button-holes in coats, the
button-hole contractor had to clear a profit after sub-contracting the work.
They had made up knickerbockers at five cents a pair. They were now
making men's pants at from 12½ to 15 cents a pair, and were supplying
the thread themselves. . . .

BUTTON-HOLE WORK.

The next shop entered was one in which a man, his wife, two children,
and a hired woman were busily engaged making button-holes in cloaks
and overcoats. For the large two-inch button-holes they were receiving a
dollar a hundred, or one cent each; for the others they got 50, 60, and 75
cents a hundred, according to the size. They had to furnish the thread and
silk themselves. The woman who was working said that she received only
$1.50 a week, and out of this paid 75 cents a week for a room. She was
entirely dependent upon herself, and had been forced to take this wage
rather than starve to death. When asked how she could possibly live on
75 cents a week she replied that it would not be long before she would
have to give up altogether. The hours were long, from eight in the morning until six every night; incessant work; no one to talk to, for the
Polish Jew who was employing her did not know much of English, and
she had scarcely enough to eat. Later on she said that she had been driven
to crime to supplement her wages, but she called God to witness that the
fact of her working steadily week after week at whatever she could get
was evidence enough to prove that she was an unwilling party to it. During the day's rounds similar stories were told by those who brought only
condemnation on themselves in the telling both by the oppressor and the
oppressed. . . .

INTERVIEWED IN BED.

The next shop called at was in another part of the city. The "boss" was in
bed with a heavy cold, but an interview was obtained with him notwithstanding. He sat up in bed, lighted a cigarette, so as to ease his throat, and
answered in a straightforward manner the questions put to him. For fifteen years he had carried on the manufacture of ready-made clothing; he
now employed fifteen hands, half of whom were women. When asked what
he paid himself he said:— "Well, I have to work hard myself, and I do the
best I can: I don't treat the men bad, but I even up by taking advantage
of the women. I have a girl who can do as much work, and as good work

as a man; she gets $5 a week. The man who is standing next to her gets $11. The girls, however, average $3.50 a week, and some are as low as $2." Later on he added that these rates were not a fair average for the year, for as a rule work could only be obtained for seven to nine months. He said that during the season he worked every day from 6 a.m.: till 7 p.m.: his wife helped him. They had four children, and it was all they could do to pay expenses. "If I come out even at the end of the year I am satisfied. Times were not always so bad as they are now. Why, a short time ago, after paying all expenses I was able to clear $2,100 in two years. Now it is different. Last week I paid in wages $119, and drew on the contract $142. My shop rent is $10 a month, the electricity for the machines is $5, and the gas for pressing, lighting, etc., is $10 a month; so you see I am not making very much. I know a contractor in Montreal who made $18,000 in one year between what he made out of his employees and the 'fake' melton of which his coats were made." He himself was making heavy winter overcoats at 60 cents each, and this, he thought, was better pay than most contractors were receiving. He had solved the riddle as to his being obliged to buy his thread from the wholesale house which furnished him with the contract. He paid $3.50 a gross for thread, and there were times when he might have bought it elsewhere at $3. However, he was told by the wholesale people that they were paying the central agency that amount for thread, and that if he wanted he could make enquiries into the matter. Accordingly he went to the central agency and asked if they would sell him thread at the wholesale rates. They offered to do so, but only made him the same price as he was paying to the wholesale house. Later on, he said, he discovered that, unknown to the rest of the world, the wholesale house was allowed at the end of the year a rebate of 33 percent, on the thread bought. He did not think contractors were making much money now. When asked about one man who was well known to be paying his hands but little, and received a good amount of work, "Oh," he said, "he has got to pay the foreman a sum of money in order to get the pick of the goods. I know myself that if he draws $200 he has to pay away a large amount to the foreman before he gets the work. How can a man pay his hands when he has got to clear his own profit above what he pays to get the job? Why when I was working for another house in the city I was refused work, bit by bit, when a new foreman was engaged. I kept asking for more, but could never get it. I wondered why it was, for my work had always been highly praised before. But one day the foreman came himself to me and said 'You see I am used to getting gold dollars under the buttons.' I refused to pay him anything and got work elsewhere. I know that any amount of the same thing is done in Toronto to-day. If I could get the money that some of the foremen are receiving simply from what people pay them who want the contract, I would drop the tailoring at once. I would pay the foreman $25 a week myself if he would give me the pick of the goods. I could more than clear this out of the best class of goods." Later on he said he knew of women who were making knicker-bockers for boys at 50 cents a dozen, and pants at $1 a dozen. . . .

The question naturally suggests itself, are such conditions of things inevitable? No one would think of asking, "are they right?" A comparison with methods pursued by other firms would suggest that even if large profits was the object mostly desired that it could be equally well attained in a right and proper way. With a view to presenting both sides fairly the representative of The Mail and Empire visited a large factory in con-nection with a leading wholesale house in the city, and was given an opportunity to see for himself, and even to inspect the books. Here it was found that men and women were employed making cloaks, but instead of wearing out their lives with a heavy machine all the machines were run by electricity. There was plenty of light, and the air was good. More than that, the employees were not driven without a moment's cessation, but were allowed, if they so desired, to work by the piece, and to receive re-muneration according to the amount done. The books showed that the average wage paid operators was $10 a week, and that in some cases it ran as high as $20. The shop was not open to the women till eight in the morning, and was generally closed at six p.m., and all Saturday afternoon. One of the poorest paid operators received $7.60 a week. . . .

A UNION SHOP.

A union "back-shop" was also visited. This is a shop where only union men are employed, and where every garment that is manufactured goes out with a union label upon it, which is a guarantee that it has been made in a shop subject to inspection, where proper sanitary conditions have been complied with, and where the hours of labour and rate of wages are such as are considered fair and right. The men were receiving 21 cents per hour for work which was scheduled as first and second-class, and 20 cents per hour for work which was classed as third. There could be no dispute about the rates, as they were in printed form, and both employer and employed had copies of them.

These last two cases are mere instances; they are sufficient, however; in the first place to prove that the evil of sweating need not exist at all; and secondly, that, where it does exist, there are means by which it may be overcome. It need not exist, because right-minded employers who have been paying a proper wage have been able to secure their profits as well; it may be overcome where it does exist, because both, in the case of the factory cited, and the union back-shop, it finds no place at all. . . .

The law in Ontario goes a certain length, but that conditions are such as have been related is sufficient to suggest that it does not go far enough. Almost every article of food is subject to inspection, and the public as well as individuals will some day wake up to the consciousness that it is to their interest to have the clothing which they wear subject to inspection as well. So long, however, as clothes are made in private houses or in shops where the most careful supervision is not exercised, both individual and public health will be in danger. . . .

The influence of the public as purchasers is one which can be made more effectual than law. It has been found in the United States that quite a number of large manufacturers have been obliged to withdraw work sent to sweating contractors, through the systematic appeals made by unions of the trade upon members of other unions and sympathizers to withhold patronage from dealers handling or keeping such goods on sale. Usually a retail clothier will cease dealing with an objectionable manufacturer rather than incur the opposition of patrons.

VALUE OF THE UNION LABEL.

In line with this method the union label has been of service. It is designed to enable people to distinguish and give preference to goods guaranteed to be made under union, fair, and sanitary conditions. Some of the retail tailors in Toronto have already adopted this label. Again the matter of reform is in the hands of the purchaser, and he can not only profit himself, but be instrumental in bringing about a better condition which will be helpful to many others by requesting that when he pays his money, he and not the shopkeeper alone, shall profit, by the price that is paid.

Under the sweating system as it now exists the retailer of ready-made goods has to make a profit out of the wholesale manufacturer, he in turn makes a profit out of the contractor, and in cases where the contract system is abused the foreman makes a profit as well. The contractor again makes a profit out of those in his employ, and in many instances this is almost extortionate, another profit is sometimes made out of the sub-contractor who undertakes the button-hole making and "felling," and he again clears a profit from those in his employ. At the bottom of the scale are the hundreds of men and women who are toiling from dawn till sundown, whose lives are being consumed with over-toil and lack of pay, and whose labour is in the last analysis practically the only labour which has added value to the garment from the time it is sewn together till it reaches the consumer's hands. Any reform which tends to bring the actual producer and the actual consumer nearer together and to lessen the number of middlemen who draw profit from a source on which they have not laboured, will not only have a tendency to secure to the man who buys a better article, which in the end must prove a cheaper one, but also bring to the one who labours most a more adequate remuneration and an opportunity for a better and possibly also a nobler life. Surely such an attainment is worthy of any strivings, and individual effort can do most to bring about the desired goal.

3 | Working-class Life

The life of the workingman in the nineteenth century was hard and, by modern standards, short. Nevertheless it undoubtedly improved somewhat during the century, at least in a physical sense. Incomes increased, food was better and more plentiful, epidemic diseases were less prevalent. The workingman in 1900, compared to his counterpart in 1800, had a rather better hope that his children would survive to adulthood, and that he would be able to feed them while they did so.

The other side of this coin was the degradation of the workingman's physical environment. To trade the farm or the small town for the city was to gain certain economic benefits; but it was also to lose the blessed escape of the countryside and the forest. It was to trade nature's beauty for the soot and filth of industry, open space for the ant's existence of the tenement. One would be hard put to strike a balance sheet for such a trade.

The obvious characteristic of the workingman in Canada, to visitors from Britain, was his sense of self-confidence and independence. However deferential his manner, however miserable his existence by our lights, the workingman of North America was the wonder of the world. He had affluence beyond the imagination of most European peasants and workers, and a sense of his worth that was in marked contrast to the semi-feudal regard for his betters of the European. Susanna Moodie, successful author and a settler at Peterborough, was a sensitive observer of this phenomenon. In the first selection below she, as a middle-class lady, wonders at and is occasionally shocked by the rude familiarity of the lower orders. But unlike most members of her class, she accepts it as natural in the Canadian environment.

The Canadian workingman was less independent than his manner might indicate. And however affluent by European standards, he had far to go to achieve a decent level of subsistence, no matter financial security. Historian J. I. Cooper gives us an overview of the life of workers in one city, Montreal in the 1850s. It was, clearly, a drab and unpleasant place for the ordinary people. It was also a dangerous place. Apart from the danger of fire (most Canadian cities were destroyed by fire at some point in the century) and disease, the city was a violent place. In addition to normal criminal violence, the bigger cities were often torn by large-scale rioting. Montreal, for instance, had seen the great riots of 1849 over the Rebellion Losses Bill, in which the provincial parliament buildings were burned. In 1853, as Cooper mentions, racial rioting broke out over the visit of Father Gavazzi. A former priest, Gavazzi toured North America denouncing the Catholic Church. His visit to Montreal was marked by riots between Catholic French Canadians and Protestant English Canadians, in which several people were killed.

The following excerpt discusses the ethnic characteristics of Montreal, and the correlation between ethnicity and other factors such as family size and income. It is drawn from the most important social study undertaken in nineteenth-century Canada, Herbert Brown Ames' *City Below the Hill*. For the first time an attempt was being made to apply the approaches of the new social sciences to the Canadian reality. It was the forecast of social research that would be undertaken in the twentieth century, and of the social engineering to be attempted by social workers.

The city in which these groups interacted was generally in deplorable condition and growing worse as more people crowded into it. Two persistent problems were clogged and unsanitary lanes and industrial filth. A report from the provincial Board of Health discusses the former problem in Montreal. The Ontario Board, in the following selection, points to abattoirs as particularly offensive industrial polluters. Industries, however, were joined by the ordinary citizens in creating health hazards and an unpleasant urban environment. Toronto, like all cities, found it difficult to police the privy pits that prevailed before indoor plumbing. The results of these conditions are to be read in the death statistics, statistics acceptable by the standards of other countries, but shockingly high by the standards of the twentieth century.

Inadequate housing was another persistent problem. A probably too optimistic view of the situation in Toronto in the 1880s is given by the mayor, W. H. Howland. The make-up of the families living in such houses is examined in another selection from H. B. Ames' *City Below the Hill*.

Food was ample in agricultural Canada. Information gathered from Saskatchewan pioneers gives unusual detail of the western diet at the end of the century in the excerpt from the article 'Bannock, Beans and Bacon.' At least one expert thought the Canadian working class ate too well. Dr W. B. Nesbitt of Toronto testified before the Royal Commission on Labor and Capital on the way in which workers pampered themselves. The porridge diet of Scottish highlanders was apparently his idea of the perfect workingman's menu. The commissioners did not think to question the good doctor on his own eating habits.

Little work has been done on the historical development of the Canadian standard of living. At best, then, all we have to go on is spotty, often subjective evidence from contemporaries. Testimony before the Royal

Commission of 1889 by a machinist in Toronto compares the standard of living in Canada and Britain, and the changes in Canada over recent years. Obviously it is easier to gain an accurate impression of real income figures. Again a basic source is H. B. Ames, who gathered detailed figures for Montreal in 1897. He also helps to draw comparisons of living standards by attempting to assess poverty levels.

Another way to determine standards is to compare what workers could buy with what they earned. The accountbooks of a tailor in Newcastle, New Brunswick, Daniel McGruar, may serve as an example. Comparing the two tables, the first on McGruar's costs, the second on his income, we find McGruar had to make a coat to buy five barrels of potatoes. On the other hand, he could also hire labour cheaply. For the price of making a frockcoat, McGruar could hire two men and two horses for half a day to haul his wood.

A very optimistic picture of the economic well-being of workers follows. Mr Patterson of the savings bank in Saint John, New Brunswick, found the living standards of people there rising steadily. The proof was the large savings many workers were able to accumulate in the bank.

Firmer figures began to emerge when the federal government created a Department of Labour charged with collecting such statistics. With these statistics it is possible to draw a 'balance sheet' for the workingman at the turn of the century. The first table compares housing costs in some major Canadian centres. The second shows the cost of certain staple food items in the same cities. The third table compares wage rates. Because some areas did not report, it was not possible to produce statistics for all cities and towns in all trades. One generalization obviously can be made from these figures. On the basis of the amount that could be bought for an hour's labour, food was comparatively much more expensive in 1900 than it is today. A somewhat soothing thought, perhaps, on our next trip to the supermarket.

THE LEVELLING PRINCIPLE

Susanna Moodie, *Roughing It in the Bush, or, Forest Life in Canada* (London, T. N. Foulis, 1913), pp. 245-51.

All was new, strange, and distasteful to us; we shrank from the rude, coarse familiarity of the uneducated people among whom we were thrown; and they in return viewed us as innovators, who wished to curtail their independence by expecting from them the kindly civilities and gentle courtesies of a more refined community. They considered us proud and shy, when we were only anxious not to give offence. The semi-barbarous Yankee squatters, who had "left their country for their country's good," and by whom we were surrounded in our first settlement, detested us, and with them we could have no feeling in common. We could neither lie nor cheat in our dealings with them; and they despised us for our ignorance in trading and our want of smartness.

The utter want of that common courtesy with which a well-brought-up European addresses the poorest of his brethren, is severely felt at first by settlers in Canada. At the period of which I am now speaking, the titles of "sir," or "madam," were very rarely applied by inferiors. They entered your house without knocking; and while boasting of their freedom, violated one of its dearest laws, which considers even the cottage of the poorest labourer his castle, and his privacy sacred.

"Is your man to hum?"—"Is the woman within?" were the general inquiries made to me by such guests, while my bare-legged, ragged Irish servants were always spoken to as "sir" and "*mem*," as if to make the distinction more pointed.

Why they treated our claims to their respect with marked insult and rudeness, I never could satisfactorily determine, in any way that could reflect honour on the species, or even plead an excuse for its brutality, until I found that this insolence was more generally practised by the low, uneducated emigrants from Britain, who better understood your claims to their civility, than by the natives themselves. Then I discovered the secret.

The unnatural restraint which society imposes upon these people at home forces them to treat their more fortunate brethren with a servile deference which is repugnant to their feelings, and is thrust upon them by the dependent circumstances in which they are placed. This homage to rank and education is not sincere. Hatred and envy lie rankling at their heart, although hidden by outward obsequiousness. Necessity compels their obedience; they fawn, and cringe, and flatter the wealth on which they depend for bread. But let them once emigrate, the clog which fettered them is suddenly removed; they are free; and the dearest privilege of this freedom is to wreak upon their superiors the long-locked-up hatred of their hearts. They think they can debase you to their level by disallowing all your claims to distinction; while they hope to exalt themselves and their fellows into ladies and gentlemen by sinking you back to the only title you received from Nature—plain "man" and "woman." Oh, how much more honourable than their vulgar pretensions!

I never knew the real dignity of these simple epithets until they were insultingly thrust upon us by the working-classes of Canada.

But from this folly the native-born Canadian is exempt; it is only practised by the low-born Yankee, or the Yankeefied British peasantry and mechanics. It originates in the enormous reaction springing out of a sudden emancipation from a state of utter dependence into one of unrestrained liberty. As such, I not only excuse, but forgive it, for the principle is founded in nature; and, however disgusting and distasteful to those accustomed to different treatment from their inferiors, it is better than a hollow profession of duty and attachment urged upon us by a false and unnatural position. Still, it is very irksome until you think more deeply upon it; and then it serves to amuse rather than to irritate.

And here I would observe, before quitting this subject, that of all follies, that of taking out servants from the old country is one of the greatest, and is sure to end in the loss of the money expended in their passage, and to become the cause of deep disappointment and mortification to yourself.

They no sooner set foot upon the Canadian shores than they become possessed with this ultra-republican spirit. All respect for their employers, all subordination is at an end; the very air of Canada severs the tie of mutual obligation which bound you together. They fancy themselves not only equal to you in rank, but that ignorance and vulgarity give them superior claims to notice. They demand the highest wages, and grumble at doing half the work, in return, which they cheerfully performed at home. They demand to eat at your table, and to sit in your company, and if you refuse to listen to their dishonest and extravagant claims, they tell you that "they are free; that no contract signed in the old country is binding in 'Meriky'; that you may look out for another person to fill their place as soon as you like; and that you may get the money expended in their passage and outfit in the best manner you can."

I was unfortunately persuaded to take out a woman with me as a nurse for my child during the voyage, as I was in very poor health; and her conduct, and the trouble and expense she occasioned, were a perfect illustration of what I have described.

When we consider the different position in which servants are placed in the old and new world, this conduct, ungrateful as it then appeared to me, ought not to create the least surprise. In Britain, for instance, they are too often dependent upon the caprice of their employers for bread. Their wages are low; their moral condition still lower. They are brought up in the most servile fear of the higher classes, and they feel most keenly their hopeless degradation, for no effort on their part can better their position. They know that if once they get a bad character they must starve or steal; and to this conviction we are indebted for a great deal of their seeming fidelity and long and laborious service in our families, which we owe less to any moral perception on their part of the superior kindness or excellence of their employers, than to the mere feeling of assurance, that as long as they do their work well, and are cheerful and obedient, they will be punctually paid their wages, and well housed and fed.

Happy is it for them and their masters when even this selfish bond of union exists between them!

But in Canada the state of things in this respect is wholly reversed. The serving class, comparatively speaking, is small, and admits of little competition. Servants that understand the work of the country are not easily procured, and such always can command the highest wages. The possession of a good servant is such an addition to comfort, that they are persons of no small consequence, for the dread of starving no longer frightens them into servile obedience. They can live without you, and they well know that you cannot do without them. If you attempt to practise upon them that common vice of English mistresses, to scold them for any slight omission or offence, you rouse into active operation all their new-found spirit of freedom and opposition. They turn upon you with a torrent of abuse; they demand their wages, and declare their intention of quitting you instantly. The more inconvenient the time for you, the more bitter become their insulting remarks. They tell you, with a high hand, that "they are as good as you; that they can get twenty better places by the morrow, and that they don't care a snap for your anger." And away they bounce, leaving you to finish a large wash, or a heavy job of ironing, in the best way you can.

When we look upon such conduct as the reaction arising out of their former state, we cannot so much blame them, and are obliged to own that it is the natural result of a sudden emancipation from former restraint. With all their insolent airs of independence, I must confess that I prefer the Canadian to the European servant. If they turn out good and faithful, it springs more from real respect and affection, and you possess in your domestic a valuable assistant and friend; but this will never be the case with a servant brought out with you from the old country, for the reasons before assigned. The happy independence enjoyed in this highly-favoured land is nowhere better illustrated than in the fact that no domestic can be treated with cruelty or insolence by an unbenevolent or arrogant master.

WORKING-CLASS MONTREAL IN THE 1850s

J. I. Cooper, 'The Social Structure of Montreal in the 1850s'. Canadian Historical Association, *Annual Report*, 1956, pp. 67-70. Reprinted by permission of the Canadian Historical Association and the author.

In discussing classes other than the established and propertied, a different approach is necessary. Biographical information is scanty, not because these classes were illiterate, but because they did not enjoy the permanence of residence which favoured the preservation of personal papers. Information derived from other sources requires careful scrutiny. This is especially so when the informant was the employer. . . . The poor were scolded, and their numerous misfortunes ascribed to intemperance or indifference. A very early note by James O'Donnell, the builder of Notre Dame Church, is apposite: "On [sic] respect to your workmen, I know well their deficiency; there are [sic] not a mechanic amongst them. . . . They are universally careless and inattentive . . . all they care for is their pay, and to do as little work . . . as they can. . . ." "He smokes his pipe, sings his song, etc. . . ." At a later time, James Hodges, one of the contractors of the Victoria Bridge, denounced the proneness of the Canadian workers to strike, "it is almost a universal custom for mechanics . . . to strike twice a year, let the rate of wages be what it may. . . ." The contagion spread to the contractors' English labourers who became quite "unmanageable". At one point a species of general stoppage of work was threatened: "The mechanics & labourers . . . on the [Victoria] bridge struck for shorter days on Saturday. . . . Yesterday & to-day they have been around to the foundries . . . telling the working men to stop or they would break their heads. Some people tried to resist them, but it was no use. . . ." A catalogue of this sort might be continued indefinitely. It may contain some truth, but it is certainly overdrawn.

An examination of censuses, and similar sources, reveals a less alarming picture. The labour force in the city was always very large compared with the total population, and also with the total employable male population. There was wide-spread employment of children, as shown by occasional detailed statements on the composition of a mill or factory staff. Women were also employed, principally as domestics, but also as "tailoresses", a designation which appears to have included fur, as well as garment, workers. Wages varied enormously between occupations. In the middle 'fifties, the best paid were the machinists employed by C. S. Rodier, the farm implement manufacturer. They received 6s 3d a day. The worst paid were women, some of whom got 10s a week. The standard wage for women garment workers was not much better, 11s 5d, a week. Nonetheless, these were improvements over the dollar-a-day wage paid to "the highest class" labourer at the beginning of the decade. As usual, increase in wages lagged behind the rising cost of living. Observers from less inflated regions were appalled by Montreal prices. J. W. Dawson, the Principal of McGill University, wrote, "£100 here is worth for domestic purchases little more than £50 in Pictou [Nova Scotia] . . . ." The working man suffered in other ways, as well. When the city was rebuilt, after the disastrous fires of 1845 and 1852, tenements, or multiple dwellings, replaced the detached houses, and obliterated their gardens. This was also the plan adopted in building the railway workers' houses in Point Saint-

Charles. They were constructed in terraces, the fronts set flush with the street line, and having scarcely more space in the rear than was required for privies, and the community well and wash house. As the city increased in area, the country and cheap farm truck receded, likewise pasture for the family cow, where that luxury existed. By the end of the 'fifties, the Montreal workingman had little recourse but his wages.

Other aspects of the wage-earning classes are less easy to set in focus. They were divided racially among French Canadians, Anglo-Canadians, and British immigrants. Except, however, in a few skilled trades, such as woodworking (virtually a French-Canadian monopoly), they were not employed on racial lines. Thus, they were in mutual competition. This factor probably generated the friction always present at [the] working-class level, and led to such outbursts as the Gavazzi riot of June 9, 1853. In this instance, two further factors contributed; first, the numerical inadequacy of the civilian police, which mustered only fifty men; second, the alarm resulting from the great fires of 1852 and the cholera epidemic of that year. The presence of a large immigrant group was a further source of weakness. It kept wages low, contributing therefore to its own exploitation, as well as to that of the native-born workers, and it posed serious problems in adaptation. The Irish, who formed the largest immigrant group, experienced these disabilities to the full. They formed two communities, separated initially by the psychological experience of the Famine, and latterly by a struggle to control community organizations, such as the St. Patrick's Society. They were even divided in place of residence: A considerable number of the pre-Famine Irish lived in "little Dublin," along Chenneville Street. Later arrivals crowded into Griffintown. The appearance of brilliant newcomers, such as Thomas D'Arcy McGee, roused the jealousy of the older Irish leaders. In a sense, many of the French Canadians, too, were immigrants, former farm people adapting themselves to urban life. "No people [are] better adapted for factory hands, more intelligent, docile, and giving less trouble to their employers. . . ." Accordingly, of labour solidarity there was little. Trade unions were really mutual benefit societies, such as l'union Saint-Joseph, formed in 1851 among stone cutters. The weakness of organization in Montreal is curious when set against the successful combinations in Quebec city of French-Canadian shipwrights and of Irish longshoremen.

One result of the stunted development of working-class organization was to place initiative in social and charitable action elsewhere. By the 'fifties, the tradition of well-to-do-leadership was established, and was evidenced by a net-work of agencies ranging from savings banks, to hospitals. An important mechanism was provided by the national societies, Saint-Jean Baptiste, St. Andrew's, St. George's, St. Patrick's, and the German Society. In 1855, St. George's Society laid out almost £300 in charity, nor was this exceptional. The societies had originated in the pre-

Rebellion era, Saint-Jean Baptiste meeting for the first time within four weeks of the moving of the Ninety-Two Resolutions. Then, they were political in aim, to hold French-Canadian or British immigrant opinion to the party line, whether reform or "constitutional". By the 'fifties, prestige, rather than political value attached to "Office-bearing". The societies served a useful social purpose in keeping together the well-to-do, who monopolized the executive posts, and the very miscellaneous persons comprising the "ordinary" membership. The annual parades, banquets, and corporate church services, cut across racial lines, since "the sister societies" were always invited. The same services, although in a much more intimate fashion, were performed by the Masonic lodges. In this period, however, Montreal Masonry was much divided on the subject of Grand Lodge allegiance, and its local importance was much less then than at earlier or later times.

ETHNIC CHARACTERISTICS IN MONTREAL IN THE 1890s

Herbert Brown Ames, *The City Below the Hill: A Sociological Study of a Portion of the City of Montreal, Canada* (Montreal, Bishop Engraving & Printing Co., 1897), pp. 68-71.

Perhaps it may not be out of place, in view of the fact that we possess considerable data regarding the various localities within the lower city and now know the predominating nationality in each, that we here turn our attention to a consideration of race characteristics to see if any such, through our series of articles, have been made apparent. I trust I may offend no one in so doing and that it will be borne in mind that I am not giving opinions but stating facts. . . .

We have treated of many subjects in previous articles, we will see how these three belts:—the French-Canadian, the Irish-Canadian and the "mixed" belt, compare with each other upon these matters.

The average size of the family (after deducting the lodgers)
in the "Mixed"   belt is 4.67 persons.
" " Irish-Canadian   " " 4.57   "
" " French-Canadian   " " 4.52   "

The average number of wage-earners per family
in the Irish-Canadian   belt is 1.43 persons.
" " "Mixed"   " " 1.41   "
" " French-Canadian   " " 1.40   "

The average number of home-tenders per family
in the "Mixed"   belt is 1.72 persons.
 "   " French-Canadian   "   " 1.48   "
 "   " Irish-Canadian   "   " 1.48   "
The proportion of children under five years of age in the average family
of the French-Canadian   belt is 16 per cent.
 "   " Irish-Canadian   "   " 16 "   "
 "   " "Mixed"   "   " 13 "   "
The percentage of school children in the average family
of the French-Canadian belt is .... 20 p.c.
 "   " Irish-Canadian   "   " .... 20 p.c.
 "   " "Mixed"   "   " .... 16 p.c.
The proportion of well-to-do families among the population
of the "Mixed"   belt is .... 26 p.c.
 "   " French-Canadian   "   " .... 12 p.c.
 "   " Irish-Canadian   "   " .... 9 p.c.
The proportion of families belonging to the "real industrial class"
in the French-Canadian belt is .... 77 p.c.
 "   " Irish-Canadian   "   " .... 74 p.c.
 "   " "Mixed"   "   " .... 66 p.c.
The proportion of regular and irregular incomes
in the "Mixed"   belt is 87 p.c. Regular and 13 p.c. Irregular.
 "   " French-Canadian "   " 79 p.c.   "   " 21 p.c.   "
 "   " Irish-Canadian   "   " 64 p.c.   "   " 36 p.c.   "
The proportion of families, living upon $5.00 per week or less, among
the total number, in the Irish-Canadian   belt is .... 17 p.c.
          "   " French-Canadian "   " .... 11 p.c.
          "   " "Mixed"   "   " .... 8 p.c.
There is a marked difference between the several nationalities which
compose our population in ability to comfortably subsist upon very small
incomes. Of the poor families especially investigated, among the French-
Canadians 62 per cent. were comfortable and independent even upon
$5.00 per week, 58 per cent. of the British-Canadians were in similar
condition, but only 51 per cent. of the Irish-Canadians of this grade were
not in need of assistance.
The average family income for all classes
in the "Mixed"   belt is .....$12.54; per individual $2.36
 "   " French-Canadian   "   " ..... 10.73; "   " 2.27
 "   " Irish-Canadian   "   " ..... 10.00; "   " 2.10
The average earnings per wage-earner
in the "Mixed"   belt amount to .... $8.89 per week.
 "   " French-Canadian "   "   " .... 7.62   "
 "   " Irish-Canadian   "   "   " .... 7.00   "
The average family income of the real industrial class only

in the "Mixed"   belt is .... $10.92 per week.
"   " French-Canadian   " " .... 9.92   "
"   " Irish-Canadian   " " .... 9.87   "
     The average wage per worker among the "real industrial class"
in the "Mixed"   belt is .... $7.92 per week.
"   " French-Canadian   " " .... 7.26   "
"   " Irish-Canadian   " " .... 6.89   "
     The average number of rooms in the "Mixed"   belt is 6.13 per family.
                          "   Fr. Canadian   "   4.50 "   "
                          "   Irish Canadian   "   4.33 "   "
     The average number of persons per occupied room
in the Irish-Canadian   belt is 1.09
"   " French-Canadian   " " 1.04
"   " "Mixed"   " " 0.86
     The average family rental
for the "Mixed"   belt is .... $12.19 per month.
"   " French-Canadian   " " .... 7.56 "   "
"   " Irish-Canadian   " " .... 6.64 "   "
     The proportion which rental takes of income
in the "Mixed"   belt is .... 24 p.c.
"   " French-Canadian   " " .... 17½ p.c.
"   " Irish-Canadian   " " .... 16 p.c.
     The average death rate
throughout the French-Canadian belt was ..... 25 per thousand in 1896
        "   " Irish-Canadian   " " ..... 21 "   "   "   "
        "   " "Mixed"   " " ..... 18 "   "   "   "
     As to the sale of intoxicants.   In the
Irish-Canadian belt there are 26 saloons and 34 liquor groceries, or one
liquor shop for every 179 persons.   In the
"Mixed" belt are 40 saloons and 24 liquor groceries, or 1 liquor shop for
every 198 persons.   In the
French-Canadian belt are 39 saloons and 29 liquor groceries, or 1 liquor
shop for every 208 persons.

     On the whole the "mixed" belt, from these comparisons, makes the best showing. Incomes and wages, rentals and accommodation, are all upon a better scale there than elsewhere. The size of the family and the proportion of the elements which compose it are very nearly the same in the French-Canadian and in the Irish-Canadian belts. Among the French-Canadians is to be found the largest proportion of families belonging to the "real industrial class." For density and high death rate the French-Canadians take undesirable precedence; for overcrowding and poverty the Irish-Canadian sections make the least creditable showing. Upon other points the comparison between these two belts is, as a rule, more favorable to the former than to the latter nationality.

CONDITION OF THE WORKING-CLASS CITY

Eighth Annual Report of the Board of Health. Quebec, *Sessional Papers*, XXXVI (1903), pt. 2, no. 6, 49-50.

Unsanitary condition of the lanes.—Since 15 years the level of certain lanes is gradually rising. Some whose level was flush with that of the surrounding streets are now from one to two feet higher, real disguised dumps surrounding the residential districts. It would be desirable that the city take over these lanes (which up to now have been private property) and pave them. This would put an end at once to the successive and permanent accumulations of filth which will almost inevitably go on unless this is done.

The causes of the unsanitary condition of the lanes are multiple. In the first place a good many families, otherwise particular about the cleanliness of their yards, have no concern whatsoever as regards the lane, which, nevertheless, borders their properties. They have no scruples about throwing all kinds of garbage right into them especially in winter, when they experience some difficulty in opening the gates of the yards. In some cases the garbage is emptied from the second or third floor of a house or shed down a wooden spout at the bottom of which a receptacle is supposed to have been placed. The second and most common cause is the tolerating of *rag-picking* in the lanes. Very often the rag-pickers, to help their work, dump the receptacles (which are there waiting for the municipal waggons to pass) and then sneak away leaving the rubbish scattered over the ground. Then along come the scavengers, but they only gather the contents of the receptacle without worrying themselves about the scattered litter. More is not apparently required of them.

In winter, especially in February and March, the lanes often are impassable and as a result, the service becomes irregular. The consequence is that the receptacles at the family's disposal no longer suffice to hold the refuse of the house. The surplus is thrown into the lanes where it remains until the snow melts away entirely in May! My observations during many consecutive winters permit me to state that in a great many cases the snow blockades of the lanes is solely due to the shovelling of the snow by the citizens to enable them to open the large gates of their yards which almost invariably open on the lanes. To remedy the situation in these cases is a very simple matter: it would suffice to oblige the proprietors to have their yard gates open on the opposite side to the lanes or as an alternative to have them cut, in the large gates (about 2 feet above the ground so as to be above the snow level during most of the winter) an opening large enough for the passage of the receptacle (an expense of half a dollar). By so doing the opening of the large gate during winter would be dispensed with. To prevent deposits of refuse in the lanes and even close to sidewalks in streets, tenants should be instructed in their duties so as to prevent them pleading ignorance. This might be done by publishing in the 3 or 4 most used languages in Montreal the municipal by-laws concerning the gathering of refuse, mentioning the penalties provided for their infraction and distributing a copy of these by-laws in every house.

Tenth Annual Report of the Provincial Board of Health. Ontario, *Sessional Papers*, XXIV (1892), V, no. 26, 99-101.

TORONTO.

Medical Health Officer's Report.

The question of an abattoir has engaged a considerable portion of our attention during the past year. The principal cities both of Europe and America pronounce strongly in favour of the abattoir system. Many diseases, such as hog cholera, trichinæ, tuberculosis, etc., otherwise propagated, are by this means effectually avoided. In this respect we are behind other cities, but it is hoped and expected that this will not long be the case. During the past year there was an outbreak of hog cholera, but happily its progress was checked in Toronto. The more recent outbreaks in other parts lead us to suspect that the authorities at Ottawa have failed to act promptly in the matter.

Although typhoid fever and diphtheria have been more prevalent in this district than in any other in the city, proving that the sanitary condition is not what it might be, there are few nuisances of sufficient importance to require special mention in this report. Complaints received both from citizens and house to house inspectors nearly always deal with minor matters, and have special reference to privy pits. The following are a few of the most important matters coming under the notice of the Department in this district:

In the vicinity of Manning avenue and Bloor street, and within a radius of a quarter of a mile, there are situated 15 slaughter houses. These have all been visited at one time or another during the past summer and have always been found to be in a scrupulously clean condition. Notwithstanding this the residents in the locality complain most bitterly of the odors arising from them, especially in the summer months. The smell is so bad that even on warm evenings the residents are compelled to keep their doors and windows closed and to remain indoors. There is such a unanimity of opinion that there can be no doubt of the truth of this. I can quite credit their statements, as even when these places are kept perfectly clean their number would be sufficient to give rise to the vile smells no matter what care may be taken to keep them in a proper condition.

Scavenger Dumps.—The neighborhood most imposed upon in this respect is also in the vicinity of the slaughter houses mentioned above. About here there are numerous ravines which they have been attempting to fill up with scavenger refuse. These ravines are so deep that it is impossible to drain them. The rain lodges in them, and as all sorts of refuse, both animal and vegetable, is deposited there the smell when decomposition sets in is something vile. Since this has been complained of the dumping has ceased, much to the relief of the residents in the vicinity.

Contagious Diseases.—Great difficulty, inconvenience and in many cases impossibility has been experienced in the isolation of cases of infectious disease owing to lack of hospital accommodation.

A house to house inspection was made of the district bounded on the south by Queen street west, on the east by Yonge street, on the west by University street, and on the north by Avenue street. A few houses remain to be inspected in this district, in which, as well as in the district mentioned above, we found privy pits which had not been cleaned for three years or more. Some of these pits were in as close proximity to the kitchen door as two feet. In several of these pits there were thirty-two barrels or more to be removed. It is to be greatly regretted that our present by-law does not provide for the removal of these pits in any case. A very striking example of this may be seen on Elizabeth street, near Queen street, where the privy pit of the house on Queen street is placed not more than two feet from the kitchen door of the house on Elizabeth street.

The Elizabeth street house is a first-class building, while the Queen street house is very inferior, yet our police magistrate holds that under the present by-law we cannot compel the removal of this privy pit. Another very striking example may be seen in the rear of Frichot street, where a row of fine brick houses cannot be rented because of a row of no less than nineteen privy pits which are only ten feet from the rear of the houses. In many large factories where many men are employed, an immense pit is in use without any adequate provision to prevent a nuisance being created.

Report of Medical Health Officer re Abolition of Privy Pits.—During the past three months we have been carefully analysing the various complaints received in this department, and find from a careful examination that from sixty to sixty-five per cent. of the complaints received, are based on nuisances caused by the presence of privy pits. In the older portions of the city the percentage is even higher. Such a complaint received, a notice is sent to the owner, the privy is emptied and the nuisance abated; but only for a time. In a few months, certainly by the end of a year, the pit is in exactly the same condition. Another notice is sent, and so it goes on. It is plain from this that sixty to sixty-five per cent. of the work of this department is of no permanent benefit. These pits are nearly all made of boards nailed together, and no attempt is made to have them water tight. The fluids consequently soak through into the earth, saturating it with filth, and remaining there after the privy is emptied. A great many people think it quite an advantage to have these loose boxes so that the liquids may run out, and will often, when ordered to empty a privy pit, complain that it is only water that is in it, and if left alone it will soak away in a short time. In certain sections privies are so numerous and so close to houses as to be a menace, if not positively dangerous to health. The denser the population the fewer the water closets, seems to be the rule, the more closely built portions having nearly all pits. In many cases there are houses built in the rear. These almost invariably have pits, and in nearly every instance the privy is placed just where the kitchen door is located, or beside it. In warm weather, especially, the air is contaminated, and the smell is distinctly perceptible. Contaminated air is heavier than pure air, and generally stinking organic vapors are heavier than, and tend, on that account, to hang around the localities from which they emanate.

DEATH RATES AT THE TURN OF THE CENTURY

Eighth Annual Report of the Board of Health. Quebec, *Sessional Papers,*
XXXVI (1903), pt 2, no. 6, 83, 85.

SYNOPTICAL TABLE OF DEATHS AMONG CHILDREN AND OLD PERSONS.

Years	Deaths among children from 0 to 1 year	Deaths among children from 1 to 5 years	Deaths among old persons from 70 years upwards
1899	8,839	5,293	3,715
1900	10,108	4,382	1,322
1901	9,149	4,186	3,696

Years	Still-born at term	Deaths due to premature birth	Children who have lived less than 24 hours
1899	1,585	475	625
1900	1,606	549	716
1901	1,637	481	490

COMPARISON WITH OTHER COUNTRIES.

Death rate per 100 of population.
Belgium in 1899 . . . .   25.4
France   " 21.1

German Empire 21.5
England and Wales 18.3
Italy   " 22.1
Ireland   " 17.6
Scotland   " 18.6
Columbia in 1901 ...... 21.83
Connecticut in 1900 .... 18.00
New York   " 18.3
Michigan in 1899 ...... 14.0
Massachusetts " 17.4
Ontario in 1900 .... 13.5
Quebec in 1901 .... 21.0 (still-born included)
Quebec   "   .... 18.5 (still-born excluded)

We give the death rate with the still-born (21.0) and that without (18.5) which is of interest to us as the great majority of countries do not include these in their calculations.

WORKING-CLASS HOUSING IN TORONTO

Canada, Royal Commission on the Relations of Labor and Capital in Canada, 1889. Evidence—Ontario, pp. 165-8.

W. H. HOWLAND, Mayor of Toronto.

Q.—Have you a pretty general knowledge of the homes of the poorer people of Toronto? A.—Yes.

Q.—You have visited them? A.—Yes.

Q.—Do you think they are as good as could be expected for people in their circumstances, or is there room for improvement in that respect? A.—Do you mean in the character of the houses?

Q.—Yes, the character of the houses first? A.—Well, there is very little system about the character of the houses; in any new place they build according to the fancy or idea of the builder, and many of them are built by the men themselves. What we know now of sanitary necessities was hardly known at all when many of them were built.

Q.—Are they large enough? Do they give the people sufficient air space? A.—I don't think the old ones do. I think the houses now being built, such as the rows of cottages you see in the newer districts of the city, are better; they are being built with high basements, good first floors, and in some cases rooms above. There is comfortable accommodation accompanied with good drainage and generally a piece of land behind them. I think there is another thing in which our Government should be more paternal. For instance, in St. John's ward you will find houses built in front and then others are built in at the back end, the result being that there is no space or air room and they are very unwholesome. Many of these rear buildings are taken advantage of for bad purposes, especially when they fall into the hands of landlords, as they are very profitable. Of course originally the additions were made when poor people managed to run up a little cottage and draw some revenue from them, but now they are largely falling into the hands of people who own a number of houses, and the system is wrong in every way. It is also wrong to put two or three families into these small houses of two or three stories, for instance. I think the whole question of artisans' dwellings should be as much under Government inspection as factories, and I think there should be prompter methods of dealing with cases where people are being crowded together to their injury and, in many cases, their positive destruction. It has taken us nearly a year to get rid of one lodging house of bad reputation here and one in which hundreds of children have been ruined.

By the CHAIRMAN:

Q.—Have these places different entrances? A.—This was an old and a large house, originally a sort of mansion house with one entrance.

By Mr. FREED:

Q.—How many rooms would one family have in these houses? A.—In some cases only one. I think that is the case, but, of course, I have not been enquiring particularly, but have mentioned these things as they came into my mind. I have heard of many cases where decent people were in two small rooms—decent people but they were being injured physically by being in such close quarters. I think that artisans' dwellings require rigid inspection for their protection. I do not say that we should have buildings which would increase the rents too much, as they are now too large under present wages, but I think the inspection should be such that all really dangerous and unsuitable places, the number of houses on one lot, and all that sort of thing, should be covered by Government supervision. You never can depend on city machinery for things of that kind.

Q.—Would it be possible to educate the people themselves as to the care of their homes and the securing of better sanitary conditions? A.—I think so, but you don't know how helpless they are. Houses just now are scarce and a man is given very short time to complain. I have never had a complaint since I have been in the city and yet I know hundreds of houses that should be complained of. Here, say, is a house at a rental of six dollars a month; it is not suitable but the tenants cannot afford to pay more and if they complain they either get the rent advanced or they are turned out.

They are not in a position to complain.

Q.—The people are afraid of their landlords?   A.—Well, they are not in a position to complain; they will tell them that if they don't want it they had better go.

Q.—How could a landlord turn them out?   A.—Well, they are only monthly tenants.

By Mr. MCLEAN:

Q.—Do I understand you to say that the landlords boycott their tenants?   A.—I would not say that, but very naturally a case of that kind would get about.

By the CHAIRMAN:

Q.—It is the law of supply and demand?   A.—If a troublesome tenant came to me and complained and I went to the sanitary office and there was a row I tell you that tenant would have a hard time. I have very often taken the responsibility myself and I have told the inspector to say that I have sent him or otherwise there would be trouble, if they thought a complaint had been sent in. Of course when a person complains of the house next to him it makes it comparatively easy, but it would be an injury to the tenant if it were done in such a way that he would be suspected of complaining. . . .

Q.—Have you any knowledge to what extent working men own their houses in Toronto?   A.—I think that up to the last few years, to a very considerable extent and I think if you reach the foundation, as to the people who own buildings in Toronto, they have nearly all been working men originally. The great majority of the buildings here have been built from wealth right from the hand.

Q.—Is the ability on the part of the mechanic to own a house less than it formerly was?   A.—Certainly; property has increased in value so much and they have to go further away, though of course the street car system has stretched out. I was surprised to find in our new addition to the city, about four miles away, so many mechanics going out to and from their work, at a place where they have a mile and a half to walk to the street cars.

Q.—It is a question of distance and not of actual increase in the value of property?   A.—It is a question of increase in value anywhere within reasonable reach. We used to have a dense population all through these streets here in this part of the city but now you will notice, these old houses are being pulled down and fine warehouses and other buildings are going up; it is the old question of a crowded population. But take a man who has been living here anywhere south of Queen street, as many working men used to do, and when you get property assessed at $100 a foot it walks into his wages, though of course he can sell it.

FAMILY STRUCTURE

Herbert Brown Ames, *The City Below the Hill: A Sociological Study of a Portion of the City of Montreal, Canada* (Montreal, Bishop Engraving and Printing Co., 1897), pp. 16, 18-19.

In the first place we will make a statistical presentation of the available data from which we are to draw our conclusions. In the city below the hill dwell 7671 families. These families include 37,652 persons. Of these persons, 25,051 are from sixteen years of age upwards and may be by us regarded as adults. These 25,051 adults are divisible into three classes: the wage-earners, male and female, numbering 10,853; the home-tenders reckoned at 11,720; and the lodgers, who either may or may not be wage earners, in number 2478. If we subtract the adults from the total number of persons, the remainder, amounting in number to 12,601, will represent the children, and this number is again divisible into children of school age of whom there are 6948 and young children of whom there are 5653.

What then is the composition of the typical family? Though it may appear strange to the eye, this can best be accurately expressed in terms of decimals. The average family contains 4.90 persons. Of this number 1.41 work for wages and are the family's support; 1.53 remain at home and contribute more or less to its care. To every third family there is assignable one lodger, who helps to swell the family income, but who, further than this, does not enter into our calculations. The average home contains 1.64 children; .91 is of school age, while .73 is an infant in the house.

These proportions may perhaps be expressed more vividly if we imagine a block to contain thirty such families. We should then expect to find in this block 147 persons, 42 of whom would be wage-earners; 46 of whom would be home-tenders; 10 of whom would be lodgers; 49 of whom would be children, of these latter 27 being of school age and 22 being infants at home. We might carry the analysis of the wage-earning portion still further. We noted in our study on employment that 77 per cent. of those employed were men and grown boys; 20 per cent. children. Of the 42 wage-earners above cited we might reasonably expect that 33 would be grown males, 8 would be women and one a child. . . .

We are accustomed to say for example that certain nationalities, especially the French-Canadian, are remarkable for large families. This may be true in other parts of the city, but it does not seem to be so for the district now under study. The three sections, Nos. 8, 10 and 6, which rank first in the matter of large families are peopled in almost equal proportions by English, Irish and French-Canadians. Of the four sections which bring up the rear section 22 is mainly Irish, section 13 is four-fifths French, whilst in sections 21 and 5 the nationalities are nearly evenly divided. Again sections 17 to 20, immediately below Notre Dame street, show much larger families than do sections 12 to 15 just above it, yet all these sections are alike preponderatingly French-Canadian. The size of the family in this part of the city does not then appear to depend upon nationality.

We have also been accustomed to think that the poorer the locality the larger the family. The poor man's chief wealth is said to consist in abundance of children. Doubtless many individual instances may be cited in support of such an hypothesis but averages for a considerable number of families, at least in the district we are examining, tend to disprove this theory. Indeed, it is the contrary, rather that appears to be nearer the truth. Three out of four of the sections remarkable for the smallness of their family averages, are at the same time localities wherein the average family incomes are among the lowest to be found. Extremely low income seems an accompaniment of especially small families. The belt below Notre Dame street, where families are large, is a region of better average incomes and fewer poor than the belt above Notre Dame street, where the families are not large. Nor, on the other hand, does the family in the best sections, such as 1, 2, 3, 6, and 9, exceed the average size, sometimes even falling below it. Hence the law which appears to the writer to be dimly apparent is in effect that neither wealth nor poverty is likely on the whole to be accompanied by large average families. These are rather to be expected among the middle industrial class, and the average number of persons per household decreases as the social status of the residents rises above or falls below this level.

Another matter which invites examination is the adult element of the average family and its occupation. Our average family was found to contain 2.94 persons no longer children. Of these 1.41 work to support the family, while 1.53 are supported at home, where probably in most cases by the performance of household tasks they contribute their part. Here a law seems fairly apparent in that the proportion of wage-earners seems gradually to diminish and the proportion of home-tenders gradually to increase as one passes from an examination of the poorer to that of the more well-to-do sections. It is probably a fact that the poorer the locality, the greater the pressure to increase the number of contributors to the family purse, while the richer the locality the larger the number of those who may be allowed to remain at home.

PIONEER FOOD

Edith Rowles, 'Bannock, Beans and Bacon'. *Saskatchewan History*, v, 1,
Winter 1952, 1-3, 5-6, 9-14. Reprinted by permission of *Saskatchewan
History* and the author, Dr Edith Rowles Simpson, Dean Emeritus, Uni-
versity of Saskatchewan.

In the early years, when there was no railroad west of Winnipeg,
all goods were hauled in carts and wagons drawn by ponies. In
the early summer the trails were bad and due to late arrivals some
shortages would occur. One time coal oil was so scarce that $10.00
a gallon was charged for it by the only dealer who had any in
stock. . . . No one carried heavy stocks . . . much business was
done by barter. Quality in many cases was not as good as now.
Jams and marmalades contained little of the fruits they were supposed to contain, and today would not sell. Prices were high in
the early years on heavy goods. In 1880 and until the railroad
reached "Troy" the freight rate from Winnipeg was $10.00 a cwt.
From 1880 to about 1892 all spices reached retailers in wooden
boxes containing five pounds and were sold in bulk.

Such are the recollections of George Ballantine, who, as the youngest
of seven children, came to Prince Albert with his mother in 1880. Prince
Albert in that year was still the largest settlement in the Territories and
Mr. Ballantine, who by the time he was eleven was working in a general
store, had an unusual opportunity to observe the problems of pioneer
merchandising and particularly the characteristics of the foodstuffs which
were handled. . . .

Large settlements such as Prince Albert and Regina may have had
stocks of varied provisions, but settlements were few and far apart, and
so the stores could not be depended upon as the only sources of food for
the settlers. Nature provided an abundance of wild fruits and game, and
the settlers supplemented these very soon by producing crops and raising
livestock. One of the most interesting reports of growing food on the
southern plains is that of Mr. and Mrs. Anthony Neville, who spent the
winter of 1883 in Regina, moving to their homestead ten miles from what
is now Lumsden in March, 1884. Mrs. L. M. Purdy of Balcarres, their
daughter, relates the story. She writes:

By 1885 father and mother had land prepared so we planted a
large garden and as soon as early vegetables—lettuce, radishes,
young carrots, etc., were fit to use we took a buckboard load to
Regina once a week. We found our best market at the N.W.M.P.
barracks, where our buckboard would be surrounded by men
hungry for fresh vegetables. We sold to the houses too, and often
the women would ask if we would trade for sugar, rice, tea, or

other things issued to them in larger quantities than they cared to use. More than one summer we got enough of the finest cut loaf sugar to do all our canning and preserves. The tea was the compressed kind, looked much like plug tobacco. We got plenty of rice, too.

There was a small hospital at the barracks, and meat and bread were issued to the amount needed if the hospital were full, so there we often got a big piece of fresh beef. They saved their dry bread, supposed to be for our chickens, but it was kept in clean cotton bags, and dry bread can be used in many ways. Mother used to put the meat into a big crock of buttermilk and if it were the least bit stale on the outside after a long drive home on a hot day, the buttermilk would sweeten it wonderfully.

Mother and I were real experts at finding and picking wild fruit, and the valleys near us provided a great quantity and variety. In 1889 we had a row of wild black currants in the garden and there was a grand crop of fruit on them and in the valley near. Mother and we girls picked twenty-four patent pails of beautiful currants and father took them to Regina and sold them for $2.00 a pail.

The year the c.p.r. was being completed mother used dried apples and wild raspberries and plenty of sugar and made many pails full of jam, selling it to the c.p.r. for twenty-five cents a pound, and the railway furnished the pails.

Father invested in a special variety of early potatoes, and got them on the market early and so was able to buy the things we needed to eat.

During several years we raised black hulless barley and had it ground to use for porridge and milk puddings. We also raised field peas for a few years, using them for soup and baking them like beans. We boiled wheat whole, ate with salt or sugar.

During several years, when we needed groceries, we would go with the wagon and pick buffalo bones and sell them in Pense, then buy flour, etc.

A typical shopping list for settlers in the earliest years (1883-1890) included sugar, tea, flour, dried apples, baking soda, salt, granulated oatmeal, rice, syrup and perhaps coffee. Many of the settlers who arrived just after the transcontinental railway was built were able to secure land close to the railway, and so they were not far from a store and post office, but earlier settlers and later ones were not so fortunate. Mrs. H. Cudmore of Manor, now ninety years of age, tells of driving one hundred miles from the station at Emerson, Manitoba, to their new home at Crystal City in the year 1881. (Crystal City is near what is now the border between Saskatchewan and Manitoba.) We have numerous records of people going by ox team fifty miles or more to get supplies. No wonder they visited stores only once or twice a year! Mrs. Edith Kinneard Horn, now of Regina, whose parents set up housekeeping near Lumsden on section 14, range 19, township 21, W 2nd, in 1882, points out that she cannot say much about what was in the stores in the early years, for she did not get to town often. She lived only fifteen miles from Regina, but had to go there with oxen. Those pioneer women who lived further from the little settlements saw the inside of a store very seldom, the husbands having to do all the shopping. Eaton's catalogue, appearing for the first time about 1896, was a welcome shopping guide for these isolated homemakers. . . .

Tea was the usual hot beverage in the early days. Brands of tea which were used included Red Rose, Gold Standard, McClary's, Blue Ribbon and Ceylon. These were often put up in fancy tin tea caddies of one, three or five pound size, but the cheapest and commonest way to buy tea was in bulk. The stores bought the tea in chests lined with lead paper and the tea was weighed out in brown paper bags. The price seems to have been about thirty-five cents a pound whether it was green or black. One householder reports buying green tea dust at ten cents a pound in 1890.

Coffee was not used as commonly as it is today. Those who told of using it were about equally divided in their purchase of coffee beans and ready ground coffee. A few bought green beans and roasted their own. Substitutes for coffee were fairly common, which would indicate that those who were fond of having coffee found it too expensive to buy. Barley, roasted and put through the food chopper, was the usual substitute; but rye and wheat were also used. One housewife reports using toast to make a synthetic coffee. Cocoa is occasionally mentioned as a beverage, but water and milk took second and third place after tea and coffee.

Then as now meat was one of the cook's chief concerns. Pemmican, used by the Indians and explorers, was not used very much by the settlers; only one of our correspondents mentions it. Mrs. Jos. Keys, now of Keystown, tells us that her parents at Wolseley in 1886 had as their meat supply, "Pemmican and the odd deer."

John Wilson, whose father settled at Saltcoats in 1883, when asked how his parents got fresh meat, replied: "With a gun." Though the buffalo disappeared from the plains shortly after the c.p.r. was constructed, there was still a variety of other game to be had. Around Prince Albert and Battleford the occasional moose or bear was brought in, in addition to the smaller game. From the early settlements in the south we have reports of antelope, deer, badger and porcupine being used as food. The variety of wild fowl was greater than today, prairie chicken, ducks and geese predominating. Mrs. Keys writes: "About 1896 the wild geese came by hundreds and were plentiful for years." Reports have been received of eating crane, grouse, partridge, plover, snipe, and wild turkey. Mrs. J. Wilkie, an 1889 bride in the Wilkie settlement, near Pense, states: "The game improved after grain was planted." John R. Bird of Broadview, who came to the west in 1882, tells us that "the meat supply in the early years was rabbit, more rabbit and still more rabbit, prairie chicken, duck, and sometimes deer." He adds that they could have fresh meat every morning out of a snare. He gives as typical menus for the years 1882-1886:

Breakfast—wheat porridge with a little molasses (no sugar), toast, rabbit stew, tea, no milk.

Dinner—rabbit, potatoes, bread and tea.

Supper—more rabbit, potatoes (fried if we had grease), bread, tea.

Settlers raised their own meat as soon as possible after getting established. Nelson Spencer of Carnduff tells us that weanling pigs were worth fifty cents to a dollar each about 1883. Everyone butchered their own meat in the fall if they had anything ready. Pork was the most common meat used, beef came next, fowl was always a standby, and very few people mention using lamb or mutton. Fresh meat was available all winter because it could be kept frozen, settlers soon learning to cut meat into useable sizes before freezing. For summer use meat had to be preserved. Some housewives fried out pork, placed it in crocks, and covered it with fat. This fresh meat, stored in the cellar, would last for several months. Salt was the most common preservative for meat. Some used dry salt, but pickling, followed sometimes by smoking, was the favourite way for preserving pork. Beef, too, was often pickled, though corned beef never became as common as pickled pork. Mrs. George Johnson, who set up housekeeping at Langenburg in 1890, reversed the process of cold storage in winter and pickling in summer. She had a deep well for keeping the meat fresh in summer, and she pickled meat for winter.

In the *Regina Leader* of March 15, 1883, the following advertisement appeared, "P.BONNEAU, corner of Lorne and Eleventh Avenue, dealer in groceries and provisions; on hand about twenty tons of fresh buffalo meat." This must have been one of the last occasions when buffalo meat was available. A few people, no doubt, bought meat occasionally in the early years, but few of our correspondents mention the store as a source of fresh meat. At Wolseley the storekeeper kept corned beef in brine in barrels, and customers took their own container to the store to bring the dripping meat home. Mr. Geo. Ballantine, of Prince Albert, states: "We bought beef and pork from farmers, prairie chicken, wild ducks, geese, moose and deer from the Indians."

Seventy-three housewives tell of drying peas for winter. Saskatoons, corn and beans were dried in more than forty homes. Other foods preserved by drying included apples, pumpkin, plums, raspberries, meat, fish, herbs, peel and kale.

Pickling and brining vegetables were common practices, and in order to make pickles many pioneers made their own vinegar. Mrs. Jordens, at

St. Hubert Mission, reports that her family made vinegar in 1885 "by using a mother of vinegar borrowed from a neighbour, adding sugar and water to fill a bottle."

Explorers in the west may have managed sometimes without flour, but as soon as homes were established flour became a necessity. Ogilvie's seems to have been the best known flour in the earliest years, and it was at first shipped in from the east, usually from Brandon. Other brands of flour used by the pioneers were Strong Baker, Five Roses, Royal Household, Purity, Harvest Queen, Four X, and Lake of the Woods. Local mills were established early. Some of the locations were: Prince Albert (Kidd's Mill), 1875; Regina, 1880's; Cannington Manor, 1882; Millwood, Manitoba, 1885; Fort Qu'Appelle, 1885; Virden, Manitoba, 1886; Wolseley, 1886; Lumsden, 1890's and Gainsboro, 1900. Millwood must have been a busy spot in the autumn. The Wilsons, living forty miles from Whitewood, took their grist sixty miles to Millwood as early as 1886. The Currys, settling in Burrows in 1888, took their wheat ten miles to the mill. There were loads of wheat from Valley View, now Tantallon, hauled thirty miles to Millwood. It was about twenty miles for the Langenburg people, and in 1890, oxcart or sleigh was used for the trip. Mrs. Emily G. Barker, of Churchbridge, states that from 1892-1897 they took their grist thirty miles to Millwood from Kinbrae (now Liscard) and brought back six or eight bags of Ivory Straights. It was usual to take a load of wheat and exchange it for flour, bran, and shorts. A year's supply of flour was what most pioneers hoped to lay by. They were aware that newly milled flour did not make as good bread as that which was aged about ten months, so it was important to lay in a good stock. Modern millers are permitted to use improvers to age the flour rapidly, but in the 1890's there was little knowledge of cereal chemistry.

Some farmers were not within reach of a local mill and so they had to sell their wheat and buy flour. Some of these farmers were able to buy a year's supply but one pioneer, settling near Stoughton in 1889, says, "We bought Harvest Queen, a second grade flour at about $2.00 for ninety-eight pounds; only one sack at a time was bought, for that was all we could afford."

To those of us who now live in the "Wheat Province" it seems strange that only about half the settlers who came before 1900 used wheat for making porridge. Some soaked the whole wheat overnight and cooked it slowly for hours but most people cracked it or ground it; sometimes they used a coffee mill, but more often a hand grinder or crusher. Many mention that they prepared wheat for the household in the same chopper that was used for preparing feed for the livestock. One careful housekeeper points out that, when preparing wheat for the family, both the chopper and the wheat were first carefully cleaned. Mr. Sam H. McWilliams writes: "I remember, as a boy of ten years, pounding wheat on a smooth flat rock with a hammer to make porridge for the family, not once, but many times." Mr. Gus Lauttamus of Tantallon states that they bought Four X flour but ground their own whole wheat flour with millstones. Some of the whole wheat flour produced in this way was made into porridge. A few people had wheat prepared for porridge-meal as part of their grist. Some of those who did not use whole wheat porridge in the early years tell us that they learned to use it later.

Out of forty-one samples of typical breakfast menus served before 1900, thirty-seven include porridge, usually oatmeal porridge. One hardy pioneer tells of porridge made from shorts, while another states that they usually ate cornmeal mush with molasses. Milk usually accompanied the porridge and often brown sugar or molasses, rarely white sugar.

Bread-making was one of the housewife's heaviest tasks, for she not only made bread for her own family, but often for the bachelors living near. Mrs. Emily Barker, living at Churchbridge since 1890, describes a wooden trough for mixing bread dough, large enough for twenty-four loaves. The pioneer breadmakers needed a cheap, reliable source of yeast, and no less than seventy-five of our informants used hops. The storekeepers kept a supply of hops on hand, but once the housekeeper had made her first purchase of these she tried to keep her own supply of yeast on hand, growing it in a jar of potato water, flour and sugar. She often called this yeast mixture "starter." Thirteen of our contributors state that they made salt rising bread. According to one of our correspondents who knew how to make both salt rising and hops bread, the salt rising bread was not as nice as the other, so she taught many of her neighbours how to use hops. When yeast cakes were available in the stores they were the "Royal" brand, and came in round cakes in little round cardboard boxes.

Substitutes for bread were bannock, flapjacks and biscuits. Mrs. E. Borwick, now of Meskanaw, writes: "In early days you could always get suet and we used it for puddings—some rendered and used it to make bannock; my husband had always been used to bannock; when he was a boy they used nothing but. He was born in Manitoba and his mother and father before him." Flapjacks were made of flour, baking soda, sour milk and salt. The hot iron griddle or frying pan was rubbed with a piece of fat pork and the flapjacks were browned, turned and browned on the other side. They were a staple for breakfast for many westerners for many years. The dough which we today bake in the oven as biscuits was, in the early days, often baked on top of the stove, either on a griddle or right on the stove lids, turned and browned (or blackened slightly) on both sides. It made a light and filling hot bread.

Most housewives used baking soda and sour milk or buttermilk for leavening their baking. Tartaric acid, rather than the cream of tartar we use today, was at first on the shelf to be used with baking soda in recipes where sour milk, molasses and other acids were not present. Twenty-one of our replies tell of the housewife making her own baking powder. A recipe from an early cook book suggests the following recipe for baking powder:

Ground rice—five ounces.
Carbonate of soda—three ounces.
Tartaric acid—two ounces.

Self-rising flour is not a new development. Mrs. Neville used to make prepared flour in the early days, sifting weighed quantities of flour, tartaric acid and soda.

Though condensed milk was available in the earliest years and has been the standby of prairie bachelors, the pioneer housewives seem to have used it rarely, instead they wanted to own a cow. This was not always easy. Robert John Hogg of Carnduff tells how, when he was eleven years old, he worked out to earn a cow for the family. In 1893 he could earn only fifty cents a day, so it took a long time before enough money was accumulated to make the necessary purchase. Once a cow was acquired, its contribution to the family was highly prized. Mrs. Purdy writes, "In July, 1883 we bought a cow and kept her milking two years before she freshened. . . ."

Our records show that there have been many changes in the merchandising of foods. In the earliest years stores stocked very little besides staples, and the supplies were kept in bins or barrels to be weighed or measured out to the customers. Even the brown paper bags are different now. Some people recall that the paper bags were "once made like envelopes; the bottom corner had to be folded to make the bottom rectangular." Butter used to be sold to the storekeeper in rolls wrapped in butter cloth or packed in crocks. Lard was packed in casks. For the customer butter and lard were gouged out of the container with a circular motion of the knife, the pieces often being sold on chipped plates. Dried apples, and later other dried fruit might be seen in the store in open containers where the customer could, and often did, help himself to a sample as he stood waiting for his order to be filled.

Granite cooking pots, tin milk pans and dippers, and heavy pottery dishes were the common kitchen utensils in every household. Heavy iron pots, dutch ovens and frying pans brought to the west by the settlers are probably still in use today. The butter bowl and paddle for working butter were of wood, and sometimes a wooden butter table with a heavy wooden arm something like a rolling pin was made for working butter. The housewife often had to manage with woefully inadequate equipment, but she learned to improvise here as well as in her cooking.

Mrs. Purdy has submitted menus typical of what her mother served in the winters, about 1885:

Breakfast—Porridge or mush, milk and brown sugar, sometimes hash or cold meat, warmed potatoes, bread, butter if we had any, stewed or canned fruit.

Dinner—Stewed rabbit with dumplings, potatoes and another vegetable, sometimes plain pudding or pie.

Supper—Variable—a hot soup, pancakes, Johnny cake with syrup, sometimes a steamed pudding, fruit, bread, hot biscuits, perhaps potatoes cooked some tasty way, often raw onions.

Mrs. A. Bishop of Broadview came to live in the west in 1885, when she was only six years old. There were five in the family. The father had helped to build the c.p.r. as far as Wolseley. Mrs. Bishop remembers that typical menus for their meals were:

Breakfast—Porridge made of ground wheat.

Dinner—Potatoes, and one other kind of vegetable, sometimes meat, bread and butter.

Supper—Bread and milk, sometimes boiled wheat with milk and no sugar.

Mrs. Mary Elizabeth Roe started housekeeping at Pense in 1893. She gives as typical menus:

Breakfast—Oatmeal porridge, fat bacon, eggs, bread, butter and tea.

Dinner—Fat pork, potatoes and other vegetable and apple pie.

Supper—Rice and egg or canned salmon or hash, buttermilk pancakes and syrup.

Mrs. Jos. Keys writes: "The breakfasts in 1886 consisted of porridge, milk, tea for the older ones, some white bread, some molasses or syrup; and the other two meals differed slightly with perhaps a small quantity of meat or fish." Mrs. Keys was one of the children in a family of nine, the children ranging in age from two to twenty-three. She tells how, in 1886, she helped to serve the first Christmas dinner for their family in what is now Saskatchewan. She says, "The menu was little different from any other day. The older members of the family were away from home working."

Mrs. Ida Hanna (nee Keys) of Keystone writes, "As to shortages in early days, if the year was poor, as many were then, it meant practically no vegetables for the winter, and often not enough potatoes, although after 1887 I think we always had some. In that case, canned tomatoes were used more than anything else to help out."

John Wilson of Springside, who, as a boy of seven, settled with his family at Saltcoats in 1883, answers the question, "Were you ever reduced to almost starvation level?" by the following statement, "Only once when the snow was so deep that we could not get out. We divided the flour up and each one got just a slice of bread three times a day, but we always had rabbits which helped a lot. It was six miles to the nearest house. The man there walked over on his snowshoes to see us. He came the next day and brought some flour."

Mrs. Ed. Wilson was a tiny child when her parents settled at Oxbow in 1892. She writes, "My father was an Anglican clergyman and I used to go with him through the country and met some pretty slim menus. I remember once it was a sort of porridge made of flour and water." One is impressed, when reading replies, at the number of times courage and ingenuity were required of our western pioneers. Many were the privations they endured. Mrs. Mary A. Jordens, married in 1887, tells of living on an Indian reserve at Fort Pelly for three years. For three months she had to cook on an open hearth, baking bannocks in front of the hot coals. Potatoes were cooked in an open kettle hanging on an iron bar over the fire. They had no cow until 1889, and the baby, until a year old, had nothing but mother's milk. Most pioneers did not suffer as many privations as Mrs. Jordens, but nearly all can mention at least one occasion when they were very short of food. It is quite remarkable how many of our contributors assure us that, once established, they were never short again. They often tell of neighbours helping one another, and over and over again we are assured that if a person was willing to work, there was no need to go hungry, even in the early years, in this land of plenty. . . .

Mrs. Jordens, recalling Christmas, 1886, writes, "There were mother, father, Frank Jordens (my fiancé), Napoleon, Midas, Virginia, Erica, Victoria, Almira, baby Frederick, and myself. We had roast pork and chicken with onion gravy, and a large plum pudding made from directions brought from England by Frank. It had to be boiled six hours steadily. We had doughnuts and raisin pies at other meals."

Mr. and Mrs. George Johnson settled at Langenburg in 1890. The earliest Christmas menu that the nine surviving members of their family can remember was: "Roast goose with raisin filling; vegetables, Christmas cake; coffee. The Christmas cake was raised with yeast and had in it peel and raisins. It was a sort of raised fruit loaf."

HOW THE WORKINGMAN PAMPERED HIMSELF

Canada, Royal Commission on the Relations of Labor and Capital in Canada, 1889. Evidence—Ontario, pp. 351-3.

Dr. w. b. nesbitt, Toronto, called and sworn.
    By the chairman:—
    q.—Will you please give the Commission your opinion in regard to foods? a.—In my opinion, in the first place, the people of the present

time are eating a great deal more than is good for them or than there is any necessity for eating; in the second place, they are paying a great deal more for the amount of nutriment they obtain than there is any necessity to pay; and in the third place, they would be able to do better work and be in much better health if they obtained their foods on a better system, and ate less. The principal difficulty is that people, as a rule, know nothing about the constituents of foods, and what they really require as food, and how to cook them; they know much less about that matter than about other subjects. Experiments, and the general run of that sort of work by a great many experimenters, have shown that living is very, very cheap.

Q.—Do not the French people live more cheaply than the English? A.— Yes.

Q.—And they live well? A.—They live better than the English people in some classes. They buy their foods better, and combine their foods better, so as to obtain a proper amount of nutriment from them. You take an ordinary meal of beef and potatoes and analyze that meat and potatoes, and also take an equal quantity of beans and peas and analyze their constituents, and you will find that there is more nutriment in the beans and peas. In the same way, take nitrogenous foods, and you will get more of every class of nutriment from them, and especially more of what is especially required.

Q.—What will be the difference in the cost between the beef and potatoes and the beans and peas? A.—Rumford, as far back as 1795, got out some tables on this subject, and looking over them and applying them to the cost of living here I find that the cost of a good meal for a hardworking man will be about three-quarters of a cent. That is the cost of a good, palatable meal, and a man would be able to do more work on it than on meat and potatoes.

Q.—Is it not a fact that in Manchester and London there are dinners provided for children at 1 cent each? A.—Yes; that is the case.

Q.—The meal, I understand, consists of bread and soup? A.—This that I have mentioned is Rumford's soup. There have been quite a number of different kinds prepared.

By Mr. HEAKES:—

Q.—What would constitute a meal costing three-quarters of a cent? A.—In this one there would be about five pounds of barley, five pounds of cornmeal, four red herrings and some salt and seasoning. The cost of the whole, together with water sufficient to make a meal for sixty-four persons, averages about three quarters of a cent, and gives about a quart of soup each.

Q.—Did that include the cost of fire and attendance? A.—There were more extensive investigations made, in which it was found that meals could be furnished at about a farthing, about a quarter of a cent each, including fire and attendance—two servants included.

Q.—Is it not a fact that given the same amount of animal food the French people can make much better use of it than the English? A.—I could give you striking instances of how little people know. If a boarding house mistress makes soup she generally throws out the meat afterwards, on the principle that all the good was boiled out of it, when, as a matter of fact, only one-third of the good is taken out of the meat when it is boiled.

Q.—Would you consider barley, indian meal and red herrings sufficient for a laboring man to do a day's work on in this country? A.—Yes; amply sufficient.

Q.—Would you like to do it yourself? A.—Yes; this is no hearsay, this is an actual fact.

Q.—You will never make the people believe it. A.—Perhaps not.

By the CHAIRMAN:—

Q.—Do not the Scotch Highlanders work on oatmeal, which they eat three times a day? A.—Yes.

By Mr. MCLEAN:—

Q.—Do you know for a fact that the Scotch have nothing but oatmeal porridge to live on? A.—Scotchmen have milk with their meals in some instances; they have it but very seldom. It is principally porridge they live on.

Q.—Do you know they live on it, and do a day's work on it? A.—Yes; it is the same way with the Irishmen living on potatoes and buttermilk. It is an actual fact that they do it; they have the nutriments and constituents of food in the proper proportions. Some of the people in New England live on fish and beans.

By Mr. HEAKES:—

Q.—Has that style of food anything to do with the destitution of the Irish people? A.—I think that is due to want of work—they have nothing to do. The system of lands there and the action of England have thrown them out of work. They have got no work to do. It does not matter whether people live on potatoes and buttermilk or on oatmeal porridge.

Q.—Do you know the amount of food furnished to a soldier in the English army? A.—I do not know the exact rations. I was looking over the tables and it is a bad system—it is not adequate. The best statement we have is that for American laborers; and, as I have said, we have tables respecting the German laborers, and I may say that the Germans have done more in this class of work than any other experimenters. The American table gives 125 grammes of proteins, 125 grammes of phosphates, and 400 grammes of carbo-hydrates. For hard work add 25 grammes of proteins.

By the CHAIRMAN:—

Q.—Do you know of what pemican, which is consumed by people in the North-West, is composed? A.—It is dried buffalo meat and fat. They take the meat and dry it, pound it in a mortar, mix some berries with it and put it in bags.

By Mr. HEAKES:—

Q.—Do you consider a soldier in the British army is over-fed? A.—I think he could do the work with less food.

Q.—Do you know what it costs to feed a soldier in Canada—how much a day? A.—I could not say.

Q.—Would you be surprised to learn that it is in the neighborhood of 23 cents? A.—I should not be surprised if it were in the neighborhood of 50 cents.

By the CHAIRMAN:—

Q.—What did it cost to feed a German soldier by the day during the war with France? A.—I do not know. The most extensive experiments were made, as I have said, by Rumford; the result was, as I have stated, that each meal cost three-quarters of a cent. The principal difficulty is that people do not know what they require and do not know how to buy.

Q.—May not others besides workingmen be placed in the same category? A.—We found, as a matter of fact, that the working classes will buy the best; for instance, they buy sirloin, when they would get just as much nutriment from the neck, and for the latter they would pay about one-third of the price.

Q.—They do not know the commercial value? A.—They do not know the respective properties.

By Mr. HEAKES:—

Q.—Taking into consideration what a man has to pay for house rent and clothing for his family, say of six people, and taking his wages at $1 a day, how much money can he afford to pay for sirloin steak? A.—It is not what he can afford but what he does spend.

Q.—What has he got to spend for sirloin steak after he has paid for fuel, clothing, house rent, and so on? A.—I will tell you as a fact, and it is the result arrived at by those who have made the most extensive investigations, that a man skrimps more on his clothing and house rent than he does on his meals.

By Mr. GIBSON:—

Q.—Who, then, buys the poor qualities of meat? A.—The people in comfortable circumstances buy cheaper meats than many poor people who are less able to afford it.

THE COST OF LIVING

Canada, Royal Commission on the Relations of Labor and Capital in Canada, 1889. Evidence—Ontario, pp. 62-4.

* * * Machinist.

WITNESS:—I do not wish my name to be published.

By Mr. FREED:—

Q.—Why do you not wish your name published? A.—There is no use leaving myself open to the condemnation of my employers. Of course, I want to protect myself as much as possible, having a living to make.

By Mr. WALSH:—

I do not think it is the wish of the Commission that any one should place himself at a disadvantage.

WITNESS:—I think it is the feeling of the workingmen; they rather object to give evidence and see their names mentioned in the papers. . . .

Q.—Are the wages in your trade higher in Toronto than in the old country? A.—When I lived there we worked nine hours a day or fifty-four hours per week at the place I left; fifty-one hours per week constitutes a week's work. Taking it by the hour I was as well off at home as here. We had as much per hour as here.

By Mr. HEAKES:—

Q.—Would the purchasing power of money in England be greater than in Canada? A.—We could live cheaper at home than here.

Q.—Money goes further there than here? A.—Yes, a great deal further. House rents are nothing there as compared with here, and coal was very cheap there.

By Mr. GIBSON:—

Q.—Did you have a good house for less money than you can get one here? A.—At home there are more tenements; you are not isolated as you are here. The working classes, especially in Toronto, like to live more on the cottage system, while at home there will be perhaps ten or twenty tenants in one building in flats.

Q.—Do you get more accommodation for less money? A.—A working-man at home has generally a kitchen and two rooms. I would sooner live the way we do here than the way they do there; at the same time houses give more comfort there.

Q.—Take the house in which you live now: would you obtain the same accommodation and the same number of rooms in the old country for the same money? A.—You would get a better house for the same money.

Q.—Then it is better in the Old Country than here? A.—Yes so far as rent is concerned.

By Mr. CARSON:—

Q.—Will you explain in what way it is that one dollar was better five years ago than it is now; is everything so dear? A.—I refer more to house rent.

Q.—You find living cheaper now than it was five years ago? A.—No.

Q.—Is it dearer? A.—No, I do not think there is much difference.

Q.—Is it about the same as it was ten or twelve years ago? A.—Yes, only I think butchers' meat is dearer than it was five years ago.

By Mr. GIBSON:—

Q.—In working over time, what are the wages in the Old Country and here? A.—In the Old Country we got one hour and a half for every one hour, from five o'clock to eight. If we worked till ten o'clock we were allowed half an hour for tea, which was not deducted from us, and we were allowed one penny beer money for every hour after eight o'clock. So from eight o'clock to six o'clock in the morning we got ten pence of beer money. So one night's work at home counts seventeen and a half hours, besides the beer money.

By Mr. BARTON:—

Q.—Do you not get any beer money here? A.—No, you hardly get time to take a drop of beer.

By Mr. GIBSON:—

Q.—Then for working all night you get double wages? A.—About double wages.

Q.—And for less time than that you get fifty per cent more? A.—Yes.

Q.—In Toronto how is it? A.—In Toronto so far as we are concerned it is this way: for from six to eight we get time and a half, and after that a time and a half up to six o'clock in the morning, but we are not allowed half an hour for tea. We are supposed to continue at work from one o'clock dinner time to six o'clock in the morning.

Q.—In the old country you get one hundred per cent and in this country fifty per cent for over time? A.—In the Old Country overtime counted from five o'clock to six in the morning. The nine hours system being in force we had one hour more.

By Mr. FREED:—

Q.—Then it is the same in England as here with the addition of the beer money? A.—I do not say it is the general rule throughout Great Britain, but it was in the district from which I came.

Q.—Where was that? A.—From Dundee.

Q.—Has your society any connection with the locomotive engineers? A.—No, not at all.

Q.—You say the accommodation and the condition of those tenement houses are not so good as the accommodation and condition of the house you live in Toronto? A.—You are more isolated here.

Q.—You have more room? A.—Yes, but of course you pay more for it.

Q.—If you had the same accommodation in the Old Country, the same amount of room you have here, how would it be? Why do they prefer to

live in tenement houses?   A.—I do not think they can get better houses.
   Q.—What rate of wages did you receive in Dundee?   A.—Thirty-six
shillings per week.
   Q.—Of fifty-one hours?   A.—Yes. There was some who received
twenty-eight shillings, thirty and thirty-two.
   Q.—What would be about the average?   A.—About twenty-eight
shillings.

INCOMES IN MONTREAL IN THE 1890s

Herbert Brown Ames, *The City Below the Hill: A Sociological Study of a
Portion of the City of Montreal, Canada* (Montreal, Bishop Engraving and
Printing Co., 1897), pp. 22-4.

We have already learned that there are 7671 families resident within "the
city below the hill." As near as can be ascertained these families receive,
each week, an aggregate amount of not less than eighty-five thousand
dollars. This means eleven dollars per week to each family. We have also
found that these families include 37,652 persons. This gives, on an average, an allowance of two dollars and a quarter per week to each individual.
*Eleven dollars per family, two and a quarter dollars per individual, these
then are the standards of average living in "the city below the hill."* . . .
   But this paper is to deal more especially with the real industrial class.
It is then necessary that we determine who belong properly to this order.
Among the families below the hill no less than 1176, or 15⅓ per cent. of
the total number, were classified by the canvassers either in accord with
their own information or because of their obviously comfortable sur-
roundings, as "well-to-do," that is in receipt of an average income of not
less than $20.00 per week, or a thousand dollars a year. This number in-
cluded proprietors, managers, professional men, store-keepers and a few
families wherein the combined income of several workers yielded a generous income. It is plain, however, that to include these, together with
their profits or salaries, when seeking to ascertain the income of the real
industrial class would unduly elevate the figures. On the other hand there
were discovered by the canvassers families to the number of 888 which,
for reasons to be studied later, were living upon incomes not exceeding
five dollars per week. These latter families and their meagre earnings
should also be deducted from the original figures in order to prevent them
from being unduly depressed by the presence of an element not properly
belonging to the class now under study. The "well-to-do" and the "submerged tenth," which together constitute twenty-seven per cent. of the

whole number, having been deducted, there remains 5607 families to be by us regarded as the real industrial class and as such examined. When then we ascertain that these 5607 families have an aggregate weekly income of $57,139.00, we conclude that $10.20 per family, or eighty cents less than the amount established as the average income when all classes were included, expresses the average weekly income among the real industrial class of the nether city. By way of further verification, were we to select the sixteen sections . . . wherein 75 per cent. or more of the inhabitants are of the class in question, we would find that the average for these was $10.07. *From $10.00 to $10.25 per week, then, is the family income of the real industrial class.* . . .

One final matter requires consideration before we abandon this subject. What is the average remuneration of the individual industrial wage-earner in "the city below the hill?" The amount previously specified as receivable weekly by all the families of this class was earned by 7794 persons giving an average of $7.33 for the earnings of each worker. Taking only the sixteen typical industrial sections before referred to and submitting their figures to a similar test the result is $7.21, or twelve cents less. We are safe then in concluding that between $7.20, and $7.35 per week, or about *$1.20 per day, is the average wage per worker*, taking as a whole the real industrial class of the west end. We have not accurate data upon which to determine the approximate wage of the sexes, but since in our second paper we learned to expect to find in each group of wage-earners 20 per cent. of them to be women, and 3 per cent. to be children, this proportion being maintained, there would be, among the 7794 mixed workers, 6000 men, 1560 women, and 234 children. If the men earned $8.25 per week, the women $4.50 per week, and the children $3.00 per week, it would account for the $57,139.00, the total amount earned by the aforesaid 7794 mixed workers. This estimate is but conjectural, yet it does not seem likely to be far wide of the mark.

POVERTY IN MONTREAL IN THE 1890s

Herbert Brown Ames, *The City Below the Hill: A Sociological Study of a Portion of the City of Montreal, Canada* (Montreal, Bishop Engraving and Printing Co., 1897), pp. 49, 53-6.

It is difficult to determine what shall constitute the low water mark of decent subsistence in our "city below the hill." Since a dollar a day is regarded as the minimum wage for an unskilled laborer, it would seem that

$6.00 per week might be taken as the point below which comfort ends and poverty commences. But a dollar a day is by no means equivalent to $6.00 per week, since few are those, among this class of laborers, who can count upon regular work throughout the year. It is also an undeniable fact that there are frugal households, not a few, wherein $6.00 per week means independence and comfort. Below $5.00 per week, however, it is hardly possible for the weekly income to fall and yet permit of proper provision being made for a growing family, and although there are those who do this also, and all honor to such as can, yet we may safely fix the limit of decent subsistence at $5.00 per week and regard such families as, throughout the year, earn no more than $260.00, as properly to be termed "the poor.". . .

It may not be at this point out of place to consider briefly the liquor question in its bearing upon the subject under examination. Whether the sale of intoxicants is the cause of irregular employment and poverty, or whether idleness and want bring into being and maintain the liquor stores we will not attempt to decide. The fact is, however, apparent to the observer, that *wherever poverty and irregularity are most prevalent, there the opportunities for drunkenness are most frequent.* Throughout "the city below the hill," there are, all told, 105 licensed saloons and 87 liquor selling groceries. Of these, 28 saloons and 9 groceries are to be found in sections 3, 5 and 11, in close proximity to the Windsor and Bonaventure stations, where it is apparent that they are sustained more by the travelling public than by the residential population. These sections can then fairly be eliminated from the calculation, thus leaving 155 liquor stores to provide for the remaining 27 sections, which means on an average one for every 45 families or one for every 219 persons. This is an exact though startling average for the "city below the hill."

Turn now to an examination of the locality between William street and the canal, and what do we find in this regard? Where every fifth family is in poverty, where two out of every five families are but irregularly employed, the population sustains one licensed—and no one knows how many unlicensed—liquor store to every 33 families, or one for every 160 persons. Look now, by way of comparison before leaving this subject, at the district beyond the canal, sections 28 to 30, with a population similar in respect to nationality to that of "Griffintown". Here one liquor store is deemed sufficient for each group of fifty families, one for every 240 persons, and here also one finds but *half* the irregularity in employment, and but *two-fifths* the proportional amount of poverty existent in the "Griffintown" district just across the canal. Let this stand as evidence sufficient that drink is inseparable from idleness and poverty and vice versa.

It will be remembered that, according to our industrial census, the total number of poor families was reckoned at 888 in "the city below the hill." Half of this number were by the writer selected as material for a second and more searching investigation, with a view of more fully examining the characteristics, conditions and causes of our west-end poverty. Four hundred and thirty-six families were sought for, and the first fact that was brought to the notice of the investigator was that 46 families, or 10½% of the above number, had left their former abodes, within the two months between the first and second canvass, drawing attention to one of the sad features of poverty's lot, viz., the constant necessity to move on because of inability to satisfy the claims of the landlord. If this ratio were maintained, and each month saw 5% of the poor evicted, in a year not half these families could be found at the former addresses.

A second fact, made apparent by the special investigation, was that our west-end poverty was not the result of recent immigration. Quite the reverse from what would have been the case in New York or Chicago, hardly a dozen families were discovered that had not been residents of the city for at least three years. The vast majority were old residents who had lived in Montreal for the greater part of their lives. The presence of poverty, then, in the nether city is not chargeable to any considerable influx of foreign elements.

In the case of 323 families inquiries were made as to the causes, assigned by the people themselves, for their indigent condition. With 109 families, or 34% the reply was "irregularity of work." The wage-earners were not without vocations but their employment was intermittent and often work ceased altogether for considerable periods. With 87 families or 28% the answer was that the wage-earners had no work whatever, nor did there seem to be any immediate prospect of getting any. With 27 families, or 9%, old age had unfitted and with a like number sickness had prevented the worker from earning the requisite support. Out of these 323 families, among the poorest of the poor, 62% claimed to be able to better their condition were employment regular and abundant. That a certain percentage of the answers given did not state the real facts of the case is quite probable. Few are the families that will admit to a stranger that drink, crime or voluntary idleness is the cause of their misery, though in 7% of the cases visited drunkenness was clearly at the bottom of the trouble. Still it is the belief of the investigator that the undeserving among the poor form a far smaller proportion than is generally imagined.

As to the composition of the family, out of 390 families, 8 were found wherein the head of the household was a widow, and 54 cases where the husband was too old or too ill to work, making in all 140 families, or 36% of the whole, that might be called "decapitated" family groups. In about two-thirds of the families, or in 64% of the cases examined, there was an able-bodied man in the house, oftimes more than one, a man able to work and professing to be willing to do so. If these proportions may be taken as fairly indicating the average among the families of the poor, it is evident that at least one-third of them are in indigent circumstances through no fault of their own. Death or disease have so crippled the family group that it can no longer unaided keep up in the fierce struggle for subsistence. Charitable effort must come to the relief of such. With nearly two-thirds of the cases, however, it is not charity that is demanded but a chance to work. Were employment obtainable these families would soon be able to adopt a comfortable scale of living. If private enterprise does not furnish sufficient opportunity for willing men to provide for their families the absolute necessities of life, during the four cold winter months, then the municipality, by carefully considered relief works conducted at a minimum wage, should come to their assistance.

A MID-CENTURY TAILOR'S ACCOUNT BOOK

Daniel McGruar Papers, 1842-1874.   PAC, MG 24, D50

Accounts
Mr. Daniel McGruar

To Daniel Wetherle

1842				
Oct 25	To 2 Barrels Turnips @ 5/		10	
Dec 14	" 17 cwt Marsh hay @ 3/	2	11	9
1843				
Feb 2	" 17½ lb Ham @ 7½			
	1 Barrel Flour 42/6	2	13	5
Oct 24	" 5 Barrels of Potatoes @ 5/	1	5	
	" Use of Bull for 1 cow 2/6		2	6
Nov 6	" pan for stove 2/6		2	6
Dec 26	" Horse & Sleigh up Northwest 15/		15	
1844				
Jany 30	" 3 cwt Meadow hay @ 3/		9	
Feb 7	" 12 cwt 2 qrs 20 lb hay @ 4/	2	10	9
April 19	" Iron work for Keel of boat 10/		10	
Aug 23	" 11¼ lb mutton @ 4d		3	9
Nov 4	" 2 Horses Man & Plough 1 day ·12/6		12	6
5	" 98 lb beef @ 3½ 8 cwt 3 qrs marsh hay			
	@ 3/	2	14	10

1845				
Feb 8	" 2 Horses & 2 Men ½ day hauling wood 10/		10	
May 15	" Horse ½ day 3/ (26) 2 Horses & Man			
	ploughing 8/		11	9
26	" 5 bbls Smelts @3/2 hauling do. 2/		17	10
30	" ½ day 2 horses & Man ploughing 6/3		6	3
June 9	" ½ bbl potatoes 2/6 ½ day horse & Cart		6	3
July 25	" Man & horse ½ day ploughing 7/6		7	6
Sept 11	" 15 lb Mutton @3½		4	4½
Oct 17	" 6 Weeks & 2 days Cow Pasturing @2/		12	8
25	" 1 bbl turnips 4/ (Dec 21) 9 cwt & 22 lb			
	hay @3/	1	11	7
1846				
Jany 5	" 1 days work horse & man 10/		10	
June 24	" Cash 20/ (Oct 1) horse & Cart			
	hauling potatoes 2/		1	2
1847				
Jany 16	" 9 cwt 17 lb hay @3/6		1	12
Feb 3	" Horse & sleigh to Douglastown 2/6		2	6
May 22	" Horse & boy ½ day hauling stone 4/6			
	horse ½ day 3/		7	6
31	" 2 horses man & plough ½ day 8/9		8	9
	" horse & boy harrowing 5/		5	
June 9	" horse & cart & boy 1 day 10/		10	
1848				
March 13	" 2 bbls Coals @2/6 (27) 2 horses & man			
	5/		10	
June 12	" Balance due on bbl Meal 9/		9	
1849				
May 9	" Waggon to Chatham		2	6
June 9	" Use of Bull for Cow 2/6		2	6
Oct 27	" 2 Horses & man 2½ days ploughing @ /14	1	15	
Nov 30	" Waggon to Chatham 1 day 2/6		2	6
1850				
Nov 7	" 1 Cow (13) 2 Horses & man			
	2 days ploughing @15/	6		
1852				
June 24	" Waggon to Chatham 1/6		1	6

1855				
Oct 29	" 12 Barrels Turnips @4/	2	8	
1856				
Oct 22	" 6 Barrels Turnips @4/	1	4	
		£ 38	1	11

Newcastle Feby 10th 1857

Miramichi

Messrs. Crane & Allison
      To Daniel McGruar

1848				
May	To Making a coat for H.B. Allison 25/	1	5	
	" Ditto a pair trousers for do. 7/6		7	6
Oct	" do a pair trousers for Jonathan Crane 7/6		7	6
	" do do do for do do 7/6		7	6
1849				
April 6	" do a frock coat for Henry Allison 10/		10	
" "	" altering a coat for Jonathan Crane 2/6		2	6
" 21	" do a pair trouser for Jonathan			
	Crane 7/6		7	6
Oct	" repairing 3 pairs trousers for			
	H. B. Allison 7/6		7	6
Nov 3	" Making OverCoat for H.B. Allison 25/	1	5	
" 7	" Seating pair trousers for J. Crane 2/6		2	6
Dec 8	" do a pair trousers for J. Crane 7/6		7	6
" 18	" do a pair trousers for H.B. Allison 7/6		7	6
1850				
May	" do a dress coat and a pair trousers for			
	J. Crane 32/6	1	12	6
June	" do a frock coat and a pair trousers for			
	H.B. Allison 32/6	1	12	6
1851				
Feby 14	" repairing a pair trousers for H.B. Allison 2/		2	
Decr 14	" To Making a suit for Jonathan Crane 35/	1	15	
1852				
Feby 14	" Making an OverCoat for J. Crane 30/	1	10	
		12	11	0

THRIFT AMONG THE WORKING CLASSES

Canada, Royal Commission on the Relations of Labor and Capital in Canada, 1889. Evidence—New Brunswick, pp. 216-18.

S.B. PATTERSON, Accountant, Savings Bank, called and sworn.
> By Mr. CLARKE:

Q. What is your business? A. I am accountant in the Dominion Savings Bank in this city.

Q. How long have you been engaged in that capacity? A. Fifteen years.

Q. What classes of people are depositors in the savings bank? A. Our customers are very largely among the working class people of the city. I mean by that that they are among the laboring and mechanical classes; possibly they are three-fourths of our customers.

Q. Can you give us any idea what is the proportion of the people who deposit their surplus earnings in the savings bank? A. The people who come regularly to the savings bank are those that we call working people —mechanics, or farmers and their families, and also some mariners. I think three-fourths of our customers are among that class of people, for we do not encourage depositors from any other class.

Q. Do they deposit frequently? A. Yes; we have a great many depositors who come regularly once a week. We look for them, at all events, once a month, and if we find they are not depositing we know there is something going wrong with them—some sickness, or trouble of that kind.

> By the CHAIRMAN:

Q. What is the lowest deposit you take? A. One dollar.

> By Mr. CLARKE:

Q. What is the limit of deposit? A. Do you mean for a year?

Q. Yes? A. Three hundred dollars.

Q. Have many mechanics reached that limit? A. Yes; a great many. The total limit is $1,000, and a great many mechanics and laboring people have reached it.

Q. In what time did they reach the $1,000 limit? A. There are a great many who reached it before the new regulations of $300 deposit in one year came in force, and who since have put in money for their children. A great many people have adopted that plan. They have put in the full limit for themselves and now they are at work filling up an account for their children, and in this way laying by money. In that way they evade the law.

Q. Do many of that class of depositors frequently withdraw their deposits? A. Yes; in the spring of the year. We will, during this month and the next, perhaps, pay out quite a large amount of money to some of those people who will want to buy a house for themselves, for just now building lots and houses are cheap, and some of those people will want to buy a piece of land. I know we are paying out a great deal of money this month for that purpose—for buying lots in this city.

By the CHAIRMAN:

Q. Do they buy vacant lots? A. Building lots.

By Mr. FREED:

Q. Are these sums paid out to mechanics or laboring people? A. To the customers I spoke of.

By Mr. CARSON:

Q. As a rule, do you ask those people what their occupation is? A. We have to ask them that when they first deposit, so as to get their names on the book.

By Mr. MC LEAN:

Q. How long does it take a mechanic to save $1,000? A. That depends upon business; some mechanics can save a great deal more money than others. If a man is steady at work and his family are earning, provided they are total abstainers, they can save $1,000 in St. John in three years.

Q. How many of a family would he have? A. Himself, with a boy and girl earning.

Q. How long would it take an individual mechanic by himself to save $1,000? A. I know mechanics who live better than I do, whose houses are better furnished than mine, and who have all the comforts and conveniences that a great many professional men have not. They have money in the savings bank; they have but little or nothing in their houses, but they put all their money in the savings bank. This they do so as to be able to get it when they want it, and until that time comes the money remains there. This they would sooner do than invest in real estate.

By Mr. CLARKE:

Q. You think that that man would prefer to invest his money in that way instead of in real estate? A. I think so.

Q. Do they think that when they are moving around they can take their bankbook with them easier than a house? A. Yes.

By the CHAIRMAN:

Q. What is the average expense of a mechanic who is not a total abstainer? A. The ordinary man, who is a moderate drinker—I mean, a man who drinks a little but does not get drunk—will find it costs him $1 a week for his liquor; that is $52 a year. He will admit that, but the unfortunate part of the case is that if the husband is fond of liquor his wife gets fond of it too, and the chances are that the children will soon follow them; if a man drinks socially and respectfully he is likely to drink too much and his children are likely to drink too, and in a very little while there is trouble in the family. I am intimately acquainted with some of those people and I often go to see them.

Q. Were you ever a mechanic, and are you able to speak from a mechanic's standpoint? A. I was a mechanic; I have employed men to work for me.

Q. What business did you follow? A. I was in the boot and shoe business.

By Mr. ARMSTRONG:

Q. You say that you know mechanics who are living in much better circumstances than you are? A. Yes.

Q. What position do they occupy? A. They are men engaged as foremen and machinists.

Q. What would their wages be? A. I do not know; I know they are able to dress their families very nice. I know a family that is in one of our cotton factories and the wages for himself and girl are among the[m] $20 a week.

Q. Do you know what their wages were before he went there? A. I do; he was once a ship-carpenter, and then he earned about $8.

Q. Could a man in St. John live economically, savingly and comfortably, and support a family, on $8 a week? A. Yes. This is a fact not generally known, that the poorer class are wasteful.

Q. What do you call the 'poorer classes—' the unskilled laborers? A. Yes; the laboring classes, and any body visiting the families of the poorer classes will see there is a waste.

By the CHAIRMAN:

Q. You mean there is a lack of management? A. Yes; there is a waste of what comes in, and a want of intelligence in producing results in the kitchen and the sewing room that works against the poor man.

By Mr. BOIVIN:

Q. Have you studied the expenses of living as between the French and English people? A. I have not, but I think that the French can live cheaper than English people. I know that the charitable societies in St. John have undertaken to take care of some families in the city, and they have managed to run the families on 90 cents a week, and give them food, which may not have been of the very best quality, but which was good and wholesome.

Q. Are the deposits made by the working people in St. John increasing, decreasing, or do they remain stationary? A. This last year, under the new regulations, they have been decreasing.

By the CHAIRMAN:

Q. That is to say under the regulations by which the amount of deposits is limited? A. Yes.

By Mr. FREED:

Q. Are their deposits decreasing from any other cause? A. I think that if it were not for that they would be increasing.

Q. Do you receive many deposits from sewing women? A. Yes.

Q. Do their deposits increase or decrease? A. Where everything is right, in the shape of good health, their deposits keep increasing; if they deposit at all they must increase.

Q. Are many persons compelled, for purposes of subsistence, to withdraw their accounts in winter? A. Not many, but there are a number of cases where it is necessary for them to do so. Our mechanics keep up depositing, perhaps not so much in January and February as they do in the other months but where everything is all right at home we do not notice that there is much difference because of the slackness of the time or work.

Q. Do you think that the number of persons who stop depositing on account of drinking is increasing or decreasing in St. John? A. It is decreasing, for we are getting as a community, more temperate.

Q. Do you, from your observation, think that the working people are less or more able to deposit money than they were ten or twelve or even fifteen years ago? A. They are more able, for the laboring people were never so comfortable in St. John as they are now, and I know this from having been among them for forty odd years.

A BALANCE-SHEET FOR THE WORKINGMAN

The *Labour Gazette* (Ottawa), II, no. 5 (November, 1901), pp. 280-1.

LOCALITY.	FLATS IN TENEMENTS OF		House of *Four Rooms.*	House of *Six Rooms.*	House of *Eight Rooms.*
	Four Rooms.	*Six Rooms.*			
	$	$	$	$	$
St. John . . .	3 to 6	5 to 7	3.50 to 6	7 to 8	10 to 12
Halifax . . .	10	14 to 16	6 to 10	10 to 14	15 to 20
Montreal . .	6 to 8	8 to 12	6 to 10	8 to 15	12 to 22
Toronto . .	10	12	7 to 10	9 to 12.50	12 to 15
Ottawa . . .	8 to 12	12 to 18	6 to 8	10 to 14	15 up.
Belleville . .	3	4	3	4	6
Winnipeg .	—	—	7 to 10	10 to 20	10 to 35
Brandon . .	2 rooms heated $10	—	5 to 8	8 to 10	10 to 15
Vancouver .	—	5 to 10 per room	10 to 15	12 to 18	18 to 30

The *Labour Gazette* (Ottawa), II, no. 5 (November, 1901), pp. 278-9.

	Bread per lb.	Flour per 25-lb. bag.	Milk per quart.	Cheese per lb.	Eggs per doz.	Potatoes per bag of 1½ bush.	Beef per lb.	Pork (fresh) per lb.	Mutton per lb.	Sugar per lb.	Tea per lb.	Coal oil per gal.	Coal (stove) per ton.
	¢	¢	¢	¢	¢	¢	¢	¢	¢	¢	¢	¢	$ ¢
St. John	3	65-75	6	16	18-22	75	10-14	8-10	8-10	6	18-40	20-24	6.00
Halifax	3½	65	6	14	22-35	85	8-15	12	8-10	5	20-60	22-25	5.50
Montreal	2⅓	55	6	10-12	16-20	70	6-12	12	10	5	20-75	18-25	6.50
Toronto	2-2½	50-60	6	12½-14	20	75	12-16	14	15	5	20-75	20	6.25
Ottawa	2½	65	5	12½-14	20-25	80	10-15	10	10-12½	5	25	20-35	7.00
Belleville	2½	50	4-5	13-15	16	45	8-10	10	10	5	30-60	20	6.25
Winnipeg	3½	60	6	12½	22	75	13	12½	12	6	40	27	10.00
Brandon	2½	57	5	14	25	53	10-12	12½	15	7	35	35	10.30
Vancouver	3⅓	70	10	15	45	75-$1	15	15	15-16	6	35-40	40	6.00

The *Labour Gazette* (Ottawa), II, no. 1 (July, 1901), pp. 46–52; II, no. 5 (November, 1901), pp. 300–5; II, no. 8 (February, 1902), pp. 453–5.

LOCALITY.	LATHERS. Average wages per week. $ ¢	LATHERS. Average hours per week.	LATHERS. Average duration working season in months.	LABOURERS. Average wages per week. $ ¢	LABOURERS. Average hours per week.	LABOURERS. Average duration working season in months.	CABINETMAKERS. Average wages per week. $ ¢	CABINETMAKERS. Average hours per week.	BLACKSMITHS. Average wages per week. $ ¢	BLACKSMITHS. Average hours per week.
New Brunswick										
St. John	9.00	54	8	7.50	54	8	10.00	54	8.50	51
Nova Scotia										
Halifax	10.00	59	7	6.25	45	7–8	13.00	59	9.00–10.00 (Windsor)	60
Musquodoboit Harbour	12.00	—	—	6.00	—	—	20.00	60	9.00	60
Quebec										
Montreal	10.00–13.50	60	10–11	6.25–6.50	59–60	8–10	9.00–12.00	60	9.00–15.00 (Roberval)	60
Yamachiche	7.50	60	—	6.00	60	8	10.50	60	9.00	60
Ontario										
Toronto	—	—	—	9.00–10.00	45–53	9	12.00–15.00	55	11.00–12.00	55–60
Ottawa	10.00	54	6	8.00–9.00	54	10	10.50–12.00	59–60	13.00	59
Belleville	9.00–1200	59	8–10	7.50	59	8–10	10.00–10.50	59	9.00–10.50	59
Manitoba										
Winnipeg	18.00	60	6	9.45	54	7	16.00	50	15.00	60
Brandon	17.00	59	7	7.50	60	7	15.00	60	13.50	60
British Columbia										
Vancouver	16.50 (Kamloops)	50	—	12.00 (Kamloops)	54	8	15.00–16.50 (Enderby)	55	14.00–16.50 (New Denver)	55
Interior	18.00	54	12	12.00	60	12	18.00	60	24.00	60

The Workingman | 4
and Social Institutions

As cities grew in population, so did the 'problem of the workingman'. For the dominant middle classes, attitudes towards the lower orders inevitably changed with urbanization. The workers, however strange and uncouth, could safely be ignored so long as they were scattered on farms or in small towns. Concentrated in large cites, the lower class was more conspicuous, and more dangerous. They disturbed public order, sometimes on a large scale as in the Orange-Catholic riots that tore Toronto in the 1850s and in 1875. They created a rising crime rate, they were vulnerable to disease (and showed a distressing tendency to spread it to the upper classes).

This chapter is concerned with the ways in which social institutions were developed to deal with the problems created by the lower orders. It is necessary to indicate some important aspects that have had to be omitted. Some social institutions that involved workingmen are not discussed. The 'national' societies—the English St George's Society, the Scottish St Andrew's Society, and the Irish St Patrick's Society—along with the ultra-Protestant Orange Order integrated workingmen with middle-class social leaders. Their activities are difficult to illustrate, however, in any understandable, and brief, way. Similarly, the churches have regretfully been omitted. Finally, the workingman's relations with the forces of law and order form too large a topic for discussion here. Suffice it to say that middle-class attitudes towards social order and towards crime mirror attitudes illustrated in other social institutions. On the other hand, criminality represented a logical enough response by lower-class people to the conditions in which they lived and to the conspicuous inequities in economic status that were so obvious in the nineteenth-century city. And violence was a useful outlet for frustration and boredom in the lower class, an inexpensive and accepted form of male recreation.

In the age of political economy, the age of *laissez faire*, the poor were expected to shift for themselves. At the same time, even early in the century, it was obvious that concentrations of the poor in cities demanded some response. The first document illustrates the former view. The response of D. B. Viger, a radical member of the Lower Canadian legislature, to the plight of indigent farmers shows the strength of *laissez faire* dogma among nineteenth-century liberals. Nevertheless, the city of Montreal found it necessary, in order to prevent epidemics, to support a hospital for the poor. The hospital's work in one-quarter of 1824 is described in its official report. That existing institutions were incapable of controlling disease was tragically established by the recurrent cholera and typhoid epidemics of the middle years of the century.

Establishing permanent bodies to deal with poverty was a slow process, given the prevailing ideology about self-help. As a letter to the *Montreal Transcript* in 1843 indicates, the city of Montreal did nothing to establish an industrial home for the poor, although a private citizen had donated money for that purpose twenty years before. Part of the problem was in devising a system that would take care of the 'deserving poor', without subsidizing the 'unworthy', the lazy and feckless. The Toronto *Globe* shows this clearly in its heartfelt sympathy for widows and orphans, and its harsh hostility to the 'whining beggars' who deserve no help. There was an obvious solution, however, to the problem of one pauper group, the immigrant poor. Mayor Howland of Toronto told the Royal Commission on Labor and Capital in 1889 that the solution was simply not to allow such people to come to Canada.

When permanent institutions for care of the poor were established, they usually operated on the principles of the English workhouse system. The indigents were expected to show their good will by working for what they received. Obviously in many cases the jobs were simply make-work rather than useful employment. But it was the principle of working for what one got, rather than the product, that was important. Excerpts from the reports of the House of Industry, the Infants' Home, and the Industrial Room in Toronto show both the functioning of these charities, and some of the philosophy behind them.

A special case, all would agree, was the child. Liberal ideas of responsibility obviously could not be applied to children. The essential problem of dealing with children was their parents. How could children be encouraged to become responsible and respectable citizens when, all too often, they were under the influence of vicious and irresponsible parents? They could not be removed from the home, given the sacrosanct status of the family in nineteenth-century thought. The usual solution to this dilemma was education, a public school system that would indoctrinate children with the proper values. The problem of the child is discussed below by perhaps Canada's leading social-welfare reformer of the age, J. J. Kelso.

As with other institutions in the society, recreation grew more organized and elaborate as the society became larger and urbanized. Early in the century, as John MacGregor shows in his description of Prince Edward Island, recreation was spontaneous and unorganized—skating, hunting, and other individual sports, frolics or bees, and other simple pleasures.

Even by the 1850s, as in Adolphus Gaetz' account of social life in Lunenburg, Nova Scotia, recreation was becoming better organized. The Prairie
West recreated the earlier frontier patterns of eastern Canada to a large
degree, although even here activity seems to have been more organized
than earlier in the century. What could not be organized, however complex the society, was the activity of small boys. Authorities tried, nevertheless. A former newspaper reporter, C. S. Clark, rather angrily describes
attempts to impose Victorian adult ideas of proper behaviour on the boys
of Toronto.

An important phenomenon in the last quarter of the century was the
rise of organized sport. There were many reasons for this development.
Concentrations of population naturally encouraged team sports, and their
popularity spread along the usual lines of influence from city to country.
In urban areas, the open fields and ponds that had been recreation centres
in the countryside were lacking; it took organization to provide facilities
there. Perhaps as much as any other factor, the Victorian age had a pen-
chant for organization, of everything and anything. It was a business-like
time, dominated by organization-minded middle-class men. Recreation
fell under the same discipline as work in their hands.

Much of the same moral imperative that was applied to work was applied to sport as well. Sports were encouraged because they toned the
mind and the body for the work of life; they imposed the sense of discipline so necessary in an industrial society; they encouraged healthy and
vigorous competition; they fostered the virtues of courage and determination. The hockey rink, then, was the broker's office writ small. Sports, too,
were useful in preoccupying and indoctrinating the unruly lower orders
of society. For the workingman, of course, many of these advantages were
not so obvious. Sports, for him, represented simply an escape from the
boredom of the factory.

In the countryside and the small towns, sports and recreation remained
mass-participation activities. Accounts of holiday events in Prince Albert,
Saskatchewan and several small towns in Ontario show how large a role
sports played in social life towards the end of the century. By this time
the imported British game of cricket, always associated with the upper
classes, was giving way in the summer calendar to North American sports
—lacrosse and baseball.

Increasingly, and especially in the cities, spectator sports were replacing
mass participation. An almost inevitable result of this was the rise of the
special sports hero. The first sport to have widespread professionalism
was rowing. Undoubtedly the most popular sports figure, and probably
the most popular of all Canadians in the nineteenth century, was the professional oarsman, Ned Hanlan. He offered something to everyone. For
the middle classes, he excelled in a sport long popular among them. For
the lower classes, there was identification with a champion who had been

a humble Toronto fisherman. The Toronto *Globe*, which had traditionally viewed sports as too frivolous to be covered by a serious newspaper, gave Hanlan front-page headlines. His 1878 triumph over the American rower, Courtney, a victory that won Hanlan a purse of $11,000, was lovingly analyzed for days by the press. The *Globe* account makes clear that the new Canadian feelings of nationalism had much to do with the enthusiasm demonstrated for Hanlan's feats.

Hanlan's successor in popular esteem was another sculler, Jake Gaudaur of Atherley, near Orillia, Ontario. Gaudaur won the world championship in England in 1896, and on his return was greeted by the largest crowd to that point in Canadian history as 100,000 Torontonians cheered him through the streets of the city.

Perhaps the fastest growing sport of the era was hockey. Although often deplored by the sophisticated for its rough tactics, hockey won mass following from workers. Hockey reached a new pinnacle when the retiring Governor General, Lord Stanley, donated a trophy for a national championship. After a good deal of bickering over the terms of the competition, the first Stanley Cup game was finally held in Montreal on March 22, 1894, with the Montreal Athletic Association besting Ottawa. The article on the game is not only of interest as an indication of mass interest in sport, but for the picture of the game as it was then played.

This section concludes with an excerpt from an article on the ideology of sport by John Weiler, an historian with the Ontario government. It is an indication of a new interest among historians in the social implications of sport.

THE EVILS OF CHARITY

Montreal Gazette, March 3, 1817.

HOUSE OF ASSEMBLY.

Debates on the Distresses of the Country Parishes.
Mr. VIGER proceeded to observe that such were the effects produced through the country and that the prospects held out to the indigent farmers could not but palsy their industry. . . . [W]as it not evident to every one acquainted with the human heart, and who had witnessed the effects produced elsewhere by similar measure that the prospect of abundant succour must paralyze industry, the suspension whereof must do as much injury as the intentions of several Members were to do good. . . .

The Hon. Members from Quebec have given us sorrowful accounts of their district as if to move our pity. Such would be laudable and necessary were they addressed to us as individuals (for as men we cannot but compassionate the afflicted,) but as Legislators we can only be influenced by the lessons of experience and the general principles of administration and political economy—but leaving aside these considerations, members from the Districts of Montreal and Three-Rivers will distinctly recollect that for several years the parishes in those districts were alternately afflicted by the failure of the harvests as at present in the lower parts of the district of Quebec. . . . He could even quote parishes where the harvest had successively failed for five years. In one of these years the lower classes in the towns and country places were reduced to the lowest extremity— the clergy and several charitable individuals by a distribution of soups had providently saved hundreds of families from the horrors of famine. No one at that time ever thought of asking the Legislature for the public money for the relief of the farmers—on the contrary they exerted themselves in procuring seed grain, in tilling their lands, improving their agriculture; and these transient evils, thanks to providence, had proved useful lessons, and had turned to their advantage, whereas had the public purse been opened, the evil must have increased as there is room to fear is already the case in this district from the fallacious prospects held out to the farmers.

ILLNESS AMONG THE WORKING CLASSES

Montreal Gazette, November 10, 1824.

MONTREAL GENERAL HOSPITAL.

Report of the Committee of management of the Montreal General Hospital, for the Quarter ending November 1st, 1824. . . .
From the report of the Medical Officers on duty during the quarter, it appears that 131 patients have been admitted into the hospital, and that 177 have received advice and medicine as out patients, which with 28 in the Hospital, August 1st, make 336 indigent sick, that have received benefit from the Institution during the quarter. Of these 12 only have been pay patients. This number is more than that of the corresponding quarter of last year, by 34.
To prevent as far as possible the intrusion into the Hospital, as paupers, persons not belonging to the parish of Montreal, an advertisement was put into the Newspapers, explaining the nature of the Institution, so that

those at a distance might not be induced to send their indigent sick and infirm, with the expectation of their being admitted into the Hospital, without their contributing to its support. . . .

LIST OF DISEASES WHICH OCCURRED IN THE M. G. HOSPITAL
FROM 1ST OF AUGUST TO 1ST NOVEMBER 1824.

Typhus Fever	13	Contusion	5
Continued do.	21	Fracture	2
Intermittent do.	1	Burn	1
Scarlet do.	1	White Swelling	1
Inflamation of the Brain	1	Fistula in Ano	1
do. of the Tonsils	1	Pelegmon	1
do. of the Eyes	2	Syphilis	3
do. of the Lungs	2	Gonorrhea	2
Dropsy of the Belly	8	Diarrhoea	3
do. of the Scrotum	1	Dysentry	4
do. of a Joint	4	Lenrorrhea	1
Anasarea	1	Amenorrhea	1
Erysipeles	1	Scald Head	1
Apoplexy	1	Impetigo	8
Delirium Tremens	1	Psoriasis	1
Palsy	1	Dysuria	2
Rheumatism	5	Scrophia	1
Sciatica	1	Indigestion	1
Tumour	1	Jaundice	1
Ulcers	11	Cough	3
Wounds	3	Debility	1

CHOLERA EPIDEMICS

Tenth Annual Report of the Provincial Board of Health. Ontario, *Sessional Papers*, XXIV (1892), V, no. 26, pp. 5, 8-11.

In this same year [1832] cholera was introduced into Canada by way of the St. Lawrence: and though it disappeared in the early autumn, its ravages were of an extended and most fatal description. It was a mysterious disease to the medical profession in Canada, and here, as elsewhere, the knowledge of its causation and method of propagation were the subject of constant speculation. Many supposed that winds of some peculiar and special character spread the disease from country to country, and the reports which had reached Canada of its westward march from India in 1827 to Russia in 1829 and later to Britain had created serious misgivings lest it should be transported to these western shores. To the end of preparing for such a contingency the Canadian Executive of Lower Canada published in October, 1831, a communication on the subject of cholera transmitted from the Colonial office in London. On its receipt a conference of physicians was called in Quebec to discuss the matter, with the result that the Government despatched M. Dr. Tessier to New York to there study the measures being adopted against the introduction of the disease.

The first Sanitary Commission instituted in Canada to deal with cholera was appointed in Quebec in February 1832, and was composed of Drs. Morrin, Parent and Perrault, and some months later a Board of Health was organized which adopted some quarantine and other regulations.

Though not appearing in epidemic form till June, the first cases of cholera arrived in the St. Lawrence on April 28th, 1832, and were landed at Grosse Isle from the ship, *Constantia*, from Limerick, having 170 emigrants of whom 29 had died on the voyage.

On May 14th the ship *Robert* from Cork arrived and had 10 deaths on the voyage.

On May 28th the ship *Elizabeth* from Dublin arrived with 145 emigrants and 42 deaths.

But the weather by June had grown warmer, and on June 3rd the ship *Carrick* from Dublin arrived having had 145 emigrants of whom 42 had died on the voyage.

This may be said to have been the beginning of the epidemic in Canada. The Grosse Isle station, having only been opened that spring, there were no conveniences, and no proper quarantine precautions. All who seemed well were allowed to pass up the St. Lawrence, disinfection was unknown, and hence all the soiled clothing of the emigrants was forwarded unwashed. Further there was constant intercourse between sailing and steam vessels westward to Montreal. It ascended the Richelieu and thence reached Lake Champlain and the Hudson.

By June 10th the disease had reached Montreal and spread rapidly to different parts of Lower and Upper Canada. It had disappeared by the middle of October, having lasted four months.

The discontent and famine in Ireland had caused an extensive emigration to American shores, and by September nearly 30,000 emigrants had come up the St. Lawrence.

Deaths amongst these people were so common from every cause, that no very special record was kept of those from cholera; but it is stated that in Quebec there occurred during this fatal summer 2,208 deaths from cholera alone, and that in Montreal 800 deaths occurred in the first fortnight and by September 1,843 had been slain by the disease.

In this brief history we have seen that some idea had been obtained of the necessity for preventing the introduction of cholera by establishing quarantine; but the results make apparent the ignorance of what was necessary to be done to attain such an end. . . .

On July 12th [1849], cholera was reported present in Toronto. The *Globe* of Saturday the 14th July, says: "The malady has appeared in our midst, but not to an alarming extent. We believe the best way is in all cases to tell the truth, the whole truth and nothing but the truth.

"As far as we have been able to learn the first case occurred on Friday of last week (July 6th), and during the intermediate days the following are believed to be an accurate report of the cases which have occurred.

	Cases	Deaths
On Scott street, 1 resident; 4 emigrants	5	2
On King street east, an emigrant	1	1
On March street, an emigrant family	5	3
On Queen street west, a carter	1	1
In Hospital, all emigrants	3	3
Emigrant shed	1	0
	16	10

"A cholera hospital will be opened today, and thanks to the activity of the Mayor every necessary precaution is being taken which the circumstances permit of."

On July 19th, Thursday, the same paper says: "There is some difference of opinion amongst the medical men whether Asiatic cholera is amongst us. Still the deaths are numerous whatever the disease."

On Wednesday, 8 a.m., the total number of new cases in the last 24 hours was 13, those previously reported being 66.

About this time Dr. Gavin Russell, Montreal, published a pamphlet "on the operation of physical agencies in the functions of organized bodies with suggestions as to the nature of cholera." His theory was that cholera is entirely occasioned by the absence or deficiency of electricity. Commenting on which the *Globe*'s sanitary editor sagely remarks, "It is a fact that thundery weather hinders butter making by causing an escape of electricity from the milk, and the same cause prevents the working of the electric telegraph."

As illustrating the changes in the newspaper barometer we quote the following from the *Globe* of July 26th, its heading is: "The Cholera—National Humiliation."

"Whatever be the natural causes employed to produce the disease, it must be regarded by every reflecting mind, as a scourge sent from the Almighty and having in it a voice calling loudly for humiliation and deep thought."

The extent and conditions attending this most serious outbreak were several years ago set forth in the records published in the Ontario Health Bulletin, 1884, and found at the end of this chapter, but the notes from various sources will be found of interest.

On July 24th the *Globe* gives the cases of cholera for the two previous days as 35 cases and 18 deaths. The next paragraph of news says: "Col. Alvah Mann's New York Broadway circus performed in this city on Friday and Saturday to crowded audiences."

The same issue of *Globe* says that the Local Board has issued a proclamation that all persons keeping pigs within the city and liberties will be fined £5.

A special order of July 25th of Central Board required local boards to have houses vacated when neglect to cleanse and crowding prevails.

The Local Board of London is recorded as having prohibited the sale of vegetable matters within the town during the prevalence of cholera.

Dr. Derry in charge of Toronto cholera hospital is referred to early in August as having resigned, his salary of $5 per diem being in his opinion wholly inadequate for the sacrifices of his private practice.

The Quebec *Mercury* has the following curious note. "Hearses and funeral carriages ply for hire in the streets of that city; a man has been seen standing with his death-carriage horsed and ready for use, the animal munching his oats and the driver on the look out for a fare."

On August 7th the Local Board of Montreal passed an order prohibiting all equestrian performances, concerts, etc., during the prevalence of the cholera. . . .

August 15th. The cases in Toronto reported to date 414, deaths 254.

August 16th. A newspaper note refers to the capture of Dr. Rolph's horse on the street at night, standing in front of a house while the Doctor was visiting a patient, by a city policeman, under an order of council prohibiting horses standing on streets at night. The Doctor had to pay 1s. 10½d. to get him out of the city pound. Complaints of imperfect records by the Board were frequently made and refuted about this time.

Montreal papers, August 24th, report a ship at Grosse Isle with typhus, 30 deaths in voyage and as many more cases landed.

In London, England, at this time cholera increased rapidly. In the last of August, 1,276 deaths occurred in a week.

The cholera was abating in Montreal by Sept. 5th. Sept. 11th the Toronto *Globe* states, we have still a few cases of cholera in the city. To date there have been 745 cases and 449 deaths.

By Sept. 22nd cholera had disappeared from Quebec, there having been 1,047 deaths there during the epidemic. . . .

With the advent of the autumn, cholera disappeared from the Province and did not reappear until 1854, its prevalence along the valley of the Mississippi and in Great Britain in 1848, made its re-appearance in 1849 to be feared, and the Province seems to have been fairly well prepared for it.

A proclamation establishing under the Act of 1849 a central Board of Health, is dated Quebec, 20th July, 1854, declaring said Act of 1849 to be in force in the Province, and to continue in force for and during the period of six calendar months. Signed *Elgin* and *Kincardine*.

Under it the Central Board issued Regulations dated at Quebec, 20th July.

They were contained in two chapters:

Chapter I contained general and personal directions to families and individuals and treated of (1) cleaning of premises, (2) keeping cellars clean and dry, (3) houses to be aired by chimney boards and stoppers being removed, (4) doors to be left open day and night, (5) bedding to be aired daily, (6) personal cleanliness by tepid bath two or three times weekly, (7) flannel vests to be worn next to skin, (8) general moderation in eating and drinking, diet light and nourishing, mainly of animal food, while fish and vegetables were to be used sparingly and green cooked vegetables, as peas, beans and cabbage to be avoided, (9) those who from principle objected to the use of spirituous or fermented drinks were recommended to take tea or toast water at meals, while those accustomed to use liquors were to use them in small quantities and of the best quality, (10) long fastings and late suppers to be carefully avoided, (11) soda water as a summer drink was recommended, (12) recommended that the sick should not be attended by more persons than absolutely necessary, thereby lessening crowding and so helping the patients while lessening the danger to the public, (13) warned the public against indiscriminate use of mineral waters and especially against the use of the many kinds of patent medicines so extensively employed, (14) recommended burning, baking and boiling of clothes, and 1 to 4 parts of chloride of lime, (15) advised against unnecessary alarm.

Successive sections advised Local Boards to pay special attention to unsound meat, to cellars, cesspools, privies, etc., stagnant pools, pig-pens, slaughter-houses and butcher stalls, skins, hides and tanneries.

Sec. XVII.—"And no interment shall be permitted within the walls of a church, or the limits of any city or town; crowding grave-yards was forbidden, and the opening of vaults having had recent interments was to be done with the utmost caution."

Undertakers, hotels and boarding-houses were most strictly regulated, and all burials were to be private and within 24 hours.

All ship captains had to report deaths on board, and Local Boards were requested to report weekly to the Central Board.

These precautions seem to have been fairly well observed, as the epidemic did not reach the proportions of previous ones.

The City of Hamilton, suffered, however, severely, a very notable number of deaths having occurred. On the 19th of July, 23 deaths occurred in Hamilton, while about the same time 56 deaths occurred daily in Montreal, while by 1st of August 832 deaths had occurred in Montreal. Domiciliary visits were then carried out regularly, and people under penalty were required to report cases. Cholera was very prevalent this year in St. John, New Brunswick.

On August 26th, 23 deaths occurred in Hamilton Hospital alone.

THE NEED FOR A WORKHOUSE IN MONTREAL

Montreal Transcript, March 2, 1843.

To the Editor of the MONTREAL TRANSCRIPT

SIR,—The attempt now being made to establish a House of Industry is very commendable. It is most astonishing that a permanent institution for the accomodation of the poor has not been in operation long ago, as nearly £2000 was left by Mr. Marteller, and other friends, for that purpose, more than twenty years ago. It is most devoutly hoped that those to whom those funds were entrusted, will exert themselves to see that they may be applied according to the design of the donors.

Can it be possible, that a city like Montreal, shall continue to allow the poor to wander from door to door seeking bread and clothing, when the labour of those destitute persons, if wisely directed, could feed and clothe them. It has been found in a neighbouring government, that the labour of the poor can furnish the necessary support; why not in Canada?

The house now occupied as the House of Industry must soon be given up for the use of emigrants, and unless an effort be made to provide other accomodations, the poor will be going about our streets begging, or stealing, as they formerly have done.

The vast importance of this object will excite the attention of all friends to the destitute. No time is to be lost. That ministers and magistrates may employ their influence in providing a house and farm for the poor of Montreal, is the prayer of

T. OSGOOD

Montreal, February 27, 1843.

THE VIRTUOUS POOR IN TORONTO

The *Globe* (Toronto), January 26, 1869.

POVERTY IN TORONTO.

———

A FEW HOURS AMONG THE VIRTUOUS POOR—SAD CASES OF INEVITABLE
MISERY AND WANT—CALL FOR SYMPATHY AND ASSISTANCE.

———

A walk among the poor people of a city with a policeman, and a walk with a City Missionary, are two very different things. The policeman delights in shewing poverty surrounded by vice and crime, and debasement in its lowest and most repulsive forms; the Missionary leads you into the lowly cottage, where, it is true, poverty like all armed men, has entered and taken possession; but where also some of the finer characteristics of humanity still linger, where virtue is not altogether eradicated, nor religion ignored and forgotten. . . .

"Honest Poverty" is a retiring thing, that "hangs the head," and seeks to hide itself from the world's gaze.

The strongest impression made on our minds that day was, that there is such a thing as "honest poverty." Many people don't believe this. Tell them of a poor family, struggling from day to day, with cold and hunger, and they will shake their heads and tell you that there must be something wrong somewhere. Describe to them the miserable condition of another family where the father, its only stay, is struck down with fever, and not even able to give his children a stove when they cry for bread; and they will discant to you on the improvident habits of the working classes and prove, or attempt to prove, that that man might have been worth money and ought to have saved something for a "rainy day,"—forgetting all the time that it has been an eternal shower with the poor mortal from the beginning, and that the great hope that has buoyed him up in the midst of his difficulties, has been that perhaps in the future was a "dry day" for him and his. Shew them a man with a naple's hat and a seedy coat, and they would as soon think of sending to the penitentiary for a clerk as admit him into their counting-house. Because vice produces poverty, it is illogically inferred that all poverty is the result of vice; and so poverty and vice are too generally looked upon as synonimous terms.

That a vast amount of honest poverty exists in the city at the present time, is a well known fact to everyone who has paid any attention to the subject. Hundreds, if not thousands, of men are out of employment, whose families are starving, and the great cry of these men is for "work"; but work they cannot get. Then, how many hideous and deserted women have we in our midst, struggling against penury? There was nothing struck us as much in the course of our visits as the sad case of many of these poor creatures. . . .

. . . [One] widow is supported by her daughter, who provides food for both, by making pants at 15 cents a pair. Let the young gentlemen who adorn King street of an afternoon, and the old gentlemen who rattle their silver in their pockets, seriously reflect on that fact.

Another is forced to send her boy, nine years of age, away, weeks at a time, on peddling excursions. . . .

In every instance amongst the widows, we found what is perhaps the best test of a woman's respectability—thoroughly clean houses. And what was more striking still, was the care almost every one had taken to ornament her humble abode. The walls, in some cases, were literally covered with adornments of various sorts. Pictorial tracts—illustrated temperance pledges—numbers of the "Workman"—valentines—cloth marks and newspaper advertisements, all entered into the list of their fine art collections; and one old lady, seemingly less fortunate in her collective faculties than the others, had taken the newspapers *holus bolus*, and utterly heedless of the aesthetic or the political, had papers of all sizes and political creeds, spread over her walls. . . .

In another house we found two immigrant families. The case of one of them might have been amusing, had it not been so sad. The wife, about four months ago, was a servant girl, who had saved upwards of a hundred dollars. She fell in love with a soldier, bought him off, and came to Canada along with him. The soldier, who has no trade, goes about the street shouldering, instead of the musket, a cross-cut saw; but somehow he cannot get any wood to cut; and the consequence is that he and his new-made wife have to live on love, or something as ethereal, for they had not a morsel of food in the house when we visited them. Love's labour lost is bad enough in a general way, but when it ends in such a universal bankruptcy as this, the case is very bad.

The case of the other family is still more sad. They arrived here in the month of August—since that time the husband has only earned eight dollars, is now in the hospital, and in all probability, will never come out of it alive. The wife and two children are thus left utterly destitute. Not a particle of food, not a morsel of fuel was in the house at the time of our visit, and as the mother, with haggard look and streaming eyes, took us to the bedside, and lifting a few rags showed us a little infant eight weeks old, dreaming little, poor thing, of the misery before it and around it. And when it woke up and cried for sustenance—little knowing of the sorrow and sadness that surcharged that breast in which it nestled—it seemed to us one of the most touching scenes of domestic misery we had ever looked upon.

CODDLING THE POOR

Daily Globe (Toronto), January 26, 1877.

HELP, BUT NOT PAUPERIZE

Toronto is in danger of becoming a centre to which all the poor of the Province gravitate. Every winter the number of outsiders who make demands upon the compassion of the charitable is increasing. From all sides they come, and every one has a more doleful story than his neighbour, with the refrain of no work to be had and no bread to eat. If this is encouraged as it has been for some time past by injudicious zeal and not over-enlightened benevolence, we shall be flooded by a large amount of sturdy and not over-deserving pauperism, which it is the interest and duty of everybody to fight against, not to foster and propagate. In the estimation of only too many who ought to know better, it seems to be a settled principle that every one who is at all necessitous ought to have everything made comfortable to his or her hand, whatever may have been the cause of destitution at first or of its continuance since. There is a feeling of maudlin pity which says, "They are ill off at any rate, though they may not be all they ought to be," and which proceeds to dispense to them in charity what ought to have been the result of personal industry and forethought. This is the case in scores of instances in Toronto alone at this present moment. There are only too many who have been earning from a dollar to a dollar and a half a day all summer, and who at the end of the season had not a farthing to fall back upon. We acknowledge that a dollar and a half is not a large sum; still it is a fact that many manage to live on it and owe no man anything. They may have to pinch and deny themselves many things they would like. Still they manage to make ends meet, and continue in the self-supporting class, while their circumstances teach them to be foreseeing and provident and self-denying to an extent and in ways they would not otherwise have thought of. Why should these —the better class in every way—have to do all this, while the drunken, the careless, and improvident are having a continual racket made about them, and are getting foolish men and women to cry out in indignation if they are not kept fully provided with the necessaries of life? It is not possible, and were it possible it would not be desirable, to remove the hardships and inconveniences of impecuniosity. To do so is to cut at the root of all that is excellent and estimable in character, to remove a chief stimulus to exertion, and to create and strengthen a spirit of wasteful improvidence and self-indulgent vice.

This is the danger with which we are at present threatened in Toronto, and if things go on as they are doing we shall in a short time have a large shiftless population with the true beggar's whine and the true pauper spirit, which is satisfied with bare existence if only it can be secured without personal exertion at the public expense. There are at this moment young married couples without children either getting weekly allowances from the House of Industry or clamouring personally or by their friends to be put on the list, though the husbands have had steady work all summer. In spite of the much-talked-of hard times, be it at the same time noticed, by the testimony of those who know the facts a great deal better than those who are raising the clamour, there has been more work for labouring men during the past summer than in some of the previous ones.

Yet, through outside pressure of unreasoning and mistaken kindness, there has already been distributed from the House of Industry more coal than has generally been sufficient for the whole winter. During the first twenty-two days of January there were given out nearly eleven hundred four pound loaves in outdoor relief, besides all that was given to casuals. The amount of rice, tea, oatmeal, and sugar has been very large, and if all the orders for these articles given by very excellent but somewhat impulsive ladies had been honoured, the establishment would by this time have been bankrupt. People are seeking relief who are no worse off than they have been any time during the last twenty years, but who have always managed to pull through, till they were advised to apply, as relief was to be had, and they might just as well as not get a share of what was going.

Is it wise, prudent, or Christian to foster such a spirit and spread such a state of things? To talk about hard-heartedness is a very cheap and easy proceeding. A very large proportion of both men and women who are the recipients of public bounty are notoriously dissipated. Though they are so, we do not advocate a system which would leave them to starve, but we do say that if they are ever to be taught economical and saving habits they must understand that the public have no idea of making them entirely comfortable in the midst of their improvidence and dissipation. If they wish to secure that they must work for it, and save and plan. Such comfort is not to be had by loafing round the tavern door, or fleeing to charity at every pinch. Too many think it is, and too many others encourage the notion. One would think that in hard times the whiskey shops would be the first to suffer. They are really the last, and a considerable proportion of their earnings comes from those who have adopted as their motto and their comfort, "The public is bound to support us." In the meantime it is not possible to lay too much emphasis on the absolute cruelty of people assisting, without enquiry, those who beg from door to door. It may appear kind to give such help. It is the very reverse. Let individuals help poor and industrious people—the aged, the young, the halt, the blind—to their utmost wish, but always so as to encourage rather than destroy that self-reliance and self-respect which are above all price. The whining beggars with their piteous stories of seven small children who have not eaten a morsel for two days, or who have, it seems, slept out of doors with the thermometer below zero, ought in any case to have a very long rope and a very short sentence, and should be dismissed without ceremony and without a copper.

THE PROBLEM OF THE IMMIGRANT POOR

Canada, Royal Commission on the Relations of Labor and Capital in Canada, 1889. Evidence—Ontario, pp. 159-61.

W.H. HOWLAND, Toronto, called and sworn.
    By Mr. FREED:
    Q.—You are Mayor of Toronto? A.—Yes.
    Q.—This is your second term in the mayor's chair? A.—Yes.
    Q.—You have been a resident of Toronto for a great many years? A.—32 or 33 years.
    Q.—As mayor, you come in contact with the poor of Toronto to a great extent? A.—Not only as mayor, but for the last eleven years I have been working among them as a matter of love, and I have a very considerable knowledge of their ways, their difficulties and circumstances.
    Q.—Are there large numbers of people in Toronto requiring assistance? A.—They require assistance from only two causes as a general rule, excepting extreme cases of misfortune, or cases where widows are left with large families. The first cause is, of course, drinking, and the second cause is the sending out to this country of people who are unsuited to make a living here—the sending out of great numbers of people who have got the poor-house taint, and who never will work or do any good anywhere.
    Q.—By whom are these people sent out? A.—They are sent out in various ways. Up to the last two or three years our government machinery was very largely used for the purposes of relieving the poor-houses—not with their consent, but their machinery was perverted from its original intention and used in that way. Then, colonies have been sent, out from time to time, with the kind intention of helping people in different districts. For instance there was a colony of a poor class sent out from some of the towns in Ireland some years ago; they are nearly all to be traced here at the present time, and to a large extent they have remained a charge on the people of this country.
    Q.—Would you rather give us a narrative respecting these people, or have us ask questions? A.—Just according to your judgment.
    Q.—Then perhaps you had better give us a narrative? A.—As a visitor of the House of Industry, I kept coming across a class of people from a certain place in Ireland; they were thoroughly unsuited for this country; they had been under the poor-house system very largely; they were demoralized, and all the spring was taken out of them for honest or faithful work. In the same way there has been progressing for sometime an immigration from England from the different poor-house Unions. You can trace them in particular streets; you come across a family at one time, sent out

by certain poor-houses, or given means to come out. I have met several cases of that kind. For instance in East London they are now sending out families, and you cannot help being sorry for them, because they sent out people with large families—eight or nine children, and sometimes more. It makes you feel that the children might have a chance, but the parents are unsuitable; having no courage, or pluck, or hope, they drop at once into the old habit of depending on chance work or assistance. They had been so much in the habit of getting help from others that they do not think of being able to help themselves; in fact they are a helpless immigration. In a great many cases they are chosen with some judgment as far as personal habits are concerned; many of those East London people that I have met with are not dissipated people, but they are corrupted with the poor-house character.

Q.—They don't know how to help themselves?   A.—They have not got any spirit; they are absolutely helpless.

Q.—Admitting this to be an evil can you suggest anything?   A.—I think we should adopt the American principle, which would prevent them being sent. I think we should stop helpless people who are going to suffer—stop them at the border. In this country the climate produces more suffering than in the old country, and I don't think it is fair to send out to us people, known to be paupers, and that we cannot make men of. I should be sorry to limit a class of immigration of which there was any chance or hope—such as young men, or those children that Dr. Barnardo and others are training. It is very wonderful how such as these fit themselves to the country and become a good population.

Q.—Is that remark made from your own observation?   A.—It is from my observation and from the evidence in the books of the agencies. And, mind you, many are sent out by the poor-law Union who have nobody to look after them, and I think that that is a very poor and wicked way of sending them out. They are sent out; somebody agrees to find them a place; they are put into a place, but if they are not well placed they drift back to the street. Some of them do well, but it is a wickedness and a hardship to send them out in this way. But when they take the children and train them a year or more in England and get them into regular habits, clothe them properly and bring them out and put them in the hands of their own agents who place them in carefully selected farm houses where they are visited regularly by the agent, and in case of the child not being suited he can be taken back to the home and then sent out again, and even in cases of extreme unsuitability can be sent back to the old country—it seems to me that that immigration is a valuable immigration.

Q.—That is the immigration of which I have been afraid and I am much pleased to hear a better account of it than I feared we would get from you?   A.—I might suggest to the Commission that they should make enquiry of these agents. There are a number of these institutions in London, such as Dr. Barnardo's and others, and there is one old philanthropic institution which has been sending out people for twelve or thirteen years, although nobody hears anything about it. Their reports from Canada are almost always favorable; and I think there is also a Scotch one besides the one at Belleville. As to the Scotch homes I forget the name of the gentleman who manages them; you don't often hear his name, but he manages them very carefully and brings out hundreds and places them with farmers. There is a Roman Catholic system which is very well managed and has its head quarters in Hamilton. I have not come across, in working amongst the children in Toronto, but one boy so far in connection with any work that we have had here that was on the street; that is of boys who came through these agencies. I came across those who are sent out by the poor-law Unions; they have some agent to find the first place and then that is the end of it, and I believe there are some places in which children have been really turned out on the street. I cannot prove it, but I have strong suspicions of it.

Q.—Are not the agents of these homes interested in sending favorable reports? A.—Well, get the books; they cannot cook the books. I think I know every boy in the city who is not in very good shape; they come to me, or I see them somewhere.

Q.—Do you believe in the law of heredity? A.—I am not entirely a believer in it, though, of course I believe it affects them physically. But my experience with children is that if they are taken at the right time they can be saved from crime. That is the way you can get them. Of course there are exceptions to everything, but I am speaking of the general principle, and my experience with children has been exceedingly favorable, when they are taken and handled in anything like a careful, kindly and intelligent way. I do not believe it is necessary that any child should be a criminal as a child; and if you get a child up to seventeen or eighteen in a good line the chances are strongly in favor of his getting on.

Q.—You think that, setting aside the higher law of humanity and putting it on the narrow ground of the good of the country, this immigration of the boys of whom we are now speaking is good? A.—I do. I tell you another thing about these children: it is the general estimation that they are children taken altogether out of bad homes, but that is not the case. In a country densely populated like the Old Country there is an immense class of people who, from age, poverty or the death of the bread-winner, are very poor and miserable, but who are perfectly respectable, and the children are right down at that point that they become part of the miserable poorhouse class unless they are dealt with. Now, a large proportion of the children taken charge of in these homes are of this class, and I think many of them are the finest children I ever saw in my life—children who have come out in that way. You find that the majority of these children are very much liked in the homes they come to in this country; I know that the people get very fond of them. I forgot to mention Miss McPherson's Home at Stratford.

Q.—And Miss Rye's? A.—Miss Rye's, I think, is for girls; but I think Miss MacPherson's is for boys. If you have a session at Belleville and Stratford, go right into the places where they have been working a long time and summon the farmers in the neighborhood; I think it would be a good thing. I have not done that myself; I have only met particular cases; but that is my judgment, as far as I have had opportunities of learning.

Q.—Have you anything further to add on that point? A.—There is another class. It often happens in the Old Country when a man is getting a little past work, when he begins to be a little bit of a charge, though he may never have been on the poor list; but he is not quite so able to make his living—people of this class are helped out to this country by private funds. This class are more helpless still. I do not say that we have any right absolutely to exclude anybody that can make a living, but, at the same time, this is a hard country for helpless people for physical and other reasons, and they should not come here; it is more cruel to bring them here than to leave them.

Q.—You think it is not right to load us with the paupers of other countries? A.—Yes; and, besides, in this country they are far more helpless and suffer more than at home, because of our climate.

Q.—It is an injury to the people and a wrong to us? A.—Certainly; the economic feature of it does not require discussion, I think.

CHARITY IN TORONTO

House of Industry, Toronto. *Annual Reports* (1857), pp. 3, 7-10; (1877), pp. 3-6; (1886), pp. 6-9; (1895), p. 9.

1857
In bringing the toils and anxieties of another year to a close, the Directors of the Toronto House of Industry rejoice in being able to review the past with pleasure and satisfaction.

Under the protection and assistance of a kind and gracious Providence, they have been enabled, notwithstanding the high price paid for wood and provisions, to relieve the squalid wretchedness, and extend the hand of mercy to upwards of 3,000 of our suffering fellow creatures who cried to them for help.

The operations of the year have been marked with great harmony and mutual goodwill. All points of friction have been so entirely removed, that the clergy of the different churches, assisted by their lay friends, have been enabled to co-operate, in the most combined and pleasing manner, for the general good. While the Directors would present their very sincere thanks to their friends and patrons for the liberal support extended to this charity, they also feel that they may cordially congratulate you upon the vast amount of good effected. Every year's experience but deepens their conviction of the importance of the institution, and every month develops new claims upon your benevolence, and brings increasing evidence of success. By your timely aid you have warmed the cold limbs of the feeble and destitute, who were perishing in their dreary abodes—fed the hungry—clothed the naked—healed the sick, and administered to the relief of the destitute and the dying. Without presumption, therefore, may you adopt the language of the benevolent Job and say—"When the ear heard me then it blessed me; when the eye saw me it gave witness unto me, because I delivered the poor that cried and the fatherless, and him that had none to help him. The blessings of him that was ready to perish came upon me, and I caused the widow's heart to sing for joy. . . ."

But the benevolence of the Board is by no means confined to the inmates of the House. There are many indigent families in all parts of the city who are feebly contending against the pinching hand of poverty, who cannot, and for many good reasons should not, break their family ties, and be removed to the wards of the House. These must be looked after at their own homes; and you will be glad to learn that no less than 200 cords of wood, and 3,176 loaves of bread have been distributed to them during the year.

The Directors are anxious, as far as the interests of the poor will admit, to discourage the very common, and in too many cases, very objectionable practice of street begging—a practice as unpleasant to the industrious and worthy receiver, as it is disagreeable to the benevolent and kind-hearted giver. If all who call at your door for alms were real objects of charity, as many of them doubtless are from adverse circumstances, it would be a pleasure for the Christian to relieve their distress; but the thought that many idle impostors, destitute alike of honesty and truth, are in the habit of thus appealing to the benevolent for very unworthy purposes, is a great drawback upon that pleasure. In the operations of this institution every precaution is taken to prevent such imposition. Doubtful cases are examined into, and improper recipients struck off the lists. Let the "Industrial Farm" be at once put in successful operation, and let the citizens of Toronto contribute to the support of your funds, "every man according to his ability," and this desirable object may soon be accomplished.

1877
The Trustees and Managers of the House of Industry beg to present, in

accordance with the Act of Incorporation, their Annual Report. The amount of relief granted during the years 1875 and 1876 was exceptionally large, but the quantity thus far distributed this season is still more so. The increase may be attributed partly to the extreme commercial depression which has existed for some time past, and partly to an influx of applicants from the outlying municipalities and the neighbouring Republic.

Cities, like individuals, must pay the penalty of their prosperity; if they do not directly generate poverty, they serve in a great measure to attract it. In the opinion of the Trustees, every municipality should be obliged by law to maintain its own poor. The enactment to this effect now on the Statute book is merely permissive; to be of any avail it should be made compulsory. Poor houses, prisons, and penitentiaries seem to be indispensable concomitants of modern civilization; our prisons and penitentiaries cannot be surpassed by those of any country; our poor houses are yet to be developed. In these days of progress when "many run to and fro, and knowledge is multiplied," people have become, to a great extent, cosmopolitan. Canada must not be outstripped in the race of nations; other countries make legal provision for the poor, and it really seems that we too will, from sheer necessity, soon be driven to adopt similar measures.

To obviate complaints that have sometimes been made of delay in the reception of relief, the number of visitors has been increased to thirty and the city divided into as many districts; blank reference cards with lists of the visitors and their respective districts are furnished to subscribers, who have thus a guarantee that the case of any applicant for assistance referred by them to a visitor, will receive prompt and due attention. Many of the gentlemen who have kindly undertaken the duty of visitor have had no previous experience; most of them are not even members of the Board; the movement is altogether experimental, and its issue is awaited with much interest by the Trustees. That means of relief may be more readily accessible to the suffering portion of the community, arrangements are being effected for the distribution of bread at two centres, in addition to the House; one in the eastern, the other in the western section of the city. Provision has also been made for the temporary reception elsewhere, of such casuals as for want of room cannot be accommodated in the outbuilding. The soup kitchen has been in active operation since the 1st inst.; soup is distributed daily (Sundays excepted), free of charge, to all applicants, between the hours of twelve and one, the daily distribution thus far averaging 170 gallons. . . .

Every visitor of experience must occasionally have found families of small children, whose parents, from various causes, were undeserving relief. In such cases his position is painful; if he withhold assistance the children suffer; if he allow it, it will almost surely be misapplied. Could not some way be devised to separate such children from such parents?

The latter are apparently irreclaimable, but the former, by judicious interference, might be saved. The question is a delicate one: who can solve it?

1886

The number of inmates in the House gives no idea of the work done by it.
The great work is the out-door relief, and the temporary assistance to
that class known heretofore as the tramp. The inmates are chiefly old and
infirm people. The retired pensioner takes kindly to our Institution, and
the managers feel that they have discovered the method of taking care of
those who in their time were the guardians of the Empire.

The OUTDOOR RELIEF is managed by a reference to the reports of visitors
who have certain sections as their territory. The city is divided into 34
districts, and every case of poverty is referred in the first instance to these
visitors. Their report goes to the extent of relief in bread, wood, or coal;
and where there is sickness in the family, of a small allowance of groceries. The reports in printed forms, come up for consideration every Tuesday and Friday before a committee appointed for that purpose, who
consider the case and learn, if necessary, further particulars from the
persons applying. This process of reporting and considering continues
during the whole year, but as may be expected, it is chiefly confined to the
winter months. Some idea can be had of the work done in this way, when
we state that it is not unusual for the Committee (three of the managers)
to dispense relief to 70 or 80 families in one day, and to sit here from
9.30 in the morning to 5.30 in the evening for that purpose.

This method of VISITING is the best that occurs to the managers, though
they are quite certain that imposition will last as long as charity lasts.
They have acted in the belief that it is better to be imposed upon at times
than to refuse relief to a person who may really be an impostor. The
rule is to give the applicant the benefit of the doubt. In the beginning of
the season the Secretary, at the instance of the Board, issued the following
circular:

> The duly appointed Visitors of the House shall have power to
> grant relief to applicants in their respective Districts to the extent
> only of 600 lbs. of coal, or quarter cord of wood, and a weekly
> allowance of bread in the proportion of 2 lbs. for each adult or
> child belonging to the family of such applicant, on their being
> satisfied that immediate relief is necessary; also, in cases of sick-
> ness, the usual allowance of groceries.
>
> Immediately on visiting a case, it shall be the duty of the Visitor
> to mail to the Superintendent of the House the usual detailed
> report, together with his reasons for granting such relief; and
> stating the quantity of fuel and bread to be allowed.

Your managers' suggestions of last year, as to the more speedy distribution of relief by delivering bread at several points in the city has

hitherto proved impracticable. They hope, however, to overcome all obstacles, and will make another effort in this direction.

TRAMPS

The other class who are a heavy drain on the resources of the House are those casual poor who seek shelter for the night and a meal in the morning. These number in the winter months on an average about 70 every night, and it was found desirable at one time to limit the number of nights in succession during which they could claim relief. Four nights were thought long enough, and afterwards a rule was made that cases for a longer period should be reserved to the Weekly Committee. This also has been found impracticable, as there is not a committee for every day in the week, and the result is, that the admission of tramps is and must necessarily be left to the judgment of the Superintendent.

Those unfortunates who have no home, many of whom are professional beggars, are a great problem in every city in America. The labour test that appeared to work well elsewhere, was put in force here in the early part of this year, but was subsequently abandoned. The report of the

COMPARATIVE STATEMENT OF THE ASSISTANCE AFFORDED TO THE POOR
BY THE HOUSE OF INDUSTRY, TORONTO, FROM 1837 TO 1857, INCLUSIVE.

| | Average Number in the House | | | | | | Wood Account | |
| | | | | | Out-door | Total | No. of Childr'n placed | To the | Con- sumed in the |
Year	Men	Women	Childr'n	Total	Poor	Relieved	out	Poor	House
1837 and 1838	4	12	26	42	864	906	54	40	90
1839	6	13	29	48	633	681	28	30	80
1840	7	12	27	46	610	656	16	32	78
1841	3	14	27	44	595	639	15	36	79
1842	7	13	27	47	752	799	18	40	90
1843	8	12	12	32	1,258	1,290	19	116	94
1844	6	10	10	26	1,029	1,029	17	124	63
1845	10	7	7	24	476	500	10	40	52
1846	12	7	5	24	676	700	11	65	57
1847	13	8	9	30	570	600	15	60	60
1848	12	9	12	33	807	849	18	60	40
1849	12	10	13	35	551	586	26	78	70
1850	12	9	18	40	804	844	23	60	50
1851	31	18	27	56	804	896	30	123	40
1852	24	23	35	81	2,760	2,841	23	172	80
1853	34	26	30	90	2,525	2,615	20	184	90
1854	38	34	18	90	1,404	2,999	16	300	90
1855	36	32	24	92	1,181	3,102	14	264	72
1856	36	37	35	108	909	2,526	20	231	68
1857	47	38	35	120	1,232	3,850	10	250	80

Committee who looked into this is brief, but it is founded on good reasons.

They "recommended temporary discontinuance of the test owing to difficulty in disposing of the wood, and other causes."

The increasing number of tramps at the office of the Mayor rendered it desirable to have a daily report of such cases sent to him. This has been attended to, and the Superintendent's experience on this point is, that parties present themselves at the City Hall in the hopes of getting more than they would get through the regular visitor of the House. It seems that those who present themselves in that way are not persons who are easily visited, and it may be reported generally that the Mayor's suggestion has worked well.

RELIEF AFFORDED AND NUMBER OF POOR
ASSISTED DURING THE YEAR 1877

Average number in the House		91
In on 1st January, 1875	89	
Admitted since	96	
		185
Discharged, 88; died, 9	97	
In the house 1st January, 1878	88	
		185
Of which are blind men	6	
Do. do. women	1	
Cripples	33	
Others	44	
Children	4	
		88
Average number in building for casual poor during the winter months, per night	30	

Out-door Poor

1,020 families—699 men, 1,003 women, 2,440 children, averaging over 4 in each family	4,112	
Temporarily relieved out-door	327	
Total relieved (exclusive of inmates) . .		4,469
Number of 4 lbs. loaves distributed to out-door pensioners	29,512	
To temporary poor out-door	463	
		29,975

Deaths in the House

8 men, 1 women—total	9

Soup given out during the winter months, 170 gallons per day. Disbursements to sick families, 277 lbs. tea; 1,043 lbs. sugar; 2,880 lbs. rice; 2,080 lbs. oatmeal.

Statement of Coal Account for 1876

Sold at half-price	4	tons.
Consumed in the house	80	"
Delivered to the poor	496	"
and 600 bushels coke.		
Total	580	"

EXPENSE OF CASUAL WARD FROM 1ST APRIL, 1894, TO 1ST APRIL, 1895.

Bread, 7,851 Loaves	$549.57
Coal, 60 Tons	294.00
Salaries	410.00
Tea, Sugar, Butter, Soup, etc.	417.04
Gas and Water Rates	164.51
Hardware, Soap, Sulphur, Lime, etc.	115.91
Camp Beds, Blankets and Dry Goods	115.10
Plumbing and Furnace Repairs	52.93
Boiler Inspection and Engineer	9.00
Sundries	9.50
Total	$2,137.56

LABOUR TEST

Worked	8,367
Refused	181
Incapable	708
Allowed to leave without working	1,029
Sundays and non-working days	290
	10,575 men

RECAPITULATION

	1889-90	1890-1	1891-2	1892-3	1893-4
Men Casuals in Wards	7,018	9,147	7,235	6,327	7,537
Worked	4,250	5,797	5,288	4,679	5,345
Refused to work	264	59	51	34	107
Incapables	363	292	241	268	461
Allowed to leave without working	1,513	808	446	571	726
Sundays, holidays, etc.	628	2,191	1,209	775	898
	7,018	9,147	7,235	6,327	7,537

Infants' Home and Infirmary, Toronto. *Annual Report* (1892), pp. 6-9, 17-18.

When listening to the stories told by applicants for admission to the Home, it would be impossible for even the most careless person not to realize that in this city of Toronto there is a vast field for philanthropic and elevating agencies. Want of moral restraint, the great ease with which alcoholic drink may be procured, the scarcity of regular employment, the low wages paid by shops, and the preference shown by young girls for factory labour, instead of entering domestic service, all these causes tend to produce a most unsatisfactory condition of affairs, most difficult to deal with, and well nigh impossible to improve; therefore so long as these evils exist, we shall hear the same stories, and the necessity will always be with us of providing a harbour of refuge, where the destitute wife or wayward girl may find shelter for the present, and take courage to face her future burden of life. The crimes of infanticide and child desertion have greatly decreased of late years; not, we are sorry to say, because people are living higher and purer lives, but for the reason that the various "homes" act as a description of prevention; these crimes being the usual outcome of friendlessness and despair. Ill treatment of infants on the baby farming system, under proper management, is greatly lessened. Owing to the improved legislative precautions, persons desiring to take infants to board, must apply for a certificate or licence.

This care for infants is entirely due to the action taken by the Infants' Home Managers in 1887, in petitioning the government and the city on the matter. Each infant life lost to this country by neglect, is a very much more serious matter than appears to the careless observer. All students of ancient history, and all professors of political economy, will tell you that those countries where infant life and training are considered, have been the foremost among nations. As an institution aiming at these first principles, the Infants' Home Managers feel that, notwithstanding the adverse criticisms cast upon their work by unthinking persons, the fruit of their arduous labours can never be in any instance wholly lost. Could we but trace the future career of the children sent out from our sheltering care, doubtless we should find that our country has greatly benefited by the men and women whose early lives have been developed under the love and care bestowed upon them in the Infants' Home. The protection of infants is part, but only part, of our work. "Let him that is without sin cast the first stone at her," was said in the past by our Divine Lord; and the words are as clear and decided to-day as in the time of old. Are we to gather our skirts and pass by on the other side, when we come in contact with a woman—far too often a child woman— who has been cruelly wronged? A thousand times no. The Managers of the Infants' Home, careful to guard against wilful known sin, open their institution to protect from themselves, and carefully watch over those weak, but far too often, much wronged fellow women who can be induced to accept the shelter offered. "Prevention is better than cure," is an old and very true proverb; give our adult inmates an opportunity to reflect over the past; also time to love and care for their helpless charges, and in almost every instance we find they leave our Home with true motherly love in their hearts, and with a strong determination to lead a new life. "Gone to service, taking her child with her;" "Gone home with her child to friends," is the usual record against our mother nurses. . . .

We are now entering upon our eighteenth year of work, during this period we have admitted and cared for 957 women, and 2,244 children, at a cost of $79,534. . . .

LADIES. The report of the Physicians of the Infants' Home and Infirmary for the year ending September 30th, 1892, presents a few somewhat unusual considerations.

The total number of admissions during the year was one hundred and ninety-six infants and twenty-nine mother nurses. This would appear to be an unusually large number considering that the Home was practically closed for about four months; but it must be borne in mind that those inmates who were sent to the Isolation Hospital during the epidemic of diphtheria, were necessarily re-entered on the books on their return from that institution, and thus the number of admissions rather over-represents the number of cases which have been treated in the Home.

The total number of deaths occurring during the year was forty-three, or twenty-two per cent. These deaths all occurred among the infants. Bearing in mind the fact that the Home during the past year sustained a most severe and deplorable epidemic of diphtheria, the smallness of the percentage of deaths may excite some surprise. The fact must not be lost sight of, however, that most of the deaths from this disease occurred in the Isolation Hospital, and consequently will properly appear on the records of that institution. The deaths from this cause being thus practically eliminated, twenty-two per cent. may be taken as representing the mortality in the Home during the past year from such diseases as may be expected to occur during an average year among children of all classes. Keeping in view the fact that most of the children when admitted, are in a very low state of health, and that others are far advanced in disease, we submit that the above figures represent in a very favourable light the work being done in the Home.

Industrial Room, Toronto Relief Society. *Annual Report* (1889), pp. 3-7.

The Industrial Room was opened in 1883; the convenor and a few other ladies deeply interested in the difficult question of helping the poor of our city, had come to the conclusion that the only true way to do so was by supplying them with work, for which a fair and right price would be paid, thus they would be enabled to retain their own independence and self-respect and prove to those from whom they asked assistance that their case was either one of worthlessness or misfortune. As several of these ladies belonged to the Relief Society the question was brought up before this Society, they kindly responded and then decided to take the Industrial Room as a branch of their own work. A Committee was formed, consisting of Convenor, Treasurer, Secretary and a representative from each Division, the Society loaning the Committee $100 to begin their new work.

For the first winter the Committee met in two small rooms on Breadalbane Street, where every week the Convenor, Miss Stark, and her Committee worked most earnestly trying to supply each applicant with sewing or knitting. Only those who were constantly at these weekly meetings can appreciate their zeal and fully understand the efforts they made. From that time the work has gone on steadily increasing; for the last three years we have rented a room in the Girls' Institute, corner Richmond and Sheppard Streets.

To those to whom the Industrial Room is new a short account of the way the work is carried on may be interesting.

The cutting out and preparing the work is of great importance; each department is undertaken by one of the committee who does all the cutting at her own home, sending the articles to the room ready to be entered in the books and then given to the women. For instance, the cutting of the night shirts is the work of one lady, the aprons of one or two others, two or three devote themselves to the children's clothing and so on through the list of articles, each lady being at the room on Thursdays to superintend the giving out of and to inspect the work as it is brought in. This certainly involves an immense amount of labor on the part of these ladies but it has been found more satisfactory than any plan we have yet tried. By and bye we hope to have a paid matron who will be at the room all the time to sell or to take orders, and who will be able to do, at all events a greater part of the cutting out. An applicant coming for work for the first time must bring a voucher or note from a member of the Relief Society, or from some reliable person known to one of the Committee, saying that the bearer is known to them, or has been visited and is in need of work.

On Thursday the women arrive very early, many being there before 9 o'clock. At 9.30 the business of the day commences. Each woman has a number given to her as she arrives, and comes up in her turn, her work is examined, she is paid for it in money, receives her work for the next week, and goes away to make room for others. In the waiting room the women are kept busy in various ways, sometimes earning a little extra by cutting and sewing the clippings of the cotton, which at the end of the season are woven into carpetings and sold. Two or three of the Committee devote themselves to this part of the work, and are always in the waiting room ready with kind words and good advice. Sometimes also they have a little music or an address, and each woman in the room at noon has a bowl of soup given to her. This they thoroughly enjoy, as many of them have had a long walk. In many cases the distance they had to come was so great and the amount received so small that it seemed as if they might think it hardly worth while to come, but the gratitude expressed by many prove that they were only too glad to get the work to do, and amply repaid the Committee for the trouble and hard work they had undergone. In some cases work was taken to the women by members of the Committee, and in the eleventh Division the representative had the work sent to her depository and given out from there.

During the winter 154 have obtained work from the Rooms, between 70 and 80 weekly, but of these 100 have not applied for work more than four times during the 9 weeks that the rooms were opened. This year the season was a little shorter than usual. Generally work is given out from January to April, as these are the months most trying for the poor.

As we aim at giving each one work to the amount of from 50 to 75 cents per week, it will readily be understood how rapidly the stock accumulates. As will be seen by the treasurer's statement, $214.60 worth of clothing was sold at the Rooms during the year, not including special sales, notwithstanding which there was $1,100 worth of clothing on hand for our sixth annual sale, which was held at Association Hall on the 27th, 28th and 29th of March last. The proceeds of these sales go to carry on next winter's work, to buy material, pay the women, etc., etc.

The improvement in sewing, and also in cleanliness is most noticeable and very encouraging, and the number of unsaleable articles wonderfully small considering that no one applying is refused work, no matter how small her knowledge of sewing may be.

The Committee would also like to be able to give the women more work each week, as 50 or 75 cents is a very small amount, but until the public more fully realize the importance of this work and come to our assistance by purchasing these garments when made, we are unable to do more.

Although a large part of the underclothing is of finer material, there is a great deal of factory cotton suitable for Hospitals, Homes, North-west Missions, and for giving to the poor, and we heartily recommend it to the charitably disposed, begging them to consider that by seconding our efforts in this way they are not only sending clothing where it will be thankfully received, but will enable us to extend our branch of the work.

THE PROBLEM OF THE CHILD

J.J. Kelso, 'Neglected and Friendless Children'. *The Canadian Magazine*, II, 1894, 213-16.

In this latter part of the nineteenth century, more attention is being paid to the causes and sources of crime than ever before. Every day it is becoming more evident that in the past, much effort has been wasted in dealing with effects rather than causes, and the most advanced thinkers now fully acknowledge that to effectively grapple with crime and vice, thought and effort must be concentrated on the children of the poor. The governing power must come to regard the child as a future citizen, and must see that it has opportunities for education and for development along the lines of industry and morality. A child's education begins from its earliest infancy, and the State has a right to insist that its training shall be such as to fit it ultimately for the proper discharge of its duties and responsibilities. We all know the difficulties experienced in influencing for good the inmates of reformatories and penal institutions, the years of labor that have been exhausted in seeking to break the chains that bind the drunkard. How much more hopeful the outlook when we deal at once and directly with the little children, and implant in their young minds aims and aspirations that shall carry them safely through life!

Very little thought has been given to these children. They have been neglected by parents, neglected by lawmakers, neglected by school boards, and only thought of by the faithful mission-worker, who, in the absence of suitable laws, and the lack of public recognition, could accomplish but little of a permanent character. It would not be too much to say that seventy-five per cent. of the criminals of to-day were made such in early childhood. It is true that occasionally a young man of good family and occupying a position of trust gives way to temptation and falls to the criminal ranks, but he seldom remains there, usually returning after a short time to law-abiding citizenship.

The habitual criminal is made such in childhood, and he continues to live by crime, not voluntarily so much as necessarily. His actions indicate the early training working to its logical conclusion. There are children on our streets at this moment who will almost surely be criminals. It is their hard and cruel fate. They are consigned to it by neglectful and vicious parents, and by the indifference and shortsightedness of the community, through its authorized representatives.

Are we justified in expecting otherwise than that evil training shall bear evil fruit?

Consider the case of a child born of drunken and degraded parents, growing up in a hot-bed of vice; hearing nothing but profanity and obscenity; learning nothing of the difference between right and wrong; no prayer whispered over its cradle; no pure thoughts of a better life instilled into its budding mind; its playground the street; its companions equally benighted with itself. It cannot attend school; it has no clothes; it is not kept clean; the mother would not take the trouble to send it, and school boards are not always sufficiently interested to provide accommodation and enforce attendance. Growing up untrained, except in evil and sharp cunning ways, the child at seven or eight years of age is sent out to sell papers or to beg, sometimes to steal, on the streets constantly, and with companions older in vice than himself. The boy learns rapidly, until at fifteen or sixteen he becomes a thief when opportunity offers, and trusts to luck to escape detection and retain freedom.

With the girl the downward course is somewhat different, though the result is essentially the same. Escape from the family quarrels and squalor is sought on the streets, where vice is easily learned, and the road to comfort and luxury made to appear comparatively easy, until by stages she sinks into a common outcast, unpitied and unloved.

Thus are the ranks of the criminal classes supplemented, and thus is perpetuated the curse of evil that stands as a constant menace to life and property, and continues to hold over every community a sense of insecurity. And where, we may well ask, lies the blame for this state of things? Not with the helpless victim of untoward circumstances, but with the parents, and with the community which failed to step in when the parents proved false to their duty.

In proposing a remedy, the first essential is education. Not education in the narrow sense of mere intellectual instruction; but education which cultivates the heart and the moral nature, which inculcates truthfulness and gentleness and modesty and calls out the purest and noblest instincts of humanity. In providing such an education it may, and often will, be necessary to remove the child from its natural parents. In this enlightened age, it is a recognized principle that no man or woman has a right to train a child in vice, or debar it from opportunities for acquiring pure and honest habits; and if parents are not doing justly by their children, they forfeit their right to continued guardianship. This principle is now a legal enactment in almost every Christian land, and it is only in the careful yet unfaltering use of this power, that we can hope for a noticeable reduction in our prison population. It is a duty we owe to ourselves; it is far more a duty we owe to the children who are thus unfortunately placed. Every resource of the law should be exercised to compel such parents to pay for the education of the children removed from their control.

For the protection of the child the removal is made; for the protection of the community, the unworthy parent should be compelled to pay to the last farthing. For all such children real homes should be sought, where they may develop naturally, and grow up in common with all other children. An institution is not a home, and never can be made such, though it may be useful as a temporary abode in which to prepare the little one for the family circle. No child should be kept permanently in an institution, however good, and this is something that cannot be too frequently pointed out, since there are orphanages that retain children for periods of from five to ten years. . . .

All successful work on behalf of neglected children must be through personal contact and sympathy. The child must feel and know by many acts and words of encouragement and kindness that he or she has at least one true friend. For this reason large classes are to be avoided, the economy that appears on the surface being really a loss and hindrance. In this thought there should be much encouragement for those earnest workers who have nothing but their services to offer. They may gather little bands around them at trifling expense, and experience the great joy of turning aimless young lives into spheres of usefulness and happiness. And surely there can be no greater service for God or humanity than in calling forth in young hearts, aspirations and hopes that lie dormant, and in removing from their path the obstacles that prevent them from achieving all that is best in their nature! Hope and joy may be brought back to crushed little hearts by love and sympathy, and if, through the reading of this article, some friendless child is gladdened and aided along life's journey, it will not have been written in vain.

AMUSEMENTS IN THE MARITIMES

J. MacGregor, *Historical and Descriptive Sketches of the Maritime Colonies of British America* (Longman, Rees, Orme Brown, and Green, 1828), pp. 67-8, 73-4.

The ice at different periods during winter offers frequent opportunities for skating, to those who delight in that amusement. Shooting and fishing are other sources of pleasure, and annual races, near Charlotte Town, are now likely to become permanent. A public subscription library, on a liberal and respectable footing, affords either to those who read for amusement, or who wish to keep pace with the growing intelligence of the world, a variety of entertaining and standard works. As the expense of keeping a horse is trifling, almost every housekeeper has one. During winter it is a favorite amusement of all classes to drive out in a cabriolle, a very comfortable open carriage, set on runners, which slip easily and rapidly over the snow or ice. . . .

The amusements of the farmers and other inhabitants settled in different parts of the island are much the same as they have been accustomed to before leaving the countries they came from. Dances on many occasions are common, families visit each other at Christmas and new year's day, and almost all that is peculiar to Scotland at the season of "Halloween" is repeated here. Among the young men, feats of running, leaping, and gymnastic exercises are common; but that which they most delight in is galloping up and down the country on horseback. Indeed many of the farmers' sons who could make a certain livelihood by steady labour, acquire a spirit for bargain-making, dealing in horses, timber, old watches, &c. in order to become what they consider (by being idle) gentlemen: those who lead this course of life seldom do any good, and generally turn out lazy, drunken, dishonest vagabonds.

The term *frolic* is peculiar, I believe, to America, in the different senses in which it is there used. If a *good wife* has a quantity of wool or flax to spin, she invites as many of her neighbours as the house can well accommodate; some bring their spinning wheels, others their cards; they remain all day at work, and after drinking abundance of tea, either go home or remain to dance for some part of the night: this is called a spinning frolic. They are on these occasions as well as at other frolics, joined by the young men of the settlement, and in this way many of their love matches are made up. When a farmer or new settler wants a piece of wood cut down, he procures a few gallons of rum to drink on the occasion, and sends for his neighbours to assist him in levelling the forest: this is again called a *chopping frolic*.

SOCIAL LIFE IN A SMALL TOWN IN THE 1850s

Adolphus Gaetz Diary, 1855-1873. PAC, MG 24, 186.

January 1856

Tuesday, 1st,—This year commenced with a mild day. This evening the Concert, got up for Miss Jan Bolman, (the blind Girl), went off exceedingly well. Doors were to be open at 7 o'clock, but long before that time the Street leading to the "Temperance Hall", was thronged with people; it became necessary therefore to open the doors before the time appointed. Upwards of 350 persons were congregated in the Hall, and the proceeds amounted to £18.7.0., which after deducting expenses, left a balance of £16.6.3., which was handed over to Miss Bolman.

The performers were,—

W.B. Lawson, bass singer
Jasper Metzler, do.
Wm. Townshend, Clarionett.
A. Gaetz, do
James Dowling, Bass Viol.
Wm. Smith, do. & Bass singer.
Miss Jane Bolman, piano Forte, & Guitar.
Miss Cossman, piano Forte.

Miss Frye; Miss Metzler; Miss Rebecca Mooney; Mrs. Wm. Smith; Mrs. Daurey, (formerly Miss Metzler); Mrs. Nichs. Zwicker. The following were the pieces performed:—

1. Anthem from luke 2 chap. There were shepherds, etc.
2. He doeth all things well. Solo by Miss Bolman.
3. Sanctus, by Fallon.
4. Mortals Awake. (christmas piece).
5. The little Shroud. Solo by Miss Bolman.
6. Haec Dies, by Webbe.
7. Great is the Lord.

Part 2nd.

1. Home Sweet Home, with Variations piano Solo by Miss Bolman.
2. The mountain Maid's Invitation.
3. Billy Grimes, Guitar accompaniment by Miss Bolman.
4. Lilly Bell.
5. They welcome me again, Solo, by Miss Bolman.
6. Mary of the Wild Moor.
7. Give me a Cot. Solo by Miss Bolman.
8. The Grave of Napoleon.
9. The little Maid. Guitar accompaniment by Miss Bolman.
10. God save the Queen.

April 1856

Wedn, 30th,—Today the ladies, belonging to St. John's Church, were busily employed, at the Temperance Hall, arranging their wares intended for sale at the Bazaar tomorrow. A large quantity of "Notions" have been made by the "sewing parties", this winter, and within these few days a goodly quantity of Confectionary such as pound and plain Cake, Jellies, etc., etc., have been baked. The Hall, now every thing is arranged, presents quite a splendid appearance, the pillars and walls being tastefully decorated with Evergreens, and the "Notions" being hung up and distributed to catch the eye. The articles made by the sewing parties will vie with any made elsewhere.

May 1856

Thurs. 1st,—The Bazaar opened at 11 O'clock, forenoon, and closed about 10 O'clock in the evening. The proceeds, which were beyond expectation, amounted to £60, besides having a variety of fancy Articles left for another occasion.

June 1856

Monday, 9th,—By proclamation, issued by the Governor, this day was recommended to the people of Nova Scotia as a public holiday to celebrate the peace, in consequence of which very little work was done in this town. The day was ushered in by firing four guns from Block house hill, and at precisely 12 O'clock noon 21 guns were fired from the same place, immediately after the first gun, the bells of the different Churches, commenced ringing a merry peal, and continued during the firing of the guns. Flags were displayed in all parts of the Town, as well as from the masts of all the Vessels laying in the harbour. In the afternoon Fiddles, fifes, drums, Tambourines and penny whistles were played by the Band through the streets, at which time numerous flags were carried and followed by nearly all the boys in the town, each one endeavouring to make as much noise as his lungs would allow him. At half past 7 O'clock in the evening, 9 guns were again fired from the Block house hill, and to end the day's celebration rockets were discharged from the Church square.

July 1856

Monday, 21st,—A Dancing school was opened this evening under the tuition of Mr. A. Ash, professor of Dancing. Terms 30/ per quarter. . . .

Monday, 28th,—In the evening an exhibition of a Magic Lantern in the Temperance Hall, by Genl. Gray of the Cold Water Army, for the benefit of Temperance.

August 1856

Wednesday, 27th,—Today the St. John's Church Sunday School pic-nic took place at the Battery point. 112 of the Scholars mustered on the Church Square at 12 O'clock, noon, and marched with flags flying to the above place where they enjoyed themselves during the afternoon; at 5 O'clock they partook of supper, at half past 6 O'clock they were again called together, and after singing a hymn and hearing an address from the Revd. Mr. Owen they were marched to town and dismissed. A large number of parents and others were present.

September 1856

Thursday, 4th,—A regatta came off at Chester, the first of the kind that has been attempted in this Country. A number of Boats were entered, and ran for the different prizes. Fireworks, Illumination, Torch light procession, and Balls closed the days entertainment. A large party went from here in the packet "Sylvia", which vessel was fitted up for the purpose.

PIONEER RECREATION

E.C. Morgan, 'Pioneer Recreation and Social Life'. *Saskatchewan History*, XVIII, 2, Spring 1965, 41-4. Reprinted by permission of *Saskatchewan History* and the author.

Beginning in 1951, the Saskatchewan Archives distributed a series of questionnaires to pioneers who settled in the Saskatchewan area prior to, and in a brief period following, the formation of the province. The questionnaire dealing with pioneer recreation and social life, completed by 287 of these early settlers, provides us with an insight into the means used to offset the hardship and loneliness which faced them. From their replies it is evident that the pioneers did not neglect to seek diversions from the drudgery of pioneer existence. "They seemed," writes William R. Allin of Eigenheim, "to keep the saying in mind 'If work interferes with pleasure, cut out the work'."

When Charles Davis settled in Whitewood in 1882, there were perhaps twelve homes within a radius of six miles, and out of these, six were homes of bachelors. Clarence D. Zeller, writes that on his arrival in the Keithville district, in the Swift Current area, there were only four homes near enough for him to visit, one being that of a bachelor settler. Thus, in such sparsely settled communities, it is not surprising that visitors were always welcome.

Visiting habits, of course, varied with the individual. John Laidlaw of Grenfell reports that he did not visit often, while Robert Sanderson of Indian Head says that his family hardly ever visited in the summer, and about every two weeks in the winter. Still others visited on the average of once a week. Formality was at a minimum in the early days, and stranger and friend alike were trusted. Doors were always left unlatched and often, if the caller found no one at home, he would light a fire and prepare a meal from the homeowner's supplies. People did not wait for invitations, and although visits may have been infrequent, callers were, according to Frank Wright of the Keithville district, welcome at "anytime." Sunday does seem to have been the favorite day for visiting although some, like Mrs. Marion Anderson of Moosomin, were not allowed to visit on Sunday, as her Methodist mother disapproved of it, though "Mother could go to visit the sick on the Lord's Day."

The pioneer was not one to stand on ceremony. "People never invited anyone" states Mrs. Richard Miles of Edenwold. Perhaps the informality was due in part to the lack of telephone communication. As Mrs. Marion Anderson says, "it wasn't easy to send word."

If you were visiting when mealtime rolled around it was taken for granted that you would stay, according to Victor C. McCurdy, a Moosomin pioneer, and according to John McCloy of Prince Albert, "to refuse was considered an insult." The variety in wording an invitation to a meal is interesting. In her home at McGuire, Mrs. John C. Knaus says it was "Sit down and have a snack," while their American neighbours would say, "Have some dinner," and the English settlers would say "Do have some tea with us." A familiar expression to many of our informants was "take potluck," while just as many said that they had never heard it used in pioneer days. The invitation to "sit in" was very common, as was "pull up your chair." In Mrs. Cristal Fern Hackett's home at Gainsborough a visitor would be welcomed by "I'm glad you came in time to get your name in the pot," while in mock apology Mrs. D. A. Moorhouse of Wallard, might have said "Stay for dinner, if we can stand it all the time, surely you can stand it once." A bachelor, on the other hand, might have apologized by issuing the challenge to "sit up and don't pass your opinion on the tack," according to Charles Davis of North Battleford.

In between meals there was always the "inevitable" cup of tea and a bite of something to eat, reports Mrs. J. Keys of Wolseley, while according to James McGuirl of Moosomin, coffee made from roasted wheat would sometimes be substituted for tea. However, Alfred Mann of Venn states that if no meal were served, there was just "a water pail."

Hospitality was widespread in the early days. Mrs. H. J. Kenyon of Pheasant Forks says that "come anytime you can was the motto of the times," and C. Evans Sargent of Garfield demonstrates the truth of this in describing a personal experience: "I recollect," writes Mr. Sargent, "as Secretary-Treasurer of the rural municipality, having to make a seizure and attach nearly everything a man had on the place. As I finished putting up the notice he came out. 'We are just sitting down to supper—you better come in and have a bite to eat with us.' I knew if I refused I would offend him far more than by making the seizure, and we had a perfectly happy meal."

The friendly spirit exhibited around the table was shown in all other areas of early pioneer life. Whenever work needing extra help had to be done, the pioneers helped one another. Houses and barns were raised, quilts made, and wells dug by means of "bees." A bee was also a social event, for it presented the women with the much-relished opportunity of getting together, no less than it did the men. While the men worked, the ladies would not be idle, for there were quilts to be sewn, and meals to be prepared. Often a bee would be organized to assist a sick neighbour by sowing or harvesting his crop, and there was almost always a bee for building a settler's first small sod, log, or frame shack or barn. In addition to these more familiar purposes, bees were also held for soap-making states Clarence D. Zeller, for logging writes George Hartwell of Pheasant Forks and for buzz-sawing wood according to Mrs. Percy Hansford of Mullingar. When a log building was being raised, Lawrence Kelly, a Rocanville pioneer, informs us that "good corner men were in demand, and there was rivalry to see who could put up the best corner."

When time permitted, card parties and dances helped to break the monotony of pioneer life. Pedro, five hundred rummy, eucher, and cribbage were the most popular card games, while old maid and snap were played by those who would not use the standard playing cards. Waltzes, squares, one step, two step, circle two step, three step, seven step, polkas, lancers and the quadrille were the dances favored in all communities, while in the Ukrainian settlement at Fenwood, waltz, koloneyko and kozaks were also popular.

Typically, dances were held in whichever home was large enough to accommodate the crowd. In most districts no formal schedule was adhered to, but Louis Demay of St. Brieux tells us that "there was a tacit turnabout, but nothing on schedule." The surprise party was a favorite. "There was no definite time," writes Mrs. H. J. Kenyon of Pheasant Forks, "but we had a party about once a month, the family chosen was not told we were coming. . . . We took our own refreshments of course, and had a lot of fun. Everybody went, old and young, no age limit."

Because of a shortage of women, dances sometimes took on a special character. David H. Maginnes of Baldwinton, remembers going to one dance about 1908 when there were 30 men present and only three women. "We danced," he says, "until the women got tired," and Charles Vavra of Scott recalls many dances at which there were only four or five women at the dance and from 20 to 30 men. There were, Mr. Vavra says, "lots of men dancing together."

In many communities, religious beliefs helped determine the type of entertainment. Dancing and card playing were enjoyed by most families, yet many shunned them. The Baptists and the Methodists frowned on either activity. C. Evans Sargent writes: "I spent a winter around Fiske where the community was split on the subject of dancing. To the Methodists it was anathema; Presbyterians danced and Anglican clergy joined in the dance with their congregations." The same conditions prevailed when it came to card playing. According to Mrs. George Brown Jameson of Melfort, "It was frowned upon by those of the Methodist faith. The Presbyterians tolerated it, and the Anglicans enjoyed their card games."

Generally, those who did not wish to dance or play cards would stay away, or sit it out and visit, and arguments would be avoided. Occasionally, however, differing beliefs would bring open conflict, as in the Roseray district where, according to Mrs. Robert Thompson, "A couple of 'them' tried to stop a dance one night by getting into the school and barricading the door," but she continues "it didn't work." While at Togo, states Sidney Stewart May "the German Lutherans objected to both, and would burn any cards taken into their homes."

After the school was built, it usually replaced the home as the center of social life. According to Mrs. D. A. Moorhouse, the school at Wallard was used for "Dances, box socials (how I remember them and the first old relic I drew as a partner when I was 14), fowl suppers, plays, public debates, picnics, Christmas trees, Church and Sunday School, funerals, and public meetings." However, in isolated instances the school was not used for such activities. Mrs. James S. Entwhistle of Wauchope writes that "School was for the children to be taught in, not for playing," Mrs. Richard Miles of Edenwold states that "All of our social life continued to emanate from our church," and sometimes, as in the case of the largely Methodist community of Hillburn, the trustees, according to Mr. William Evans, did not allow the school to be used for dances or card parties.

With the advent of community halls, the school was usually replaced by the hall, as the focal point of social life. This was, however, not always the case. If the hall was located in a village or town, distance would often dictate that the rural school remain the scene of most social activities.

Most of the community halls were of log or frame construction, but a surprising number were built of brick, the latter being a feature of some of the larger towns. The town of Estevan erected a brick hall, measuring 90 x 40 feet about 1912, and the town of Arcola built a brick hall with a seating capacity of over 300 in 1905. Funds for building a hall were usually raised by the sale of shares or from contributions. The Grain Growers at Red Deer Hill, sold shares to members at $5.00 each, to construct in 1916, a frame hall measuring 24 x 30 feet. The Orangemen built a 24 x 50 frame hall at Summerberry in 1888, and this hall was also financed by selling shares. At Ladstock, the settlers organized a bee, in 1915, to construct a log hall measuring 20 x 40 feet.

BOYS WILL BE BOYS

C.S. Clark, *Of Toronto the Good. A Social Study* (Montreal, Toronto Publishing Co., 1898), pp. 4-6.

Some years ago a number of baths were presented to the city by a one time resident at a cost of some $5000.00, and they were certainly a boon to the boys of the city. A storm, however, destroyed their utility and for a long time there was only the beach where they could go, including the sand bar opposite Queen's wharf. It is currently reported that some stately lady used to sit at the hotel window and survey the boys in bathing through an opera or field glass, until she made a complaint with the result that bathing without trunks was prohibited by the police. Like all such prohibitive legislation, however, it is to be remarked that it was regularly and systematically set at defiance. On Sunday mornings in summer the sand bar was alive with boys and young men who strip themselves and throw their clothes in a boat. If a policeman looms in sight they take to the boats and I have never heard that anyone has been arrested yet.

During the past summer, Mr. W. J. Gage made an offer to the city council to build a swimming bath in a central locality, if the city would furnish the site. A special committee was appointed to consider the matter and confer with Mr. Gage, and recommend to council such plans and methods as they may find practicable and desirable to secure the best possible results from the liberal propositions made by Mr. Gage.

The Mayor's experiment, by which the city provided a steam tug to ferry the boys of the city across the Bay to the sand bar for bathing lessons proved a huge success. On one Saturday no less than 3000 boys were taken over, and as there was an experienced swimmer in charge, and all necessary appliances on hand at the expense of the city, the bathing is absolutely safe, and the departure is proving an immense boon to the boys in the hot weather.

Besides the bathing afforded by the island it is the terminus of all the boats that leave the slips at night. All the water front comprises interminable lengths of boat houses both private and public, and the houses owned by organizations such as the Royal Canadian Yacht Club are perfect palaces in their way. Aquatic sports comprise very largely the principal diversion of Toronto's men and boys, and there is scarcely a boy in the city whose sympathies are not enlisted in some of the great summer events.

This seems to be a matter which is the legitimate outcome of events. The bay seems to be the only place belonging to the city that is not consecrated. The parks are for walking in, not for athletic sports, the streets for traffic, and woe to the boy who is caught desecrating them by playing upon them. If he is under the age of sixteen years, and enter a billiard room, he is liable to arrest again, so that his opportunities for enjoying life are very limited indeed, and with the restrictive legislation passed for his benefit, he has not much opportunity for playing, with the result that pernicious amusements are at a premium.

A child eleven years old appeared in the Police court charged with the offence of playing ball on Sumach street. The ball, a small rubber affair, was produced in court and the boy when asked why he did not bring the bat also, explained that he had no bat, and was playing with the ball and a piece of a stick when the policeman interrupted him. There was no question as to the guilt of the accused. Hugh Miller, J.P., fined the boy $2 or ten days in goal. A good hearted justice of the peace like Mr. Miller could not go against the by-law, but the by-law forbidding ball playing in the street should be enforced against children with a good deal of discretion. By-laws that deal with graver offences than ball playing are not enforced at all. The child who was playing with a soft rubber ball on Sumach street was doing nobody any harm, and the city has something else to do with its money than to pay policemen to run down children who in their innocence think it no sin to try and enjoy themselves.

A squad of boys, the oldest of whom was thirteen, were playing ball in front of their home on Victoria street, opposite the Normal School grounds, when Police Constable 195 ordered them to desist and took their names. The officer did his work civilly enough, and the protest is not against him, but rather against the folly of employing policemen for the persecution of small boys. Not that the Toronto small boy is an angel. By no means. He is rude and mischievous. His mania for damaging trees and defacing property may be explained by the fact that it is unsafe for him to attempt to enjoy himself in any more innocent way. A hundred property owners can bear witness that the police have not come between the small boy and his enjoyment of the game of tearing down fences or breaking the windows of vacant houses. But let a few children start a game on a quiet street with a lawn tennis ball such as those boys on Victoria street used and immediately a policeman interferes. When the street becomes the playground of youths or grown men some body is liable to get hit with the hard ball they use. It ought to be easy to avert this danger without perpetuating a by-law which permits the police to exclude children from the streets and to terrify them with threats of Police Court prosecution for the heinous offence of playing with a soft ball.

A HOLIDAY IN THE WEST

Prince Albert Times, May 25, 1888.

THE QUEEN'S BIRTHDAY.

The morning though dark and gloomy brightened up about 9 o'clock, and the remainder of the day was beautiful. Flags were flying from every flagstaff in town and all places of business, except the candy and fruit stores and saloons, were closed. The only persons who did not appear to honor the day as a holiday were those on the government works at the Court House. . . .

At 8 o'clock in the morning the band turned out, for a couple of hours, on the Presbyterian Church square and played the national anthem and a number of select airs. In the afternoon they again played during the second innings of the cricket match. . . .

The first sporting event of the day was the cricket match between the P.A. and the N.W.M.P. Cricket Clubs in which the former were badly worsted by an inning and twenty-eight runs in favor of the police. . . .

After the cricketers were through a lacrosse match took place between the benedicts and bachelors of the P.A. Lacrosse Club which was keenly contested, and in which the former came out second best. During this match one of the players was severely hurt and others more or less so. Some of the players are altogether too rough in playing and appear to think that the game consists of slashing and the roughest possible play.

These matches were witnessed all day by a large assembly of ladies, both on foot and in carriages, who evinced a keen interest in both games. . . .

In the evening a concert was given in St. Paul's Church by the Fuhrer family, who arrived in town from Qu'Appelle the day previous. The building was crowded to overflowing long before the concert commenced. Col. Sproat occupied the chair. The programme consisted almost entirely of instrumental music, piano and violins.

THE PASTIMES OF THE PEOPLE

The *Globe* (Toronto), July 3, 1900, p. 9.

At Perth.

Perth, July 2.—About six thousand people from Almonte, Carleton Place, Smith's Falls, and the surrounding country witnessed the Crescent Lacrosse Club's celebration here to-day. At 10 o'clock this morning a monster trade procession was given, and the many turn-outs were unique and up-to-date. After this aquatic sports took place on the basin and were well contested, especially those in which the boys took part. In the afternoon proceedings were resumed at the athletic grounds. The first number was a baseball match between Smith's Falls and Perth, and resulted in a win for the latter by 10 runs to 6.

The horse races were the next feature. In the 2:40 class there were four entries. . . .

The Boys' Brigade of Smith's Falls gave an exhibition of fancy drilling, which made quite a hit with the people present.

The lacrosse match between the Crescents of Perth and Almonte was the main feature of the day. This was an Eastern League game, and was the first time these two teams met this year. The play was fast all through. The score at the finish was 7 to 3 in favor of the Crescents.

At Milton.

Milton, July 2.—Dominion Day was celebrated with great enthusiasm by the Miltonians and a great number of visitors which the morning trains brought to town from Hamilton and Toronto and intermediate points. The weather was fine and cool. Excellent music was furnished by the 13th Battalion Band of Hamilton and the local brass and reed band, the 13th also giving a grand open air concert in the evening, which was much enjoyed by a large audience.

In the grand fancy and military drill contest the first prize of $100 was secured by the St. Thomas Canton, while Hamilton Canton captured the second prize.

The 10-mile amateur foot race for a $20 silver cup was won by Sherring of Hamilton. . . .

The three mile open bicycle race was very hotly contested but T.R. Thompson of Hamilton succeeded in gaining first place and so won the $15 cup.

NED HANLAN AND NATIONAL PRIDE

The *Globe* (Toronto), October 4, 1878, p. 1.

It would indeed have been strange if any sporting event that ever took place on this side of the Atlantic had ever aroused the enthusiasm that the present contest has. Hitherto anything in the way of an international contest between Canada and the United States has begun, and ended, with the odds largely in favour of the latter, and from the outset a large majority of the Canadian people have regarded a Canadian defeat as a foregone conclusion. True, the record of the famous Paris crew proved an exception to this rule, while Joe Dion in his palmiest days managed to command many friends and backers, although later on he found more than his match, and the billiard championship passed out of the hands of a Canadian holder. . . . In lacrosse the Americans would not dispute the question of superiority with our people. On the other hand, we have been badly beaten on the turf, both in trotting and running, while in cricket, yachting, and rifle shooting our representatives have cut but a sorry figure in international contests. In these sports defeat was confidently looked for by the majority of Canadians, and the results were not disappointing. In sculling, too, it seemed as if the fortunes of war were against us, until the result of the [U.S.] Centennial contest [in 1876] showed Canadians what a wonder they had on their own soil. Even this was not sufficient to settle the question of superiority and as the American championship was still held at Pittsburg, it remained for Hanlan to go to the champion's own water and beat him there. How this was done every reader of THE GLOBE has had the opportunity of learning, but it had not been accomplished before the air was full of rumours of the proposed match between the great Union Springs sculler and the Toronto man. . . . [I]t was to Courtney that all eyes turned as the defender and upholder of American supremacy in aquatic contests. . . .

At last the great international scullers' race is over, and Canada wears the laurels. The great battle was fairly and squarely fought out from start to finish, and Hanlan has proved himself the better man. No one can now question either his technical or equitable right to the title and honour belonging to the championship of America, and there are very many who think that the modest young fisherman of two years and a half ago is now in a fair way to become the champion of the world.

The *Globe* (Toronto), September 23, 1896, p. 10; September 8, 1896, p. 6.

ROUSING RECEPTION TO JACOB GAUDAUR.

A UNIQUE DEMONSTRATION.

TEN MILES OF PROCESSION,
TEN MILES OF PEOPLE.

A proud and happy man, indeed, should be Jacob Gill Gaudaur of Orillia, who, having reached the goal on which he long ago set his ambition, is told by a hundred thousand of his fellow-countrymen that they had sympathy with his efforts and have glory in his success. . . .

All the city turned out to do the world's champion honor last night. . . . Leading the procession proper came the long string of trolley cars, stretching from Church almost to Sherbourne street. The first car, which was brilliantly lighted up by a hundred or so vari-colored incandescent lights, was occupied by the Grenadiers' Band. The next car held the portly forms of the city fathers. Immediately behind it came the float in which the champion stood. It was literally a mass of verdure, the body of the float, which was the truck of a fire reel, being covered with maple leafs. . . .

The climax of the achievements of Canadian representatives in aquatic and athletic sports came . . . when Jacob Gaudaur of Orillia, following the plucky efforts of Edward Hanlan and the late William O'Connor, succeeded where they failed, and won back from an Australian the rowing championship of the world. It is nothing short of marvellous that with our short rowing season and scanty population, we have been always in the front rank in aquatics, and are to-day once more at the very top. The prac-

tice and popularity of athletics are a sign of a vigorous and healthy community, and we may be happy that they flourish exceedingly with us.
They bring out some of the best qualities of human nature—generous
rivalry, self-control, patient endurance and steadfast determination, together with fiery zeal and great courage. The lessons of sport are to be
stout of heart and straightforward, respectful to authority, strong in emer-
gency, modest in success and considerate to the beaten.

THE FIRST STANLEY CUP GAME

Toronto Daily Mail, March 23, 1894, p. 8.

Montreal, March 22.—The hockey championship was decided to-night,
and never before in the history of the game was there such a crowd present at a match or so much enthusiasm evinced. There were fully 5,000
persons at the match, and tin horns, strong lungs, and a general rabble
predominated. The match resulted in favour of Montreal by 3 goals to 1,
and the contest was the hardest and best ever seen here. The ice was fairly
good. The referee forgot to see many things. The teams:

Montreal.		*Ottawa.*
Collins	Goal	Morell
Cameron	Point	Pulford
James	Cover-Point	Young
Routh	Forward	Kirby
Mussen	"	J. McDougall
Hodgson	"	S. McDougall
Marlow	"	Russell

Referee, W. Scott, Toronto. Umpires, Messrs. Anderson and Irwin.

In the first half the play was of the rushing order, with Montreal getting
slightly the better of it. The Ottawas, however, found an opening after
about ten minutes' play and Russell scored. As soon as the puck was sent
off again Hodgson carried it to the Ottawa end, but the Ottawa defence
were on the alert, and saved the goal. A hard struggle ensued, and after
ten minutes' of rushing and hard hockey Montreal scored. No other goal
was taken this half, and when the second half was commenced everyone
settled down to see a great contest, and they were not disappointed. The
Ottawas played with more vim, and made it lively for their opponents.
The Montrealers were more fortunate, and thanks to the efforts of Hodg-

son and Barlow two more games [goals] were taken, and the match concluded in a victory for the local team by three goals to one.

ORGANIZED SPORT

John Weiler, 'The Idea of Sport in Late Victorian Canada'. Paper delivered to the Canadian Historical Association, Kingston, June, 1973, pp. 1, 14-17, 21-6. Reprinted by permission of the author.

One of the most fascinating legacies of our late Victorian heritage was the incredible rise of organized sport and athletics. . . .

The amelioration of "moral" abuses in sporting pastimes was . . . often concerned with the refinement of inter-personal conduct. By far the most pervasive idea in this regard was the insistence that sport be "gentlemanly". Though all sporting pastimes were supposed to enhance an amicable relationship among competitors, sportsmen soon realized that their activities, especially bodily contact games, could lead to quite the opposite. Consequently, brute force was denigrated as "unmanly". It was an educated strength, manifested in speed and agility, which marked the true sportsman.

The term most commonly used to describe the concept of gentlemanly conduct was "scientific play". An excellent example of this idea can be found in W. K. McNaught's *Lacrosse and How to Play It* [1880]. It was emphasized throughout this book that any man of ordinary health could play lacrosse, if he approached the game scientifically. Science was consistently defined as carefully studied and practiced physical reactions. . . .

The way to insure that sport was scientific, and therefore fit for gentlemen, was for sporting clubs and associations to enact rules strictly prohibiting unnecessary violence. The Canadian Hockey Union, for example, went so far as to explicitly outlaw "unmanly methods" in its founding constitution. . . .

Another way for sporting associations to insure gentlemanly conduct was to inculcate in its [sic.] members a "manly" attitude toward victory and defeat. As one enthusiast with poetic pretensions put it: "set the cause above renown and love the game beyond the prize". W.A.H. Kerr aptly demonstrated this idea while describing the responsibilities of the Ontario Hockey Association. "A friendly spirit of the most undoubted kind", he said, "should be fostered by its members toward their competitors and the game should be played for its own sake and not entirely for the sake of winning. . . ."

Besides being extremely interested in eradicating "moral" abuses in their activities, sportsmen were equally enthusiastic about the virtues which sport produced and its benefits for society. Sports and athletics were viewed as a conditioning for "the race of life". The basis of this idea was the assumption that the rigor of sport and athletic discipline, both physical and mental, required the same sort of qualities needed for the struggles of business and professional pursuits. One sports advocate, for example, saw rugby football as the best formative experience a man could possibly wish for.

> The sina qua non of a good footballer is grit, and in after life the grit cultivated by the hard knocks of the football field will stand men in good stead in contests of business and professional life. . . .

Although the idea of sport and morality was an important concern, there were two more pressing issues for sportsmen. Who should participate in organized sporting pastimes and how important were these pastimes relative to other activities in society? Both of these questions were featured in the most heated sporting controversy of the times—professionalism.

Professionalism was viewed by many sporting advocates as a curse, an evil to be stamped out lest it corrupt all legitimate sport. The secretary of the Ontario Hockey Association, for instance, declared that "the most regrettable feature which has become apparent of late in hockey, and in other sports, is the growth of the professional element . . . and it must be admitted that the executive cannot be possessed of too extensive powers for dealing with such an evil. . . ."

Most sporting organizations explicitly outlawed professionalism and often formulated elaborate definitions of amateur status in their constitutions. The amateur codes varied slightly; but the only concession ever given to the athlete, regarding monetary affairs, was in reimbursement for hotel or travelling expenses incurred while in the pursuit of his sporting activities. . . .

Why were many organized sportsmen so concerned about the "evils" of professionalism? Part of the answer lies in the fact that sport was considered legitimate only as a minor aspect of life. Sport could never be sanctioned as a full time occupation. It must always be kept subordinate to the serious. An excellent statement of this concept was made by Goldwin Smith, an active member of the Toronto Athletic Club, not to mention his other claims to fame.

> With games no one seems to doubt their value as an element of education, so long as they are not allowed to become too absorbing, to interfere with the serious work of life, or give birth to a

false standard of merit; so long, we must add, as they are kept clear of the professional and betting element which seems to creep in and is fatal to the liberal character of sport.

However, anti-professionalism was more than simply a belief in a subordinate role for sport in society. It was also a manifestation of class exclusiveness. Unlike the business and professional middle class, the great mass of Canadians could not afford the expense, nor the time, to participate in organized sporting activities, without some monetary reward. Amateur codes were therefore an effective device for excluding the less prosperous sections of society from sport and athletic clubs. Although the class exclusiveness idea is extremely difficult to prove conclusively, it can be illustrated from various inferences contained in the sporting literature of the times.

The organizers and promoters of sport sometimes referred to the cheapness of a particular game, implying that it was therefore open to all. Occasionally, there appeared a platitudinous avowal of the non-exclusive nature of an individual sport. This was especially true of curling, a sport which was the virtual preserve of the more prosperous members of the community. In these comments writers seemed to be apologizing for egalitarian principles which in practice they tacitly ignored.

Probably the most revealing evidence is to be found in the middle class notion of the gentleman sportsman. Factory workers, with little or no education, were not very likely to "intellectualize" or "refine" their sporting pastimes. Is it not plausible that many middle class sports enthusiasts feared the destruction of gentlemanly conduct if they had to compete against "uncouth", "ignorant" and "brutalized" workingmen? It may be tentatively asserted, therefore, that an important number of articulate sporting exponents did not look favourably upon the participation of workingmen in organized sport.

It would be an exaggeration, however, to insist that all sportsmen viewed amateur codes as an effective means of keeping out the lower classes. It would be equally misleading to claim that professionalism itself was uncategorically despised. A particularly interesting case is to be found in the game of cricket. Cricketers constantly argued that imported professionals were needed to train Canadian teams and therefore raise the level of play. Some cricket enthusiasts, most notably G.G.S. Lindsey, also claimed that only the introduction of pay for cricket players could improve the quality of the Canadian game. Lindsey contended that this was essential because Canada lacked a large wealthy leisure class necessary to provide raw material for good cricketers.

Moreover, several sportsmen viewed professionalism as an inevitability that would not destroy or corrupt sports. J.P. Roche, writing about lacrosse, clearly illustrated this view.

The advent of out and out professionalism is a long way off, but when it does come it will not be an unmixed evil, for it will do no more harm to our national game in Canada than it has done to amateur baseball in the United States or to cricket in the old country. When we have professional teams the amateurs will go and see them play and no doubt learn something from the experience of experts.

It is significant that this comment was made in 1896. At the turn of the century sporting activities were attracting increasingly large numbers of spectators and this growing appeal demanded ever improving quality of play. Implicit in Roche's argument was the idea that skill was directly related to specialization of activity—professional sportsmen were experts. If sport was to be expertized, athletes must be engaged in their skill on a full time basis and incentives provided to encourage excellence. Money could accomplish both. The attitude toward professionalism was clearly being transformed by the exigencies of an expanding and changing industrial-urban society.

5 | Organizing the Workingman

The argument over the benefits and disadvantages of industrialization will probably never be settled. But one aspect of it is indisputable: working people gained important advances in terms of wages, hours of labour, and working conditions because they organized to demand them.

Canadian labour organization developed as it did in response to three factors. One, of course, was the objective circumstances of the Canadian industrial scene. The others were British and American influences. British influence was felt first as workers emigrating from Britain brought trade-union ideology to Canada. This element was dominant within Canadian labour until after Confederation. In the latter nineteenth century, however, the influence of American unionism began to rise towards the dominance it has enjoyed in the twentieth century. In some measure this was because of the friendly imperialism of American unions, anxious to spread their benefits to their Canadian brothers. At least as often, the initiative was taken by Canadians. American unions were closer than British ones, their success was more obvious, and their style of organization apparently more suited to North American conditions. So in many cases American unions expanded into Canada on the invitation of Canadian workers. Whatever the merits of our contemporary arguments over the need for Canadian national unions, workers in the late nineteenth century saw real merit in the so-called international unions, those with headquarters in the United States. A very mobile labour situation, with workers moving freely back and forth across the border; the increase of American 'branch plant' companies being established in Canada; the apparent similarity in labour problems on both sides of the border—these were compelling arguments for international unions.

Labour organization in the nineteenth century touched only a small percentage of workers. It was essentially limited to the 'aristocracy of labour', skilled workers such as printers, carpenters, shoemakers, and the like. Ordinary unskilled labourers rarely even attempted to organize and when they did the efforts were usually short lived. Only the skilled had the education, traditions of co-operation, job security, and sense of self-worth to join together successfully. Only they had real ability to coerce employers;

unskilled workers could all too easily be replaced from the ever-present stock of unemployed.

Under these circumstances it is not surprising that unions tended in the nineteenth century to be rather conservative, limited in their goals, and self-centred. Nevertheless, desperate times sometimes did produce desperate responses. The hard depression of the 1840s, for example, called forth Canadian echoes of the 'Luddite' movement that had caused large-scale rioting in Britain early in the century. Fearful of the impact of machinery on their careers, Montreal shoemakers engaged in machine-smashing, destroying the shoemaking machines that threatened to throw many of them out of work. Railway workers engaged in many bitter strikes that led to rioting and destruction of property. The frequency of such outbreaks was limited, however, by the ruthless methods employed to suppress labour demonstrations. Government troops were used on dozens of occasions, not only to put down riots or stop destruction of property, but also simply to break extended strikes. Whatever its growing liberalism in labour legislation, government made clear that its real sympathies lay with management by its use of the full coercive power of the state to restrain labour.

Phillips Thompson, the author of the poem that opens this chapter, was the most articulate spokesman for the radical tendencies that began to influence labour at the end of the century. Editor of the Toronto newspaper, the *Labour Advocate*, Thompson was a leader in the Knights of Labour in the 1880s, and a major figure in radical unionism in the United States as well as in Canada. His egalitarian views were in sharp contrast with those of early trade-union leaders. The carpenters and joiners of Toronto were among the first to organize, and their 1833 plea for public understanding of the union is a measure of their moderation. Their equally moderate colleagues in Montreal, however, nevertheless met unyielding resistance from their employers, as illustrated in our third document. Some trades, such as the ship labourers who loaded ocean-going vessels at Quebec, had more coercive power. The timber trade was a high-risk activity with a short shipping season. The workers' threats to disrupt this season gave them real power. An article by J.I. Cooper, a McGill historian, discusses the rise of the successful Ship Labourers' Benevolent Society, which grew from an organization providing accident and burial benefits for workers into a powerful trade union.

The nature of nineteenth-century union organization can best be illustrated by observing some of the more important strikes of the period. Two have been selected: the strike on the Lachine canal works near Montreal in 1843; and the strike of Toronto printers in 1872. The Lachine strike is particularly revealing for a number of reasons. Public works, canals, and railways were key factors in Canadian economic development in the nineteenth century. They were also major employers of labour. The importance of such works meant that both employers and governments were likely to be even less sympathetic than usual towards labour disruptions. Yet labour unrest was also more likely on public works. Large numbers of workers were gathered together for extended periods of time, making organization easier. The importance to the economy of their work made them more conscious of their worth. And, in a system in which parts of the work were sub-contracted to small capitalists, abuses were frequent— inadequate pay, difficulties in getting regular payment of wages, severe discipline on the job—as small contractors attempted to achieve maximum profits on their sections of the works.

The Lachine strike showed that skilled and unskilled workers, under the proper circumstances, could successfully combine. But these documents demonstrate the obstacles they faced. The hostility of their employers was joined by the hostility of the authorities and the press. The workers' grievances were often denigrated or distorted. In the case of the Lachine strike, the popular interpretation was that it was simply a riot caused by imported animosities among the workers themselves, conflicts between traditionally warring groups of Irishmen. Samples are given of the viewpoints of the workers, the employers, and the press. A modern economic historian, H.C. Pentland of the University of Manitoba, sums up the strike in the concluding selection.

Of greater long-range impact was the Toronto printers' strike of 1872. In emulation of their British and American counterparts, the Toronto printers struck to win a nine-hour working day. They were vigorously opposed by the newspaper publishers, led by George Brown of the *Globe*. Brown went so far as to have the strike leaders arrested under a nearly forgotten law forbidding union organization. Since Brown was also the former leader of the Liberal Party the strike took on important political connotations. In a bid to win labour sympathy (and ultimately votes), the Tory Prime Minister, Sir John A. Macdonald, had a law passed legalizing trade unions. His strategy won the adherence of many workers to the Conservative Party for the next decade.

The documents show that the implications of the Toronto strike went far beyond the immediate, local issues. The *Globe* editorials denouncing the strikers demonstrate the liberal nineteenth-century image of Canada as a land of opportunity, a land in which any restraint on capitalist initiative was inappropriate and dangerous to the nation's well-being. On the other side, the workers expressed a growing consciousness of what could be accomplished by united action. While still moderate, still stressing their 'respectability,' they gave hints of a coming militancy. The barriers still to be surmounted, however, were highlighted at the trial of the strike leaders. The magistrate, Alexander Macnabb, was probably typical of middle-class hostility towards organized workers. The report also illustrates the use of detectives to protect strikebreakers and to harrass unionists. All of this is in contrast to the attitudes of a Conservative newspaper, the Toronto *Mail*, commenting on the question of the legal status of unions. Despite its generous attitude on this issue, however, the *Mail* shared characteristic establishment views on higher wages and shorter hours of work.

Out of the struggle of the printers grew in part the movement to establish a national labour congress in Canada, a body to increase labour's power by giving it a united voice. On the call of the Toronto Trades Assembly, a convention met in Toronto in September 1873 to form the Canadian Labour Union. Despite its ambitious name, the union was entirely Ontario based. Among the goals of many workingmen, disillusioned by the way in which labour interests were disregarded by middle-class politicians, was the election of workers to parliament. A resolution calling for support of labour candidates was passed at the first convention of the Canadian Labour Union, after the speech of Toronto printer William Joyce, reproduced below. A sampling of other labour concerns is given in the following document, drawn from the proceedings of the third CLU convention in 1877.

The CLU did not live out the decade, a victim of depression and labour's lack of a sense of co-operation. The idea lived on, however. In 1886 the first meeting of a national association was held. The Trades and Labour Congress would live on, but in the nineteenth century it would represent only a small portion of even organized workers, no matter workingmen at large. And although in 1898 it elected a British Columbian, Ralph Smith, as president, the TLC remained in the nineteenth century largely a Quebec and Ontario organization.

Some of the TLC programs are illustrated in two reports from its 1897 convention in Hamilton. Unlike the Canadian Labour Union, the TLC was primarily concerned with seeking legislation favourable to labour. It was not an easy task. The Montreal *Witness* expressed a common belief in 1875 in its lack of enthusiasm for even giving the vote to workers. But during the 1880s and 1890s labour did make some legislative gains. Two pieces of legislation were especially important. The Ontario Factories Act of 1884 began to drag Canada—kicking and screaming—towards a realistic assessment of the needs of working people in the industrial age. While hardly a radical document, it did provide some protection for women and children in factories, and established a network of inspectors to check the worst abuses in workplaces. Labour wished to go further; the views of the Toronto Trades and Labour Council on an abortive federal factories act, a bill the Conservative government allowed to die in the Senate, are given in an account from the Toronto *Globe*. It is worth noting how far the *Globe* itself had moved since the death of George Brown. On the federal level, the most important piece of legislation was the Dominion Conciliation Act of 1900. The TLC had been pressing for compulsory arbitration of labour disputes to end long and punishing strikes. The Conciliation Act fell far short of that in creating a system of voluntary conciliation. At any rate, the TLC would soon realize compulsory arbitration was not to labour's advantage, and in 1902 would reverse its position. What was of great significance in the Act, however, was the creation of a federal Department of Labour, charged with collecting statistics on labour and with publishing a monthly *Labour Gazette*.

In its insecurity, organized labour was mightily exercised about the threats posed by immigration. During the lingering depression that lasted from the early 1870s to the mid 1890s, workingmen were angered by a continuing influx of immigrants into an already overstocked labour market. They saw immigration as a concerted policy by government and employers to keep down wages and discourage unionization. This feeling was all the more intense when immigration involved strange, distrusted peoples. One of labour's most fervent crusades was against oriental immigration, which had started on a significant scale when Chinese coolies were imported to build sections of the Canadian Pacific Railway. The Chinese, and later Japanese and East Indians, were seen as an 'Oriental menace' that threatened not only jobs, but the very way of life of Canadian workingmen. The Orientals would work at wages below the subsistence, they would take on jobs of the most demeaning and dangerous kinds. As a result, they were threats to the standards Canadian workers had fought to achieve. More, they seemed a threat to Canadian morality. Orientals were alleged to be opium addicts, to engage in white slavery, to live—by choice—in the most degrading physical environments. It was in British Columbia, home of most of the eastern immigrants, that the fight against the menace was most vigorously carried on. In the first decade of the next century, the fight would be carried into the streets, in widespread anti-Oriental riots.

Two documents are presented on this theme. The first, from the Sessional Papers of the Provincial Parliament, concerns the enforcement of the anti-Oriental law of 1897, which prohibited the employment of Orientals in the province's mines. That anti-Oriental feeling was widespread is indicated by an editorial from a radical labour newspaper, the *Industrial Banner* of London, Ontario, a city hardly over-run with hordes of Chinese.

Even at the end of the century unionists still had good reason to feel insecure. Unions were still weak and still represented only a very small proportion of workers. The very existence of trade unions remained a matter of controversy. The next group of documents attempts to show the two sides of this controversy, both among employers and workers.

If unions generally were still controversial, this was much more true of the most daring labour experiment of the age, The Noble and Holy Order, Knights of Labor. The Knights expanded into Canada from the United States, setting up a local assembly in Hamilton in 1881. The Order's growth was rapid, especially in Quebec. As a secret society with elaborate ritual, the Knights of Labor had the appeal of mystery. More important was the Order's idealistic program, stressing education of its members, co-operative economic activity, political action, land and money reform. In the United States the Knights collapsed in the late 1880s. They were victims of the internecine quarrelling in the labour movement: the American Federation of Labor was hostile and undermined the Knights; and the Knights themselves split between traditionalists who supported the Order's opposition to the strike as a labour weapon, and radicals who became involved in bitter and bloody strike action.

With the collapse of American assemblies, the Knights of Labor became virtually an all-Canadian organization. It declined after the early 1890s, but some local branches continued well into the twentieth century. The Knights had an important impact in Canada, increasing labour radicalism and organizing workers previously untouched by traditional craft unions. As much by its secret nature as by its program, the Order won widespread opposition in Canada. The grounds of this opposition are well-expressed in an excerpt from the Toronto *Week*, a journal published by the prominent liberal intellectual, Goldwin Smith. In contrast is the testimony of a Cornwall, Ontario, spinner, John Bickley, supporting the aims of the Knights of Labor.

By century's end, labour had experience with attempting to make gains within the existing social and economic structure. The experience had not been a pleasant one for labour leaders. Labour was sufficiently established to have a core of professional organizers and to have created a professional labour press. Organizers and labour journalists had the time and the opportunity to think about the implications of their struggle. And they had ample guidelines for that thought. In Britain socialist parties were springing up. In the United States radical and attractive solutions were being offered to the problems of the workingman, notably the popular call of Henry George for a 'single tax' on land.

The result was a growing militancy and radicalism in some parts of the labour movement and in the labour press. Two comments from the *Industrial Banner*, and another from Phillips Thompson's *Labour Advocate*, give some of the variety of this new radicalism.

THE POLITICAL ECONOMIST AND THE TRAMP

Phillips Thompson, *The Politics of Labor* (New York, Belford, Clarke & Co., 1887), pp. 160-1.

THE POLITICAL ECONOMIST AND THE TRAMP

Walking along a country road,
    While yet the morning air was damp,
As unreflecting on I strode,
    I marked approach the frequent tramp.

The haggard, ragged, careworn man,
    Accosted me in plaintive tone:
"I must have food—" he straight began;
    "Vile miscreant," I cried, "begone!

" 'Tis contrary to every rule
    That I my fellows should assist;
I'm of the scientific school,
    Political economist.

"Do'st thou not know, deluded one,
    That Adam Smith has clearly proved,
That 'tis self-interest alone
    By which the wheels of life are moved?

"That competition is the law
    By which we either live or die?
I've no demand thy labor for,
    Why, then, should I thy wants supply?

"And Herbert Spencer's active brain,
    Shows how the social struggle ends:
The weak die out—the strong remain;
    'Tis this that Nature's plan intends.

"Now, really, 'tis absurd of you
    To think I'd interfere at all;
Just grasp the scientific view—
    The weakest must go to the wall."

My words impressed his dormant thought.
   "How wise," he said, "is nature's plan!
Henceforth I'll practice what you've taught,
   And be a scientific man.

"We are alone—no others near,
   Or even within hailing distance;
I've a good club, and now right here
   We'll have a 'struggle for existence.'

"The weak must die, the strong survive—
   Let's see who'll prove the harder hittist,
So, if you wish to keep alive,
   Prepare to prove yourself the fittest.

"If you decline the test to make,
   Doubting your chances of survival,
Your watch and pocketbook I'll take,
   As competition strips a rival."

What could I do but yield the point,
   Though conscious of no logic blunder?
And as I quaked in every joint,
   The tramp departed with his plunder.

AN EARLY TRADE UNION

Canadian Correspondent, York, June 15, 1833. Quoted in Edith G. Firth, ed., *The Town of York, 1815-1834* (Toronto, University of Toronto Press, 1966), pp. 77-8.

ORGANIZATION OF CARPENTERS AND JOINERS

WE the JOURNEYMEN CARPENTERS and Joiners, having formed ourselves into a Body for the purpose of assisting any of our Members who may sustain loss by Fire or Robbery, or who is deprived of the means of Subsistence by Sickness or any other accidental cause; and likewise, to enable us to carry our laudable objects into effect, we have called upon our Employers for more punctual payments than what we have had in time past, (all that we demanded of them was 5 dollars per week, on account, and a settlement at the end of each month) we appointed a Committee to wait upon them to arrange existing differences between them and us. A few of our employers have acceded to our moderate demands, but the majority have thought proper to resist them. We, therefore, thought ourselves justified in not returning to our employment, and have come to the determination of taking work on our own account, and we are confident in asserting that we can execute work committed to our care, with credit to ourselves and satisfaction to those who employ us, and moreover, we can do so, at least as cheap and expeditious, if not more so, than has hitherto been done. We are aware that the public mind is, in a certain degree, prejudiced against us, and we in justice to ourselves, as well as to those who haved employed us, and we in justice to ourselves, as well as to those who have employed public, confident in doing so, that we will receive their favour and support.

WILLIAM JAMIESON,
Secretary.

P.S. The Public, perhaps, are not aware that this Society comprises most, if not all, the best workmen in York.

York, June 10, 1833

OPPOSITION TO UNIONS IN THE 1830s

Montreal Gazette, March 4, 1834.

It is hereby intimated to the Public in general, and to JOURNEYMEN CARPENTERS in particular, that in consequence of the recent conduct of JOURNEYMEN CARPENTERS and joiners in this city, and of a COMBINATION entered into by them, it has been deemed necessary to obtain the general sentiments of the

Masters who have unanimously adopted the following RESOLUTIONS, viz:

1st. That the Trade of Carpenters and Joiners, has from the earliest date to the present day, been considered by all nations and countries as one of the most useful and ornamental.

2nd. That in order to support its respectability it is the duty of Masters to agree in the establishment of such rules and orders, as will most effectually protect it from any arbitrary impositions either by the Journeymen or others who have not its interest at heart.

3d. We view with distrust the combined exertions of those Journeymen who have lately formed themselves into a Society called "The Mechanics' Protecting Society of Montreal," who by their conduct last year most decidedly injured both their Masters and themselves, without any advantage resulting to the public, and who, by their present conduct, are bringing further discredit upon themselves and ruin upon the Trade generally.

4th. We did not last year oppose the journeymen in their demand of reduced time, with a continuance of their former summer wages, because they took advantage of the season after our general work was engaged, and it would have greatly retarded our business; we, therefore, suffered an average loss of about fifteen per cent upon all labor on contracts engaged, and of course the public suffered the same proportion in the accounts of days' work.

5th. We now, in consequence of the present combinations consider ourselves called upon to make a stand against their arbitrary and injurious conduct, and after mature and calm deliberation, have resolved that the long established custom of this place previous to last year is the best, and that it shall remain unaltered; we have, therefore, agreed that from the first of April to the first of November a day's work shall consist of eleven working hours; and from the first of November to the first of April a day's work shall be regulated by the old established custom, and we have confident reliance in the concurrence of the public, to enable us to carry these regulations into effect.

6th. We find from our comparative statements of journeymen now in employ, that the disaffection is not unanimous, nor so general as has been supposed. Out of ninety Society-men now at work there are only twenty-five who have not expressed themselves dissatisfied with the conduct of the Society, and satisfied, according to verbal agreement, to continue work until the first of April, without alteration; furthermore, we find that we can very well dispense with any or all of those men who have left their work, until they may be willing without opposition to continue their services as formerly. . . .

8th. We are further unanimous in declaring our opinion that the Society calling itself the "Mechanics' Protecting Society," is calculated to produce the worst consequences; such a body of men cannot be considered competent to what they have undertaken, neither are they likewise to confine themselves to decent and becoming order, they are therefore dangerous to the peace and safety of good citizens. They have already attempted, by combined threats, to force peaceable men to leave their working employ; not wishing to create difficulty and dissension we have hitherto overlooked the circumstance, which we hope will not occur again.

Montreal, March 1, 1834.

A SUCCESSFUL MID-CENTURY UNION

J. I. Cooper, 'The Quebec Ship Labourers' Benevolent Society'. *Canadian Historical Review*, xxx, 4, December 1949, 338-43. Reprinted by permission of the author and of the publisher, University of Toronto Press.

. . . [I]n 1857 hard times settled on Quebec, and even French-Canadian labour, long-established and relatively well paid, felt pinched. Successive issues of local newspapers carried long accounts of workers' meetings in St. Roch, and of processions through the Lower Town protesting against unemployment and reduced wages. It was out of this situation that the Ship Labourers' Society grew. . . .

The term "Benevolent" in the Society's title signified its earliest objective. It provided a number of modest benefits, including accident coverage and burial expenses. These varied; at one time, the Society paid $6.00 a week for a period of thirteen weeks to a member injured on ship board. Such benefits came entirely from fees, which at the start were very low, 25 cents a month for six months of the year. Fees were collected monthly, when the treasurer issued a receipt or "ticket" which showed that the member was in good standing. At some point an initiation fee was adopted, and from this fee combined with the monthly dues, and fines, the charitable work of the organization was sustained. In its benevolent character, the Ship Labourers' Society looked back to a very remote period when occupational groups sought to protect their members from the age-old horrors—accident, unemployment, destitution, death.

What may be inexactly described as the trade union phase of the Ship Labourers' Benevolent Society followed upon, and probably developed from, its charitable activities. This statement is based on the sequence of the Incorporation of the Society in 1862 and the great strike of 1866. In midsummer of that year, a crisis blew up when the Society attempted to establish uniform rates of pay for various categories of work. It had the temerity to publish its new schedules, and when they were disregarded, it called a strike, or, as it was usually described by contemporaries, "a combination." Since the Quebec press covered the episode fully, no doubt because of its novelty, we can follow events adequately. The contest resolved itself into a determined struggle of shipmasters, stevedores, and timber merchants pitted against the Ship Labourers' Benevolent Society. The immediate response of the embattled masters was to move vessels in the process of loading to Lévis, where the workers were only partially organized. The Society thereupon called a complete stoppage of work on both shores of the river, and set out to make up the Lévis labourers' minds for them. This was accomplished, and was attended by one highly dramatic incident in which the Quebec men invaded the sacred precincts of the Davy yard, actually pushing aside John Davy, the proprietor of the yard and one of the most important Quebeckers of his day, in an effort to get at the scabs he employed. By the third week in July, opposition to the strike began to collapse. The first to capitulate were, significantly, the shipmasters, who had become restive in the unrewarding role of cats' paws. In a meeting at Noonan's "Imperial Hotel," on July 23 they agreed to the Society's terms. The following day the merchants met, and, after saying rude things about the action of the skippers, accepted too. The merchants' meeting was an illuminating affair, attended by Sharples, Wilson, Ross, Dean, Bickell, and Jeffery, a veritable roll-call of the old St. Peter Street oligarchy. As outraged capitalists, the merchants were scandalized by the successful revolt of labour, and as the Quebec ruling class, they were dismayed by the defection of their allies, the shipmasters. The use to which the workers had put their benevolent society was bitterly denounced as "not only illegal, but unreasonable," "decidedly and undeniably illegal." It was moved that parliament should be petitioned to repeal the obnoxious Act of Incorporation. Fortunately for the good sense of the gathering, the motion failed, but the men were warned sternly that ". . . Labour was simply a commodity, like everything else, and was regulated by the same laws. . . ." How the Ship Labourers celebrated their victory is not known; probably soberly enough, for three weeks without wages must have left them very low indeed. Throughout, they had acted with great restraint in the face of general hostility and the action of the merchants in employing bluejackets and marines as strike-breakers. The secretary of the Society, and presumably the strategist of the strike, was James Paul. He must have been unusually clear-headed and forceful to realize the commanding position his men occupied, and yet to restrain them till success was won.

At a later time, the Society enlarged its objectives by refusing to use steam-driven machinery in handling certain types of freight, and by stipulating the number of men to be employed on a given job. This produced violent reactions among the shippers, and an angry discharge of letters from the Harbour Commissioners and the Board of Trade. They protested against interference in the conduct of "their" business, and solemnly warned the Ship Labourers' Society that it was ruining the trade of the port of Quebec. . . .

These prosperous days were symbolized by the great midsummer parades, which were such a feature of Quebec life. They were held on July 23, the anniversary of the foundation of the Society. The place of assembly was the Mariners' Chapel, whence the marchers ("four deep"), perambulated the Lower Town, climbed Palais or Mountain hills, made a circuit of the Upper Town, and so back to the coves by way of the Plains. That was quite a step, approximately eight miles, and two directives of the Society made it even more spartan. Members who did not walk were fined, and members who sought to refresh themselves at taverns *en route*, or who fell in refreshed, were fined and might be expelled. The parade was punctuated by bands and was garnished with flags and banners. The great banner of the Society was a splendid affair, bearing the representation of a ship in the process of being loaded, and carrying the motto, "We support our infirm; We bury our dead." The marchers were dressed in their best clothes, and their appearance was further enhanced by cockades and cascades of rosettes of various colours. The townsfolk replied in kind: for example, in 1873 one of them hid his house behind ". . . a colossal figure of Marshal MacMahon . . . dressed in the Sarsfield uniform," a triumph, surely, of decoration and diplomacy. An agreeable feature of the march was the serenades "dispensed" to friends and well-wishers of the Society. The proprietor of the *Morning Chronicle* was one such, and, at various times was regaled by a "bouquet of lively tunes," "Should auld Acquaintance be Forgot," and "The Rising of the Moon."

In its relations with other bodies of organized workers, the Ship Labourers' Benevolent Society was usually happy. Until the late seventies, the division of labour on "racial" lines, which made ship-building French Canadian and longshoring Irish, held good. As ship-building declined, however, the French Canadians were forced into what had been the Irish workers' preserve. Some of them entered the Society; others set up an organization of their own, L'Union Canadienne. Friction rapidly developed on both counts. Within the old Ship Labourers' Society, jealousy flared up when the French-Canadian members sought to secure a political influence and a division of work such as their numbers warranted. With L'Union Canadienne, the crisis mounted, culminating in sanguinary rioting in the summers of 1878 and 1879. In August of the latter year, a miniature pitched battle took place in Champlain Street, which the Ship Labourers' barricaded and defended with cannon. The *Canadian Illustrated News* featured several spirited cuts picturing the clash, the French-Canadian longshoremen, some in top hats (a most awkward headgear to wear to a riot), defending their banner from the more functionally attired Irish. Peace was patched up between the two organizations, and the Ship

Labourers' turned to the more delicate task of accommodating their own French-Canadian members. This was effected by the adoption of a by-law which provided for the employment of an equal number of French-speaking and English-speaking workers on a job. Thus the old Society was transformed from a virtually exclusive Irish-Canadian organization.

THE LACHINE STRIKE OF 1843

Montreal Transcript, January 26, 1843.

There was something of a riot on Tuesday last, among the workmen of the Lachine Canal—and a "strike" for higher wages. We have heard very contradictory statements in regard to the cause of the outbreak—one party casting the blame on the contractors, on account of the jobbing character of their dealings with the workmen in relation to their pay; and the other laying it to the turbulent and grasping spirit of a few ringleaders among the workmen, who had excited the outbreak without any just cause of complaint. It is difficult to learn who are really at fault in the matter; at all events such illegal and riotous proceedings as were lately enacted in the neighbourhood of St. Catherines, should be prevented by a speedy and effectual punishment of the offenders.

As near as we can learn a number of the workmen left on Tuesday, and took with them those who were willing and even anxious to remain at the rate of wages allowed. This the discontented party would not allow; threatening to use violence against those who remained.

The contractors were certainly to blame in not stipulating the amount of wages to be paid to the workmen before the engagement, and although we think the workmen ought to be paid in *money every week*, still if monthly payments are to be made, any provisions furnished to the workmen should be afforded of a given quality, and at a certain price—and that price should be as low as like provisions can be obtained in market. Whether the stores are under the direction of the contractors or not, and whether the goods and provisions are as good and cheap as could be procured elsewhere, such stores are uniformly a cause of discontent among workmen, when they procure cheques upon the stores in lieu of money, and previous to the day of payment. Such a method of payment ought not to be tolerated.

The common workmen, we are informed now demand 2 s. 6d. per day, and the borers and blasters 3 s. This is certainly fair wages when we take into consideration the time of the year and the cheapness of provisions, and to good workmen it is not too much.

We are informed that a party of 14 or 15 attacked a person who is engaged in putting up sheds or barracks for the workmen, and beat him very severely, pushing his horse into the ditch.

Montreal Transcript, January 31, 1843.

To the Editor of the MONTREAL TRANSCRIPT.

SIR,—A long time has elapsed since the Irish laborers in the new world obtruded themselves on the columns of a Public Journal, to vindicate themselves from calumny and misrepresentation of the worst kind, which appeared in your invaluable journal, and also in the *Morning Courier*, and which appeared in your paper by one of the Sub-Committee of the House of Industry, dated 26th January, which probably they were led to believe were facts.

1st. Then, with respect to the wages of the labouring men at Lachine, it was studiously kept a secret between the contractors and their overseers, each man setting into work when employed in the full but delusive hope of getting the usual wages given at public works in this Province, say 3 s. per diem for good labourers, drillers, blasters, and excavators in proportion.

2dly. They did not anticipate negroe-like cruelty or treatment and disrespect from foremen, which subsequently we experienced at their hands, and which was connived at and sanctioned by the Contractors or those who represented them. As proof of the same the foremen who did not use this severity to the men in their charge were dismissed without ceremony, and the said cruelty used by incompetent foremen who were as ignorant of a man's labour in canalling as they were of astronomy or navigation, much less blasting or excavation.

3rdly. Doubtless we may be told that it would be too much to expect as much wages now as in summer; but we poor labourers beg to state that the severity of the weather, together with the number of hours we wrought, entitled us to the highest wages given in summer; for we wrought from dark to dark, without being allowed the usual hour for breakfast.

4thly. The informant of the *Morning Courier* states that the Committee of the House of Industry is fearing that the city would be flooded with applicants for charity. We beg to state in reply thereto, that we are all, with very few exceptions, healthy young men, without families; our earning and industry for the last few years, together with the moral precepts of the Very Rev. T. Mathew, has rendered us independent of charity, thanks to Providence. We further state that notwithstanding the hopes entertained by our enemies, we are all fully determined to steer clear of any infraction of the law.

In conclusion, we beg to state, that we are perfectly indifferent as to whether or not the canal may ever be made, as our last pay fell far short of paying our board; besides, each man's loss, or gain thereby, when taken into consideration, is of little consequence, as the Spring will soon set in when there will be enough of employment, for all hands, but particularly as the paltry and junior Contractors of Montreal, would feign make a fortune by the poor self expatriated Irish, who expects you will give insertion to the above.

I remain, dear Sir,
Your obedient and humble Servant,
For Self and Fellow Laborers,
JOHN COX.

Lachine, Jan. 28, 1843.

Montreal Transcript, February 7, 1843.

The disturbances among the labourers employed at the Lachine Canal have continued to excite a good deal of alarm in the minds of persons resident on the spot, and the threats of violence proceeded so far that on Saturday last two companies of the 71st and a detachment of the Dragoon Guards were ordered to proceed to the scene of the disturbances. On their arrival at Lachine a search was made of the houses in and near the village, and large numbers of persons were found crowded together, some of them armed with sticks, others with guns. About 27 of the latter were arrested and lodged in jail, in order to await their trial. . . . Prevention is better than cure, and perhaps the report that about 200 men were being drilled in the woods may have accelerated the civil authorities in invoking military aid. There had been a good deal of marching and counter-marching with flags during the week, and in one or two instances assaults had been committed by the rioters, but there does not appear to be any foundation for the reports of loss of life which have been floating through the city for the last day or two.

The disputes arose perhaps more from old enmities between the Corkonians and Connaught men, than from disputes with the Contractors. One would suppose that in a strange land, in the depth of winter, with want staring them in the face, all local jealousies between persons from rival counties would have been laid aside, but unfortunately for the labourers the reverse has been the case, and the results may easily be imagined. We cannot but hope that now that the leaders are in custody, the mass will return to their employment.

THE LACHINE RIOTS

Montreal Transcript, March 11, 1843.

Peace has been restored between the contending parties, by the intercession of a number of gentlemen deputed for that purpose, and the exertions of the Very Reverend Patrick Phelan, who, on Wednesday last, addressed about 2000 of the laborers after mass, and succeeded in inducing them to come to a reconciliation. A large number of guns were given up, and a subscription made by the laborers on behalf of those who had suffered during the riots, to which Mr. Benjamin Holmes added, on behalf of the St. Patrick's Society, £10, and ten dollars as his own subscription, an example which was followed by several other gentlemen of the delegation. Among those who were active in putting an end to this disgraceful tumult, in addition to Mr. Phelan, whose great influence over his countrymen was as heretofore exerted on the side of peace and good order, were Messrs. Holmes, Driscoll, Dunn, Evans, Lett, Collins, Curley, Tully, Murphy, Casey, and O'Grady. This last gentleman, the author of 'The Emigrant,' and other poems, mainly contributed to the success of the mission, by bringing several hundreds of the Corkonians to the spot, where a reconciliation was effected. He received the warm applause of his countrymen. At present, therefore, the work goes on quietly, and it is to be hoped will so continue, although there is but too much reason to fear an opposite result. Feuds of so long standing, and after having been carried to such dangerous extremes, are not likely to be suddenly stopped, and a spark may at any moment again light up the fires of passion in all their fury. The *Courier* of yesterday, speaking of the reconciliation between the contending parties, says:

"Even the manner in which the disturbance is quelled is scarcely creditable to the Province, however honorable it is to the gentlemen whose kind offices have been so usefully employed. At the best it can only be regarded as a compromise with men who have broken the laws, and who therefore deserved punishment. We rely at present on the forbearance of two parties whose feuds have disturbed the peace of the Colony, and not on the power of the law to suppress those feuds. Is this a state of things which ought to exist in a British Colony, and above all in Canada? We think not, and we regret exceedingly that so dangerous a precedent should be afforded."

It is even said that no persons are to be employed on the Canal except those who have made oath that they have no dangerous weapons in their possession, and also sworn *that they will not commence new riots*! Such a burlesque on the inefficiency of the authorities, to whom is confided the duty of enforcing the law, is as glaring as it is disgraceful. But what other course than conciliation was left open? The power of the law was despised —contests with firearms were going on in open day—houses were broken into and whole families were driven from their homes in terror—passengers on the highway were stopped and searched—the troops called forth to maintain peace were, by the pusillanimity of certain Magistrates, marched *from* the scene of unrest—the trials which had been brought on before King's Bench had terminated favorably for the rioters—in short it seemed as if full . . . licence had been given, and premiums offered for tumult and breaches of the peace, so that the public may be thankful that peace is restored by any means, and that the rioters have *made oath* no longer to disturb the public, and beat and maim each other.

Montreal Transcript, March 25, 1843.

The "strike" alluded to in our last number by the workmen on the Lachine Canal has been attended with still further investigations into the complaints against the contractors.

The complaints, we understand, are:

1st.—The wages are too low to furnish the labourers a comfortable subsistence, and lower than the contractors can well afford to give.

2d.—The wages are held back, paid only at the end of a fortnight—consequently not paid in money but often in *Store* pay.

3d.—Those of the laborers who wish to leave the works cannot get a settlement from the contractors (unless by orders on the stores, with which they cannot settle their board bill) only at the expiration of the fortnight.

Affidavits to the above effect were taken before B. Holmes, Esq. and others, by whom a statement of the case is to be laid before the Executive.

Two shillings a day for common labourers, and 2s. 6d. for borers and barrow men, are the wages given; 2s. 6d. to 3s. 9d. and 4s. are the wages demanded. Whether the Contractors can afford to give more or not, we have no accurate means of knowing; and as they are about giving a counter statement to that of the workmen, we shall wait to hear what they have to say.

Taking into consideration the price of provisions, the scarcity of money, and the rate of wages, we think the workmen cannot complain of the rate of wages. Two shillings is now equal to three at this time last year; and when able bodied men can be obtained in the country for 1s. 3d. a day, exclusive of board, although the wages of the workmen on the canal will not give them many of the comforts and luxuries, if properly paid it will furnish them with all the necessaries of life. The second complaint, if true, is a grievance of the gravest nature. The workmen should be paid at least every week *in money.* Granting that the contractors furnished the articles required as cheap as they possibly could be procured in town, still this method of store pay will always furnish ground of complaint. The contractors should avoid it.

The third complaint is also a grievance.—The contractors should instantly pay up the wages of every man who is desirous of leaving the work. That pay should be furnished in money. We shall allude to the subject again when the statement of the contractors appears.

Montreal Transcript, March 28, 1843.

TO THE EDITOR OF THE GAZETTE.

SIR,—In consequence of numerous *exparte* and injurious statements, made at public and private meetings, and in the columns of your contemporary newspapers, with respect to the disturbances at the Lachine Canal; I am, in vindication of my own, and the characters of those interested with me in the completion of the work on the Lachine Canal, compelled to ask your kind aid in making the following statement of facts public, through the medium of your columns. I am your very obedient servant,

HENRY MASON, Contractor.

Lachine, March 23, 1843.

STATEMENT

The men, principally natives of Ireland, were put on the work early in January last, at the rate of wages then being paid to labourers on the Lachine Canal by the Board of Works, viz: two shillings per day, payable once a month as is the practice on public works, and as is now being paid at Beauharnois and elsewhere—and which pay-day is in all cases lost to the work and at about which period I am paid for work performed—or once in about forty days. As the necessities of the men became apparent, I altered the pay day to once a fortnight, at which intervals the men have since been regularly paid—not, as has been injuriously stated by many, in *truck* or *store pay*, but in money. At the request of nine-tenths of the men put on the work, I arranged with Mr. Bethune for supplying the men with bread from the public Bakery, at Montreal prices, as well as with pork, flour, &c., and became personally responsible for all orders for such articles given by my foreman, between pay days.

The Rev. Father Phelan asked many of the men, when collected near Norton's, at Lachine, whether they could obtain bread, &c., on the foreman's orders, from the store on the works, kept by Messrs. Bethune & Kittson, as cheaply, and of as good quality, as they could elsewhere for money? The answer in the affirmative,—given in presence of J. Somerville, Esq, and many others—should alone be sufficient evidence that no real cause of complaint as to the "store pay," as it has been called, existed. . . .

As is known to many, the men employed by me, struck for an advance of wages. Witness their placards, several of which I can produce, by which strike the work was stopped for many days, to my direct loss and serious inconvenience, and left in such a state, that during the hard frost which followed, from four to five hundred men only could be employed by me: thus were nearly a thousand men thrown out of work, by their own act. Of this thousand, I put in, as frequently as possible, gangs of from twenty, thirty, or forty men, *solely* with a view to enable them to *obtain the means of living* till the work could be opened again. These men were paid every day or two, as they were necessarily discharged, and becoming discontented in consequence, amused themselves by fomenting disturbances among the men actually at work. These discharged men retained the tools in many instances, which tools were invariably taken from them (being furnished by me) on paydays, as they were in hopes of being taken on the work again, sooner than they could be otherwise, or in preference to men having no tools. Many of these men were the loudest in the complaints at not being paid on the regular pay-days, when in fact they did not ask for it or appear at the office. The paymaster has not been absent from the work an entire day since it was opened, and has always been prepared with money to complete pay-lists; or pay discharged men at any working hour. . . .

I have been, among other things, much complained about by the men employed, and by others, for the exorbitant rate, charged for very wretched lodgings at and near the works. I had nothing whatever to do with lodging the men employed by me. Their own number materially enhanced the value of shelter in the neighbouring farmers' houses and outbuildings, and in the cabins, erected by their own countrymen on speculation; but I have now the account before me, of Messrs. Goudwillee and Wark, in which the main item is, a charge of £152 16s. "for the erection of barracks and a cook house," which, since they were completed, have been occupied by the workmen and their families, without the payment to me of a single farthing of rent, nor has a farthing been kept from the men, by way of rent of these buildings.

Montreal Transcript, April 1, 1843.

The *Times* probably was not aware that only last week there was an outbreak between the Connaught men and the Corkonians on the Beauharnois Canal, and that it did not require the labourers to "*break the atmosphere of Lachine*" to renew their ancient bickerings.

We were informed on Tuesday, by a gentlemen who lives in Beauharnois, and whose business called him to the place of the works in that county, that he was stopped by a band of the Connaught men (there the stronger party) and only with great difficulty and after submitting to be questioned and badgered about his business, intentions, birth and destination, was he permitted to depart unharmed. These facts show that it is something other than "the atmosphere of Lachine," however improbable this may appear to the *Times*, which has caused the disgraceful proceedings we have been compelled latterly to notice.

We previously mentioned that we suspected, and had been informed, that the laborers, as the *Times* says, had been "instigated and fomented by crafty individuals with an ulterior intent" to renew their ancient disputes; we should be glad to believe that the instigators and fomenters of these disturbances were not rather to be found among a different class of men than that pointed at by the *Times*. If the Irish laborers would only continue, in some way or other, to work in quietness for the future, there is no disposition to revert to bygone disturbances, which are so little creditable to themselves and to the public authorities; we sincerely hope that this may be the case, for we are quite sure that the laborers have need of all they can earn by their uninterrupted labor, to preserve themselves and families from inconvenience, if not from actual want.

We are sorry to learn that fresh disturbances have broken out among the workmen on the Lachine Canal, originating in the discontent of such as struck for higher wages—that the Contractors had employed Canadians at the rate of 2s. 6d. a day, the wages previously offered to the rioters. The Canadians were driven from the works—some of them said to be severly beaten and injured—and it is supposed they cannot be again induced to return to a place where they are exposed to be maltreated on account of previous misunderstandings between the Contractors and their workmen, with which they had nothing to do, and for which they certainly ought not to suffer. Whether the Contractors or the workmen were to blame in the previous riots, certainly this can have nothing to do with the present unjustifiable attack. The Contractors have the right to employ whomsoever they please, and it is absolutely ridiculous to suppose that they will pay 3s. and 3s. 6d. when they can hire laborers for 2s. 6d. per day, who may accomplish an equal amount of labor, and be less likely to create disturbance. A mis-statement in relation to the causes of the former outbreaks, in yesterday's *Times*, appeared in the following extract:

> Now, admitting to the fullest extent, for the sake of argument, that Corkmen and Connaughtmen viewed each other then with jealousy, it is very improbable that ancient disputes would be renewed on the banks of the Lachine Canal unless instigated and fomented by crafty individuals with an ulterior intent. Some fifteen hundred men were attracted to the works: of these, many have laboured during the summer on the Beauharnois Canal,

peaceably, quietly, and perseveringly. Corkmen and Connaught-men evinced no antipathy to each other at the Beauharnois Canal; yet no sooner do they break the atmosphere of Lachine, than we learn their ancient bickerings are renewed.

H. C. Pentland, 'The Lachine Strike of 1843'. *Canadian Historical Review*, XXIX, 3, September 1948, 273-7. Reprinted by permission of the author and of the publisher, University of Toronto Press.

Of documents dealing with the Lachine strike, those which seek explana-tions and solutions are of most significance to this paper. For perhaps the first time in Canada, men grappled seriously with the problems of em-ployer-employee relations under free wage labour. Some of the opinions expressed show more anger than insight, and some are decidedly partisan. All may be useful, nevertheless, to demonstrate the atmosphere in which discussions took place.

Some observers, like the mayor and magistrates of Montreal, blamed the leaders: "It is too clear that on this, as on all similar occasions the mass was peaceably disposed but they were deceived and irritated by a few—Entering into details of former real or imaginary wrongs these self constituted chiefs impelled their followers to breaches of the peace. . . ." One person laid the blame on the Irish, as Irish: "I am decidedly of the opinion that all the difficulties which have occurred, originated with the men. They are a turbulent and discontented people that nothing can satisfy for any length of time, and who never will be kept to work peaceably un-less overawed by some force for which they have respect . . . ." One observer found the difficulty entirely outside employer-employee relation-ships, in the internal feuds of the Irish: "I believe the Lachine riots to have principally arisen from an old quarrel which took place last year on the long Suel Canal. The parties call themselves Corksmans and Con-naughtmen . . . ."

Three commentators, however, offered analyses more fundamental than those above. One of these, Major-General J. A. Hope, commanded the forces in Canada East, and was the director of the inquiry that provided much of the data for this paper. His own positive contribution is slight, but will serve to give the flavour of his approach. He believed, on the one hand, in amelioration:

. . . If public works are to be carried on during the Winter, which has not taken place till this year—the Labor is likely to be impeded by the severity of the weather . . . many of the men may thus be thrown out of employment & left to their own resources. During Summer the Laborers can gain better wages, probably more than sufficient for their maintenance. I cannot help therefore thinking that if a branch of a saving Bank were established in the neighbourhood of these Works to enable the men to lay up part of their wages during the favorable season, the perfect security of these Deposits being explained by persons in whom the men reposed confidence, that such a measure would be attended with a good effect.

On the other hand, the general was a soldier, and was far from advocating any right of labour to strike: "It appears to me . . . that the Evil arises from there not being an adequate civil power maintained on the line of Works of a proper description." While the context makes it clear that the "Evil" referred to, is the use of troops for civil purposes, the general implies that force is the immediate solution, and its absence the immediate cause, of strikes.

The two remaining observers are Captain Charles Wetherall, who had been and was in future to be a police magistrate; and Charles Atherton, superintendent of engineers at Lachine. Both men prepared analyses of the Lachine labour situation that show much insight. Captain Wetherall wrote as follows:

> The Public Works throughout the Province, are given by the Board of Works to Contractors; and the labour is invariably performed by Irishmen, who work in Gangs; and having no other mode of gaining their livelihood, seem to monopolize all the labour on the Public Works, both here and in the United States:— They are considered the best labourers; consequently it is the interest of the Contractors to employ them, in preference to Canadians:—The only difficulty is to manage them, and from their peculiarities, and general opinions of a Contractor, it becomes next to impossible for him to do so.
>
> They look on a Contractor, as they view the "Middle Men" of their own Country, as a grasping, money-making person, who has made a good bargain with the Board of Works for labour to be performed; and they see, or imagine they see, an attempt to improve that bargain at their expence, by giving them too low a rate of pay, or by compelling them to receive their wages in Store Pay; in other words, that they are obliged to purchase all the necessaries of life from Stores, established by the Contractors.

Wetherall's solution to the Lachine situation is really a part of his analysis. He proposed that the conditions of employment be laid down in detail by the Board of Works, with a single enforcing superintendent clothed with wide powers, to ensure compliance and uniformity:

It should be his [the superintendent's] duty to ascertain that a fair rate of Pay was given by the Contractor, and that every part of his agreement is well understood by the parties, and rigidly performed . . . . [Then] there would be no inducement for the men to leave one work in the hope of getting more wages or better treatment on another; and there would be a wholesome check on Men by Knowing, that if discharged for misconduct, they would not find Government employment elsewhere . . . . The basis would be a fair price of labour, and punctuality of payment on one hand, and on the part of the labourer, a rigid performance of his engagement; but all arrangements however good will fail, unless the labourer receives his Pay without any deduction, and is at liberty to spend it where he chooses—that I am satisfied is the subject on which all the difficulties hinge, and never will be got over, as long as the Contractor has any interest in the supply of their wants. While the work is in the neighbourhood of a Village where there are Stores, *bons* could be issued by the Contractor, which would be cheerfully received by any of the Storekeepers *without depreciation*, and on an engagement on the part of the Contractor to redeem them at fourteen days.

Charles Atherton's discussion of the Lachine strike reads:

For some years past, the Public Works, both in the United States & in Canada, have been carried on almost exclusively by Irish Labourers, who have been accustomed to flock in masses from Work to Work; & thus a large proportion of the Labourers on the Lachine Canal Improvements are men of unsettled habits, having no established home and consequently not bound by the moral ties which influence a settled population. In such Bands certain Individuals soon acquire influence thus an unity of Action is effected, capable of disturbing the *ordinary* rules which subsist *individually* between the Labourer and his Employer, & this power is wielded as the views of a few Individuals may dictate.
. . . [T]he violent proceedings to which 1,500 men, homeless & poverty stricken, may be suddenly instigated, can only be promptly arrested by measures which may be considered incompatible with the ordinary State of peaceable Society. The putting down such an outbreak demands unusual steps, the more so as the skill with which it is conducted baffles the authority of the Law. The *prevention* of such outrage should in my opinion be

sought in the adoption of regulations, whereby such masses of destitute men, should not be induced or allowed to congregate in one Locality.

As to the Origin of the Evil,—In my humble opinion, one of the chief causes has been the delusive expectations which Emigrants have been led to form on leaving their native land. Food should be looked forward to as the fruits of Emigration rather than Money alone, but the reverse has been the case, & Emigrants on their arrival in Canada have seldom followed steady agricultural Labour, yielding the natural remuneration of *food*, with *moderate* wages in Cash, such as Agriculture can afford, but generally those pursuits have been sought which yield temporary high wages payable in Coin. Hence their misery,—for the highest rate of wages to be earned at a temporary Public Work, is but poor compensation for a wandering life. Poverty and Discontent are the natural consequences of such an error. Public Works are demoralizing at best, & should in my opinion be carried on as far as possible by the local population, & be regarded as the mere *helping hand*, not the *dependence* of the Emigrant.

The opinions on labour relations presented in this paper are thought to give a fair picture of Canadian opinion in the eighteen-forties. It should be borne in mind that there was in this instance a good deal of public sympathy for the labourers—probably more than was usual in such cases. Racial and political groupings, turning on the isolation of the merchant class in Montreal, help account for this. However, this sentiment was displayed chiefly by illiterate portions of the population, and finds no expression in this symposium.

Aside from this unlettered opinion of wage-earners and habitants, there seem to have been two groups: the merchants-employers, represented by Henry Mason, Norman Bethune, and the Montreal magistrates; and the governing class, rooted in feudal England, with General Hope, Captain Wetherall, and Charles Atherton for its spokesmen.

It is clear that neither of these groups thought of the labourers as human beings in their own image, but considered them rather as machines for doing work. In the employers' case, the result was a feeling of rage that the machine did not run according to specifications; both the working class and the employing class in Canada were as yet naive, undisciplined, and irritating to the other. This mechanical approach, however, may have assisted members of the governing class to remain detached in their appraisal of industrial difficulties. Particularly was this possible because the governing class had little higher opinion of the employers than of the employed. The rise of the large railway corporation in the eighteen-fifties was to destroy this attitude of impartial superiority;

but government officials seem to have been able, in the eighteen-forties, to discuss industrial relations with a calm that is almost academic.

While the canal contractors and canal labourers were the forerunners of the modern Canadian capitalist and working classes, the bureaucrats were representative of an old order about to be swept away. The public works, which they strove so hard to build, helped destroy that order, in favour of new economic and political groups. The eighteen-forties was thus a decade of transition, marking the rise of wage-labour on a large scale, and of a milieu that would forge labour into a self-conscious independent force.

THE PRINTERS' STRIKE OF 1872

Daily Globe (Toronto), March 23, 1872.

PRINTERS' ASSOCIATION

Toronto, March 10, 1872

The undersigned Master Printers of the City of Toronto, in view of the action taken by the Typographical Union with regard to the internal arrangements of their Offices, feel themselves compelled for the first time to unite in self-defence; and hereby agree to adopt regulations for the internal conduct of all their offices, the wages of their employees, the price at which work shall be executed, and all other matters affecting their common interests.

We further agree that the term of daily labour in our offices shall be ten hours; that the price of composition by the piece shall be thirty cents per thousand ems for day hands, and thirty-three and one-third cents for night hands on morning papers; and that the MINIMUM wages of efficient compositors, when employed by the week, shall be ten dollars.

We further agree that in the event of the threatened action of the Typographical Society, taken on Wednesday, 18th March, being carried into effect, and our hands strike work, we shall declare all our establishments non-union offices.

We further pledge ourselves that in the event of a strike, we shall all unite to complete the work unfinished in our several offices, and to bring out all the newspapers as usual.

We further agree that in the event of a strike, we shall act unitedly in resisting all demands inconsistent with this agreement; that we shall meet together daily and stand by the determinations from time to time come to by a majority of the parties to this agreement.

GEO. BROWN, *Globe Printing Company.*

J. ROSS ROBERTSON, *The Daily Telegraph.*

JAMES MOYLAN, *The Canadian Freeman.*

J. B. COOK, *The Express.*

E. R. STIMSON, *Church Herald.*

S. ROSE, *Christian Guardian.*

W. H. FLINT, *Pure Gold.*

PATRICK BOYLE, *Irish Canadian.*

COPP, CLARK & CO.

DUDLEY & BURNS.

MC LEISH & CO.

BELL & CO.

HUNTER, ROSE & CO.

ROWSELL & HUTCHISON.

P. H. STEWART.

GEO. O. PATTERSON.

M. J. GRAND.

PRINTERS WANTED.

COMPOSITORS CAN RECEIVE
PERMANENT ENGAGEMENTS

In the undermentioned Toronto Printing Offices, at the following rates of wages:

33 1/3 cents per 1,000 ems, for work on morning papers.

30 cents per 1,000 ems, for day work.

$10 to $15 per week, of sixty hours, for Job Hands.

THE GLOBE OFFICE.

THE DAILY TELEGRAPH OFFICE.

THE EXPRESS OFFICE.

THE CANADIAN FREEMAN OFFICE.

THE CHURCH HERALD OFFICE.

THE GUARDIAN OFFICE.

THE PURE GOLD OFFICE.

THE IRISH CANADIAN OFFICE.

THE ONTARIO GAZETTE OFFICE.

COPP, CLARK & CO.

DUDLEY & BURNS.

MC LEISH & CO.

BELL & CO.

HUNTER, ROSE & CO.
ROWSELL & HUTCHISON.
P. H. STEWART.
GEORGE C. PATTERSON.
M. J. GRAND.
Toronto 22nd March, 1872

THE NINE HOURS MOVEMENT

Daily Globe (Toronto), March 23, 1872.

We have no sympathy with those who object to organized movements for increasing the wages of the artisan or the elevation of his social position. On the contrary, our sympathy goes heartily in favour of whatever contributes to those ends. The best interests of the whole community are promoted by every fair and temperate step tending to increase the comfort and happiness of any large section of the people.

But to carry with it public sympathy, every such organized movement must have a clearly defined object in view; that object must be openly and honestly stated; and the demand made must be shown to be based on justice, common sense and the public well. No claim based on such grounds can be resisted for many days by any body of employers, however powerful, wealthy or united—in Canada at any rate, whatever may be done in other countries. And no claim that cannot stand examination by those tests can be permanently enforced.

We are glad at last to have an authoritative statement of what is the aim and scope of the Nine-hours movement. A gentleman has been brought specially from the United States to explain it to us, and on Wednesday of last week he told us the whole story in the Music Hall. Mr. Trevellick is President of the National Labour League of the United States, and one of the lecturers hired by the said League to peregrinate the United States and Canada and explain the objects of the Nine-hours movement. We shall not err, therefore, in accepting his utterances as official and authoritative.

We have to thank Mr. Trevellick for having met two, at least, of our preliminary conditions. He has told us clearly what is wanted—and he has told it openly and candidly. Here, in brief, are his demands:

1. He demands from the employers of labour "the adoption of the nine-hours system," to "come into operation on the first Monday of June,

1872"—and that they shall give their answer, yes or no, to "the Trades Assembly," by "the first of May."

2. He tells us, however, very frankly—speaking, of course, authoritatively for the National Labour League:—"He did not believe in nine hours; every breath in his body called out for eight hours." (Loud applause) But he would not "ask the men of the Dominion to *call* for eight hours. Let them get these things step by step."

3. He explains that "by working men they did not only mean those who worked by their hands, but also the men of science who taught them how to subdue the forces and bring machinery under the guidance of men. They wanted justice—justice to the brain, and justice to the muscles."

4. He gives warning to objectors that this thing is to be done "if fifty years" are necessary to do it—that "by studying the principles of legislation, if those who villified them would not grant their reasonable demands, they, the people, would do it for themselves." If "the law would not give them their rights, they must trip up the law and take them."

5. And with equal candour he tells us how the Press is to be muzzled if it ventures to dissent from the *dicta* of the President of the National Labour League of the United States: "He tendered the working men this advice—if a paper shot too hard at them they should neither take that paper, nor buy dry goods at any store advertising in that paper. (Applause.) If the working men of Toronto would only say, 'Let him alone,' that would kill him; he would commit suicide. The papers could not live without wind, and it was their money which gave them the wind."

It will be seen, therefore, that "the Nine-hours Movement" is merely one step in the march of progress. When that step has been accomplished, it is to be followed up by a second step, in the shape of an eight-hours movement;—and every breath in the body of the National Labour League of the United States calls aloud for eight hours! *at the wages of ten, of course.* Nay, while telling us so much, Mr. President Trevellick omitted to assure us that even the eight-hours movement would be a finality—that is, in its turn, shall not be followed up by other steps downward, until that grand climacteric in the march of laziness is reached, when everybody shall "wear large boots," "give select parties," "live by chance on the labour of somebody else," and be "of no more use to society than so many bull-frogs." We quote the words of Mr. President Trevellick. . . .

But let us not forget for a moment the impudence of the thing. Let us look at the proposal to restrict all daily labour to nine hours, on its merits. . . .

How is it possible to fix the duration of daily labour of all descriptions by one cast-iron standard? Sir Benjamin Brodie, we think estimated the exhaustion from mental labour to be three times as great as that from physical labour. How, then, can the same duration of work be suitable for both? . . . On the very face of the thing the same rule cannot be applied to all occupations. There is no inherent virtue in any particular number of hours, showing it to be right and all others wrong. As well may you attempt to pay all men the same wages, as to make all work for the same time. The good sense of mankind has heretofore regarded ten hours for work, seven for sleep, and seven for food, enjoyment and improvement, as a wise and healthful distribution of time for an able-bodied man engaged in ordinarily laborious avocations; and the more closely the matter is examined, the nearer the truth, we fancy, will this term be found to be. But it would be nearly as absurd to fix ten hours for all, as nine. There are many avocations too exciting, too hot, too cold, too exposed, too hard, to be wisely or profitably continued for either of these terms; but in the vast majority of industrial pursuits in Canada, the man who thinks ten hours hurtful or oppressive, is too lazy to earn his bread; and in the name of all the women of Canada, we protest against sending home such a fellow to pester his wife, loafing around for another hour daily. She has enough of him already, poor woman.

We earnestly object to the impression which such professional agitators as Mr. Trevellick seek to stamp on the popular mind—that labour is a thing to be disliked, shunned, striven against—that the man who works hard and is well paid for it, is a victim of the rapacious capitalist—that the shorter the hours the happier the man. On the contrary, we believe that the man who has full steady employment for a length of time daily, not inconsistent with robust health and the discharge of all family and public duties—who has occupation for every minute of the day—and who goes home to his wife at night with the glad consciousness that he has done a good day's work, and added to the comforts of his household, is a far better, healthier, happier man than his neighbour who has one or two hours daily of idle time to consume. Show us the man who is always ready to give a helping-hand to any public good; to give up a day or an hour at the call of a friend; to subscribe of his limited means liberally to the cause of religion or philanthropy—and we will show you a man, be he labourer or capitalist, merchant or mechanic, who works up to the full limit of his time, and thanks God he has the strength to do it.

We are not forgetful of the great mental improvement that might be achieved by everybody, if in addition to the fourteen hours that remain (after working ten hours) for sleep, food and improvement, a fifteenth hour were taken from labour, and devoted by everybody to study, and lectures, and scientific researches. No doubt. But does a healthy man want more than seven hours for sleep? or more than one hour for food?—ah! we forgot; is Mr. Trevellick an Englishman? let us say *two* hours for food,— and one hour for going to and returning from work. There still remain four hours per day for relaxation, enjoyment or study, according to inclination. If the subject is really desirous of mental improvement, is not that enough? But is the number who are ardently bent on high mental cultivation or scientific acquirement really so very great among us that all the rest of the population must stop work for one hour per day to let them do it? . . .

But let us get quit of a glaring absurdity in the "tall talk" of Mr. President Trevellick about the crushing exactions of the capitalist and the grinding down of the working man. In Canada, at any rate, all this is absolute rant. To hear his nonsense, one might fancy him to be not a Yankee, but an Englishman—an English professional orator—fresh caught from an Islington stump, and brimful of all the tyrannies and disabilities which men of large souls like himself endure at the hands of the "blawsted aristocrats." Evidently, Mr. President Trevellick is profoundly ignorant of how the social fabric of Ontario is constituted. Evidently he does not know that when you speak of the working man in Ontario, you include everybody. We all work. We all began with nothing. We have all got by hard work all we own—and the richest among us work on still, and like to do it. There is probably no country on earth where the whole people are more industrious or more reasonably frugal. Not many large fortunes are accumulated among us; but in very few countries, if in any, are there so large a proportion of the workers who achieve an ample independence. We have no such class as those styled capitalists in other countries. The whole people are the capitalists of Canada. The earnings of our prosperous farmers provide the means to settle their sons on new lands and subdue the forest. The savings of our mechanics and business men build the houses and warehouses of our towns and cities. The small yearly accumulations of all classes furnish capital for our banks, saving societies and other sound monetary institutions—and these in turn distribute it among merchants and manufacturers and set the wheels of industry moving over the land. We have no Rothschilds in Canada—no Jacob Astors, no Vanderbilts, no Tweeds, no Goulds, no Jim Fisks. But we have thousands of small investors, and these are our only capitalists. The demand for workmen of all descriptions from every corner of Ontario is constant and urgent—the supply is never equal to the demand—and as a consequence the wages are high, the employee is master of the situation, and he rules his employer with a rod of iron.

In such a country it is utterly ridiculous to talk of the rapacity and despotism of the employer. The tyranny of the employed over his master would be an infinitely truer version of the case. In countries where the large mass of the people live from day to day on the wages of others, and in dread of the loss of work—excessive hours of labour and other injustice may be forced on the employed by the employer. But how can this ever be in a country where so vast a proportion of the people work for themselves—where so small a portion work for others, and can so readily find employment. . . .

We respectfully submit to the President of the National Labour League of the United States that before he makes his next speech in Canada he had better learn something more of the character and employments of our people and he will not talk so croucely [coarsely?] about tripping up laws and crushing newspapers. Not a fraction even of the forty thousand men who are within reach of his nostrums, we venture to affirm, have a particle of sympathy with him in the movement—and assuredly if the number was much more, they are mistaken if they flatter themselves for a moment that the other million and a half of their fellow-citizens, who do a full day's work for fair compensation, will be coerced by any strikes or threats into paying them ten hours' wage for eight hours' work—or nine hours' either.

One word more for Mr. President Trevellick, of the National Labour League of the United States. Not only are the people at large the real capitalists of Canada, but his flights of oration about the political subjection of the working man are as ridiculous as his ideas on monetary despotism. The men who make our laws, who govern our Province, who administer our excellent institutions, who dispense justice admirably— almost to a man came from the people, are of the people still, and not a few of them are among the hardest-worked men in this or any other community. The people have entire political power in their own hands—what they wish done, must be done. All men stand here on an equal footing. No laws of primogeniture or entail build up privileged classes; no hereditary rights bar the way to the elevation of the man of ability. The poorest man may rise to the highest office in the State, and there are among us many living evidences of the fact. We have no doubt our political strifes and feuds like other people, and we fight them out keenly enough; but we all unite heartily in teaching our children that honest labour is honourable, that industry, perseverance and energy are noble virtues, and that laziness is detestable.

The *Mail* (Toronto), April 4, 1872.

MASS MEETING IN THE ST. LAWRENCE HALL.

The St. Lawrence Hall last night was crammed with workingmen on the occasion of a united demonstration in favour of the nine hour movement. The proceedings began at 8 o'clock. The chair was taken by Mr. Williams, President of the Trades' Assembly. . . .

Dr. A. A. RIDDELL was the next speaker. Apologizing for the shortness of time, he moved:—"That this meeting hereby give expression to their condemnation of the unjust and oppressive attempt of the Master Printers to destroy the Typographical Union, and consider it an encroachment upon the rights of the men, and an effort to prevent the formation of Trades' Unions for the protection and benefit of the men." He did not regret the share he had taken in the formation of Trades' Unions. He believed that workingmen had a perfect right to join together for the sake of obtaining an increase in wages. If that were not the case, the employee had no rights as a citizen. If it could be said that there was one law for the employer and another for the employed, then there was no liberty in the country. (Cheers.) The laws which oppressed the workingman ought before long to be swept from the statute book. . . . He believed that, if possible, strikes should be avoided; but still he believed that workingmen had as much right to place a price upon their labour as has the farmer to put a price upon his produce. (Cheers.) It was for the mutual advantage of the nation that the workingmen should be well paid for their labour; and that the shortest hours should prevail. As the hours went at present, no time was given to the workingman to show that he was a citizen or anything removed from a bondsman. (Cheers.) . . .

Mr. DANCE (Ironmongers' Union), in seconding the resolution, proceeded to remark on the inconsistency of the *Globe.* Six months ago, when a strike was in progress at Newcastle-on-Tyne, the *Globe* was in favour of nine hours. The *Globe* said it then because it was 3,000 miles away; but when the ball was kicked from Newcastle to Hamilton, it couldn't see it all. (Cheers.) No good argument had been adduced, bearing on the Masters' case. After describing the origin of the strike in Wilson, Bowman & Co.'s factory at Hamilton, Mr. Dance proceeded to say that the real opponents of the nine hours' movement acted solely for the sake of opposition. It was all right for the *Globe* to organize for political purposes, but it was wrong to organize to carry out the purposes of the workingman. (Cheers.) He trusted that at the next election only those members would be returned who would vote for the passage of a law for the protection of Trades' Unions.

The *Mail* (Toronto), April 16, 1872.

MASS MEETING OF WORKINGMEN IN
THE QUEEN'S PARK.

———

SPEECHES BY MR. BEATY, M.P., AND OTHERS
PROCESSION IN THE EVENING.

The Trades' Assembly of Toronto held a monster procession yesterday to celebrate the inauguration of the nine hour movement, and the granting of it by the Great Western Railway authorities at Hamilton. About half-past one the procession was formed at the Moulders' Hall, on King-street west. About 1,200 representatives of the different trades in the city took part in it. The music was supplied by four bands, including the band of the 10th Royals which turned out in uniform. . . .

The sidewalks along the route were crammed with spectators. The procession marched from the Moulders' Hall to Brock street, thence to Queen, down Queen to George, then by George to King st., where a halt was made and cheering given in front of the *Leader* office. Marching up King st., the procession turned up Yonge, thence to the platform in the Queen's Park, when the procession resolved itself into a meeting. It was calculated that nearly 6,000 people were present. On the platform were the officers of the Trades' Assembly, Messrs. James Beaty, M.P., Ald. Hallam, E. King Dodds, Dr. C. B. Hall, Dr. A. A. Riddell, and others.

Mr. Williams, President of the Trades' Assembly, presided. During the whole of the meeting a fierce snow storm raged. . . .

Mr. E. KING DODDS said that seldom in the history of Toronto had a greater gathering of her citizens been witnessed than upon the present occasion. This was no mere local question. It must be an issue of great national importance which had brought so many thousand working men together. The meeting to-day was a precursor of the great but peaceful social revolution which would remodel the entire industrial system of the country (Cheers.) The handwriting on the wall was plain; the fiat had gone forth that nine hours was the limit of a day's toil. The question in Toronto was being agitated in a fair and straightforward manner; and the workingmen stepped forward in the open light of day and proclaimed to the country their request. They might double the police force of the city, but it was unnecessary. The agitators were peaceful and honourable citizens, whose agitation was but the echo of a universal sentiment. It was not, as its opponents say, an American plea, but a principle which having been found successful in England is firmly implanted in the minds of Canadian citizens. The *Globe* in alluding to the condition of workingmen in Warwickshire, England, applauds unions as the probable means for the elevation of their condition, and trusts that many of the labourers in that part of the country may be induced to immigrate to Canada where labour is better appreciated and where the working man occupies a more dignified and independent position. While paying this just tribute to the benefits of united organization in Warwickshire, it condemned the principle when it came nearer home and clashed with the interests of "Master Printers." While painting in such glowing colors the superior freedom and independence enjoyed by the workingman in this country it in another column prints the manifesto of the employers, most of them put forward by George Brown, to declare against the nine hours movement, and thus stifle the honest desire of the working-men of Toronto. Historians claim that in England there stands "a power behind the throne." That power is the workingmen of England. We have not the throne in this country, but the power nevertheless rests in the hands of the people, whose energy, perseverance and toil make them the true aristocracy of the land. (Cheers.) Fifty-four hours a week was sufficient for any man to work. No physical force or riotous conduct had been introduced into the consideration of this question. The pioneers of this reform—the printers of Toronto—had conducted themselves in a most orderly manner. They laid their case before their employers, and if their request be not granted they will go elsewhere where intelligence as well as muscle was appreciated. (Applause.) Remembering the motto, "Union is strength," the artizans of Toronto were supported by the sentiment of the country. He did not desire to introduce politics into this matter, but it rested with his auditors to send men to represent them in Parliament who would fight the battle of the workingman. He called upon them to take no shuffling promise, but insist upon a fair and straightforward promise that their interests should be properly agitated. He did not advocate class legislation, but a broad, liberal and comprehensive policy in the interests of the whole people. Last evening he read with great pleasure that the Great Western Railway had granted the nine hours' movement. He felt it most appropriate that the first important admission of the principle underlying this great reform had been made by a corporation like the Great Western Railway. This was a movement not to crush but to advance. Men would do as much in nine hours as was now accomplished in ten, it would not be detrimental to the interest of employers, while it would be elevating to the condition of the labourer. He defended the principle of Trades' Unions, and stated that when the honest workingman once placed his foot down there was no such word as fail. The power of the people must succeed. The union of workingmen the world over has proved in the past a rampart of strength. Workingmen's hands around the globe are on this question clasped in friendly strength; the link of a common brotherhood unites them, and united they are invincible. The speaker withdrew amid immense applause.

Daily Globe (Toronto), April 19, 1872.

THE PRINTERS' STRIKE.

THE CHARGE OF CONSPIRACY BEFORE THE POLICE MAGISTRATE

The thirteen printers who were arrested on Tuesday for conspiracy and were admitted to bail, were again brought up yesterday before Mr. Alexander Macnabb. The court was crowded at the hearing.

The names of the prisoners were: Edward Ward, G. J. McMillan, John Armstrong, James Gillespie, William Lovell, James A. Lanfear, George Huson, James Macdonald, William Meredith, Edward Clark, Thomas Gibson, John Casson, James S. Williams, and John H. Lumsden, and the charge against them was that, "being workmen and labourers in the act or occupation of printers, and employed as such artificers, workmen, and labourers in the said art and occupation, by the usual number of hours in each day, and not being content to work and labour in that art and occupation by the usual number of hours, did unlawfully conspire, combine, confederate, and agree together, by divers subtle means and devices, to induce and persuade artificers and workmen who had contracted with the said master printers to serve them in the said art or business, for certain times and periods in that behalf agreed upon between them and the said employers, and so having entered into the services of the said employers, unlawfully to absent themselves from the said service, without the consent of the said employers, before the respective terms of their services were completed, to the great damage of the said master printers, to the evil example of others in like case offending, and against the peace of our Lady the Queen, her Crown and dignity."

The warrant included 10 other names, but the parties had not yet been arrested.

On the entrance of the prisoners, a cheer was raised from the crowd on the outside of the bar.

The MAGISTRATE instantly ordered that part of the Court to be cleared. . . .

The crowd was then ejected from the court, and the proceedings from that time were of an orderly character.

Mr. K. Mackenzie, Q.C. and Mr. Falconbridge prosecuted; and the prisoners were defended by Mr. A. W. Lauder, Mr. C. McMichael, and Mr. Dixon. . . .

The case was accordingly proceeded with, Mr. McKenzie calling his witnesses without any introductory remarks.

WILLIAM B. PARKS, sworn—I am a printer. There is a union existing in Toronto called the Toronto Typographical Union, No. 91. The rules produced are the rules and regulations of 1869. I believe some new ones have since been issued, but those produced form the constitution and byelaws. . . . A strike occurred among the printers on the Monday before Easter. They stopped work on the 25th March. A great many men took part in the strike. Some printers in THE GLOBE office did so, some also in the *Telegraph, Express,* Hunter, Rose & Co.'s, Copp, Clark & Co's, Dudley & Burns', and Rowsell & Hutchison's. He did not know about the other offices. The strike took place because the Union as a body made certain demands for the shortening of hours of labour from 10 hours a day to nine hours. Except in one or two instances, the employers refused to grant the demands. The last meeting of the Union I was at, it was decided that the news hands should strike or stop work on the following Monday. This was carried by a majority of the votes. The strike took place in consequence of this, the nine hours not being conceded. The defendant Mc-Millan was in the chair, and I think several of the other defendants were present. I went on the strike myself, because I obeyed the majority. I continued on it for eight working days. When I returned to Dudley & Burns, I was told to leave the Union, but not by any of the defendants.

Mr. LAUDER objected to any evidence not relating to the defendants being given.

The MAGISTRATE said it had been proved that there was a combination of men for a certain purpose, and the rates and papers thereof had been put in. The defendants were members of the society, and the proposed evidence referred to the action of the society·

Mr. MC KENZIE said the law provided that, in cases of this kind, "the acts of other conspirators may be given in evidence against them if done in furtherance of the common object."

WITNESS—One member of the Union named Benjamin Loeman told me I was a mean man in going back to work.

Mr. DIXON. I think he was right.

WITNESS—He insinuated that when things were settled, I should have a tough chance of getting work. Another member Courtenay, told me that, as the close of this thing, a black list would be published, and my name would appear in it. Several other members have been at me, telling me I had done wrong and that in the long run, I should suffer for it. There was a printer at the office named Robert Ridley, whom they called a "rat," which I understand to mean one who works for lower wages. Ridley never struck, and I was told I could not be allowed, as a union man, to go back to work with a "rat." This took place at the committee-room of the Union. There were three men present named McGillicuddy, Bleith, and I think, Meredith, when this took place. I know a boy named John Thompson, who is an apprentice in Dudley & Burns' employment. He came out on strike. I saw him paid on Easter Monday by William Lovell. He got a dollar and a half from the funds of the Union to help support him. In each office, there is a committee called a "chapel" is formed of those men, one of whom is called the "father of the chapel." I was once appointed on a committee of three by Edward Clark, the chairman of the Vigilance Committee; we were to go to the *Telegraph* Office in reference to something connected with the strike; I don't recollect what.

The MAGISTRATE—Why can't you tell us right now?

Mr· LAUDER—I think the witness is willing enough; He has no business to be brow beaten by the court.

WITNESS—We went to the *Telegraph* Office to try and arrange between the Union men and the *Telegraph*; I was at a meeting just previous to the one I have spoken of, but I don't recollect what took place.

Cross examined by Mr. LAUDER—I was a member of the Union, which has existed since 1844. The master printers knew of its existence. I believe most of the proprietors knew of the "chapels." When the masters thought demands reasonable, they had generally given way previously.

The MAGISTRATE—Does that make it legal?

Mr. LAUDER—We want to show the custom.

The MAGISTRATE—If a man meets you on the street, and demands your watch does your giving it to him make it legal? Here is an illegal act showed and you say because the other party acceded to it, it became legal.

Mr. LAUDER—But we say it is not illegal.

The MAGISTRATE—By law it is illegal to conspire for certain purposes.

Mr. LAUDER—We say that has to be proved.

The MAGISTRATE—There is no need to prove the law. It is not a foreign law, it is the law of the land.

WITNESS—The proprietors have I believe united together and formed an association.

Mr. LAUDER—Give their names.

The MAGISTRATE—What has that to do with it? We are not trying these other parties. . . .

Mr. LAUDER asked the witness a number of questions which the Magistrate decided were irrelevant.

Mr. MC MICHAEL asked the witness a question, and the Magistrate decided that the answer was not important. Mr. McMichael asked that the answer might be taken down, but the Magistrate refused to note them. After long argument, Mr. Lauder asked that the objection might be noted, his Worship declined to accede to this.

Mr. LAUDER—What, doesn't your Worship note objections of counsel?

The MAGISTRATE—No, because there are no counsel here as a matter of law, but only as a matter of courtesy.

Mr. LAUDER—That is the first time we have heard that doctrine.

The MAGISTRATE—Then you had better read the Statute, and you will find it.

EDWARD DOUDIET, sworn—Was a printer employed by Hunter, Rose & Co. Had been a member of the Typographical Union until the 26th of March, when he sent in his resignation. The strike took place on the 25th of March. Attended the meeting of the union on Saturday, March 16th, and one subsequently. Witness knew all the prisoners except one. He identified Lanfear as a member of the union. At the first meeting he attended, McMillan was in the chair. The object of the union was to keep up the rate of wages, and regulate the time of labour. At the meeting on the 16th of March it was decided that the news hands should apply for an increase from 30 to 33 1/3 per cent, per thousand ems. At that time it was not thought advisable that the whole society should strike.

The MAGISTRATE said the witness had sworn that the object of the society was to fix wages and regulate time, and regulating time was only another way of fixing wages. That was an illegal combination. What was the object of giving the proceedings at any one meeting of the society?

WITNESS, cross examined—The demand for an increase of wages was granted, in some offices.

The MAGISTRATE said that, whether the Master Printers acceded to the request of the Union or not, it did not make it legal. If this was an illegal combination, did the fact of any establishment, or the whole of the establishments in the city of Toronto, acceding to the demand do away with the illegality?

Mr. LAUDER—If they have acceded to the demand, why prosecute?

The MAGISTRATE—You must ask them about that.

Mr. LAUDER said nothing had yet been proved of an illegal character. At all event, what had been shown would be quite legal in England.

Mr. MACKENZIE observed that in 1825 a statute was passed in England legalising these unions to a certain extent. Soon after, however, another one was passed repealing the former one. But this had nothing to do with the state of things in Canada, where the only law on the subject was common law.

Mr. LAUDER said that was the misfortune of these men, who were not aware that they had been so remiss as not to pass an Act here in reference to unions.

EDWARD J. O'NEIL, sworn.—Am a detective, know where the union meets No. 93 King street West; attended some of the trains coming in to Toronto—about 13; have seen men coming in to work for the GLOBE Printing Company; saw other parties go up and ask these men if they were printers, and if they said yes the others said we are printers too, and we have struck work here in the city for nine hours, and would ask them if they were union men to go up to the committee rooms and join; I told these parties not to speak to the men I had with me as they were going to work in THE GLOBE office; followed these men and saw them go up stairs to the union rooms and enter where I would not be admitted. On the 30th March I received instructions to meet some parties coming in by train and proceeded to London and met these men, Merrick, Flynn and Longan; brought them to the GLOBE office; this was on Saturday; I made a verbal agreement with these men on the train between London and Hamilton and a written agreement was made afterwards to work in the GLOBE office for one year; saw these men at work to THE GLOBE office on the Sunday and Monday following; about noon on Monday saw two men whom he knew to be printers with Merrick between them going into the Union on King street; went on down to the St. James' Hotel, and a few minutes after J. V. Thompson came in followed by Merrick and Wm. Lovell; Lovell demanded Merrick's bill at the bar and paid it and then the three men went over to the Grand Trunk platform, did not then arrest Merrick but telegraphed to Hamilton and Merrick was arrested there. I got on a train and went to Hamilton where I got track of Flynn whom I followed and arrested at Paris, and brought him back to Toronto; I found nothing on Flynn in connection with the Union; searched Merrick and found a ticket of membership of the T. T. U. No. 91. . . .

Cross-examined by Mr. LAUDER—I live in Ottawa; my superior sent me to Toronto; will not say who they were; I refuse to say who sent for me to come to Toronto. Mr. Lauder wished to know if the witness was not compellable to reveal who sent for him.

His WORSHIP said he was not, as it did not affect the case. . . .

Mr. LAUDER said there was no doubt George Brown was at the bottom of the whole thing.

Examination resumed—I said to Merrick that if any one offered him violence he was to notify me; on the way to the train no physical force was employed with the men who left;

His WORSHIP here stopped the examination, as being entirely useless. He said the case tried was whether this combination was illegal; it had to be proved that there was a Union.

Mr. MACKENZIE said he had a number of witnesses to prove overt acts, but, for the present he would not call them. He said they had proved combination, and that it was a fact that there had been a strike. It might be settled at once as it did not appear that their evidence could be displaced.

Mr. LAUDER asked for an adjournment.

Mr. MACKENZIE said it was a bailable offence, and he would take any, the very lightest bail.

It was finally decided to adjourn the hearing till Monday fortnight; the defendants being admitted to go on their present bail.

LEGAL STATUS OF UNIONS

The *Mail* (Toronto), April 19, 1872.

We are heartily glad to see that Sir John Macdonald gave notice yesterday of his intention to introduce a bill assimilating the law of Canada to that of England in the matter of strikes and Trade Unions. The modification to which the harsh old English law has been submitted at home, are even more necessary and suitable to the circumstances of Canada where capital and labour are not separated by impassible lines, old traditions and the relics of feudalism. It is our delight to call ourselves a free country, and no country can be really free where a man is not at liberty to do the best he can with his labour, where and when he likes. There is an element of bondage in the law as it stands here, and as soon as it attracted the notice of our Minister of Justice, with the promptness that characterizes all his efforts in the way of remedial legislation, he instantly set about abating the evil.

The *Mail* (Toronto), April 25, 1872.

THE LABOUR QUESTION.

If Canada has hitherto neglected to repeal the old, harsh and cruel laws against Trades combinations, the fact is due to their having become obsolete and their very existence forgotten. An attempt to revive them, to put them into force, was no more thought of than any rational person would think of putting into force the old English law which requires everyone, under penalty, to attend church once every Sunday. Such a case, to the surprise of almost every one, has actually occurred; and a real necessity has arisen formally to modify a law which every rational man who knew of its existence believed to have become a dead letter. It is quite time to take from any man or body of men the power to treat as a criminal conspiracy a mere combination to raise the rate of wages. When such combinations lead to coercion or violence these acts must be treated as criminal just as if they had been done under any other circumstances.

The merits of the question involved in the nine hours movement is another matter. The refusal of a number of work men to work beyond a limited number of hours a day should be based on some good reason. If nine hours' work exhaust the system, and be as long a working day as is compatible with the preservation of health; if longer hours would reduce workmen to a condition of mere animalism; if the workshops necessarily, or in fact, are charged with noxious gases or impure air, to breathe which more than so many out of the twenty-four impairs the health and debilitates the constitution; if any of these or any similar results would come of making a greater number of hours a day's work, then a case would be made out for a shorter number of hours. To talk of making the length of the working day uniform, in all occupations, is to overlook the differences in the effects of different employments on the health; and is not a whit more sensible than would be a proposal that all men of whatever height should wear clothes of uniform length. There are occupations in which men cannot safely work nine hours a day; among them may be ranked glass blowing, the desiccation of certain kinds of excrementitious matters, and mixing paints. But are there not undoubtedly others at which healthy men can work, without detriment to their frames, ten hours a day? Indeed we believe it will be generally found to be true that ten hours' labour is perfectly consistent with the preservation of health; and that any curtailment of them would be at least as injurious to the workmen as to the employers. Even the same employments are more or less injurious, according to the conditions under which they are followed. Book printers, who do their work in the day can work longer than printers engaged in the production of morning papers, whose labour must be done in the night.

We take it for granted that, in a normal condition of society, the hours of labour should not be so long as to abridge life or to make it a burthen. There may be states of society in which the lot of the workman is necessarily miserable. But we ought not to find this in new countries, where the gifts and bounties of nature yield as certainly as here in Canada to the labour of man.

The production of wealth is not everything. Man is not a mere physical machine out of which so much labour is to be ground, and which has no further use. His moral and social nature requires cultivation. If this be neglected, society will be the loser. . . . One of the pleas for a shortening of the hours of labour is the necessity that there is to obtain time for the mental improvement of the workmen. The usual reply is that the cases in which the extra time taken from work would be used for mental improvement are very rare; that, as a rule, it would not be so used; and that if a man be particularly anxious for such improvement he will not allow ten hours' labour to bar his way to knowledge. In this there is much truth; but it is not the whole truth, and it scarcely puts the case fairly. We must take the average workman as he is; and we fear we must admit the probability of the extra hour taken from labour being generally used for some other purpose than mental improvement. But that of itself is no reason why the opportunity should be withheld. And if the manual toil be prolonged so as to exhaust the frame, the desire and the power of mental exertion will be wanting: drowsiness will supervene, and repose appear to be the greatest earthly good. . . .

The moral right of workmen to combine for the purpose of getting the highest price for their labour is as clear as any right which freemen can exercise; and any old laws that prevent its exercise ought to be repealed. For nearly three centuries British legislation was directed against Trades' Unions. But it failed to put them down; and nearly half a century ago (1826) this policy was abandoned. Since then any combination of men has been at liberty to say for what wages and on what conditions its members would work, and to use persuasion to induce others to act upon their views. That is their right. But they enjoy this liberty on the same condition that others enjoy theirs. Coercion is incompatible with the enjoyment of liberty; and whoever resorts to that forbidden weapon seeks to destroy the conditions on which his own liberty rests. The punishment of this wrong is in the interest of society, to which liberty is as necessary as air and water. While one man has a moral right to refuse to sell his labour at a certain price and on certain terms, another has the same right to accept that price and to waive those terms. For a combination of men to interfere by violence or intimidation to prevent the latter is just as tyrannical as for the legislative authority to interfere to compel the former.

The workmen who value their own liberty should respect that of others. They can hardly be said to do this when they insist on providing against future imaginary evils in the shape of an excess of labour by assuming to abridge the liberty of their employers in restricting the number of apprentices they shall take. This seems to be a remnant of the old system of corporate exclusion, which existed when workmen and capitalists were combined in the same persons. Then the restriction was the conspiracy of a class against the general public; now, when capital and labour have been divorced, it is the conspiracy of labour against capital. . . . Much has been said, and often truly, of the tyranny of capital over labour; but if this is not the tyranny of labour over capital, of employed over employer, it would be difficult to say what it is. It is by insisting on such things as this that workmen put themselves in the wrong. The Celestial emperor has far more show of right when he refuses to allow outside barbarians to trade with his subjects. Nothing that is not reasonable can succeed in the long run; and every folly of labour is the ground of a victory for capital.

If the mere fact of workmen uniting to raise the rate of wages ought to continue to rank among our laws as a crime, a combination of employers to keep down wages would have to be placed in the same category. The liberty of combination must either be refused or granted both to employers and employed. Justice has not two scales, one for labour and another for capital. Combinations among merchants to keep up the price of particular articles would have to come under the common rule, whatever it might be. . . .

The shortening of the hours of labour has the effect of raising wages in two ways. First, by giving less labour for the same money, unless it can be shown that the shorter hours give as good a result as can be got out of the longer; and second by increasing the competition among employers. A manufacturer employs one hundred hands. By shortening the hours of labour, the hundred men do no more than ninety did before. He wants ten more men, and he finds all his neighbours in the same position. To attract these ten from other shops, he must offer higher wages, and as he cannot pay the increased rate to the ten without paying it to the other ninety, the general wage-rate in that employment goes up. Or if the additional hands cannot be obtained, production is lessened while the cost remains the same; the profits of capital are reduced and the cost of the particular manufacture is raised. In that case, and supposing the reduction of production to be general, there would be a general rise of prices and the workman would have to pay more for almost everything he consumes. He would, in fact, have succeeded in duping himself when he thought he was merely wresting from capital a further share of profit.

The labour question can only be satisfactorily regulated by allowing both parties the greatest liberty; and we are glad to see that a movement has been made by the Minister of Justice to expunge a law which is a disgrace to the statute book, and which the British Parliament repealed nearly half a century ago.

FOUNDING A NATIONAL LABOUR BODY

The *Mail* (Toronto), September 25, 1873.

The Canadian Labour Congress re-assembled yesterday morning at eight o'clock, Mr. J. W. Carter in the chair. . . .

The Committee on the Constitution and Rules brought up their report drafting a portion of the Constitution as follows:

THE CONSTITUTION.

Whereas the workingmen of the Dominion of Canada, in common with the intelligent producers of the world, feel the necessity of co-operation and harmonious action to secure their mutual interests, just compensation for their toil, and such limitations in the hours of labour as may tend to promote their physical and intellectual well-being, and believing that the causes which have operated in the past to the detriment of labour may nearly always be traced to the want of proper organization in the various branches of industry: Therefore to unite the energies of all classes of labour in this Dominion of Canada for the purpose of guarding their inherent rights, we, the representatives of the workingmen of the Dominion of Canada in convention assembled, do hereby enact and adopt the following constitution:—

DESIGNATION AND OBJECTS.

ARTICLE 1.—Sec. 1. This body shall be known and designated as the Canadian Labour Union.

Sec. 2. Its objects shall be to agitate such questions as may be for the benefit of the working classes, in order that we may obtain the enactment of such measures by the Dominion and Local Legislatures as will be beneficial to us, and the repeal of all oppressive laws which now exist.

Sec. 3. To use all means consistent with honour and integrity, to correct the abuses under which the working classes are labouring, as to insure them their just rights and privileges.

Sec. 4. To use our utmost endeavours to impress upon the labour of the country the necessity of a close and thorough organization, and of forming themselves into unions wherever practicable.

LABOUR AND POLITICS

The *Mail* (Toronto), September 26, 1873.

Mr. Wm. Joyce, seconded by Mr. Levesley, moved "That it is essential to the recognition and establishment of the just and equitable rights of the workingmen of this country that they should have their own representatives in the Dominion Parliament, and with this idea in view, it is the opinion of the Congress that a workingman's platform should be put before the industrial classes of the country, and that the President do appoint a committee to draw up such a platform." In moving the foregoing resolution, Mr. Joyce said that the one great question in his mind was how shall the social and moral elevation of the working classes be best accomplished? True, a ready answer may be given by securing the united action of all branches of industry, skilled and unskilled, on this great issue. But that was the great sticking point. Were the working masses as united as either of the great political Parties of the day, then success would be certain. Lockouts, strikes, etc., with their concomitant evils, would happily be a thing of the past, for they should send their own representative to the National Parliament, there to demand and get justice. But ere they could reach this acme of their desires the public must have thorough training. The general who takes a poorly drilled and equipped army into the field against an enemy perfect in all that appertains to war, is foolish indeed, and but invites defeat. And so it is with workingmen. They have their Unions 'tis true, but they are scattered, weak, and disconnected. This Congress of Labour was a stride in the right direction. They must drill their army to fight manfully at the great battle-ground—the polls—and teach the enemy that election funds are of no avail against men determined not to sell their birthright for dollars. It had been whispered in his ear: "Look out for anything like Communism or the attempt to make a political machine of the Congress." Well, he thought this Canada of ours could get along without the Commune as can any other free country where the masses are not goaded into desperation by the despotic acts of their rulers. If they would continue to send men to Parliament whose only objects were the exaltation of their Party and the furtherance of their schemes of self-aggrandizement, the workingmen have only themselves to blame. As for politics he went heart and soul for the workingman's ticket, knowing neither Reformer nor Conservative, and would vote only for that man who pledges himself to support any measure brought forward for the amelioration of the toiling masses, and would watch that he fulfil his pledge. (Applause.)

TRADE UNION DEMANDS

The *Daily Globe* (Toronto), August 10, 1877.

Mr. J. C. MC MILLAN submitted the following motion:— "That in the opinion of this Congress it will be advisable and tend to the improvement of trade if the hours of labour were reduced in every branch of industry from ten to nine hours; and it would be followed by the advancement intellectually and morally of the working classes. . . ."

Mr. GIBSON believed that if all the men in Toronto were as true to their interests as their fellow-workmen in England they would easily secure their object. He fully approved of the motion; indeed, he would go further, and vote for a reduction to eight hours. He believed in the "four eights"—"eight hours' work, eight hours' play, eight hours' sleep, and eight shillings a day." (Hear, hear, and laughter.). . .

The following motion was submitted by Mr. J. S. WILLIAMS and seconded by Mr. R. RUDDY:—

"That this Congress is of opinion that the application of the principle of arbitration and conciliation in trade disputes is one well calculated to advance the prosperity of the trades, and promote amicable relations between employers and employed, and would urge upon all branches of trade the desirability of establishing such Boards wherever possible. . . ."

Mr. JURY held that what was wanted was a Mutual Board. Let the employers meet and support so many delegates and the Trades Unions do likewise. He thought it was well that the public should know that this Congress disapproved of strikes. They were, however, a necessary evil, and until mutual or Government boards were appointed the only way of testing their strength was that of brute force. . . .

The following motion was submitted by Mr. JURY, and seconded by Mr. BENTLEY:—

Whereas it is impossible to secure thorough representation on the floor of the House of Parliament of the working classes until we are represented by men of our own class;

Therefore be it resolved that this Congress pledge itself to use all legitimate means in its power to secure the election of workmen to Parliament, and to support any workingman's candidate nominated by the Parliamentary Committee or the local labour organization of the locality in which they reside.

Mr. JURY held that the presence of a dozen workingmen in Parliament would have a most beneficial effect, and would lead to that class being better treated than at present. This was not class legislation; it was trying to break down class legislation. There was class legislation at present for every class save that of the workingman. They wanted to introduce universal representation by introducing the only class which was not at present represented. The Licensed Victuallers were represented in Parliament, and surely the workingman was quite as important to the community as these gentlemen. The temperance party were represented, and the lawyers were in Parliament in great force; but the labouring classes had only one man, and they had only half of him. (A laugh.). . .

Mr. WILLIAMS said that the principle of co-operation might be called the panacea for all the evils of the workingman. As far as his knowledge had gone he thought the great drawback to the success of the principle was not anything in the idea itself, but in the lack of confidence in each other existing amongst workingmen. . . .

It was moved by Mr. MOFFAT,

"That this Congress believes that the principle of co-operation in both production and distribution are of the greatest importance to the working classes, and until we put this principle into practice we can never hope to place ourselves in that position in society to which our usefulness and industry entitle us."

Daily Mail (Toronto), September 15, 1897.

Hamilton, Sept. 14.—(Special.)—Although the Trades and Labour Congress was in session only a few hours this morning considerable business was transacted. The meeting opened about 9 o'clock and the members plunged into their work. The report of the Committee on Standing Orders presented, and adopted, after which the Congress considered a series of resolutions. . . .

The question of a weekly wage payment was brought up by the introduction of the following resolution:

Moved by S. Fitzpatrick, seconded by R. Keys: "That we strongly condemn the monthly payment system as now in vogue in the Government works and other large corporations, it being detrimental to the workingmen and their families to wait so long for their hard-earned wages, thereby compelling them to run on the credit system for their requirements. That this congress representing the working classes of the Dominion, petition the Governments, both Federal and Local, to pay all their employees weekly, and in any contracts for public works or otherwise given out by the Governments, that it will be one of the conditions that the men employed by them shall receive what is due them weekly."

In the discussion which followed, Representative O'Donaghue said he would like to see the resolution broadened, but a majority of the delegates concluded that it would be unwise to make the change proposed for fear it might cause opposition from the smaller employers of labour. The resolution was passed in the shape in which it was introduced.

UNION LABEL GOODS.

It was moved by William V. Todd, seconded by J. Sim: "Whereas, a large number of labour organizations have adopted union labels for the purpose of designating the product of their labour, to the end that members of organized labour and those who are in sympathy with the cause might, by demanding the union label, aid very materially in creating and sustaining a demand for union made goods; and whereas, experience has demonstrated that it is of the first importance in the agitation for the use of union labels that organized labour, individually and collectively, should lead in making the demand for these labels; therefore, be it resolved, that in the opinion of this congress, it is the duty of organized labour to demand the union label to the extent of refusing to trade directly or indirectly with dealers who neglect or refuse to handle union label goods."

Mr. Todd referred to the difficulty of being able to get members of union organizations to support the union label, and hoped union men would realise that they were just as powerful as consumers as they were as producers. The union man seemed to be actuated by the idea of buying in the cheapest way possible. That sort of thing was all wrong. If, as it was said, the labour fight of the future was to be on the union label, union men would have to turn around and realise their power as consumers.

In seconding the resolution, J. Sim said that the garment workers had not been able up to date to get any clothing manufacturers either in Hamilton or Toronto to adopt the union label.

The resolution was passed.

A SECRET BALLOT.

There was no discussion over a resolution introduced by Delegate Hastings, to petition the Government to introduce an absolutely secret ballot, unmarked in any way, which was carried further than the explanation from Mr. Hastings that the absolutely secret ballot was necessary for the protection of the workingmen.

Moved by H. Robinson, seconded by D. Hastings:—"That all public works under the control of the Federal Government should be carried out by it by day labour, as far as possible, and that on all such works, whether done by day labour or contract, the hours of labour should not exceed eight per day."

Moved by Edward Williams, seconded by D. Hastings: "That the property qualification for all civil and municipal offices should be abolished."

Moved by H. Robinson, seconded by E. Williams:—"That the practice of requiring deposits from candidates for the Dominion Parliament should be abolished."

Moved by J. C. Scott, seconded by D. J. Marsan:—"That it be an instruction to the Quebec Executive to urge upon the Government of the Province of Quebec the advisability of having the books of all the Public schools made uniform. . . ."

All the foregoing resolutions were carried.

The morning session adjourned about eleven o'clock. After luncheon the delegates were the guests of the Local Council, and were taken to the Beach on the Radial railway, and up the famous mountain on the Incline railway.

The congress will resume its session to-morrow morning.

By invitation of Bandleader Robinson a number of the delegates attended the concert given by the 13th band this evening.

NATIONAL VS INTERNATIONAL UNIONS

The *Daily Mail and Empire* (Toronto), September 16, 1897, p. 2.

The Committee on Standing Orders reported unfavourably on a resolution, presented by Delegate Hay in favour of the formation of a Canadian Federation of Labour. Mr. Hay spoke strongly in favour of the resolution, arguing that the time had come when Canadians should teach the national and not the international idea. . . .

Fred Walker . . . said that during the moulders' strike in Hamilton there had come to Hamilton to the moulders no less than $19,000, of which fully $1,000 was from Detroit alone. For every cent paid into the international body by the Hamilton men they had drawn out at least three cents. . . .

Several other delegates favoured the international idea. . . . It was argued by them that Canada was not large enough in many branches of labour to maintain a national organization, and that it was advisable to be affiliated with the American organizations. . . .

Delegate Keys held that there was no necessity for internationalism; Canadians could afford to be independent. He could not agree with the other delegates as to the beauties of internationalism. He knew of independent unions in Montreal that had engineered strikes and engineered them successfully. He knew of international unions in the same city which had undertaken strikes and had made failures of them. . . .

Delegate Donnelly introduced a resolution in favour of the amendment of the Municipal Act, to make every male subject 21 years of age or over entitled to vote at municipal elections.

An amendment was moved by Delegate Horwood, to the effect that the words "male subject" be struck out, and the words "every citizen in Canada, both male and female," be inserted in their place. There was no discussion, and when the vote was taken 22 hands were raised for the women, and but four against them.

SHOULD THE WORKING CLASS VOTE?

Daily Witness (Montreal), December 24, 1875.

MANHOOD SUFFRAGE.

The question has been before the Ontario Legislature, having been brought up by Mr. Currie, of Welland, a Liberal of good abilities and independent character. The subject, however, does not seem to be a very pressing one, for only one of the members, Mr. O'Donohue from Ottawa, thought it worth while to speak on the motion, and no one seemed to think it necessary to oppose it. It was negatived by a vote of two to one after Mr. Robinson, of Kingston, had caused some laughter by saying that he should like to see the females vote. The principal reason urged was, of course, that every one interested in the law should have some voice in making it, and this is a very strong one. Mr. Currie estimated that in his county one-fourth of the males above the age of twenty-one years were debarred from the franchise under the existing laws, which is perhaps a larger proportion than most people thought was the case. There never has been any very pressing demand for manhood suffrage in Canada, and the reason, no doubt, is that there are no class grievances, and that the extension of suffrage to all men of legal age, would not make any appreciable difference in the government of the country. When there is no practical evil flowing or likely to flow from any course of action to which they have been accustomed, or when there is no practical good likely to result from a change, agitation does not seem to the British mind to be worth while, and Canadian principles, or rather instincts, in this as in so many other directions, agree with those of the mother country, as they might naturally be expected to do, for the controlling element springs from practically the same people. A conservative feeling in this matter also is, no doubt, aided by the fact that the bulk of the voters are farmers owning their own land, who do not consider those having, as they think a less stake in the country, are so well entitled to a voice in the management of its affairs as themselves. At any rate they cannot be expected to feel enthusiastic in the matter, and stump orators who may feel inclined to lay stress on a movement in this direction meet with so cool a reception that they soon learn to confine themselves to other topics. For the Dominion Parliament manhood suffrage is undoubtedly more called for than for the Provincial Legislatures, for it has more to do with general questions affecting all alike, and its revenues, raised principally by customs and excise duties, are levied from all. The Provincial Legislatures have the right of legislation in respect to real estate and municipal matters and would, in the last instance, have to resort to direct taxation for revenue, so that there are better reasons for confining the franchise, so far as they are concerned, to property holders and a more conservative class generally. They, however, derive the greater portion of their revenue from indirect taxation in the shape of the subsidy from the Dominion, and they have extensive powers in legislating in regard to personal matters, such as the administration of justice, which cannot but furnish a ground on which to claim suffrage for all. In municipal matters least of all is there any right to claim manhood suffrage. The franchise in this direction is now sufficiently general, if indeed it is not a great deal too much so. Money has to be raised by direct taxation and those paying it should have the greatest voice in its disposal, which they hardly have at present. If municipalities were more restricted in their powers to legislate regarding personal matters, and the suffrage more restricted also, it might be found to result in great advantage. As the Anglo-Saxon nature is not influenced to any great extent by mere ideas, manhood suffrage will not probably make any rapid progress in the popular affections. At the same time if either the Dominion or Provincial Governments brought forward a bill in favor of it, it might not meet with very much opposition. Ontario has already made a step in this direction by adopting the income franchise, which, however, except in the cities, did not bring in many voters, and that province may therefore be naturally expected to be first to go further in this direction.

THE ONTARIO FACTORY ACT OF 1884

The *Globe* (Toronto), March 19, 1884, p. 5.

The House went into Committee on Mr. Fraser's bill for the protection of persons employed in factories, to be known as "The Ontario Factories Act of 1884." The first section, taken from the Imperial Act, provides that a child, young girl, or woman, who does any work in a factory is to be deemed employed in the factory. The fifth clause is from the Dominion Act, though it appears to have been based on the Imperial Statutes. It provides that a child, young girl, or woman, is not to be employed where permanent injury to health is likely, and whoever so employs any child, young girl or woman, shall upon summary conviction thereof, incur and be liable to imprisonment in the common gaol of the county wherein the offence has been committed, for a period not exceeding six months, or to a fine of not more than $100, with costs of prosecution, and in default of immediate payment of such fine and costs, then to imprisonment as aforesaid. Clause 6 and its subsections provide that a child under twelve years of age shall not be employed in a factory except upon the possession of a certificate stating its age. No child between twelve and fourteen shall be employed; no child, young girl, or woman, shall be employed more than ten hours in one day, nor more than sixty hours a week; not less than an hour shall be allowed for dinner. Clauses 7 and 8 relate to the closing of machinery, and permitting time lost by reason of accidents to machinery to be made up by the employees working overtime. Clauses 9 and 10 relate to minor particulars as to posting notices, and 11 provides for procuring an efficient sanitary condition of the building in which the children and young women are employed. By section 13 the inspector may take a physician into a factory. Under section 14 a penalty of not more than $500 can be imposed upon any owner or employer for keeping a factory so that the safety of the persons employed is endangered. The 15th section provides for the fencing of machinery and hoistways, and the following section provides for the prevention of fire. The parent of a child or young girl employed contrary to the act is liable to a penalty under section 19, and section 25 and sub-sections define the power of the Inspector.

The *Globe* (Toronto), March 25, 1884, p. 4.

A return laid before the House of Commons on motion shows that the Toronto Trades and Labour Council, at a meeting held on the evening of February 1st, resolved to suggest several amendments to the Factory Bill. These amendments are almost exactly the same that were suggested by the *Globe* when a copy of the bill reached us. Indeed, in some cases, they, the suggestions of the T.T. and L. Council, are in effect that the provisions contained in previous bills, and omitted in this Government's measure to please the proprietors of factories, should be restored. They ask that places in which less than twenty persons are employed be not exempted from the operation of the Act. They ask that children under fourteen shall not be employed in factories; that when children from fourteen to seventeen are employed the employer be required to hold a certificate showing the child's age at the date thereof. If the Government resolve to adhere to the age of twelve as the minimum, they ask that the following be added to one of the sections:

"And in no case shall any child under the age of fifteen years be employed in any factory or place covered by the provisions of this bill, unless such child has been attending school at least twenty weeks in each year, including the fifteenth, and of which attendance satisfactory evidence must be furnished the inspector."

They ask that women and children work only nine hours a day and only fifty-four hours a week, and they ask that a suitable dining-room be provided for the operatives by their employers free of expense. They suggest various other amendments, all of which are manifestly very valuable. One of these is that no door leading to the principal entrance of the factory, or to the tower, staircase, or fire-escapes, be locked, bolted, or barred during working hours. Section 22 provides that if an offence under this Act be committed without the personal consent, concurrence, or knowledge of the employer, the person who actually committed such offence may be summoned, convicted, etc. This clause the T.T. & L. Council ask should be expunged, as it would enable the employer in most cases "to evade the spirit of the provisions of this Act, as well as the penalties for the infraction thereof."

As we have already said, former bills contained nearly all that the workingmen now suggest. It is very improbable therefore that those suggestions will have any weight with a Government which is so much under control of the manufacturers that at their instance they made the bill what it is. The men now in power at one time pretended to have the interests of the working classes much at heart. That pretence has almost been abandoned. Everyone now knows that it is but a pretence. They treat the working classes as if fine words were enough for them, and as if they should be quite content to make great fortunes for a few friends of the Government. The bill was introduced early in the session as if to prove that the Government were at last very much in earnest about this matter. The probability is that they will trouble themselves very little about it; but should it pass it will not, we fear, contain many of the amendments which the Trades and Labour Council so properly suggested.

LABOUR LEGISLATION

Labour Advocate (Toronto), December 26, 1890, p. 28.

Several measures in the interest of labor have lately been introduced into the Quebec Provincial Legislative. One of the most important is a Government bill, introduced by Premier Mercier, to amend the Factory Act. It creates two new classes of factories, in regard to which the age at which children can be employed is raised. In unhealthy factories, which includes all manufactories of tobacco and cigars, the age is fixed at fourteen for boys and fifteen for girls. In factories classed as both unhealthy and dangerous, which are left to be specified by the Government, the age is put at sixteen for boys and eighteen in the case of girls. There is also a provision that the day of ten hours shall not begin before six in the morning, or end later than nine in the evening.

THE DOMINION CONCILIATION ACT OF 1900

The *Globe* (Toronto), June 28, 1900, p. 5.

Mr. Mulock introduced a bill to aid in the prevention and settlement of trade disputes and the publication of statistical industrial information.

In reply to a request by Mr. Foster, Mr. Mulock said one of the objects of the bill is by the aid of boards of conciliation to promote the settlement of trade disputes and of differences that arise from time to time between employers and employed and between different kinds of employers. It is hoped that the different application of this principle may prevent strikes and lockouts, and if, unfortunately, that extreme measure has been reverted to in the case of such disputes, the adoption of this method of bringing about a more satisfactory and permanent settlement of the subject matters of these disputes. Another object of the bill is to establish a Department of Labor. It will be the duty of the Department of Labor to gather statistical and other information affecting labor and to provide for its publication and for its being made accessible to the public generally. In order to carry out that object the department will publish a monthly gazette, a labor gazette, which, as regards labor, will fill the same place as does the report of the Minister of Agriculture as regards agriculture and the report of the Minister of Trade and Commerce in the commercial world. . . .

My hon. friend (Mr. Davin) asked me to explain the machinery of the conciliatory portion of this bill. I may say that is not anything new, but is an echo largely of the conciliation act which has been in force in Great Britain for some four years. . . . The act provides for the Board of Trade of England keeping a register of the conciliation boards and arbitration boards throughout Great Britain, and in that way being in connection with the machinery for conciliation, which machinery can be set in motion whenever the occasion arises. These conciliation boards are selected by the interests concerned. The act provides that, if the interests desire it the Board of Trade in England—it will be the minister charged with the carrying out of this act in Canada—may, if requested, appoint conciliators or arbitrators. (Cheers.) There is nothing from the beginning to the end of the act of a coercive character, but, the whole principle rests upon the theory of consent both in the organization of the board, in their taking any part whatever by way of intervening in disputes and ultimately in arriving at decisions. Failing conciliation, the Imperial act—and so will this bill—provides for reference to arbitration. (Cheers.) There is, however, a wide difference between determining a dispute by a board of conciliators and determining it by a board of arbitrators. In the case of the reference of the dispute to a board of conciliators, the conciliators are the party to to the dispute themselves. The employers or their representatives, and the employees and their representatives, constitute the board. (Hear, hear.) There is not, as in the case of arbitration, the delegation of powers to settle the dispute to an outside tribunal, which may or may not be composed of persons in any way directly interested in the trade concerned, but the persons directly interested in the difference are the persons to settle that difference. (Cheers.) If the conciliators arrive at a conclusion it is a consent conclusion. The parties concerned meet together, employers and employees, around the same table; they exchange views; they become perhaps better acquainted, each side with the other; a better spirit is evoked, and the result is that ultimately consent is reached. In the case of arbitration, it is a delegation of authority to an outside tribunal, whose decision, not being the decision of the parties concerned, is accepted perhaps as binding, but not with the same degree of alacrity and perhaps sullenly. . . .

. . . It will be possible for the machinery to be set in motion either by the parties to the difference themselves or by the Department of Labor.

Any of the parties can evoke it, endeavor to secure its good offices for the bringing about of a settlement.

THE ORIENTAL MENACE

Return to an Order of the House for . . . all correspondence . . . in connection with the employment of Chinese or Japanese labour below ground in the metallurgical mines of this Province, British Columbia. *Sessional Papers*, 1898, pp. 769-70.

Letter from A. A. Forbes, J.P., to Attorney-General,
Dated 15th September, 1897.
I beg to inform you that a party came to me to lodge information against the Van Anda Mining Co., of Texada, the complaint being the above Company are employing Chinamen underground in defiance of the law. Consolidated Statutes, 1897, Cap. 27, Act 12.

Having heard that there has been a decision given in the Courts against the above Act I deemed it best not to take the information until I could communicate with you on the subject.

Will be obliged for instructions on the matter. This question is of grave importance up here amongst the miners. . . .

NANAIMO, B.C., 4th January, 1898.

DEAR COLONEL BAKER,—I am informed by reliable correspondents on Texada Island that Mr. Blewett, of the Van Anda mine, is discharging all of his white miners and substituting in their places Chinese miners, contrary to the spirit and provisions of the "Metallurgical Act" passed last session. From what I can learn the wages of the whites were reduced to the sum of $2.00 per diem, out of which $1.00 per diem was deducted for board. Apart from the attempt to lower wages which, of course, is a matter strictly of the company's concern, but which in the interest of labour should, if possible, be prevented, I am also told on the very best authority that previous to the last visit of Mr. Carlyle, most of the miners were Chinese, and further *that not one of these heathens was possessed of a mining licence*, whereby the Province lost a considerable sum to the revenue. Mr. Bate, the assessor and collector for the district of North Nanaimo, collected a poll tax which, by the way, was paid by Mr. Blewett with or by a cheque which, on presentation at the bank, was refused acceptance, and it was some time before the amount was finally made good. From all I can hear they are a "snide" outfit, and of little good to the country. What I would take the liberty of suggesting is that some person be authorised to at once proceed to Texada, and if any difficulty is found in enforcing the "Act" so far as it deals with "Chinese" above or below ground, that he (the authorised person) should at least see that no Chinese person is allowed to work around the mine unless he has paid and has the necessary licence to do so. But some steps should also be taken to guard against impersonation. There cannot be the least shadow of a doubt but that each and every Chinese person will (and be assisted to a certain extent by the Company) endeavour to make one licence do duty for more than one. In fact, I very much fear that some attempt might be made to make these licences, the property of the company should the original owner leave the employ, to do duty for any that might take their places. In the meantime much dissatisfaction has existed among the white miners during the whole of last summer because they have been compelled to have licences while the Chinese have escaped "scot free." I am not surprised at it. I hope that this matter will receive the attention of the Department so that the miners of Texada Island may have their minds disabused of the idea that the laws of this country are, so far as the Government is concerned, administered only in the interests of the Mongolian. The remarks that I have made allude, with equal force, to other parts of the Province where Chinese are permitted to work in metalliferous mines.

Wishing you a happy and prosperous New Year, believe me to be

Yours, etc.,

(Signed)   W. WYMOND WALKEM.

Lt.-Col. the Hon. James Baker,
Minister of Mines, Victoria, B.C.

Industrial Banner (London, Ont.), October, 1897.

The Curse of Chinese Immigration
──────────
What It Has Done for Other Countries and
What It is Doing for Canada.

In a large measure the people of eastern Canada are blind to the grave menace that Chinese immigration is to the interests of the country. The action of the Dominion Trades and Labor Congress in asking the Dominion Parliament to raise the tax on Chinamen entering Canada from $50 to $500 is a step in the right direction. A great deal of false sympathy is expended on behalf of John by people who have never investigated the question or asked why organized labor seeks to prevent the unrestricted immigration of Chinamen. We are assured that if we wish to make a Christian of John we should welcome him with outstretched arms and try to do him good; but we candidly confess, without any apology, if those are the only terms on which he can be Christianized he had better remain a heathen, for a little while longer at any rate.

Now, as a matter of fact, every country that has suffered through the immigration of the Mongolian race has had sooner or later to take active steps to combat the evil. While in Colorado some years ago the editor of the BANNER had ample opportunity of studying the Chinese, and will say that if he were to tell all that had come under his own personal observation he would hardly be credited. We have it on the authority of a prominent clergyman, who made a study of the question as it affected San Francisco, that for every Chinaman converted to Christianity in that city he was confident that, at a very low estimate, twenty Americans went to hell. Children in that city, to his personal knowledge, were in hospitals through the contraction of loathsome vices and diseases as a direct result of their contact with Chinamen. In the Chinese quarters of the city the inhabitants are herded like rats, an ordinary room in many cases having as many as two additional floors placed in it so as to make three with not space for a man to stand upright; and here, packed like sardines in a box, the Chinaman lives, works, eats and sleeps. He can subsist on a few cents a day; and this is the kind of competition that self-respecting white labor is asked to meet.

As more directly affecting Canadians we can state that at the present times the Chinese are increasing in British Columbia to an alarming extent, and they are bringing with them the same vices that have worked such dire effects in San Francisco. They are entering all avenues of trade and are slowly, but surely, displacing white labor on every hand; they are in the mines and canneries, and, in fact, it is hard to find an avocation that sooner or later they do not enter. Even the clergymen in British Columbia are standing shoulder to shoulder with organized labor, as indeed do all classes of the community, for there, where the evil is recognized, no maudlin sentimentality or false sympathy is wasted.

It is not only British Columbia that is threatened but the whole Dominion. Mr. Chinaman does not stand still; once he has secured a footing he gradually works his way, and, once established, it is next to impossible to get rid of him. During the last year the increase of the Chinese in Winnipeg, Manitoba, was over 25 per cent, and even there people are beginning to realize the danger. Here in London, and in points further east, we have them, and though as yet in no great numbers they are increasing. So far they have confined themselves to the laundry business; this is always the first step, but, inevitable as fate, when the time comes they will invade other fields, and when too late the people of the east will realize that the people of the western provinces should have had their support before the evil had gained too great a footing. Australia has had to grapple with this question and they have already done what the Dominion Trades and Labor Congress has asked the Dominion Parliament to do.

Wherever free and slave labor has come into competition, free labor has always inevitably been forced to the wall. Living as he does under the most degrading conditions, subsisting on the outlay of a few cents a day, the Chinaman is in a position to take a situation for a pittance that no self-respecting white man could live on, leave alone support a family. The Chinaman has no desire to be raised to a higher position or plane of life; he has no intention of becoming a citizen; on a miserable pittance he can live and accumulate what will be a fortune when he returns to China. It is because of this that the people of the Pacific province are crying out for relief. It is for this that the Dominion Trades and Labor Congress has asked for an increase of the tax. Canadians cannot, at this time, afford to waste sympathy where it is not needed. Organized labor has been actuated by no narrow or contracted spirit, it has no fight with the Chinaman because he is a Chinaman or foreigner but because of the grave menace which his presence is to the welfare of the country. Shall we stand idly by and see free labor displaced by slave labor, because slave labor means a larger profit for those who employ the Chinese; or shall we insist that Canadian labor shall be protected and stem this tide that threatens such dire calamities to the working classes. Agitate this question everywhere until the government shall be compelled to act and stem the tide of undesirable Mongolian immigration.

We will have more to say on this matter in the future for we believe that if not resolutely encountered now it will have to be faced when it has grown to more alarming proportions. Now is the time to crush the danger, and it cannot be undertaken a moment too soon.

THE VALUE OF UNIONS

Canada, Royal Commission on the Relations of Labor and Capital in Canada, 1889. Evidence—Ontario, pp. 51-3, 57-9.

JOHN CALLOW called and sworn.
    By the CHAIRMAN:—
    Q.—What is your business?   A.—I am a carpenter in Seaton Village, Toronto.
    Q.—How long have you been here?   A.—Eight years, since 1879.
    By Mr. HEAKES:—
    Q.—Are you connected with organized labor in this city?   A.—Yes; I have gone in for it recently. When in the old country I belonged to a

union. I could not, however, get admission here at first; I had to wait for some time, and I only got introduced into the brotherhood four or five weeks ago.

Q.—The brotherhood of carpenters? A.—Yes. I belonged to the general union in England before I came here.

Q.—Do you know whether the principles of the Trades Unions are opposed to capital? A.—I never knew that the principles of Trades Unionism were opposed to capital; I considered them both to run in the same channel.

Q.—Do you consider that organization among workingmen is a benefit to them? A.—I do, when rightly administered.

Q.—Do you think organization amongst workingmen is an injury to employers? A.—I do not, but that it is a very great benefit. The shop where I worked in England always had the working rules posted up, and allowed society meetings to be held in the shop. That was at the shop of Alderman Neill, of Manchester. In 1877 and 1878 there unfortunately happened to be a strike, and some time afterwards I left the country.

Q.—Does organization among workingmen have a tendency to cause strikes? A.—I never knew it, so far as my experience has gone. Of course, there are some fire-eaters among workingmen as there are among other classes, but my experience has been what I have said.

Q.—I am speaking of the organization of workingmen as a body? A.— I never knew it to be detrimental or injurious in any way.

Q.—You think that organized labor is a benefit alike to employer and employé? A.—I do, when justly administered.

Q.—Have you any knowledge of instances where disputes were settled by a conference between employers and employed? A.—I have known several disputes settled by what are called deputations or delegations of employers and men meeting together. A number of men were selected from each party and they were appointed to transact the business.

Q.—Do you know that cases of that kind have occurred in Toronto since you have been here? A.—I have not had a very great knowledge of the society since I have been here.

Q.—Since you have been in Toronto how do you find wages as compared with wages in the old country? A.—The wages in the old country when I was there were eight and a-half pence, or seventeen cents per hour.

By the CHAIRMAN:—

Q.—Where? A.—In the city of Manchester.

By Mr. HEAKES:—

Q.—Do you know what they are there now? A.—I do not. I do not know what the rates have been since I left. I left in 1879, after the great strike which lasted twelve months.

Q.—Do you think the wages in this country as good as the wages there? A.—I do not want to speak in depreciation of Canada, but I do not think they are so good here. Money has a much greater purchasing power in the old country than it has here.

Q.—A man can live for less there than here?   A.—Yes. A man can get a good substantial brick cottage for six shillings per week, one having four or five rooms.

Q.—Is there anything in connection with your society such as a black list?   A.—I could not speak as to that.

Q.—You have not heard of anything of the kind?   A.—I do not go by anything I hear, but by what I know by my own experience.

Q.—Does your society prohibit union men from working with non-union men?   A.—I cannot speak of that.

Q.—You have never known it to be done?   A.—I have not examined the rules sufficiently—I do not know of it. . . .

Q.—With respect to the settlement of disputes, do you favor arbitration?   A.—I would favor Government interference. The Government build asylums and workhouses for people who cannot assist themselves and they make the rest of the people pay the taxes, and therefore they ought to protect workingmen. I am not wishing to speak too strongly in behalf of workingmen, but so far as I can judge he is in this country the victim every time.

Q.—You would believe in the Government compelling the settlement of dispute?   A.—Yes, and that they should protect those classes that cannot protect themselves.

By the CHAIRMAN:—

Q.—You are in favor of arbitration?   A.—Of Government interference under whatever name it is called. They make us pay taxes, and we are entitled to their protection; but we do not get it.

Q.—What is the effect on a trade when men have been on strike at any time?   A.—I do not know that it has any further effect than delaying the work and rather disturbing that branch of society.

Q.—Do you know any good results to ever come from strikes?   A.—I do not think there are any—not really tangible good results.

Q.—Nothing lasting?   A.—There is nothing lasting in it. A strike only compels employers to do a little more justly to the men, but it passes away like a morning cloud. And after a time they return to their evil doings and the wages of the men come down again.

Q.—Does organization tend to increase wages?   A.—It may do so, but it is the shortening of hours that would increase wages in my judgment, because there is a preponderance of population, and the population increases so rapidly that there must be a reduction in the hours of labor or some other means found to employ the surplus population.

Q.—What I want to get at is this; would the wages be as good if there were no organization amongst the men?   A.—I think that would largely depend on the surplus labor in the country. I do not think that organization would affect it altogether; it might have a slight effect, but the surplus population is what I think would affect it. It is supply and demand all the way through; when the supply is greater than the demand wages come down; when supply is less than the demand wages go up. To answer your question more directly I would say that organization might slightly affect it, but I do not think it does altogether. . . .

Q.—You said some time ago that you had recently joined the union in Toronto? A.—Only about four or five weeks ago.

Q.—Was it because you did not agree to join the union? A.—No, it was because I could not get in. There is no branch of the general union to which I belonged when in England; there was only what is called the Amalgamated Carpenters', and I was too old to join. Consequently I was left out. In 1882, the Brotherhood was established, and I was admitted to that four, five or six weeks ago; I cannot tell the exact day.

Q.—Is it to your advantage to belong to the union? A.—I consider it an advantage, because it brings me more among the men at the meetings and makes me better known.

Q.—Can you get work more easily? A.—I think so. I consider it has a tendency to rub away the rough edges and bring me into work; besides, there is the sick and the death benefit, which I think a great deal of.

Q.—Do you get better wages as a member of the union? A.—I think I do; I am recognized as a member and get better wages. . . .

Q.—You were talking about strikes, and you thought that strikes did little or no good. Now is it not a fact that, although an individual strike may prove a failure, yet in consequence of the strike wages are kept higher than they would have been without a strike? A.—Could you give me that in another way so that I may grasp the idea more correctly.

Q.—Let me put it this way: Do you suppose carpenters' wages are higher because of the effect of strikes? A.—I do not know. I will tell you what I think about it. In my experience in eight cases out of ten the employers infringe on the men's rights and privileges. That is my experience during the last seven or eight years.

Q.—If the workmen were not united, were not in unions, would not the employers infringe in their rights more? A.—I think they would, for they are a grasping lot. I am not speaking in any way improperly as to employers, but taking them as a rule they are a very grasping set of men.

By the CHAIRMAN:—

Q.—Are not all people grasping? A.—There are some exceptions.

Q.—Is not everybody grasping? A.—I cannot say they are; no, I find some gentlemen very liberal in giving.

By Mr. FREED:—

Q.—What qualifications are required of a man who joins the carpenters' union? A.—That he be a competent workman.

Q.—How do they determine that? A.—There are men who have worked with the applicant, and those men have to recommend them for initiation. If they do not know from their own experience that he is a good workman they would not recommend him. I had to get two men to vouch for me, although I have worked here seven years and am well known in the city. They are very particular.

Q.—You consider that all the men belonging to the union are qualified workmen?   A.—I could hardly say that; that is putting a leading question into my mouth. But as a rule I might say that seven-eighths of them are qualified workmen.

Q.—Why then did the union object to that clause requiring employers to pay twenty-two and a half cents per hour to qualified workmen only? A.—Because they wanted the wages to be higher, and they did not want that to be a ground for restricting the rate from going up. They wanted things to be elastic, so the men could get advanced wages and not continue to be kept down. Employers would keep all the men down at that grade; I find they go as far in that direction as they can.

Q.—Did the men require the employers to pay twenty-two and a half cents per hour to men not qualified?   A.—No; the society does not require that.

Q.—Then what is the object of the qualification clause?   A.—Because the employers drew it up and introduced it into the agreement. It was an innovation and had no right to be there, and when the agreement was made the year before there was nothing of that kind in it. When, however, a new agreement was proposed it was introduced, and that was the cause of the late strike.

Q.—If the men work shorter hours than you do, do you think they should get higher wages?   A.—We simply demanded what was right. Supply and demand will always regulate the wages. When men are difficult to be had wages will go up.

Q.—Will that increase the cost of production?   A.—I do not know that it will very seriously; it might affect it a little. . . .

By Mr. FREED:—

Q.—Let us go back a little. If unqualified workmen got into a union and were employed in a shop could not the employer discharge them and keep only qualified workmen?   A.—It is this way: they would keep the men who offered to labor the cheapest. That is the best answer I can give.

Q.—Will the union permit the cheap man to continue at work?   A.—I do not think the union can always help it.

Q.—Are the men who are thoroughly skilled workmen employed more than those who are unskilled?   A.—It depends on the wages. There might be a skilled workman who would work for fifteen cents and he would get the preference over a man who might be better skilled, but who wanted $1.75 a day.

Q.—Does the union permit men to work for fifteen cents an hour?   A.—

I do not know that it does; I cannot speak about that. But I presume there are some working at that rate, if it were known.

Q.—I understood you to say that twenty-two and a-half cents was the minimum? A.—It is supposed to be, but there are a great many not getting that or anything like it. It is, however, supposed to be the minimum.

By Mr. CARSON:—

Q.—That is the minimum wages of the union? A.—Yes.

LABOUR TROUBLE ON THE DOCKS

Canada, Royal Commission on the Relations of Labor and Capital in Canada, 1889. Evidence—New Brunswick, pp. 207, 209-10, 212, 214-15.

SAMUEL SCOFIELD, Ship-broker, called and sworn.

By Mr. CLARKE:—

Q. What is your business? A. Ship-broker and agent. . . .

Q. Have you had any labor troubles in connection with the loading of vessels in the port of St. John? A. We have.

Q. Were they settled by consultation or arbitration? A. They were settled in different manners. Sometimes we have gone on and carried our point, and sometimes we have had to give into the labor combinations, but I do not remember of a time when there was an arbitration or understanding arrived at.

By the CHAIRMAN:—

Q. How were the troubles finally settled? A. Sometimes we settled it one way, sometimes another; sometimes the laborers had their way and sometimes we had ours. We have had serious trouble. We have had steamers laying at the wharf in St. John, being discharged by what are called outsiders, and also by the crew, interrupted in their work by these society men, because we would not agree to give them their exorbitant demand of $5 a day. These laborers have gone on the steamer by hundreds, completely crowding her, and terrorizing our men, who have quit work and left us, leaving the steamers perfectly idle. And this is a matter I should like to see this Commission take hold of. There was an Act passed last year by the Dominion Government, called the Quebec Act, the object of which was to meet difficulties of that kind which had arisen at Quebec. I have seen the Act and think it is very good; but so far as our experience here goes, I consider this Act insufficient for our purposes. It provides penalties and imprisonment with hard labor for a term not exceeding three months, for any person that interferes with laborers about vessels or makes threats, but it does not provide for the difficulty we have experienced in this city. We have had men at work beaten here in this city while at work, and they have been made to go away from our city on account of treatment received at the hands of this laborers' society. This laborers' society, when they wish to prevent any vessel being loaded by outsiders, knock off work on all vessels in the harbor, and congregate by hundreds, perhaps 600 or 700 on the wharf watching and talking. They may offer no violence to any body, and perhaps say nothing that could be construed into being illegal, but it is a species of intimidation, the effect of which is that these outsiders are so frightened that when they get home, at night they are afraid, and will not come back to work. They are also afraid when going home that they will be attacked. It strikes me that this Act ought to contain a provision to prevent the men massing together in such large numbers with the evident intention of intimidating, for their actions strike terror into the minds of those who are at work on these vessels.

By Mr. FREED:—

Q. How can you prevent the men from assembling on the streets? A. We can; our policemen can move people from the streets when congregated together in numbers larger than three. Therefore, we feel that a section of that nature should be introduced into the Quebec Act and enforced. I think it would be the only thing that would apply to those difficulties.

By Mr. CLARKE:—

Q. Have these labor troubles seriously militated against the port? A. Undoubtedly they have. We do not object to any man refusing to work for a less rate of wages than he wants to, but we do think that while that is the right of every man that this intimidation and crowding at special wharves is wrong. It is a right that every man has to charge what he sees fit for his services, but we do object to this intimidation in any shape or form, and I think that the law ought to be so arranged that intimidation of all kinds will be impossible. That is what I refer to; I think that the Quebec law is insufficient in that respect for us here.

By Mr. KERWIN:—

Q. Did not the members of the Ship-laborers' Union meet the merchants and arrange a scale of prices to be paid by them? A. Yes; but there was no general meeting; such I would infer from your question. The ship-laborers went around to the different ship-brokers and owners and saw them separately.

Q. It is not the document signed by them separately? A. Yes.

Q. Is it not signed as a joint statement? A. Yes; they all signed the same document.

Q. Did the Ship-laborers' Union follow up that document and do just as they stated they would? A. Yes.

Q. Have there been any labor troubles since that document was signed? A. There have not.

Q. Are not the Ship-laborers' society this year following out the terms of that document—is it not true that some of the shipping merchants of this port have signed a document to something of the same effect for the coming year? A. I have heard so; I think that they have signed a document to the effect that they will pay the laborers $3.60 a day on steamers. . . .

Q. Can you tell why it is that the majority of ship-owners in St. John are willing to pay $3.60 on steamers and only $2.50 a day for loading sailing ships? A. I think it is very ridiculous, and I have told the society so, because I know from my own experience there is more labor involved in loading steamers with the same quantity of deals than sailing vessels; therefore the ship-laborers, instead of looking upon steamers, should view them in an opposite light. A few days ago I asked this question of a stevedore, and he said he thought the coming of steamers to this port was an advantage to the port. If all the deal were carried by steamers the laborers would get more than they do now. We consider the charging of $3.60 a day on steamers exorbitant, and last year we agreed on $3 as a compromise arrangement.

Q. Were the merchants who signed the agreement for this year compelled to do so? A. No; they are not compelled to sign, but it might be possible that the laborers would say, if you do not give us this agreement and pay $3.60 a day you will have to pay $5 some other day. The labor market is limited here, and with the intimidating that is done on the part of the Ship-laborers' Union we find it extremely difficult to get people to work outside the union.

Q. Are not some ships and other crafts loaded in this harbor by non-union men at the present time? A. There are some little crafts that are, but the ship-laborers let them go by; but it is only small crafts; occasionally a large ship may do so. There is a struggle going on all the time between the union and non-union men, but the greater part of the work is done by the union men. We, in St. John, prefer to work with the union men, provided their rate of wages are only reasonable. Speaking for myself, I would say I consider $3.60 a day, not to talk of $5, is entirely too high to pay for labor, for there is no laboring-man can earn that sum of money. . . .

Q. Could you suggest any means to the Commission any system of arbitration whereby these labor troubles might be avoided? A. Of course, if arbitration could be made compulsory by law it would be all right, but I do not see how you could interfere with the rights of the subject, because if a man chooses to ask a certain rate of wages Parliament will never interfere with him doing so. Every man has a right to ask whatever he likes for his services, and the only extent that Parliament can deal with this matter is by preventing unlawful combination or combinations, which act injuriously to trade. I have indicated one way in which I think they could remedy this evil. This Act before me (Quebec Act) was got up by some gentlemen to meet existing labor troubles there, and with a little amendment it might be made to work in St. John. We have an Act passed by the New Brunswick Legislature which is very good to a certain extent, but I do not see what it can do beyond preventing these combinations by law from doing overt acts.

By Mr. CLARKE:—

Q. Has arbitration ever been suggested to you in reference to any of these troubles? A. No; we have talked the matter over ourselves with the society and I am of opinion that where they and the steamship owners cannot agree there is no one else will make an agreement for them; we have tried all we could, when these difficulties have been up, to meet the laborers, and have, at times, conceded a great deal but still we have, at times, failed to accomplish our object.

By Mr. FREED:—

Q. When you speak of any Legislature making combinations illegal, do you refer to trades unions? A. I mean laborers' unions, such as we have here, for I suppose that was the only thing I was asked to reply to.

Q. Do you think that Parliament ought to make it illegal for any body of men to associate together to protect their own interests? A. I think they ought to be allowed to do that, but where they intimidate other men from working, that ought to be prevented and, those sort of intimidations should be stopped in all their various forms.

Q. If they ask the privilege of assembling together and offer violence to no one does not the law protect those persons and punish the guilty if they are discovered? A. Yes; this Quebec Act covers that ground.

Q. Then you say that at present the police authorities have power to prevent any illegal assembly and compel persons to move on the street? A. I think that our police have authority to that effect.

Q. What other power is necessary to deal with these cases like you have in view? A. I think that the Quebec Act ought to have provisions in it dealing with such troubles as we experience with the Ship-laborers' Union in St. John.

Q. What power has charge of the police regulations? A. I suppose the police regulations are made by the local authorities.

Q. Do you think that the Dominion Government has power to give the police authority to interfere with any assemblages that do not go so far as to offer violence to people? A. I think the Dominion Parliament is supreme, and can do anything.

By Mr. ARMSTRONG:—

Q. Cannot a man who commits an overt act or an act of intimidation be punished by the common law? A. Yes.

Q. Is not that the law of the land to-day? A. Yes.

Q. Do you require a special law for that purpose? A. No; I would ask for this Quebec Act to be amended. There is no law to punish men who congregate in large numbers, crowding the wharf.

Q. What do you call large numbers? A. Five or six hundred people; the mere fact of their being there on the wharf intimidates the men who are working; so I do not see but what there ought to be a law passed to stop that practice. The Government passed this Act in 1887; it was introduced by a member from Quebec.

Q. Is that the Act that the Minister of Justice got passed? A. Yes.

Q. Do you prefer it to the Amyot Act? A. I did not know that Act. We have had labor difficulties here, and all the work on shipping has been stopped at once, just from sheer intimidation by the men congregating in large numbers on our wharves.

By Mr. KERWIN:—

Q. Do you want a law made against these people? A. No; to interfere with such proceedings.

Q. And with large congregations of people? A. Yes.

Q. Would you want to apply that to a political meeting? A. That is a matter that might require consideration; I am speaking about the laborers congregating in large numbers on our wharves.

Q. Do you approve of the plan that the laborers have adopted of holding a meeting every year, between themselves and the merchants, and fixing the rate of wages to be charged for the ensuing twelve months? A. That is a very good plan, and the great majority of the merchants agree to their demands when they are at all reasonable, but I think the wages the men are asking this year are unreasonable, for $3.60 a day all the year through is too high.

OPPOSITION TO UNIONS

Canada, Royal Commission on the Relations of Labor and Capital in Canada, 1889. Evidence—Nova Scotia, pp. 16-18.

ROBERT TAYLOR, manufacturer of boots and shoes, sworn.

Q. Have you ever had labor troubles with your men? A. Not for about 12 years. There was something then but never since.

Q. How did you fix it, or how would you fix it in a similar case now? A. We fixed it then by letting them go about their business and they came back with their fingers in their mouths wanting work again.

Q. Do you think that would be the best course to pursue again? A. That is what I would do if it happened again.

Q. What was the cause of the labor trouble you referred to? A. They had what is called a Crispin organization; we discharged a man and the others insisted upon his being allowed to work.

Q. Did you discharge him because he belonged to the organization? A. No; because his work did not suit.

Q. How long was he working before you found out that he did not suit? A. I think about a year.

Q. Does it take you a year to find out that a man does not suit? A. He did something—I don't remember what it was, that did not please the foreman.

Q. And because he was discharged the other men struck? A. They insisted upon his being allowed to work.

Q. Was there any communication between you before they struck? A. No.

Q. They struck abruptly because the man was not re-instated? A. Yes. . . .

Q. Has the foreman power to employ men at will? A. Yes.

Q. Has he objections to employing men belonging to labor organizations? A. Yes.

Q. If you knew men belonged to such organizations would you employ them? A. No.

Q. What objection have you to them? A. I think there is no necessity for them, and for that reason I would not employ men belonging to them.

Q. Do you employ a man for what he is worth according to your opinion? A. Yes.

Q. Has not a man the right to put a price on his labor? A. Yes; and I have the same right.

Q. Would not men be better if they engaged as a body, than if they engaged singly? A. No; I think such combinations are a mistake. If men are treated well they are better off without them.

Q. Did you ever know the members of any labor organization to be of the same opinion? A. No.

Manitoba Morning Free Press (Winnipeg), January 24, 1894, p. 2.

VANCOUVER, Jan. 19. Those laboring men who do not belong to any labor organization in British Columbia and are therefore called collectively unorganized labor, waited upon the government yesterday, and were received with open arms, and as a result of their interview there is no doubt their suggestions will be carried out. They did not assume the rather dictatorial manner of organized labor at their recent interview and were consequently more successful with the government. Their spokesmen said they wished to do away with strikes altogether. They did not wish to force a strike if an employer proved to them that he was obliged to cut wages to make a living profit himself. They have passed resolutions in council that councillors and arbitrators be appointed by parties in dispute, and if the council disagree the matter to be finally referred to arbitrators; that when one of the parties in the dispute makes application to have the matter referred to council, then the other party shall be obliged to name their councillors and arbitrators, or failing to do this, that the government appoint them within four days.

Canada, Royal Commission on the Relations of Labor and Capital in Canada, 1889. Evidence—Nova Scotia, pp. 40-2.

ALBERT TANNER, tailors' cutter, sworn and examined.

By Mr. WALSH:—

Q. How long have you been in your present position? A. About two years.

Q. What is your pay as a cutter? A. It depends on how I work, as I work by the piece.

Q. Are you the principal cutter in the establishment, or is there more than one? A. We have more than one cutter. We have no principal cutter.

Q. What wages do you receive on an average as a cutter? A. I cannot give a correct average. I can name a figure, and should say about $13 a week. . . .

Q. Is your room ventilated well in every particular? A. Splendidly ventilated.

Q. Have you water closets on your flat? A. No.

Q. Where are the water closets that you have to visit? A. Upstairs; the ones before named.

Q. Those are the only closets in the house? A. Yes.

Q. For all the hands downstairs? A. Downstairs in the bank there are closets, but they alone have access to them.

Q. Do you consider your position healthy—no complaints with regard to the ventilation, or anything of that kind? A. I do not see that any complaint could be justly made as to ventilation or anything like that—high ceilings in the rooms, and they are splendid rooms.

By Mr. KELLY:—

Q. Do you get your wages weekly? A. No; we are paid fortnightly.

Q. You say that you work piece work? A. Yes.

Q. Are all the other gentlemen working piece work? A. Yes.

Q. And is the price about the same? A. We are all paid the same.

Q. I suppose you generally work as hard as you possibly can? A. Yes; if they are well. It depends a little upon what is on their mind. Their wages would be much about the same.

Q. Do you live in a tenement house or do you board?   A. I board.

Q. What is the usual price of board per week here?   A. I live at home.

Q. If you had to pay for board outside about the same as you get at home, what would it cost you?   A. I could not expect to get it less than four or five dollars a week.

Q. You do not pay any taxes, I presume?   A. No.

By Mr. HEAKES:—

Q. How many hours a day do you work?   A. Nine.

Q. What days in the week?   A. We have Saturday afternoons off.

Q. Do you prefer taking Saturday afternoon off to working and getting paid for it?   A. Certainly we do....

Q. Is there any labor organization among the tailors in Halifax?   A. Not that I know of; I am glad there is not.

By Mr. KELLY:—

Q. Why is that; do you think every man should be paid according to the work he performs?   A. Yes; according to his ability and his work. I think it is the part of the employer to regulate prices.

By Mr. ARMSTRONG:—

Q. Do you think that the workman has a right to say how much he will sell his labor for?   A. Certainly he has the right to give his opinions, but not to enforce his views.

Q. Do you not think that if there was an organization, that that organization would be the best judges of price?   A. In some cases it is and in some cases it is not.

Q. Was there ever an organization of tailors in Halifax?   A. Not that I know of.

Q. Did you ever work outside of Halifax?   A. No.

Q. As regards the benefits of an organization in relation to prices generally, you do not know whether it would be so or not?   A. I only give my opinions as to what I read in the papers about labor societies in connection with tailors' establishments in the United States.

By Mr. KELLY:—

Q. Did you ever know of any person not paid proportionately to their worth?   A. I hardly understand that question.

Q. I mean as to their ability?   A. Well, you see my experience has been very small indeed.

Q. You have had some years' experience, I presume?   A. A few; I am quite young yet. I think every one should be paid according to their ability. I think they are.

By Mr. ARMSTRONG:—

Q. Do you think you get sufficient wages for your work?   A. I do not complain. I think it is very good; certainly I would take more.

Q. Then you are not satisfied?   A. Perfectly satisfied; I would not think of asking for more, but I would take it if were offered to me.

Q. Do employers often give more wages without being asked? A. No; they are not inclined that way.

By Mr. KELLY:—

Q. Do you think you are paid proportionately with the price of the goods as they are sold? A. I do not know how they are sold, so I cannot answer; I do not know the selling price.

Q. Judging from your general knowledge and experience in the shop you would know the prices at which these goods would be sold, then I ask you: do you think you are paid a fair proportional part of that price for your labor? A. I do not know, this is outside of my province, as it were.

THE KNIGHTS OF LABOR: TWO VIEWS

The *Week* (Toronto), March 18, 1886, p. 248.

THE organization of Knights of Labour is, as was said before, far more formidable than a Trade Union. It is secret, and sure in the end to fall into the same sort of hands into which other secret societies have fallen; it extends over the whole continent, having its centre in New York; it avows itself political, and has already appeared in that character; by laying a trifling tax on its innumerable members it can command almost any sum of money for its operations; it is aggressive in the highest degree, and as every column of commercial intelligence shows, has already kindled war at many points of the industrial world. In an attempt to exclude it from their establishment, the Toronto Street Car Company have brought on a great strike which was attended with rioting, the strikers, or people acting in their interest, having used violence to prevent the Company from running its cars with other hands. The right of men to leave their employment, either individually or in a body, whensoever they please is indisputable; but so is the right of other men to take the place, and that of the employer to say whom he will employ. If an employer is not to be at liberty to say whom he will employ, commercial enterprise must cease. If the work which one man declines or gives up another is not to be allowed to take, freedom of labour must come to an end and be replaced by the most oppressive of monopolies. That no one but the members of a particular association shall be permitted to earn his bread by the work of his hands would be a class law to which the community, which lacks power of organized resistance, might be compelled for a time to bow, but which in the end it would refuse to endure. The obligation of contracts is also obviously vital to those interests of commerce and industry which are common to masters and men; yet it has been very lightly treated on this occasion by certain organs of opinion. It was said that the Street Car Company had broken its charter: that it had broken the rule requiring the rails to be kept level with the road every one who crosses the track is made painfully aware; but this was a totally different question. The usual cry was also raised against Monopoly. A monopoly the Street Car Company is and must be unless the streets can be so widened as to admit competing lines; but it is not an uncontrolled monopoly, and it is assuredly a great blessing to the citizens, above all to our artisans, whom it enables to live at a distance from their places of work, in better air and where house-rent is lower. Let its charter be strictly enforced by all means, but to set the roughs upon it is really to set them upon public property, little as people may see the matter in that light. We unfortunately needed no further proof of the amenability of magistrates elected by popular suffrage to the popular influence of the hour, or of the subserviency of party journals to anything in the shape of a "vote." The police and those immediately in command of them loyally did their duty. On this occasion mediation has happily brought about a compromise; but apparently dark times are coming for industry and trade. To make the workingman understand theoretically the ultimate effect of labour disturbances on the interests of labour is almost impossible, especially as industrial demagogues have exclusive possession of his ear; and experience in this case will be a costly teacher. It will be costly to the workingman and costly to us all.

INDUSTRIAL warfare is the natural offspring of the Old World. There is less necessity or excuse for it on this continent, because under democratic institutions political power is in the hands of the working-class, and the workingman, if he is wronged, can do himself right in a regular way. . . . It is happily impossible that in Canada or the United States legislative injustice should be done to the workingmen, or that they should be deprived of any liberties which are fairly theirs. Here it is rather the other class that is in danger of unfair treatment. By the Mechanics' Lien Act, the owner of a house which is being built is compelled to pay the wages of mechanics whom he has not employed, who have not trusted him, and to whom he is under no sort of obligation, in order that they may not lose by the failure of their employer, to whom he has already paid the money for the work done. Such a law passed by the master-class in its own favour would be denounced by the workingmen as unjust. It is surely a conclusive proof that the interest of the artisan does not go to the wall. It might have been hoped that in a community so liberally organized as ours peace with justice would not be unattainable; unfortunately in the industrial world, as in the world at large, there are people to whom justice is not an object of great solicitude, and who subsist by disturbing peace.

IT is almost heartbreaking to consider the gross and palpable character of the fallacy by which the bulk of the artisans who take part in these labour insurrections are misled, and under the influence of which they may in the end lay destructive hands on the trades by which they live. The enemy against which they are waging war is Capital, which they are taught by their chosen guides to regard as a tyrant robbing them of their bread. Suppose they are completely victorious in the war, as, after a struggle more or less protracted, they are pretty sure to be—suppose the capitalist, finding that all his profits are gone, that nothing but the risk of loss and vexation is left, retires discomfited from the field, realizes whatever remnant of property may remain to him, transfers it to some community where commercial liberty still exists, and shuts up his works or mill, what will follow? Will the artisans without capital, with nothing but their bare sinews, and, perhaps, without the means of subsistence for a week, be able to set up works, or a mill of their own? If not, what can they do but remain unemployed and starve? The expulsion of all capital from the country is the goal towards which these agitations ultimately lead. Does any sane artisan believe that his condition would be really improved by that result?

Canada, Royal Commission on the Relations of Labor and Capital in Canada. Evidence—Ontario, pp. 1083-5.

JOHN J. BICKLEY, Cornwall, called and sworn.
I have for some years followed the occupation of an overseer in the spinning mills. I am not doing anything at present.
By Mr. HEAKES:—
Q.—You are a spinner by trade? A.—Yes.
Q.—Are you acquainted—connected—with any organization of workingmen? A.—I am now and have been for some years a member of the Knights of Labor.
Q.—Do you know if there is any feeling on the part of employers in Cornwall not to employ members of that order? A.—I have heard at different times, from different men, that there was. I could not positively state that such was the case, although I have frequently heard from the men that employers refused to employ them because they were Knights of Labor.
Q.—Did anyone say anything to you about being a member? A.—Yes.
Q.—Would you tell us the circumstances, please? A.—I was dismissed from my situation, and I was given to understand that I was dismissed because I was a Knight of Labor, and because I took an active part in labor matters.
Q.—Since you have been a member of this organization have you ever

seen anything in its principles that would be an injury to the workingman?
A.—I have not. If the teachings of the order were lived up to, nothing but
good could come to the workingman; the result would be good.

Q.—Do you know if they have any principle laid down for the settlement of disputes between capital and labor? A.—Yes; that is one of the
twenty-two articles of the preamble, to try and bring about a settlement
of strikes and difficulties by arbitration.

Q.—That is a fixed rule of the order? A.—Yes.

By Mr. MC LEAN:—

Q.—What do you do when out on strike? Do you take any means of
deciding how to go back, or whether you are to go back to work? A.—All
local assemblies have an executive board. That executive board tries to
bring about a settlement of the difficulty. They try to meet the manager
or employer, and try and effect a settlement, and that is one of the things
that the executive board at all times tries to do—to have the case settled
by arbitration.

By Mr. HEAKES:—

Q.—Do you know whether strikes are more frequent in towns that are
not organized or towns that are organized? A.—I know that strikes are
less frequent in towns where they are organized than where they are not.
My experience has led me to believe that if labor is properly and thoroughly organized strikes will seldom occur. For instance, if the hands
employed at one of these mills were Knights of Labor, the Knights of
Labor would have control over them and could keep them at work, but as
they are partly organized and partly disorganized we can exercise no control over those that are not organized.

Q.—Is there any "boycotting" or "black-listing" in this town? A.—I
know of one case; that is my own. I was given to understand that I would
be "black-listed" all over Canada.

Q.—For what reason? A.—For being a Knight of Labor and taking part
in labor matters.

Q.—Did you have anything to do with the settlement of labor disputes?
A.—I had considerable to do with it, and took an active part all through,
and finally acted as arbitrator for the help.

Q.—Can you state if the agreement entered into after the first difficulty
was carried out? A.—It was not. Mr. Knight, of the Canada Cotton Mills,
refused to live up to that agreement when waited upon with the price-list
of the Merriton Mills. It was a true list of the wages of the employés, to
which was attached the signature of every overseer of that mill. He refused to recognize it, and refused to agree to the terms already agreed to.

Q.—Would the second strike have taken place if they had lived up to
the first agreement? A.—I feel safe in saying it would not.

Q.—How much of a reduction in the prices paid to weavers took place?
A.—As I understand it, it ran from 28 to 33 per cent.

Q.—Are you able to tell us what wages they earned previous to the reduction? A.—I cannot say the whole. I can give it just as I heard it, just as I heard others state. I heard weavers state that they could not make more than $4.50, and they set up the claim that they were first-class weavers. I know that there are weavers in the town who made $9, and others who made $8.50, and some $7. Some do fairly well, and others are poorly paid.

Q.—Over what part or department were you overseer? A.—Spooling, spinning and warping.

Q.—What were your average wages? A.—The last I had to do with was a small mill, and could not be taken to set prices from. In that mill, for spooling, spinning and twisting, the average wages were 90 cents a day, taking the whole mill, superintendent and all. There were about twenty hands employed.

Q.—Was the agreement, finally between yourself and the mill, a satisfactory one? A.—When I made the statement to the operatives I can say that I heard but very few complain. There are among the men a few that were dissatisfied, but very few, when you take into consideration the number engaged in that strike.

Q.—If the mill owners had resorted to arbitration previous to forcing the people out on a strike, would there have been a necessity for a strike? A.—I do not think there would be; I do not think the strike would have occurred.

Q.—Were the mill owners furnished with a copy of the arbitrators' award? A.—Yes. When I refer to the usefulness of labor organizations, as an instrument for promoting peace in the times of excitement—for instance, I might say: I have known cases where certain persons who are in authority in the mills, would have been severely dealt with had it not been for members of the order of the Knights of Labor. I know one particular case where the Knights of Labor were instrumental in preventing a visit to the house of an overseer for the purpose of molesting him. I know of people being very outspoken as to what they would do to men in the mills, and I know that the Knights of Labor went in and prevented trouble. I know that the Knights of Labor, down at Cornwall, met and prevented much difficulty; and people, in talking about the late strike, were surprised that it was conducted so quietly. There was no trouble, and they claimed that it was due to the Knights, in a very great measure, that there was no trouble—no difficulty. Without having access to the books at the present moment, I feel safe in stating that since the formation of the organization in Cornwall, now bordering on three years, upwards of $500 has been paid out in relieving distress and furnishing sustenance to individual citizens of the town. I know of many cases where the Knights relieved this distress. Had it not have been so, the town of Cornwall would have very likely have had to do it through its treasurer.

By Mr. MC LEAN:—

Q.—When your society are out on strike do they have any ability to decide and say whether they will go back or not?   A.—To answer that, I will give you the plan laid down by the Knights, and what they follow: We will take, for instance, the Stormont Mill. We will say, for the sake of argument, that it is thoroughly organized, and that there are grievances. Grievances are sometimes imaginary and sometimes real. If there are any grievances the Knights state the case to the executive board of the local assembly. They investigate the matter, and if the grievance was found to be real they would try and effect a settlement with the manager. They would then lay the case before the executive board of the district and bring about a settlement, if possible. If they found they could not, and that the manager would not agree to anything, the executive board could call the help out. From the time the executive board calls the help out they are entitled to the support of the order and always receive it, but they cannot receive any support until they are so called out; so that you see, if a place is organized they cannot jump up at the spur of the moment and leave the company's service. If they did so, they would do it at their peril, because the order would give them no support.

THERE IS A REASON FOR IT

Industrial Banner (London, Ont.), February, 1897.

A sermon was recently delivered by a clergyman in this city in which he contrasted the condition of affairs to-day with what existed at the commencement of the century, and among other things he stated that the artizan did not labor as many hours as he used to do. While this is true, it is as well to understand how it has come about. It has been accomplished not because humanity and civilization has advanced so much as because labor was organized. The reduction of the hours of toil has been gained as the price of unceasing conflict and unrelenting determination on the part of the Trades Unions.

They have been resisted and opposed at every turn by capital and the capitalistic class. Every concession gained has been wrung from unwilling hands; and at the present moment the same conflict is being waged for an eight-hour day, and it is being just as resolutely opposed, and by the same class of people as have stood in opposition all along. Therefore, if the mechanic and laborer is working a less number of hours per day now than he was fifty years ago, he can thank the organizations of labor that such is the case. Without organization the capitalist would not hesitate to make him work his twelve or fourteen hours straight. It is a fact, however, that workingmen are working too many hours as it is.

With the multiplication of labor-saving machinery the science of production has advanced with such tremendous strides that one man can now turn out as much material as demanded the skill of twenty men a few short years ago, and hence as a result thousands of unemployed abound in the land.

The only possible chance to place this class at profitable employment is to reduce the hours of toil to keep pace with the increased power of production, and this is what the employing class is resisting, tooth and nail.

It is no virtue for the pulpit to inform the producing classes that they work less hours now than they used to do. Rather let them boldly proclaim the truth, and acknowledge that the conditions under which workingmen and workingwomen now earn a livelihood are more onerous than when they worked twelve hours a day.

The struggle for a bare existence is more bitter at this moment than it ever was before. More workers are out of employment, and their ranks are constantly swelling. Work in the past was at best reasonably sure; not so in the present.

And, pray, who is fighting the battle for shorter hours now—the pulpit, the press, the universities, the employers, or the men of business? Most certainly not. It is the workingman himself, and he is met with opposition on every hand. In the future, we doubt not, when progressive trade unionism has succeeded in still more materially reducing the hours of toil, some preacher will arise and tell the producers how much better off they are than we to-day. If the organizations of labor had never existed, it is safe to say no preacher could take such unction to his soul as to think humanity was advancing, and point to these decreasing hours of toil as a proof.

If workingmen are better off in this respect to-day than formerly, they know whom they have to thank. They are intelligent enough to understand that the working classes must work out their own salvation; that if they have gained concessions in the past it was because they were in a position to demand them and able to enforce the demand. They are not so ignorant as to believe that the leopard will change his spots, or the lion become a lamb. They recognize that the class who have antagonized their legitimate claims for justice in the past will likewise oppose them in the future; that any concession they may gain will be conceded only when the opposing class is powerless to withhold it. In a word, the laborer is becoming aware that only as he becomes organized and intelligent has he any show whatever of securing the least recognition in the community, or any consideration of his rights.

Because the hours of labor have been reduced in the past it would be unsafe to say that humanity was getting better. First recognize how and why they have been reduced, and then ask yourself the question: "Why should men even work eight hours a day when the advanced mechanical skill and productive power of the world is sufficient to feed, clothe, house and provide every luxury requisite to happiness with less than four hours of toil a day?" Is it not a fact easily proved that even at eight hours a day, the worker is just toiling four hours too long?

It is well to recognize that the reason why so many men are in poverty, with no work to do is because they who do the work have to toil so long.

LABOUR DEMANDS EQUAL RIGHTS

Industrial Banner (London, Ontario), October, 1897.

How persistently the world sticks to old ideas; how sacred even injustice becomes if sanctioned by age and antiquity. A hundred years ago it was looked upon as treasonable to argue that a mechanic or laborer should have a vote. Workingmen to-day enjoy the privileges of the franchise only because they have forced the concession, after years of bitter struggle, from a class who believed and taught that it was divinely ordained that property should rule; and the same privileged class to-day teach the same doctrine, and enact it whenever possible.

If you doubt this assertion, just ask yourself how it is that so many workingmen are only part citizens, with only a partial and unequal say in the institutions of their own towns and cities.

No man, however intelligent or capable, can sit in the mayor's chair, or even aspire to the dignity of a petty alderman, nor vote on any question involving the expenditure of public money, unless he is possessed of a certain amount of real estate, but must be content to act the role of a partial citizen at best. . . .

The law requiring property qualifications for the holding of public office is a relic of feudalism and one that is destined to be swept away as have other abuses before it. The number of intelligent men who are ashamed to defend such a system is rapidly growing larger. The artisan class has had to overcome hostility, persecution, ridicule and abuse in the attainment of the ballot, and the same battle is going on to secure the privileges of full citizenship, a battle that will end with the same results— the triumph of justice. . . .

Every citizen should have equal rights; character should count for more than money, and brains for more than property. The electorate should have the right to nominate whoever they wish for office, and no law enacted for the benefit of a privileged class should have the power to hinder them.

While feudalism itself has passed away, a few decaying old relics still remain, and one of the hardest to die is the ancient and fossilized idea that the possession of property should confer special rights and privileges on its possessor. The time is coming, aye, cannot be much longer delayed, when the system that requires property qualifications will be only a memory of the past. It will be laid away to rest without hope of resurrection in the grave that so fitly awaits it—let it die.

THE RISE OF SOCIALISM

Labour Advocate (Toronto), September 4, 1891, p. 361.

The Trades and Labor Congress for the Dominion began its annual session on Monday last in Quebec. . . . It is to be hoped that in arranging the programme of measures for which the labor organizations are to be asked to agitate, much more advanced ground will be taken than in the past. It is high time that the workers in Canada felt the impulse of the "new unionism" which has entirely transformed the character of the labor movement in Britain. Canadian workingmen ought surely to be capable of learning, as the workers of other countries have learned, that the thing to be aimed at is not merely a little more wages, or a few hours in the week less work for the men of this or that craft, but the overthrow of the various forms of monopoly and social injustice which keep the worker in an inferior and dependent position. It is folly to expect any material change for the better, either by trying to squeeze a little more out of the employers or clamoring for a few miserable inadequate legislative palliatives which leave the root of social abuses untouched.

If the labor movement is to be anything but a donkey-engine for this or that political party, and a bitter disappointment to those who are sincere in desiring the emancipation of the workers—the efforts of its councils and congress must be directed towards securing thorough going radical reforms in the direction of the national control of industry. They must not be content with labor bureaus, factory and shipping inspection, anti-Chinese laws, or any such wretched makeshifts which the Government throws to the labor organizations from time to time as sops to a hungry and troublesome dog. They should demand nothing less than the abolition of land, money, and transportation monopolies, and the recognition of the right of the worker to all he produces. No one expects, of course, that social revolution of this kind can come suddenly or without long years of agitation. But what we do say is, that no labor reform organization in this day is worthy the name which does not clearly realize and boldly proclaim that the reorganization of the industrial system is the end they have in view, and demand such immediate measures of legislation as tend in that direction.

The address of welcome by Mayor Fortier of Quebec . . . should be a warning to labor bodies to avoid the mistake of inviting partizan politicians and capitalistic flunkeys to take part in their proceedings. "Those whom you have invited to join," said this functionary, "magistrate, capitalists, and others, prove that your object is not really against authority or capital." If the Labor Congress does not belie this twaddle by its actions, and show that it is emphatically against capitalism, it might as well dissolve for all the good it will ever accomplish. And for the future, labor organizations in order to avoid being placed in a false position, will do well to avoid seeking the patronage of self-seeking politicians and others whose interests are identified with the existing order of things.

BIBLIOGRAPHICAL NOTE

The working man has received little attention in Canadian historical studies. But the ways in which the historical problem can be attacked are well illustrated in the more sophisticated British and American studies now available on working-class life in those countries.

The logical starting point would be E. P. Thompson's brilliant study of the workers' response to English industrialization, *The Making of the English Working Class* (London, 1963). The works of E. J. Hobsbawm are equally important; see, for example, *Labouring Men* (London, 1964). Some of the most important insights into the self-consciousness of working people have come from the study of working-class violence. Especially recommended are: Hobsbawm, *Primitive Rebels* (New York, 1949) and Hobsbawm and George Rudé, *Captain Swing* (New York, 1968).

There is now a rich literature on the American working class. An excellent collection of essays, illustrating the variety of approaches and subject matters, is Herbert G. Gutman and Gregory S. Kealey, eds, *Many Pasts: Readings in American Social History*, 2 vols (Englewood Cliffs, N.J., 1973). Stephan Thernstrom has made important contributions to writing history 'from the bottom up'. See especially his study of a small industrial city, Newburyport, *Poverty and Progress: Social Mobility in a Nineteenth Century City* (Cambridge, Mass., 1964). Broader approaches yet are to be found in Henry Nash Smith, ed., *Popular Culture and Industrialism, 1865-1890* (New York, 1967).

There is not a great deal even of general social history in Canada. Two general social histories that help somewhat in putting the working-class experience in context are Arthur R. M. Lower, *Canadians in the Making: A Social History of Canada* (Toronto, 1958) and G. P. de T. Glazebrook, *Life in Ontario: A Social History* (Toronto, 1968). General works in recent years have paid greater attention to social questions. For example, among the more useful are: J. M. S. Careless, ed., *Colonists & Canadiens, 1760-1867* (Toronto, 1971); J. M. S. Careless and R. C. Brown, eds, *The Canadians, 1867-1967* (Toronto, 1967); G. M. Craig, *Upper Canada: The Formative Years* (Toronto, 1963). The one major attempt to create a general Marxist interpretation of Canadian history, in which the history of the working man can be placed, is that of Stanley Ryerson, in *The Found-*

ing of Canada: Beginnings to 1815 (Toronto, 1960), and *Unequal Union: Confederation and the Roots of Conflict in the Canadas, 1815-1873* (Toronto, 1968).

Recently there have been some efforts to provide a general framework for the study of the working class. A group of young Marxist scholars have had a go at it in Gary Teeple, ed., *Capitalism and the National Question in Canada* (Toronto, 1972). So has the Ontario Waffle in a recent collection of essays, *(Canada) Ltd.* (Toronto, 1973), edited by Robert Laxer. Especially interesting in this volume are Mel Watkin's 'The Trade Union Movement in Canada' and 'Populist and Socialist Movements in Canadian History' by John Smart. An extremely important essay, analyzing Canada along the lines of E. P. Thompson's work on Britain, is Steven Langdon, 'The Emergence of the Canadian Working Class Movement, 1845-75', *Journal of Canadian Studies*, VIII (1973). An older, but equally important work, is H. C. Pentland's 'The Development of a Capitalistic Labour Market in Canada', *Canadian Journal of Economics and Political Science*, XXV (1959).

The aspect of working-class experience that has been most thoroughly surveyed is unionism. The traditional history of the union movement is Harold Logan, *Trade Unions in Canada* (Toronto, 1948). A partisan left-wing view is offered in Charles Lipton, *The Trade Union Movement of Canada* (Montreal, 1959). An equally committed socialist interpretation is Martin Robin's *Radical Politics and Canadian Labour, 1880-1930* (Kingston, 1968). Bernard Ostry has surveyed the attitudes of politicians towards labour in two significant articles: 'Conservatives, Liberals and Labour in the 1870's', *Canadian Historical Review*, XLI (1960), and 'Conservatives, Liberals, and Labour in the 1880's', *Canadian Journal of Economics and Political Science*, XXVII (1961). Another view of that relationship is to be found in D. G. Creighton, 'George Brown, John A· Macdonald, and the Workingman', *Canadian Historical Review*, XXIII (1943).

There have been some excellent specialized studies on unions. Excerpts from two of those are found in this collection: H. C. Pentland, 'The Lachine Strike', *Canadian Historical Review* (1948); and J. I. Cooper, 'The Quebec Ship Labourers' Benevolent Society', *Canadian Historical Review* (1949). The militant Knights of Labor have been studied by Douglas R. Kennedy, *The Knights of Labor in Canada* (London, Ont., 1956). It was already obvious by the end of the nineteenth century that labour would be most radical in British Columbia. The history of the movement there is found in William Bennett, *Builders of British Columbia* (Vancouver, 1937). The roots of the social conflict in B.C. are exhaustively treated in Martin Robin's two-volume history, *The Company Province* (Toronto, 1972-3).

There have been some useful studies on the immigration of working-class people. The standard work is Helen I. Cowan, *British Emigration to*

British North America (Toronto, 1961). Another important general study is Norman Macdonald's *Canada, 1763-1841: Immigration and Settlement* (Toronto, 1939), which was followed by his *Canada: Immigration and Colonization, 1841-1903* (Toronto, 1966). Several books written early in the twentieth century throw light on the problem of immigrant adjustment in Canada. Some have been reprinted in the excellent Social History of Canada series, edited for the University of Toronto Press by Michael Bliss. Worth attention in that series are J. S. Woodsworth's *My Neighbor* and *Strangers Within Our Gates*, and Ralph Connor's *The Foreigner*. The same series has reprinted the best look at the problem of the agrarian, *Rural Life in Canada* by John MacDougall.

Staying with the Bliss series, one can find some of the best material on the urban worker. The first sociological study of the Canadian working class in many ways remains the best. H. B. Ames' assessment of Montreal in the 1890s has been cited several times in our collection; the entire book has been reprinted by the University of Toronto Press. An equally basic source is the Royal Commission on the Relations of Labor and Capital, 1889. In 1973, the Bliss series published a one-volume selection from the Commission, edited by Greg Kealey. A new work that provides an excellent, rounded picture of working-class life is Terry Copp, *The Condition of the Working Class in Montreal, 1897-1929* (Toronto, 1974). A funny and informative account of Toronto social life is to be found in C. S. Clark, *Of Toronto the Good* (Montreal, 1898), now available in an inexpensive reprint from Coles.

The social life of Montreal has been treated better than that of any other Canadian city. As well as Ames and Copp, some other important works include: J. I. Cooper, 'The Social Structure of Montreal in the 1850's', Canadian Historical Association *Annual Report* (1956); and G. R. C. Keep, 'Irish Adjustment in Montreal', *Canadian Historical Review*, xxxi (1950). M. Sheehy has looked at 'The Irish in Quebec', in the Canadian Catholic Historical Association *Report* (1943). Michael Katz is engaged in a huge computerized study of Hamilton between 1851 and 1871. Some of the early results of that project are to be seen in his essay 'Social Structure in Hamilton, Ontario', in Stephen Thernstrom and Richard Sennett, eds, *Nineteenth Century Cities* (New Haven, 1968). Michael Cross has described some aspects of working-class organization in the Ottawa Valley in two articles: 'Stony Monday, 1849: the Rebellion Losses Riots in Bytown', *Ontario History*, lxiii (1971); and 'The Shiners' War: Social Violence in the Ottawa Valley in the 1830's', *Canadian Historical Review*, liv (1973). Perhaps the most thoroughly studied of any group of workers in the nineteenth century are the timberers. The most important works are those of A. R. M. Lower: *Settlement and the Forest Frontier in Eastern Canada* (Toronto, 1936); and *Great Britain's Woodyard: British America and the Timber Trade, 1763-1867* (Montreal, 1973).

The French-Canadian lower class is coming in for more detailed study. In the plethora of material, two works may be cited as especially interesting: Fernand Ouellet, 'Les Insurrections de 1837-38: un phénomène social', *Social History*, II (1968); and William F. Ryan, *The Clergy and Economic Growth in Quebec, 1896-1914* (Québec, 1966). The best source for the study of working-class life in the Atlantic Provinces is the extensive publication program of the Nova Scotia Archives.

Only a start has been made on the questions of welfare and labour legislation. The standard studies on welfare are Elisabeth Wallace, 'The Origin of the Social Welfare State in Canada', *Canadian Journal of Economics and Political Science*, XVI (1950), and R. B. Splane, *The Development of Social Welfare in Ontario* (Toronto, 1965). A useful work on labour legislation is Eugene Forsey's 'Notes on the Dominion Factory Bills', *Canadian Journal of Economics and Political Science*, XIII (1947).

Proletarian culture and ideology has received little attention. The most impressive working-class ideologue of the nineteenth century in Canada was Phillips Thompson, labour agitator and editor. His views are to be read in *The Politics of Labor* (New York, 1887) and *Labor Reform Songster* (Philadelphia, 1892). Two helpful assessments of labour ideology are: Ruth McKenzie, 'Proletarian Literature in Canada', *Dalhousie Review* (1939); and Frank Watt, 'The National Policy, the Workingman and Proletarian Ideas in Victorian Canada', *Canadian Historical Review*, XL (1959).